LEVIATHAN

Parts I and II

broadview editions
series editor: L.W. Conolly

LEVIATHAN

Parts I and II

revised edition

Thomas Hobbes

edited by A.P. Martinich and Brian Battiste

broadview editions

Library and Archives Canada Cataloguing in Publication

Hobbes, Thomas, 1588-1679
    Leviathan. Parts I and II / Thomas Hobbes ; edited by A.P. Martinich and Brian Battiste. — Rev. ed.

(Broadview editions)
Includes bibliographical references and index.
ISBN 978-1-55481-040-6

    1. Political science—Early works to 1800. 2. State, The—Early works to 1800. I. Martinich, A. P. (Aloysius P.), 1946-
II. Battiste, Brian III. Title. IV. Series: Broadview editions.

JC153.H652 2010   320.1   C2010-905986-7

Broadview Editions
The Broadview Editions series represents the ever-changing canon of literature in English by bringing together texts long regarded as classics with valuable lesser-known works.

Advisory editor for this volume: Martin Boyne

Broadview Press is an independent, international publishing house, incorporated in 1985.

We welcome comments and suggestions regarding any aspect of our publications—please feel free to contact us at the addresses below or at broadview@broadviewpress.com.

North America
PO Box 1243, Peterborough, Ontario, Canada K9J 7H5
2215 Kenmore Ave., Buffalo, New York, USA 14207
Tel: (705) 743-8990; Fax: (705) 743-8353
email: customerservice@broadviewpress.com

UK, Europe, Central Asia, Middle East, Africa, India, and Southeast Asia
Eurospan Group, 3 Henrietta St., London WC2E 8LU, United Kingdom
Tel: 44 (0) 1767 604972; Fax: 44 (0) 1767 601640
email: eurospan@turpin-distribution.com

Australia and New Zealand
NewSouth Books
c/o TL Distribution, 15-23 Helles Ave., Moorebank, NSW, Australia 2170
Tel: (02) 8778 9999; Fax: (02) 8778 9944
email: orders@tldistribution.com.au

www.broadviewpress.com

This book is printed on paper containing 100% postconsumer fibre.

Typesetting and assembly: Eileen Eckert, Calgary, Canada.

PRINTED IN CANADA

Contents

Acknowledgements

Help for the original edition of this work was provided by Jo Ann Carson, Leslie Martinich, Reid Pillifant, and especially Sharon Vaughan. For the revised edition, John Deigh provided many helpful suggestions. The editors want to thank Leonard Conolly and Tara Trueman of Broadview for their great help.

Introduction

Thomas Hobbes's *Leviathan* is generally regarded as the greatest work of political philosophy in English, even greater than John Locke's *Two Treatises of Government* (1689) and the modern classic, John Rawls's *A Theory of Justice* (1971). Although *Leviathan* was published in 1651, more than 350 years ago, it remains an important treatise because of its compelling answers to some of the most fundamental questions of political theory. Before discussing these questions and his answers, let's say something about the person.

Hobbes: His Life and Works

Hobbes was born outside Malmesbury, Wiltshire, on Good Friday, as he noted in one of his autobiographies, 5 April 1588, the year of the Spanish Armada. Rumors of the Spanish invasion circulated in the preceding months, and Hobbes claims that his mother gave birth to him prematurely, along with a twin, fear. In fact, fear played an important part in Hobbes's later life, and the concept of fear is important to his philosophy. His father, also named Thomas, was a relatively uneducated Elizabethan clergyman, with a penchant for drinking and brawling. In 1604, after punching the vicar of Foxley in the head, he fled the area and disappeared from history. Hobbes went to Magdalen Hall, a poor relation of Magdalen College, Oxford, in 1604, thanks to the generosity of his uncle Francis.

Hobbes had distinguished himself as a student at an early age. His intelligence was matched by his willfulness, and he took pride in skipping formal instruction and proving logical problems in his own way. As Hobbes approached graduation, the principal of Magdalen Hall recommended him to the first earl of Devonshire to be officially a tutor to his son, William Cavendish. In fact, being only two years older than William, he was more a companion than a tutor. During 1614 and 1615, Hobbes toured France and Italy with William, a standard journey for a well-to-do Englishman of the time.

Back in England, Hobbes associated with several distinguished intellectuals due to the prominence of William and his cousin, also named William. Hobbes occasionally was also a secretary to Francis Bacon, an associate of the Cavendishes, and Hobbes is the source of the story that Bacon died, presumably of pneumonia, after stuffing a chicken full of snow in order to test the preservative power of cold air. Hobbes's helping of William included soliciting loans for the spendthrift nobleman. William became the second earl upon the death of his father in 1626, but died two years later, at the age of 38. Hobbes nominally dedicated his first major publication, a translation of Thucydides' *History of the Peloponnesian War* (1629), to the third earl, but it was clearly done in honor of William.

William's wife, Christian Bruce, daughter of the first Lord Kinloss, partially blamed Hobbes for her husband's spendthrift ways; and she let him go. In 1629-30, Hobbes was employed by a neighbor, Gervaise Clifton, to be the tutor of and guide for his son during another tour of the Continent. Hobbes credited his love of geometry to an incident during this trip, but his desire to search for the causes of things already existed in 1626 when he wrote a long poem, *De mirabilibus pecci* (*On the Wonders of the Peak*). After reconciling with Christian, he became the tutor of William's son, the third earl of Devonshire, in 1631. In the 1620s and 1630s, Hobbes was also a member of the circle of intellectuals formed by the cousin William mentioned above, the future first Duke of Newcastle.

Hobbes's third tour of Europe, officially as the tutor of the third earl, was the occasion for Hobbes's meeting with Galileo (1564-1642) in Italy, and Marin Mersenne (1588-1648) and other members of Mersenne's impressive circle of philosophers and scientists in France in 1634. Because Hobbes impressed Mersenne with his abilities, he was sent a pre-publication copy of René Descartes's *Meditations on First Philosophy*, and wrote the Third Set of Objections, which were published along with the *Meditations* in 1641. Hobbes and Descartes had a low opinion of each other. Descartes wanted none of his unpublished work sent to Hobbes because he feared Hobbes would plagiarize it, and, according to John Aubrey, Hobbes said that while Descartes was a good mathematician, his "head did not lie for philosophy."

As the 1630s progressed, strained political and religious relations between King Charles I and parliamentary supporters increased. When the prospect of a parliament to be called for 1640 arose, Hobbes stood for the House of Commons but was not selected. His manuscript, *The Elements of Law, Natural and Politic*, circulated in that year and earned the ire of supporters of parliament and limited sovereignty because of Hobbes's pro-royalist stand. Because he feared for his life when a new parliament was to begin in late 1640, Hobbes left England for France, the "first of those that fled," as he put it in his verse autobiography. Rather than being ashamed of what might have been seen as cowardice, Hobbes saw fear of death as a fundamental part of being human. In *Leviathan*, he said that allowances had to be made for people of "feminine courage" (21.16).

In France for all of the 1640s, Hobbes published *De Cive* in 1647, which included notes replying to objections made to a privately printed edition of 1642. *De Cive* was supposed to be the last part of his three-part general philosophy, *Elementa Philosophica*. He said that the events of the English Civil War (1641-49) made it incumbent on him to publish it first, but he also had difficulty putting the first part, *De Corpore*, into a form that satisfied him, even though he worked on it extensively during this time. It eventually appeared in 1655. The second part, *De Homine*, was published in 1658.

This tripartite structure of his philosophy is misleading at best because Hobbes divides reality into two basic parts: natural bodies and artificial bodies. Artificial bodies are primarily civil states; as for natural bodies, these include humans and other animals as much as rocks and flowers. It is not the creation of human beings, but the creation of civil states that introduces something new into the world, as Hobbes explains in the Introduction to *Leviathan* (see below, pp. 35-36).

In Paris, in 1645, Hobbes and Bishop John Bramhall debated the issue of free will and predestination at the request of William Cavendish, the duke of Newcastle. Hobbes defended predestination, Bramhall free will. Neither participant wanted his contribution published. For Hobbes's part, he, like other Calvinists, thought that predestination should be taught from the podium but good works preached from the pulpit, and was concerned about the effect that the truth might have on ordinary people. When Hobbes's manuscript was given to a young man, it was published in 1654 as *Of Liberty and Necessity*, without Hobbes's approval. Irate because he believed Hobbes had acted dishonorably, Bramhall replied with *Defence of True Liberty from Antecedent and Extrinsical Necessity* in 1655. Hobbes replied to that with *Questions Concerning Liberty, Necessity, and Chance* in 1656. This debate was important for at least two reasons. One is philosophical: Hobbes showed how the necessity that holds between cause and effect was compatible with freedom or liberty. Liberty, he said, is nothing more than absence of external impediments, and will is merely the last desire before an action. Much contemporary compatibilism stems from Hobbes's work. The other reason is largely historical. As a Calvinist, Hobbes emphasized that God is omnipotent and the ultimate explanation of everything. These properties entail, in Hobbes's opinion, that God is the cause of everything; this includes every human action, even the sinful ones.

For a time, he tutored the Prince of Wales, the future Charles II, in mathematics, and regularly discussed the epic poem *Gondibert* (1650-51) while it was being composed by its author William Davenant (1606-68). He was seriously ill in 1647 and confessed his sins to Dr. John Cosin, later bishop of Durham. Some have speculated that part of the etiology of his illness was the stress resulting from his inability to write *De Corpore* to his satisfaction. In addition to Davenant and Cosin, Hobbes was involved with such notables as Henry Bennet (1618-88), Kenelm Digby (1603-65), and Edward Hyde (1609-74). Hobbes returned to England in early 1652, not long after the publication of *Leviathan*, partly because Mersenne had died in 1648 and his friend, Pierre Gassendi (1592-1655) had moved to the south of France, but also because the French Roman Catholic clergy were unhappy with his attacks on that church in *Leviathan*, and the English court in exile was unhappy with his treatment of the Church of England and the terms of sovereignty.

In the 1650s and 1660s, he divided his time between life in Derbyshire with the third earl of Devonshire and London, where he associated with some of the most distinguished English intellectuals, such as William Harvey and John Selden, not to mention his occasional discussions with Charles II after the Restoration. His political writing was largely behind him, and he returned to the study of science and mathematics. He engaged in acrimonious debates with John Wallis and others about his own flawed attempts to solve the problem of squaring the circle, using only straight-edge and compass, and with Robert Boyle about the existence of a vacuum, supported by experiments using a newfangled air pump, which allegedly extracted air from a glass globe. Hobbes disdained the empiricism of the Royal Society, incorporated in 1662, and tried to cast doubt on the reliability of the machinery and the inferences made by Boyle. For Hobbes, natural science should be deductive and ideally geometrical, not experimental. His distaste for experimentation is expressed in this passage: "not everyone that brings from beyond seas a new gin, or other jaunty device, is therefore a philosopher. For if you reckon that way, not only apothecaries and gardeners, but many other sorts of workmen, will put in for, and get the prize."[1] Hobbes offered to the Royal Society his scientific services, which were ungraciously declined.

Hobbes's acerbic and stubborn temperament, the flaws in his mathematical proofs, and his nonstandard religious views contributed in large part to a decline in his reputation during the late 1660s and 1670s, although he remained admired by many intellectuals on the Continent. Hobbes's scientific replies to his critics were published in his lifetime, while most of his defenses of his religious views were published posthumously. His appendix to the Latin translation of *Leviathan* (1668) is a notable exception. By 1676, Hobbes was spending most of his time at the residences of the third earl, Chatsworth (not the current house) and Hardwick Hall. His translations of Homer's *Iliad* and *Odyssey*, which appeared in 1676 and 1677, have been widely criticized as wooden and so colloquial as to be unworthy of those classic works. However, Homer's own language was not elevated, and in blind "taste tests" of Hobbes's translations against those of Chapman and Pope, Hobbes's is often preferred. He was nowhere near the poet Pope was, but his translations are clear and vigorous. In 1679, his history of the English Civil War, *Behemoth*, was published, as were new editions of several of his other works.

Hobbes's final illness began in October 1679. The final blow was a stroke he suffered about a week before he died that left him paralyzed. He died, at peace, on 4 December, at the age of 91. According to James Wheldon, Hobbes's amanuensis and companion during the latter part of his life, Hobbes had received "the Sacrament" several times before his last illness with "devoting, and in humble, and reverent posture." He is buried near Hardwick Hall, within the walls of the local parish church in Ault Hucknall, Derbyshire.

Leviathan

In *Leviathan*, Hobbes answers some of the fundamental questions of political philosophy: Why do human beings need laws and governments? What makes them legitimate? Hobbes's answer is that if there were no laws or government of any kind, then every action would be permissible; and if every action were permissible, then each person would have the right to everything that another person had, including that person's life. With everyone having a

---

1 *Consideration upon the Reputation, Loyalty, Manners, and Religion of Mr. Hobbes* in *English Works*, ed. William Molesworth, volume IV, p. 437.

right to everything every other person has, a war of each against all is inevitable. One might think that there was never a time when no laws of any kind existed. For example, moral laws are eternal. Hobbes agrees about the moral laws, which he calls "the laws of nature."[1] But his description of the consequences of there being no laws of any kind is part of a thought experiment. By thinking about such a situation, people can come to understand why moral laws are necessary. That is a great achievement.

Hobbes's idea of the natural condition of human beings, which includes a right to everything that people believe they need to preserve themselves, is probably the single most misunderstood part of his philosophy. The misunderstanding began soon after *Leviathan* was published. Robert Filmer (1588-1653) wrote,

> I cannot understand how this right of nature can be conceived without imagining a company of men at the very first to have been all created together without any dependence one of another, or as mushrooms (*fungorum more*) they all on a sudden were sprung out of the earth without any obligation to one another.... The scripture teacheth us otherwise, that all men came by succession, and generation from one man: we must not deny the truth of the history of creation.[2]

Filmer's mistake is to think of the state of nature as primarily historical and descriptive of the very earliest time in human history. In fact, Hobbes denies that the first humans, Adam and Eve, began in the state of nature. He thinks that the state of nature actually exists in three situations: among people too primitive to have a government, during civil wars, and between sovereign nations.

Hobbes wanted his theory to be not empirical but rather scientific, according to a model of science that takes Euclidean geometry as paradigmatic. He did not go around collecting evidence for how people actually behave in certain situations, and he criticized the Royal Society for its empiricism, as we saw above.[3] For him, geometry begins with definitions, from which one deduces logical consequences. If this seems an odd model of science, one must remember that the new science was in its infancy in the seventeenth

---

1 These are not laws of physics.
2 *Observations on Mr. Hobbes's Leviathan: Or his Artificial Man: A Commonwealth*, section 3.
3 Hobbes's definitions are empirical, however, in the sense that the terms of his definitions denote objects in the physical world.

century, and no dominant concept of science or scientific method had been developed. What Hobbes knew was that geometry produced necessary truths. So we may say that Hobbes began with a series of definitions of which the salient ones for political philosophy are the definitions of the natural condition of humans, the right of nature, and a law of nature; and he then deduces the consequences. More will be said about these laws and their deductions below.

One might wonder why the first law of nature—in effect, "You do not make war"—is necessary. Wouldn't war be avoided if each person stayed out of every other person's way? This might actually occur if population was sparse and there was enough naturally occurring food and shelter for everyone. But the first problem is that the mere fact that people might not be at war with each other does not amount to a law against making war on others. Laws are normative, and facts are not. Also, in fact human populations often have a density and scarcity that makes war not only possible but inevitable. Human beings desire to preserve their lives; even people with painful, terminal illnesses usually try to stay alive as long as possible. It may seem that we are talking about empirical facts now and not definitions or their consequences. Although Hobbes does not explicitly say anything about population density and scarcity, it must be working in the background. Concerning human beings and their desire to stay alive, Hobbes holds that self-preservation is the greatest good for each person and the good is what is desired. Although he sometimes recognizes that life can be so painful that a person desires to die, because the desire to live is so dominant he in effect defines an animal as a body that desires its own self-preservation. Sometimes, in his typically dyspeptic way, he indicates that the desire for self-preservation is the desire not to die, which people think causes the "greatest of all bodily pains."[1]

If people desired the wrong things or did not desire anything, they would die. But even the desires that are necessary for life produce conditions that threaten life. If there is one apple and two people who desire it because they are hungry, then the two people will have interests that conflict. This is the first cause of war.

The actual human condition is even more serious than described so far. In addition to conflict being unavoidable, everyone would know that other people are in competition with them. So it makes sense for each person to try to kill or otherwise neutralize

---

1   *The Elements of Law, Natural and Politic* I, chapter 16.4.

other people preemptively. Further, each person knows that other people are or could be thinking the same thing; so each person is at greater risk than that caused by simple competition. This means that each person has even more incentive to preemptively kill or neutralize others.

There is still a third cause of conflict. Some people try to dominate others because they enjoy having power over other people. It gives them glory.

It is obvious that it is necessary for human beings to get out of this natural condition of no laws, and of course people have done so. The question is how they could have done it, and how in fact they did. Government is the answer. But how can we get from a condition of no laws to a government? What are needed are laws of nature. So let's consider Hobbes's notion in more detail. He defines the term "law of nature" as a precept or action-guiding proposition, discovered by reason, not empirical investigation, by which a person is forbidden to do what will destroy his life and required to do what will preserve it. From this definition, Hobbes claims the first law of nature follows: "Make peace." Hobbes could have used a common technique of geometrical reasoning, *reductio ad absurdum*, to prove it. Suppose for the sake of argument that a person does not make peace. Then it follows that the person will remain in the state of nature and hence will likely soon die. But this contradicts the definition of a law of nature. It follows, therefore, that people make peace.

The second law of nature explains how they can make peace: each person lays down his right to all things. For the proof, again suppose that people do not lay down their right to all things. Then they do not make peace. Since this contradicts the first law of nature, the supposition must be false. Therefore, each person lays down his right to all things. This law does not mean that a person lays down or loses every right that he has, although Hobbes may sometimes give that impression. It means that people have to give up some of their rights, perhaps many or most of their rights. They do this by making a covenant with each other. Each person agrees to let some designated entity govern them. Hobbes calls this entity, the government, the "sovereign." The sovereign is a construct of the people who covenant with each other to have that artificial person govern them. When that sovereign is constituted by one human being, the government is a monarchy; when it is constituted by several, but not all the human beings of the civil state, it is an aristocracy; and when it is constituted by all, it is a democracy. He does not think there was any difference in meaning between "monarchy" and "tyranny," between "aristocracy" and "oligarchy," or between "democracy" and "anarchy." The difference is merely one of tone or connotation. "Tyranny," "oligarchy," and "anarchy" are the words used when one does not like the government. While Hobbes prefers monarchy over the other two forms of government, he recognizes that the other two are equally valid forms.

A difficult issue is whether Hobbes's deductions of the laws of nature involve means/end reasoning or not. Sometimes Hobbes gives the impression that means/end reasoning is always the product of experience. If someone wants to buy some clothes (the end or goal), the person has to go to a store that provides clothes (the means). This is something that is learned. Hobbes's deductions of the laws of nature are not supposed to be empirical, and hence not the product of experience. But it seems that means/end reasoning also applies to geometrical reasoning, and for Hobbes such reasoning is scientific. For him, a circle is a plane figure that was possibly produced by drawing a closed line that is equidistant at every point from a given point inside the figure. This kind of scientific means/end reasoning seems to be at work in the deduction of the laws of nature. If one has the goal of getting out of the state of nature, the means are to make peace. If one has the goal of making peace, the means are to lay down one's right to all things.

So far, Hobbes's theory seems plausible or insightful. But there are problems. One is that he believes in absolute sovereignty, which we may define as the view that the sovereign has the right to all the political power and the right to control almost every aspect of life.[1] Hobbes's argument for absolute sovereignty may be sketched as follows. Whoever has a right to the end has a right to the means necessary to that end. The end of a sovereign is to protect his subjects. Having all the political power and having a right to control every aspect of life are the means necessary to achieving the sovereign's end. Therefore, the sovereign has the right to all the political power and control over every aspect of life. In contrast with absolute or unlimited sovereignty, liberal democracies believe in limited sovereignty. In the United States, for example, political power is distributed among three branches of the federal government (although one could argue that these are

---

1 According to another interpretation, absolute sovereignty is unlimited sovereignty. In this sense, absolute sovereignty is consistent with a separation of such sovereign powers as the executive, legislative, and judicial branches of government.

simply three aspects of one sovereign, the People of the United States), state governments, and municipal governments. Also, the Bill of Rights guarantees that the government does not have the right to encroach upon certain aspects of life. Can Hobbes's theory be changed to accommodate limited sovereignty? Should it be changed?

Other difficult questions can be asked. What exactly is the relationship between subjects or citizens and the sovereign? Is it really the case, as Hobbes sometimes says, that the sovereign has no obligation to his or her subjects? If subjects or citizens actually give up or lose or alienate certain of their rights, is there also a sense in which the sovereign represents the subjects and exercises their own rights for them? But if the sovereign exercises subjects' own rights, they must not have given them up. (To give a modern analogy, when a real-estate agent represents a client and exercises the client's right to buy a piece of property, the real-estate agent does not buy the property; the client does. It is the client who pays the purchase price and takes title to the property.) Hobbes's answers to these questions are not always clear and not always cogent. Such deficiencies are characteristic of even the greatest philosophers. But puzzling over and trying to improve on the ideas of a great philosopher are also two of the joys of doing philosophy.

Leviathan is much more than a great work of political philosophy. Its opening chapters adumbrate a worldview that is thoroughly materialist, mechanistic, and reductionist. Everything that exists is a body; all changes occur through the contact of one body against another; life is nothing but a certain kind of complex motion; human life is strictly analogous to the motion of machines; and qualitative experience of the world is reducible to motions in the brain and heart. In short, Hobbes challenged the most basic beliefs of his contemporaries. The first words of the Introduction, "Nature ... [is] the Art whereby God hath made and governs the world," deconstruct the distinction between what is natural and what is artificial. Nature, the paradigm of what is natural, is artificial, because what is artificial is something made by a person; and God, who is a person, made the world. The deconstruction continues with Hobbes's assertions that machines are alive and human beings are machines.

Equally as contentious is his position that man is not naturally a social or political animal, *pace* Aristotle. In their natural state, human beings are "solitary," as sketched above. The political or civil state is artificial, made by human beings themselves in a creative act. That is, humans create government just as God created the world. The commonwealth he calls "Leviathan," after the monster described in the book of Job as "king over all the sons of pride." All humans are guilty of pride because they are disinclined to obey legitimate authority. Leviathan is also a "mortal god, to which we owe, under the immortal God, our peace and defence," as Hobbes says in chapter 28. Hobbes gives to the sovereign properties that are similar to divine ones, namely, the power to judge what is true and false and what is good and evil, the power to make laws and to save people from the dangers of the state of nature. So Leviathan is a savior god because it does for humans what individually they cannot do themselves. If one thinks about how much Western liberal democracies provide for people, one may see why some political thinkers say that the government has effectively replaced the role of God.

As indicated above, *Leviathan* was written in France mostly during 1650, the year after King Charles I had been beheaded. About the earliest critics of *Leviathan*, a few points are worth making. First, most are respectful of Hobbes as a person and thinker, as the selections in the appendices from Robert Filmer (Appendix A) and Edward Hyde (Appendix G) make clear. The second point is that this praise was often tempered with negative judgments. Hyde wrote that *Leviathan* would "produce much mischief in the world," and that "it has been always a lamentation amongst Mr. Hobbes his friends, that he spent too much time in thinking, and too little in exercising those thoughts in the company of other men of the same or of as good faculties." And Filmer, after endorsing Hobbes's conclusions about government, says, "but I cannot agree to his means of acquiring it. It may seem strange I should praise his building, and yet mislike his foundations; but so it is." The third point to be made about Hobbes's earliest critics is that they rarely read his words sympathetically or engaged him in debate. Their minds ran in the ruts of their time and they often simply denied rather than refuted his arguments. To a large extent, their criticisms are a record of the conventional wisdom of the time. Related to the second and third points is a fourth. Many of his critics think that Hobbes regularly contradicted himself, which in fact does seem to be true. In part this is due to the difficulty of the problems he was trying to solve. Yet some good can come out of the bad of self-contradiction. The reader may be stimulated to select the best consistent theory to be found or reconstructed in the work.

The appendices to this book contain representative criticisms from several seventeenth-century thinkers. Some of the criticisms seem to be fair, but many are unfair, based either on misinterpretations or on unsound arguments. But readers need to decide for themselves whether this is true and, if so, to what extent. They will be assisted by Hobbes's own defense of some of his views, which is reproduced in Appendix H, against the criticisms of Bishop John Bramhall.[1]

---

1   A.P. Martinich wishes to thank Brian Battiste for his comments on the Introduction.

Thomas Hobbes: A Brief Chronology

1588	5 April: Hobbes born in Malmesbury, Wiltshire, England; "invasion" of the Spanish Armada
1608	graduates from Magdalen Hall, Oxford, and becomes tutor to William Cavendish, the future second earl of Devonshire
1614-15	tours Continent (France and Italy) with William Cavendish
1619-23	sometime secretary to Francis Bacon
1622-24	stockholder in Virginia Company, probably by the grace of William Cavendish
1628	William Cavendish dies
1629	publication of Hobbes's translation of Thucydides' *The Peloponnesian War*
1629-30	second tour of the Continent, with Gervase Clifton
1634-36	third tour of the Continent, with William Cavendish, the third earl of Devonshire; associates with Marin Mersenne, Pierre Gassendi, and others in Paris
1636	visits the aged and ill Galileo under house arrest; returns to England in October
1640	spring: *Elements of Law, Natural and Politic*, circulated in manuscript
1640	November: Hobbes flees to the Continent
1641	contributes to *Objections* to Descartes's *Meditations*
1642-49	English Civil War
1642	*De Cive* published; 1647: second edition
1646	debates the issue of free will with John Bramhall in Paris; debate published in 1654-55
1648	December: Pride's Purge
1649	January: execution of Charles I
1649-60	The Commonwealth
1651	about May: *Leviathan* published
1652	February: returns to England; Robert Filmer, *Observations on Mr Hobbes's Leviathan*
1654	*Of Liberty and Necessity* published
1655	*De Corpore* published
1656	English translation of *De Corpore* published
1656	*The Questions Concerning Liberty, Necessity and Chance* published
1657	George Lawson, *An Examination of the Political Part of Mr Hobbes His Leviathan*

1658	*De Homine* published; John Bramhall, *The Catching of Leviathan, or the Great Whale*; death of Oliver Cromwell
1660	Restoration
1661-65	Clarendon Code
1662	*Mr Hobbes Considered in his Loyalty, Religion, Reputation and Manners* published
1663	William Lucy, *Observations, Censures, and Confutations of Notorious Errours in Mr. Hobbes His Leviathan*
1666	bill introduced into the House of Commons to prosecute Hobbes for atheism; no action taken
1667	Edward Hyde, the earl of Clarendon, dismissed by Charles II, flees to the Continent
1668	Latin version of *Leviathan* published
1670	Thomas Tenison, *The Creed of Mr. Hobbes Examined in a feigned Conference between Him and a Student in Divinity*; Samuel Pufendorf, *Of the Law of Nature and Nations*
1673	translation of the *Odyssey* published
1675	leaves London for the last time; last years spent at Chatsworth and Hardwick Hall
1676	translation of the *Iliad* published; Edward Hyde, *A Brief View and Survey of the Dangerous and Pernicious Errors to Church and State in Mr Hobbes's Book, Entitled Leviathan*
1679	4 December: Hobbes dies, buried in the parish church near Hardwick Hall
1679-81	Exclusion Crisis
1680	*An Historical Narration Concerning Heresy, and the Punishment Thereof* published
1682	*An Answer to a Book Published by Dr Bramhall*, published
1688	Glorious Revolution

A Note on the Text

Since this is an edition for students, we have changed those things that we think unduly interfere with understanding and have retained some things that give the flavor of seventeenth-century grammar and typography, with one exception. The "Review and Conclusion" at the end of *Leviathan* is presented in this edition with its original spelling and punctuation. For the rest of the book, we have modernized the spelling of most words (including changing "then" to "than" when appropriate). Greek words have been transliterated into the Roman alphabet. We have modernized punctuation, fully aware of the dangers of doing so. (In this matter, we follow the practice of the great scholar J.C.A. Pocock in his edition of James Harrington's political works.) In the original edition of *Leviathan*, italics were often used for proper names, emphasis, and to indicate a quotation. We have retained italics to indicate a quotation, sometimes retained them for emphasis, but rarely, if ever, use them for proper names. Hobbes's name was spelled in various ways, e.g., "Hobbs." We have typically kept the original form unless its form is an apparent typographical error.

Internal references to the Bible have often been moved to the more natural position at the end of a quotation. Biblical references in the margins remain there. In Hobbes's original edition, these were often preceded by an asterisk that correlated with an asterisk in the body of the text. The asterisks have been removed. Some references have been expanded and some corrected silently. Books of the Bible are set in Roman type.

Since many scholars now refer to *Leviathan* by chapter and paragraph number, we have inserted paragraph numbers into this edition, even though they do not appear in early editions. Since Hobbes's seventeenth-century critics referred to a 1651 edition of *Leviathan*, we have provided the original page numbers in brackets. (It is crucial to remember this when reading references to *Leviathan* in the appendices.) In the 1651 Head edition (and thus in our numbering) two pages are each numbered 247 and 248; and no pages are numbered 84, 194, 257-60, 332, and 388. The original page references also help one to find the same passage in other editions of *Leviathan*. No one interested in political philosophy should own just one edition of *Leviathan*.

Among the things that we might have changed but did not are the verb-ending *-eth* and the full capitalization of words that

Hobbes put in capitals, for example, "HONOUR" and "ENEMY." But we have changed to lower case most nouns that were capitalized; for example, "Commonwealth," "Honour," and "Nature" become "commonwealth," "honour," and "nature."

All items in brackets are our editorial additions to the text.

Words and phrases in brackets in the text either indicate the meaning of an unfamiliar word (e.g., "propriety [property]") or help to fill out Hobbes's syntax a bit (e.g., "for such [men] know"). The context should make clear which is which.

When we refer to other parts of *Leviathan* in the footnotes, the instruction "See also" means that other passages deal with the same topic. "See" usually means that we are giving a reference that the text requires. "Cf." ["confer"] means that other passages give a different treatment of the same topic.

With a few exceptions, we have limited cross-references in the footnotes to other passages in *Leviathan*.

The critical edition of *Leviathan*, edited by G.A.J. Rogers and Karl Schuhmann (Bristol: Continuum, 2003) provided valuable information about textual variants.

We have prepared not a postmodern edition of *Leviathan* but a minimalist one.

Note to the Revised Edition

For this revision, changes have been made to the punctuation in order to increase the clarity of the text. New notes and emendations have been added to help readers understand the text, and unhelpful or misleading notes have been eliminated.

Substantially more cross-references have been provided for the reader. A new appendix, containing selections from Hobbes's reply to Bishop John Bramhall's *The Catching of Leviathan*, has been added.

Some Tips on Understanding Hobbes's Language and Grammar

• Sometimes an independent clause or even a sentence begins with the word "which," referring to something mentioned in the preceding clause, often something quite complex. For example,

No man can know by discourse that this or that is, has been, or will be; *which* is to know absolutely, means

> No man can know by discourse that this or that is, has been, or will be; *to know by discourse that this or that is, has been, or will be* is to know absolutely.

- Sometimes "which" occurs as if it were an adjectival pronoun. For example,

> All which causes ... do manifestly appear in the examples following

means

> All the causes [of religious changes, which were discussed in the preceding six paragraphs] do manifestly appear in the examples following.

- Sometimes the word "that" means "in order that." For example,

> to make known to others our wills, that we may have the mutual help of one another

means

> to make known to others our wills, in order that we may have mutual help.

- Sometimes the word "even" means "that is," as in this passage

> the restorer of the kingdom of God, even our Blessed Saviour.

- Sometimes the word "that" is used where we would use "who." For example, "The man that studies hard" or "The Romans that had conquered the greatest part of the then known world."

- Hobbes sometimes reverses what we consider the normal word order. For example, where he says, "in the body natural," we would say, "in the natural body."

- Often he uses "but" where we would use "nothing but," e.g., "multiplication is but adding together of things equal."

Editions of 1651

Three editions of *Leviathan* purport to have been published by Andrew Crooke with the date 1651. While all three were published during Hobbes's lifetime, two of them were actually later than 1651. The three editions are referred to by the printer's ornament that appears on the title page: Head (a head on a capital), Bear, and 25 Ornaments. The Head edition was the very first. It appeared in two large paper versions. The pages of one of these two contain a border formed by a red line. The Bear edition was probably printed in Holland at an unknown date. The 25 Ornaments edition was probably printed in London about 1680. The Bear and 25 Ornaments editions contain various corrections, modernizations, and even some modifications of the text of the Head edition. While we generally follow the Head edition, some of our readings come from the Bear and 25 Ornaments editions. We also incorporate readings from a vellum manuscript of *Leviathan*, which was probably a gift from Hobbes to Charles II and currently located in the British Library.

Abbreviations

Abbreviations Used for Hobbes's Books

Lev.	*Leviathan*
DC	*De Cive*
Q	*The Questions Concerning Liberty, Necessity and Chance*

Abbreviations Used for Books of the Bible

Acts	Acts of the Apostles
Apoc.	Book of the Apocalypse [= Revelation]
Chron.	Chronicles
Col.	Colossians
Cor.	Corinthians
Dan.	Daniel
Deut.	Deuteronomy
Eccles.	Ecclesiastes
Eph.	Ephesians
Esth.	Esther
Exod.	Exodus
Ezek.	Ezekiel
Gal.	Galatians
Gen.	Genesis
Heb.	Hebrews
Is.	Isaiah
Jer.	Jeremiah
Jon.	Jonah
Josh.	Joshua
Judg.	Judges
Lev.	Leviticus
Matt.	Matthew
Mic.	Micah
Num.	Numbers
Prov.	Proverbs
Ps.	Psalms
Rom.	Romans
Sam.	Samuel
Thes.	Thessalonians
Tim.	Timothy
Zech.	Zechariah

LEVIATHAN

OR

THE MATTER, FORM, & POWER

OF A

COMMON-WEALTH

ECCLESIASTICAL

AND

CIVIL

BY THOMAS HOBBES OF MALMESBURY

Thomas Hobbes, *Leviathan* (1651) illustrated title page.
Harry Ransom Humanities Research Center,
The University of Texas at Austin.

TO MY MOST HONOR'D FRIEND
MR. FRANCIS GODOLPHIN OF GODOLPHIN[1]

Honor'd Sir,

Your most worthy brother Mr. Sidney Godolphin, when he lived, was pleased to think my studies something, and otherwise to oblige me, as you know, with real testimonies of his good opinion, great in themselves, and the greater for the worthiness of his person. For there is not any virtue that disposeth a man, either to the service of God, or to the service of his country, to civil society, or private friendship, that did not manifestly appear in his conversation, not as acquired by necessity, or affected upon occasion, but inherent, and shining in a generous constitution of his nature. Therefore in honour and gratitude to him, and with devotion to yourself, I humbly dedicate unto you this my discourse of commonwealth. I know not how the world will receive it, nor how it may reflect on those that shall seem to favour it. For in a way beset with those that contend on one side for too great liberty, and on the other side for too much authority, 'tis hard to pass between the points of both unwounded. But yet, me thinks, the endeavor to advance the civil power, should not be by the civil power condemned; nor private men, by reprehending it, declare they think that power too great. Besides, I speak not of the men, but (in the abstract) of the seat of power (like to those simple and impartial creatures in the Roman Capitol, that with their noise defended those within it, not because they were they, but there) offending none, I think, but those without, or such within (if there be any such) as favour them. That which perhaps may most offend, are certain texts of Holy Scripture, alleged by me to other purpose than ordinarily they use to be by others. But I have done it with due submission, and also (in order to my subject) necessarily; for they are the

---

1 Sidney Godolphin (1610-43) was an MP in both the Short and Long Parliaments and died, as Hobbes says near the end of *Leviathan*, "by an undiscerned, and an undiscerning hand" ("A Review and Conclusion," 314). Hobbes may have met Godolphin when the latter was a member of the Great Tew Circle (see headnote to Appendix G, below). In his will, Godolphin left Hobbes 200 pounds sterling, which was to be paid by his brother Francis. Hence the dedication.

outworks of the enemy, from whence they impugn the civil power. If notwithstanding this, you find my labour generally decried, you may be pleased to excuse yourself, and say [that] I am a man that love my own opinions, and think all true I say, that I honoured your brother, and honour you, and have presumed on that, to assume the title (without your knowledge) of being, as I am,

    Sir,

    Your most humble, and most obedient servant,

    Thomas Hobbes.

    Paris. April 15/25, 1651

THE CONTENTS OF THE CHAPTERS

1. NATURE (the art whereby God hath made and governs the world) is by the *art* of man, as in many other things, so in this also imitated, that it can make an artificial animal.[1] For seeing life is but a motion of limbs, the beginning whereof is in some principal part within, why may we not say that all *automata* (engines that move themselves by springs and wheels as doth a watch) have an artificial life? For what is the *heart*, but a *spring*; and the *nerves*, but so many *strings*; and the *joints*, but so many *wheels*, giving motion to the whole body, such as was intended by the Artificer? *Art* goes yet further, imitating that rational and most excellent work of nature, *man*. For by art is created that great LEVIATHAN[2] called a COMMONWEALTH, or STATE[3] (in Latin, CIVITAS), which is but an artificial man, though of greater stature and strength than the natural, for whose protection and defence it was intended; and in which the sovereignty is an artificial *soul*, as giving life and motion to the whole body. The *magistrates* and other *officers* of judicature and execution [are] artificial *joints*. *Reward* and *punishment* (by which fastened to the seat of the sovereignty, every joint and member is moved to perform his duty) are the *nerves* that do the same in the body natural. The *wealth* and *riches* of all the particular members are the *strength*. S*alus populi* (the *people's safety*) [is] its *business*. *Counsellors*, by whom all things needful for it

---

1 Hobbes is showing that normal beliefs do not pass scrutiny. Nature is actually artificial; machines are alive and humans are machines. Our beliefs must be reconsidered.

2 Cf. 17.13 and 28.27.

3 Comparing the state to a living body was common in the late sixteenth and the seventeenth centuries: "The head cares for the body, so doeth the King for his people. As the discourse and direction flowes from the head, and the execution thereunto belongs to the rest of the members, everyone according to their office: so it is betwixt a wise Prince and his people" (James VI of Scotland, "The Trew Law of Free Monarchies," [1598]); and "As in natural things, the head being cut off, the rest cannot be called a body: no more can in politick things a multitude or commonality, without a head be incorporate" (Anonymous, *Examples for Kings: or Rules for Princes to Govern By*, [1642]).

to know are suggested unto it, are the *memory*. *Equity* and laws [are] an artificial *reason* and *will*. *Concord* [is] *health*. *Sedition [is] sickness*. And *civil war* [is] *death*. Lastly, the *pact*s and *covenants* by which the parts of this body politic were at first made, set together, and united, resemble that *fiat*,[1] or the *let us make man*, pronounced by God in the Creation.

[2]   2. To describe the nature of this artificial man, I will consider

First, the *matter* thereof, and the *artificer*; both which is *Man*.

Secondly, *how*, and by what *covenants* it is made; what are the rights and just *power* or *authority* of a *sovereign*; and what it is that *preserveth* and *dissolveth* it.

Thirdly, what is a *Christian Commonwealth*.

Lastly, what is the *Kingdom of Darkness*.

3. Concerning the first, there is a saying much usurped of late that *wisdom* is acquired, not by reading of *books*, but of men. Consequently whereunto, those persons, that for the most part can give no other proof of being wise, take great delight to show what they think they have read in men by uncharitable censures of one another behind their backs. But there is another saying, not of late understood, by which they might learn truly to read one another, if they would take the pains; and that is *nosce teipsum*, *read thyself*, which was not meant, as it is now used, to countenance either the barbarous state of men in power towards their inferiors or to encourage men of low degree to a saucy behaviour towards their betters. But [it was meant] to teach us that for the similitude of the thoughts and passions of one man to the thoughts and passions of another, whosoever looketh into himself and considereth what he doth when he does *think, opine, reason, hope, fear*, etc., and upon what grounds, he shall thereby read and know what are the thoughts and passions of all other men upon the like occasions. I say the similitude of *passions*, which are the same in all men, *desire, fear, hope*, etc., not the similitude of the *objects* of the passions, which are the things *desired, feared, hoped*, etc.; for these the constitution

---

1   *Fiat* is Latin for "Let there be." *Fiat lux* means "Let there be light." *Fiat homo* means "Let there be man." These are some of God's words of creation in the Vulgate or Latin version of the Bible.

individual and particular education do so vary, and they are so easy to be kept from our knowledge that the characters of man's heart, blotted and confounded as they are with dissembling, lying, counterfeiting, and erroneous doctrines are legible only to him that searcheth hearts. And though by men's actions we do discover their design sometimes; yet to do it without comparing them with our own and distinguishing all circumstances by which the case may come to be altered is to decipher without a key and be for the most part deceived by too much trust or by too much diffidence, as he that reads is himself a good or evil man.

4. But let one man read another by his actions never so perfectly, it serves him only with his acquaintance, which are but few. He that is to govern a whole nation must read in himself, not this or that particular man, but mankind, which though it be hard to do, harder than to learn any language or science; yet when I shall have set down my own reading orderly and perspicuously, the pains left another will be only to consider if he also find not the same in himself. For this kind of doctrine admitteth no other demonstration.

PART I

OF MAN

Chapter I

Of Sense

1. Concerning the thoughts of man, I will consider them first singly and afterwards in train or dependence upon one another. Singly, they are every one a representation or appearance of some quality or other accident of a body without us, which is commonly called an *object*. Which object worketh on the eyes, ears, and other parts of man's body, and by diversity of working, produceth diversity of appearances.[1]

2. The original [origin] of them all is that which we call SENSE (for there is no conception in a man's mind which hath not at first, totally or by parts, been begotten upon the organs of sense). The rest are derived from that original.[2]

3. To know the natural cause of sense is not very necessary to the business now in hand; and I have elsewhere written of the same at large. Nevertheless, to fill each part of my present method, I will briefly deliver the same in this place.

4. The cause of sense is the external body or object which presseth the organ proper to each sense either immediately, as in the taste and touch, or mediately, as in seeing, hearing, and smelling; which pressure, by the mediation of nerves and other strings and membranes of the body, continued inwards to the brain and heart, causeth there a resistance or counter-pressure or endeavour of the heart to deliver itself, which endeavour, because *outward*, seemeth to be some matter without. And this *seeming* or

---

1 Hobbes is conceding that there is qualitative experience of the world, as he also does in 1.4

2 A standard philosophical view, usually associated with Aristotelian philosophy, is that "nothing is in the intellect that was not first in the senses."

CHAPTER I: OF SENSE 39

fancy is that which men call *sense* and consisteth, as to the eye in a *light* or *colour figured*; to the ear in a *sound*; to the nostril in an *odour*; to the tongue and palate in a *savour*; and to the rest of the body in *heat, cold, hardness, softness*, and such other qualities as we discern by *feeling*. All which qualities called *sensible* are in the object that causeth them but so many several motions of the matter by which it presseth our organs diversely.[1] Neither in us that are pressed are they anything else but divers motions (for motion produceth nothing but motion).[2] But their appearance to us is fancy, the same waking [as] that dreaming. And as pressing, rubbing, or striking the eye makes us fancy a light, and pressing the ear produceth a din, so do the bodies also we see or hear produce the same by their strong, though unobserved action. For if those colours and sounds were in the bodies or objects

[4] that cause them, they could not be severed from them, as by glasses, and in echoes by reflection, we see they are where we know the thing we see is in one place, the appearance in another. And though at some certain distance the real and very object seem invested with the fancy it begets in us; yet still the object is one thing, the image or fancy is another. So that sense in all cases is nothing else but original fancy, caused (as I have said) by the pressure, that is, by the motion of external things upon our eyes, ears, and other organs, thereunto ordained.

5. But the philosophy schools, through all the universities of Christendom, grounded upon certain texts of Aristotle,[3] teach another doctrine; and say for the cause of *vision*, that the thing seen sendeth forth on every side a *visible species*, (in English) a *visible show, apparition*, or *aspect*, or *a being seen*, the receiving whereof into the eye is *seeing*. And for the cause of *hearing*, that the thing heard sendeth forth an *audible species*, that is, an *audible aspect*, or *audible being seen*; which, entering at the ear, maketh *hearing*. Nay, for the cause of *understanding* also, they say the thing understood sendeth forth an *intelligible species*, that is, *an intelligible being seen*; which coming into the

---

1 The qualitative properties that people naturally think of as in bodies are actually only motions of very small bodies.

2 Qualitative experiences in humans are also nothing but motions. Cf. 1.1. Thus, the Aristotelian view is false; see 1.5.

3 Hobbes is thinking primarily of Aristotle's *Metaphysics*.

understanding, makes us understand. I say not this as disapproving the use of universities, but because I am to speak hereafter of their office in a commonwealth, I must let you see on all occasions by the way what things would be amended in them, amongst which the frequency of insignificant [meaningless] speech is one.

Chapter II

Of Imagination

1. That when a thing lies still, unless somewhat else stir it, it will lie still for ever is a truth that no man doubts of. But that when a thing is in motion, it will eternally be in motion, unless somewhat else stay it, though the reason be the same (namely, that nothing can change itself), is not so easily assented to. For men measure, not only other men, but all other things, by themselves; and because they find themselves subject after motion to pain and lassitude think everything else grows weary of motion and seeks repose of its own accord, little considering whether it be not some other motion wherein that desire of rest they find in themselves consisteth. From hence it is that the schools say heavy bodies fall downwards out of an appetite to rest and to conserve their nature in that place which is most proper for them, ascribing appetite, and knowledge of what is good for their conservation (which is more than man has) to things inanimate, absurdly.

2. When a body is once in motion, it moveth (unless something else hinder it) eternally; and whatsoever hindreth it cannot in an instant but in time and by degrees quite extinguish it. And as we see in the water, though the wind cease, the waves give not over rolling for a long [5] time after, so also it happeneth in that motion which is made in the internal parts of a man, then, when he sees, dreams, etc. For after the object is removed or the eye shut, we still retain an image of the thing seen, though more obscure than when we see it. And this is it the Latins call *imagination*, from the image made in seeing; and [they] apply the same, though improperly, to all the other senses. But the Greeks call it *fancy*, which signifies *appearance*, and is as proper to one sense as to another.

IMAGINATION, therefore, is nothing but *decaying sense*[1] and is found in men and many other living creatures, as well sleeping as waking.

3. The decay of sense in men waking is not the decay of the motion made in sense, but an obscuring of it, in such manner as the light of the sun obscureth the light of the stars, which stars do no less exercise their virtue by which they are visible in the day than in the night. But because amongst many strokes which our eyes, ears, and other organs receive from external bodies, the predominant only is sensible; therefore the light of the sun being predominant, we are not affected with the action of the stars. And any object being removed from our eyes, though the impression it made in us remain; yet [with] other objects more present succeeding and working on us, the imagination of the past is obscured and made weak, as the voice of a man is in the noise of the day. From whence it followeth that the longer the time is after the sight or sense of any object, the weaker is the imagination. For the continual change of man's body destroys in time the parts which in sense were moved, so that distance of time and of place hath one and the same effect in us. For as at a great distance of place that which we look at appears dim and without distinction of the smaller parts, and as voices grow weak and inarticulate; so also after great distance of time our imagination of the past is weak; and we lose (for example) of cities we have seen many particular streets, and of actions many particular circumstances. This *decaying sense*, when we would express the thing itself (I mean *fancy* itself), we call *imagination*, as I said before. But when we would express the decay and signify that the sense is fading, old, and past, it is called *memory*. So that imagination and memory are but one thing, which for divers considerations hath divers names.

Memory.

4. Much memory, or memory of many things, is called *experience*. Again, imagination being only of those things which have been formerly perceived by sense, either all

---

1 Hobbes's goal is to show that mental states and events, for example, imagination, are reducible to a few basic things, and ultimately matter in motion. Thus, imagination is really decaying sense, and a sensation is a motion in the brain. Memory is imagination, which is decaying sense, which is motion.

at once or by parts at several times. The former (which is the imagining the whole object, as it was presented to the sense) is *simple* imagination, as when one imagineth a man or horse, which he hath seen before. The other is *compounded,* when from the sight of a man at one time and of a horse at another, we conceive in our mind a centaur. So when a man compoundeth the image of his own person with the image of the actions of another man, as when a man imagines himself a Hercules or an Alexander (which happeneth often to them that are much taken with reading of romances), it is a compound imagination and properly but a fiction of the mind. There be also [6] other imaginations that rise in men (though waking) from the great impression made in sense. As from gazing upon the sun, the impression leaves an image of the sun before our eyes a long time after; and from being long and vehemently attent [attentive] upon geometrical figures, a man shall in the dark (though awake) have the images of lines and angles before his eyes, which kind of fancy hath no particular name, as being a thing that doth not commonly fall into men's discourse.[1]

5. The imaginations of them that sleep are those we   Dreams. call *dreams.* And these also (as all other imaginations) have been before either totally or by parcels in the sense. And because in sense the brain and nerves, which are the necessary organs of sense, are so benumbed in sleep as not easily to be moved by the action of external objects, there can happen in sleep no imagination and therefore no dream, but what proceeds from the agitation of the inward parts of man's body; which inward parts, for the connexion they have with the brain and other organs, when they be distempered, do keep the same in motion; whereby the imaginations there formerly made, appear as if a man were waking, saving that the organs of sense being now benumbed, so as there is no new object which can master and obscure them with a more vigorous impression, a dream must needs be more clear in this silence of sense than are our waking thoughts. And hence it cometh to pass that it is a hard matter, and by many thought impossible, to distinguish exactly between sense

---

1   Philosophers today call this kind of fancy an "afterimage."

and dreaming.[1] For my part, when I consider that in dreams I do not often nor constantly think of the same persons, places, objects, and actions that I do waking, nor remember so long a train of coherent thoughts dreaming as at other times, and because waking I often observe the absurdity of dreams, but never dream of the absurdities of my waking thoughts, I am well satisfied that, being awake, I know I dream not, though when I dream, I think myself awake.

6. And seeing dreams are caused by the distemper of some of the inward parts of the body, divers distempers must needs cause different dreams. And hence it is that lying cold breedeth dreams of fear and raiseth the thought and image of some fearful object, the motion from the brain to the inner parts, and from the inner parts to the brain being reciprocal, and that as anger causeth heat in some parts of the body when we are awake, so when we sleep the overheating of the same parts causeth anger and raiseth up in the brain the imagination of an enemy. In the same manner, as natural kindness when we are awake causeth desire and desire makes heat in certain other parts of the body, so also too much heat in those parts, while we sleep, raiseth in the brain an imagination of some kindness shown. In sum, our dreams are the reverse of our waking imaginations; the motion when we are awake beginning at one end, and when we dream, at another.

Apparitions or Visions. [7]

7. The most difficult discerning of a man's dream from his waking thoughts is, then, when by some accident we observe not that we have slept; which is easy to happen to a man full of fearful thoughts, and whose conscience is much troubled, and that sleepeth without the circumstances of going to bed or putting off his clothes, as one that noddeth in a chair. For he that taketh pains and industriously lays himself to sleep, in case any uncouth and exorbitant fancy come unto him, cannot easily think it other than a dream. We read of Marcus Brutus (one that had his life given him by Julius Caesar, and was also

---

1 A partial response to Descartes. It is significant because Hobbes does not try to identify a criterion to distinguish dreaming from waking. Such a criterion would be useless, because one would need another criterion to judge whether one was correctly applying the first criterion, and so on.

his favourite, and notwithstanding murdered him), how at Philippi, the night before he gave battle to Augustus Caesar, he saw a fearful apparition, which is commonly related by historians as a vision. But, considering the circumstances, one may easily judge to have been but a short dream. For sitting in his tent, pensive and troubled with the horror of his rash act, it was not hard for him, slumbering in the cold, to dream of that which most affrighted him; which fear, as by degrees it made him wake, so also it must needs make the apparition by degrees to vanish. And having no assurance that he slept, he could have no cause to think it a dream, or anything but a vision. And this is no very rare accident; for even they that be perfectly awake, if they be timorous [timid] and superstitious, possessed with fearful tales and alone in the dark, are subject to the like fancies, and believe they see spirits and dead men's ghosts walking in churchyards; whereas it is either their fancy only or else the knavery of such persons as make use of such superstitious fear to pass disguised in the night to places they would not be known to haunt.

8. From this ignorance of how to distinguish dreams and other strong fancies from vision and sense did arise the greatest part of the religion of the Gentiles in time past that worshipped satyrs, fauns, nymphs, and the like; and nowadays the opinion that rude people have of fairies, ghosts, and goblins, and of the power of witches.[1] For, as for witches, I think not that their witchcraft is any real power, but yet that they are justly punished for the false belief they have that they can do such mischief, joined with their purpose to do it if they can, their trade being nearer to a new religion than to a craft or science. And for fairies and walking ghosts, the opinion of them has, I think, been on purpose either taught or not confuted to keep in credit the use of exorcism, of crosses, of holy water, and other such inventions of ghostly[2] men. Nevertheless, there is no doubt but God can make unnatural

---

1 Scholars dispute whether Hobbes wanted to restrict this problem to pagan religions or to extend it to Christianity also. Many Protestant theologians lamented the widespread superstitions of most people.

2 "Ghostly" may mean either spiritual or religious. In either case, Hobbes is being sarcastic. See also 47.24.

apparitions. But that he does it so often as men need to fear such things more than they fear the stay or change of the course of nature, which he also can stay and change, is no point of Christian faith. But evil men, under pretext that God can do anything, are so bold as to say anything when it serves their turn, though they think it untrue. It is the part of a wise man to believe them no further than right reason makes that which they say appear credible. If this superstitious fear of spirits were taken away and with it prognostics from dreams, false prophecies, and [8] many other things depending thereon, by which crafty ambitious persons abuse the simple people, men would be much more fitted than they are for civil obedience.

9. And this ought to be the work of the schools, but they rather nourish such doctrine. For (not knowing what imagination or the senses are) what they receive, they teach, some saying that imaginations rise of themselves and have no cause, others that they rise most commonly from the will and that good thoughts are blown (inspired) into a man by God, and evil thoughts by the Devil, or that good thoughts are poured (infused) into a man by God, and evil ones by the Devil. Some say the senses receive the species of things and deliver them to the common sense; and the common sense delivers them over to the fancy, and the fancy to the memory, and the memory to the judgement, like handing of things from one to another with many words making nothing understood.

Understanding.	10. The imagination that is raised in man (or any other creature endued with the faculty of imagining) by words or other voluntary signs is that we generally call *understanding*, and is common to man and beast. For a dog by custom will understand the call or the rating of his master, and so will many other beasts. That understanding which is peculiar to man is the understanding not only his will, but his conceptions and thoughts, by the sequel and contexture of the names of things into affirmations, negations, and other forms of speech. And of this kind of understanding I shall speak hereafter.

Chapter III

Of the Consequence or Train of Imaginations

1. By *Consequence* or TRAIN of thoughts, I understand that succession of one thought to another, which is called (to distinguish it from discourse in words) *mental discourse*.

2. When a man thinketh on anything whatsoever, his next thought after is not altogether so casual as it seems to be. Not every thought to every thought succeeds indifferently. But as we have no imagination whereof we have not formerly had sense in whole or in parts, so we have no transition from one imagination to another whereof we never had the like before in our senses. The reason whereof is this. All fancies are motions within us, relics of those made in the sense. And those motions that immediately succeeded one another in the sense continue also together after sense; in so much as the former coming again to take place and be predominant, the latter followeth by coherence of the matter moved in such manner as water upon a plain table is drawn which way any one part of it is guided by the finger. But because in sense, to one and the same thing perceived, sometimes one thing, sometimes another, succeedeth, it comes to pass in time that in the imagining of anything, there is no certainty what we shall imagine next. Only this is certain, it shall be something that succeeded the same before, at one time or another. [9]

3. This train of thoughts or mental discourse is of two sorts. The first is *unguided, without design*, and inconstant, wherein there is no passionate thought to govern and direct those that follow to itself, as the end and scope of some desire or other passion; in which case the thoughts are said to wander and seem impertinent one to another, as in a dream. Such are commonly the thoughts of men that are not only without company, but also without care of anything, though even then their thoughts are as busy as at other times, but without harmony; as the sound which a lute out of tune would yield to any man, or in tune to one that could not play. And yet in this wild ranging of the mind, a man may oft-times perceive the way of it and the dependence of one thought upon another. For in a discourse of our present civil war, what could seem

Train of thoughts unguided.

more impertinent than to ask, as one did, what was the value of a Roman penny? Yet the coherence to me was manifest enough. For the thought of the war introduced the thought of the delivering up the King to his enemies; the thought of that brought in the thought of the delivering up of Christ; and that again the thought of the 30 pence, which was the price of that treason; and thence easily followed that malicious question; and all this in a moment of time, for thought is quick.

Train of thoughts, regulated.

4. The second is more constant, as being regulated by some desire and design. For the impression made by such things as we desire or fear is strong and permanent, or (if it cease for a time) of quick return; so strong it is sometimes as to hinder and break our sleep. From desire ariseth the thought of some means we have seen produce the like of that which we aim at; and from the thought of that the thought of means to that mean; and so continually, till we come to some beginning within our own power. And because the end by the greatness of the impression comes often to mind, in case our thoughts begin to wander they are quickly again reduced into the way; which, observed by one of the seven wise men, made him give men this precept, which is now worn out: *respice finem*;[1] that is to say, in all your actions, look often upon what you would have, as the thing that directs all your thoughts in the way to attain it.

5. The train of regulated thoughts is of two kinds: one, when of an effect imagined we seek the causes or means that produce it; and this is common to man and beast. The other is, when imagining anything whatsoever, we seek all the possible effects that can by it be produced; that is to say, we imagine what we can do with it when we have it. Of which I have not at any time seen any sign, but in man only; for this is a curiosity hardly incident to the nature of any living creature that has no other passion but sensual, such as are hunger, thirst, lust, and anger. In sum, the discourse of the mind, when it is governed by design, is nothing but seeking, or the faculty of invention, which the Latins call *sagacitas*, and *solertia*, a hunting out of the causes of some effect, present or past, or of the

[10]

---

1 See Plato, *Protagoras* 343a-b; Chilon according to repute said, "Look to the end."

effects of some present or past cause. Sometimes a man seeks what he hath lost; and from that place and time wherein he misses it his mind runs back, from place to place, and time to time, to find where and when he had it; that is to say, to find some certain and limited time and place in which to begin a method of seeking. Again, from thence, his thoughts run over the same places and times to find what action or other occasion might make him lose it. This we call *remembrance* or calling to mind. The Latins call it *reminiscentia*, as it were a *re-conning* [re-examination] of our former actions.

Remembrance.

6. Sometimes a man knows a place determinate, within the compass whereof he is to seek; and then his thoughts run over all the parts thereof in the same manner as one would sweep a room to find a jewel, or as a spaniel ranges the field till he find a scent, or as a man should run over the alphabet to start a rhyme.

7. Sometimes a man desires to know the event[1] of an action; and then he thinketh of some like action past, and the events thereof one after another, supposing like events will follow like actions. As he that foresees what will become of a criminal re-cons [recalls] what he has seen follow on the like crime before, having this order of thoughts: the crime, the officer, the prison, the judge, and the gallows. Which kind of thoughts is called *foresight*, and *prudence*, or *providence*, and sometimes *wisdom*; though such conjecture, through the difficulty of observing all circumstances, be very fallacious. But this is certain: by how much one man has more experience of things past than another; by so much also he is more prudent, and his expectations the seldomer fail him. The *present* only has a being in nature; things *past* have a being in the memory only; but things *to come* have no being at all, the *future* being but a fiction of the mind, applying the sequels of actions past to the actions that are present; which with most certainty is done by him that has most experience, but not with certainty enough. And though it be called prudence when the event answereth our expectation; yet in its own nature it is but presumption. For the foresight of things to come, which is providence, belongs only to

Prudence.

---

1 "Event" here may mean effect, result, or outcome, as suggested by the Latin version of *Leviathan*.

him by whose will they are to come.[1] From him only, and supernaturally, proceeds prophecy. The best prophet naturally is the best guesser; and the best guesser, he that is most versed and studied in the matters he guesses at, for he hath most *signs* to guess by.[2]

Signs.   8. A *sign* is the event antecedent of the consequent, and contrarily, the consequent of the antecedent, when the like consequences have been observed before; and the oftener they have been observed, the less uncertain is the sign. And therefore he that has most experience in any kind of business has most signs whereby to guess at the future time, and consequently is the most prudent. And [he is] so much more prudent than he that is new in that kind of business, as not to be equalled by any advantage of natural and extemporary wit, though perhaps many young men think the contrary.

[11]   9. Nevertheless, it is not prudence that distinguisheth man from beast. There be beasts that at a year old observe more and pursue that which is for their good more prudently than a child can do at ten.

Conjecture of the times past.   10. As prudence is a *presumption* of the *future*, contracted from the *experience* of time *past*, so there is a presumption of things past taken from other things (not future but) past also. For he that hath seen by what courses and degrees a flourishing state hath first come into civil war, and then to ruin, upon the sight of the ruins of any other state will guess the like war and the like courses have been there also. But this conjecture has the same uncertainty almost with the conjecture of the future, both being grounded only upon experience.

11. There is no other act of man's mind that I can remember naturally planted in him so as to need no other thing to the exercise of it but to be born a man and live with the use of his five senses. Those other faculties, of which I shall speak by and by and which seem proper to man only, are acquired and increased by study and industry, and of most men learned by instruction and discipline, and proceed all from the invention of words and speech. For besides sense and thoughts and the train of thoughts, the mind of man has no other motion, though

---

1 I.e., God.

2 See also 12.19.

by the help of speech and method, the same faculties may be improved to such a height as to distinguish men from all other living creatures.

12. Whatsoever we imagine is *finite*. Therefore there is no idea or conception of anything we call *infinite*.[1] No man can have in his mind an image of infinite magnitude, nor conceive infinite swiftness, infinite time, or infinite force, or infinite power. When we say anything is infinite, we signify only that we are not able to conceive the ends and bounds of the thing named, having no conception of the thing, but of our own inability.[2] And therefore the name of God is used, not to make us conceive him (for he is incomprehensible, and his greatness and power are unconceivable), but that we may honour him. Also because whatsoever (as I said before) we conceive has been perceived first by sense, either all at once or by parts, a man can have no thought representing anything not subject to sense. No man therefore can conceive anything, but he must conceive it in some place and endued with some determinate magnitude; and which may be divided into parts; nor that anything is all in this place and all in another place at the same time; nor that two or more things can be in one and the same place at once. For none of these things ever have or can be incident to sense, but are absurd speeches, taken upon credit, without any signification at all, from deceived philosophers and deceived or deceiving Schoolmen.

Chapter IV

[12]

Of Speech

1. The invention of *printing*, though ingenious, compared with the invention of *letters*, is no great matter. But who was the first that found the use of letters is not known. He that first brought them into Greece, men say, was Cadmus, the son of Agenor, King of Phoenicia. A profitable invention for continuing the memory of time past

Original [origin] of speech.

---

1 See also 12.6, 31.28, 45.12, and 45.15.
2 Infinite magnitude or number is as hard to understand as infinite goodness.

and the conjunction of mankind dispersed into so many and distant regions of the earth; and withal [in addition] difficult, as proceeding from a watchful observation of the divers motions of the tongue, palate, lips, and other organs of speech, whereby to make as many differences of characters to remember them. But the most noble and profitable invention of all other was that of SPEECH, consisting of *names* or *appellations*, and their connexion, whereby men register their thoughts, recall them when they are past, and also declare them one to another for mutual utility and conversation, without which there had been amongst men neither commonwealth nor society nor contract nor peace no more than amongst lions, bears, and wolves. The first author of speech was God himself, that instructed Adam how to name such creatures as he presented to his sight, for the Scripture goeth no further in this matter. But this was sufficient to direct him to add more names, as the experience and use of the creatures should give him occasion, and to join them in such manner by degrees as to make himself understood, and so by succession of time so much language might be gotten as he had found use for, though not so copious as an orator or philosopher has need of. For I do not find anything in the Scripture out of which, directly or by consequence, can be gathered that Adam was taught the names of all figures, numbers, measures, colours, sounds, fancies, relations; much less the names of words and speech, as *general, special, affirmative, negative, interrogative, optative, infinitive*, all which are useful; and least of all, of *entity, intentionality, quiddity*, and other insignificant words of the School.[1]

---

1 By "School," Hobbes is referring to the tradition of medieval Aristotelian philosophy that dominated Europe in the thirteenth and fourteenth centuries. It was influenced to a greater or lesser extent by Aristotle (384-322 BCE), Thomas Aquinas (c. 1225-74), John Duns Scotus (c. 1265-1308), and William of Ockham (c. 1288-c. 1348). Although this tradition was in decline in the seventeenth century, it was still influential. Spanish scholastic philosopher Francisco Suarez (1548-1617), for example, is sometimes singled out for criticism by Hobbes. Many of Hobbes's opponents, notably Bishop John Bramhall (see Appendix C), were scholastic philosophers.

2. But all this language gotten and augmented by Adam and his posterity, was again lost at the Tower of Babel, when by the hand of God every man was stricken for his rebellion with an oblivion of his former language. And being hereby forced to disperse themselves into several parts of the world, it must needs be that the diversity of tongues that now is, proceeded by degrees from them in such manner as need (the mother of all inventions) taught them; and in tract of time grew everywhere more copious.

3. The general use of speech is to transfer our mental discourse into verbal or the train of our thoughts into a train of words, and that for two commodities, whereof one is the registering of the consequences of our thoughts, which being apt to slip out of our memory and put us to a new labour, may again be recalled by such words as they were marked by. So that the first use of names is to serve for *marks* or *notes* of remembrance. Another is when many use the same words to signify (by their connexion and order) one to another, what they conceive or think of each matter and also what they desire, fear, or have any other passion for. And for this use they are called *signs*. Special uses of speech are these: first, to register what by cogitation we find to be the cause of anything, present or past, and what we find things present or past may produce or effect, which, in sum, is acquiring of arts. Secondly, to show to others that knowledge which we have attained, which is to counsel and teach one another. Thirdly, to make known to others our wills and purposes, that we may have the mutual help of one another. Fourthly, to please and delight ourselves and others, by playing with our words for pleasure or ornament, innocently.

4. To these uses, there are also four correspondent abuses. First, when men register their thoughts wrong by the inconstancy of the signification of their words, by which they register for their conceptions that which they never conceived, and so deceive themselves. Secondly, when they use words metaphorically, that is, in other sense than that they are ordained for, and thereby deceive others. Thirdly, when by words they declare that to be their will, which is not. Fourthly, when they use them to grieve one another, for seeing nature hath armed living creatures, some with teeth, some with horns, and

The use of speech.

[13]

Abuses of speech.

some with hands, to grieve an enemy, it is but an abuse of speech to grieve him with the tongue, unless it be one whom we are obliged to govern; and then it is not to grieve, but to correct and amend.

5. The manner how speech serveth to the remembrance of the consequence of causes and effects consisteth in the imposing of *names*, and the *connexion* of them.

Names proper and common.

6. Of names, some are *proper*, and singular to one only thing; as *Peter*, *John*, *this man*, *this tree*. And some are *common* to many things, as *man*, *horse*, *tree*, every of which, though but one name, is nevertheless the name of divers particular things, in respect of all which together,

Universal.

it is called a *universal*, there being nothing in the world universal but names, for the things named are every one of them individual and singular.[1]

7. One universal name is imposed on many things for their similitude in some quality or other accident. And whereas a proper name bringeth to mind one thing only, universals recall any one of those many.

8. And of names universal, some are of more and some of less extent, the larger comprehending the less large. And some again [are] of equal extent, comprehending each other reciprocally. As for example, the name *body* is of larger signification than the word *man*, and comprehendeth it; and the names *man* and *rational* are of equal extent, comprehending mutually one another. But here

[14]

we must take notice that by a name is not always understood, as in grammar, one only word, but sometimes by circumlocution many words together. For all these words, *he that in his actions observeth the laws of his country*, make but one name, equivalent to this one word, *just*.

9. By this imposition of names, some of larger, some of stricter signification, we turn the reckoning of the consequences of things imagined in the mind into a reckoning of the consequences of appellations. For example, a man that hath no use of speech at all (such as is born and remains perfectly deaf and dumb), if he set before his eyes a triangle and by it two right angles (such as are the corners of a square figure), he may by meditation compare and find that the three angles of that triangle are equal to those two right angles that stand by it. But if

---

1 A clear statement of Hobbes's nominalism.

another triangle be shown him different in shape from the former, he cannot know without a new labour whether the three angles of that also be equal to the same. But he that hath the use of words, when he observes that such equality was consequent, not to the length of the sides, nor to any other particular thing in his triangle, but only to this, that the sides were straight, and the angles three, and that that was all for which he named it a triangle, will boldly conclude universally that such equality of angles is in all triangles whatsoever and register his invention in these general terms: *Every triangle hath its three angles equal to two right angles*. And thus the consequence found in one particular comes to be registered and remembered as a universal rule and discharges our mental reckoning of time and place, and delivers us from all labour of the mind, saving the first; and makes that which was found true *here* and *now* to be true in *all times and places*.

10. But the use of words in registering our thoughts is in nothing so evident as in numbering. A natural fool that could never learn by heart the order of numeral words, as *one, two,* and *three,* may observe every stroke of the clock and nod to it or say *one, one, one,* but can never know what hour it strikes. And it seems there was a time when those names of number were not in use; and men were fain to apply their fingers of one or both hands to those things they desired to keep account of; and that thence it proceeded that now our numeral words are but ten, in any nation, and in some but five, and then they begin again. And he that can tell ten, if he recite them out of order, will lose himself and not know when he has done. Much less will he be able to add and subtract and perform all other operations of arithmetic. So that without words there is no possibility of reckoning of numbers, much less of magnitudes, of swiftness, of force, and other things, the reckonings whereof are necessary to the being or well-being of mankind.

11. When two names are joined together into a consequence or affirmation, as thus, *A man is a living creature,* or thus, *If he be a man, he is a living creature*; if the latter name *living creature* signify all that the former name *man* signifieth, then the affirmation or consequence is *true*; [15] otherwise *false*. For *true* and *false* are attributes of speech, not of things. And where speech is not, there is neither

truth nor *falsehood*. *Error* there may be, as when we expect that which shall not be or suspect what has not been; but in neither case can a man be charged with untruth.

12. Seeing then that *truth* consisteth in the right ordering of names in our affirmations, a man that seeketh precise truth had need to remember what every name he uses stands for and to place it accordingly; or else he will find himself entangled in words, as a bird in lime twigs; the more he struggles, the more belimed. And therefore in geometry (which is the only science that it hath pleased God hitherto to bestow on mankind), men begin at settling the significations of their words, which settling of significations they call *definitions*, and place them in the beginning of their reckoning.[1]

13. By this it appears how necessary it is for any man that aspires to true knowledge to examine the definitions of former authors and either to correct them, where they are negligently set down, or to make them himself. For the errors of definitions multiply themselves, according as the reckoning proceeds, and lead men into absurdities, which at last they see, but cannot avoid, without reckoning anew from the beginning, in which lies the foundation of their errors. From whence it happens that they which trust to books do as they that cast up many little sums into a greater, without considering whether those little sums were rightly cast up or not; and at last finding the error visible, and not mistrusting their first grounds, know not which way to clear themselves, but spend time in fluttering over their books, as birds that entering by the chimney, and finding themselves enclosed in a chamber, flutter at the false light of a glass window for want of wit to consider which way they came in. So that in the right definition of names lies the first use of speech, which is the acquisition of science, and in wrong or no definitions lies the first abuse, from which proceed all false and senseless tenets, which make those men that take their instruction from the authority of books and not from their own meditation to be as much below the condition of ignorant men as men endued with true science are above it. For between true science and erroneous doctrines, ignorance

---

1 These definitions may be stipulative and need not be descriptive of actual use.

is in the middle. Natural sense and imagination are not subject to absurdity. Nature itself cannot err; and as men abound in copiousness of language, so they become more wise or more mad than ordinary. Nor is it possible without letters for any man to become either excellently wise or (unless his memory be hurt by disease or ill constitution of organs) excellently foolish. For words are wise men's counters; they do but reckon by them; but they are the money of fools, that value them by the authority of an Aristotle, a Cicero or a Thomas, or any other doctor whatsoever, if but a man.

14. *Subject to names* is whatsoever can enter into or be considered in an account and be added one to another to make a sum, or subtracted one from another and leave a remainder. The Latins called accounts of money *rationes*, and accounting *ratiocinatio*. And that which we in bills or books of account call *items*, they called *nomina*, that is, *names*. And thence it seems to proceed that they extended the word *ratio* to the faculty of reckoning in all other things. The Greeks have but one word, *logos*, for both *speech* and *reason*; not that they thought there was no speech without reason, but no reasoning without speech. And the act of reasoning they called *syllogism*; which signifieth summing up of the consequences of one saying to another. And because the same things may enter into account for divers accidents, their names are (to show that diversity) diversely wrested and diversified. This diversity of names may be reduced to four general heads.

Subject to names.

[16]

15. First, a thing may enter into account for *matter* or *body*, as *living, sensible, rational, hot, cold, moved, quiet*, with all which names the word *matter* or *body* is understood; all such being names of matter.

16. Secondly, it may enter into account or be considered for some accident or quality which we conceive to be in it, as for *being moved*, for *being so long*, for *being hot*, etc.; and then of the name of the thing itself, by a little change or wresting, we make a name for that accident which we consider, and for *living* put into the account *life*, for *moved, motion*, for *hot, heat*, for *long, length*, and the like. And all such names are the names of the accidents and properties by which one matter and body is distinguished from another. These are called *names abstract*, because severed, not from matter, but from the account of matter.

17. Thirdly, we bring into account the properties of our own bodies, whereby we make such distinction. As when anything is *seen* by us, we reckon not the thing itself, but the *sight*, the *colour*, the *idea* of it in the fancy; and when anything is *heard*, we reckon it not, but the *hearing* or *sound* only, which is our fancy or conception of it by the ear: and such are names of fancies.

18. Fourthly, we bring into account, consider, and give names to *names* themselves, and to *speeches*; for, *general*, *universal*, *special*, *equivocal*, are names of names. And *affirmation*, *interrogation*, *commandment*, *narration*, *syllogism*, *sermon*, *oration*, and many other such are names of speeches. And this is all the variety of names positive, which are put to mark somewhat which is in nature or may be feigned by the mind of man, as bodies that are or may be conceived to be, or of bodies, the properties that are or may be feigned to be, or words and speech.

Use of names positive.

19. There be also other names, called *negative*; which are notes to signify that a word is not the name of the thing in question, as these words: *nothing, no man, infinite, indocible [unteachable], three want four*, and the like; which are nevertheless of use in reckoning, or in correcting of reckoning, and call to mind our past cogitations, though they be not names of anything, because they make us refuse to admit of names not rightly used.

Negative names with their uses.

20. All other names are but insignificant sounds, and those of two sorts. One, when they are new and yet their meaning not explained by definition, whereof there have been abundance coined by Schoolmen and puzzled philosophers.

Words insignificant.
[17]

21. Another, when men make a name of two names, whose significations are contradictory and inconsistent, as this name, an *incorporeal body*, or (which is all one) an *incorporeal substance*, and a great number more. For whensoever any affirmation is false, the two names of which it is composed, put together and made one, signify nothing at all. For example, if it be a false affirmation to say *a quadrangle is round*, the word *round quadrangle* signifies nothing, but is a mere sound. So likewise if it be false to say that virtue can be poured, or blown up and down, the words *inpoured virtue, inblown virtue*, are as absurd and insignificant as a *round quadrangle*. And therefore you shall hardly meet with a senseless and insignificant word

that is not made up of some Latin or Greek names. A Frenchman seldom hears our Saviour called by the name of *Parole*, but by the name of *Verbe* often; yet *Verbe* and *Parole* differ no more but that one is Latin, the other French.

22. When a man upon the hearing of any speech hath those thoughts, which the words of that speech and their connexion were ordained and constituted to signify, then he is said to understand it, understanding being nothing else but conception caused by speech. And therefore if speech be peculiar to man, as for ought I know it is, then is understanding peculiar to him also. And therefore of absurd and false affirmations, in case they be universal, there can be no understanding, though many think they understand, then, when they do but repeat the words softly, or con [examine] them in their mind. — Understanding.

23. What kinds of speeches signify the appetites, aversions, and passions of man's mind and of their use and abuse, I shall speak when I have spoken of the passions.

24. The names of such things as affect us, that is, which please and displease us, because all men be not alike affected with the same thing, nor the same man at all times, are in the common discourses of men of *inconstant* signification. For seeing all names are imposed to signify our conceptions and all our affections are but conceptions, when we conceive the same things differently, we can hardly avoid different naming of them. For though the nature of that we conceive be the same; yet the diversity of our reception of it, in respect of different constitutions of body and prejudices of opinion, gives everything a tincture of our different passions. And therefore in reasoning a man must take heed of words, which, besides the signification of what we imagine of their nature, have a signification also of the nature, disposition, and interest of the speaker; such as are the names of virtues and vices. For one man calleth *wisdom* what another calleth *fear*; and one *cruelty* what another *justice*; one *prodigality* what another *magnanimity*; and one *gravity* what another *stupidity*, etc.[1] And therefore such names can never be — Inconstant names.

---

1 One person calls the death penalty justice, another calls it cruelty. See Hobbes's translation of Thucydides' *History of the Peloponnesian War* 3.82. It is odd that Hobbes should include the words "fear" and "justice" among those names that "can never be true grounds of any ratiocination," since (Continued)

true grounds of any ratiocination. No more can metaphors and tropes of speech; but these are less dangerous because they profess their inconstancy, which the other do not.

Chapter V

Of Reason and Science

Reason what it is.

1. When a man *reasoneth*, he does nothing else but conceive a sum total from *addition* of parcels, or conceive a remainder, from *subtraction* of one sum from another; which (if it be done by words) is conceiving of the consequence of the names of all the parts to the name of the whole, or from the names of the whole and one part to the name of the other part.[1] And though in some things (as in numbers), besides adding and subtracting, men name other operations, as *multiplying* and *dividing*; yet they are the same; for multiplication is but adding together of things equal, and division but subtracting of one thing, as often as we can. These operations are not incident to numbers only, but to all manner of things that can be added together and taken one out of another. For as arithmeticians teach to add and subtract in *numbers*, so the geometricians teach the same in *lines*, *figures* (solid and superficial), *angles*, *proportions*, *times*, degrees of *swiftness*, *force*, *power*, and the like. The logicians teach the same in *consequences of words*, adding together two *names* to make an *affirmation*, and two *affirmations* to make a *syllogism*, and *many syllogisms* to make a *demonstration*; and from the *sum* or *conclusion* of a *syllogism*, they subtract one *proposition* to find the other. Writers of politics add together *pactions* [contracts] to find men's *duties*, and lawyers, *laws* and *facts* to find what is *right* and *wrong* in the actions of private men. In sum, in what matter soever there is place for *addition* and *subtraction*, there also is place for *reason*;

---

they are central to his political philosophy. His point presumably is that when they are used with "inconstant signification," they cannot be "true grounds of any ratiocination."

1 Reasoning is computation. Reason does not tell a person what to do; that is the job of desire. Reason only tells one how to do what one desires.

and where these have no place, there *reason* has nothing at all to do.

2. Out of all which we may define (that is to say determine) what that is which is meant by this word *reason* when we reckon it amongst the faculties of the mind. For REASON, in this sense, is nothing but *reckoning* (that is, adding and subtracting) of the consequences of general names agreed upon for the *marking* and *signifying* of our thoughts; I say *marking* them, when we reckon by ourselves; and *signifying*, when we demonstrate or approve our reckonings to other men.

Reason defined.

3. And as in arithmetic, unpractised men must, and professors themselves may often err and cast up false, so also in any other subject of reasoning, the ablest, most attentive, and most practised men may deceive themselves and infer false conclusions, not but that reason itself is always right reason, as well as arithmetic is a certain and infallible art. But no one man's reason nor the reason of any one number of men makes the certainty, no more than an account is therefore well cast up, because a great many men have unanimously approved it. And therefore, as when there is a controversy in an account, the parties must by their own accord set up for right reason the reason of some arbitrator or judge, to whose sentence they will both stand, or their controversy must either come to blows or be undecided, for want of a right reason constituted by Nature, so is it also in all debates of what kind soever. And when men that think themselves wiser than all others clamour and demand right reason for judge; yet seek no more but that things should be determined by no other men's reason but their own, it is as intolerable in the society of men, as it is in play after trump is turned, to use for trump on every occasion, that suit whereof they have most in their hand. For they do nothing else, that will have every of their passions, as it comes to bear sway in them, to be taken for right reason, and that in their own controversies, bewraying [revealing] their want of right reason by the claim they lay to it.

Right reason where.

[19]

4. The use and end of reason is not the finding of the sum and truth of one or a few consequences, remote from the first definitions and settled significations of names, but to begin at these and proceed from one consequence to another. For there can be no certainty of the last

The use of reason.

conclusion without a certainty of all those affirmations and negations on which it was grounded and inferred. As when a master of a family, in taking an account, casteth up the sums of all the bills of expense into one sum, and not regarding how each bill is summed up by those that give them in account, nor what it is he pays for, he advantages himself no more than if he allowed the account in gross, trusting to every of the accountant's skill and honesty. So also in reasoning of all other things, he that takes up conclusions on the trust of authors and doth not fetch them from the first items in every reckoning (which are the significations of names settled by definitions), loses his labour and does not know anything, but only believeth.

Of error and absurdity.

5. When a man reckons without the use of words, which may be done in particular things (as when upon the sight of any one thing, we conjecture what was likely to have preceded or is likely to follow upon it); if that which he thought likely to follow follows not or that which he thought likely to have preceded it hath not preceded it, this is called error, to which even the most prudent men are subject. But when we reason in words of general signification and fall upon a general inference which is false, though it be commonly called *error*,[1] it is indeed an absurdity or senseless speech. For error is but a deception in presuming that somewhat is past or to come, of which, though it were not past or not to come, yet there was no impossibility discoverable. But when we make a general assertion, unless it be a true one, the possibility of it is inconceivable. And words whereby we conceive nothing but the sound are those we call *absurd, insignificant,* and *nonsense.* And therefore if a man should talk to me of a *round quadrangle,* or *accidents of bread in cheese,* or *immaterial substances;* or of a *free subject,* a *free will,* or any *free* but free from being hindered by opposition, I should not say he were in an error, but that his words were without meaning; that is to say, absurd.

[20]

6. I have said before (in the second[2] chapter) that a man did excel all other animals in this faculty, that when he conceived anything whatsoever, he was apt to enquire

1 See 4.11.
2 Actually, it is the third chapter.

the consequences of it and what effects he could do with it. And now I add this other degree of the same excellence, that he can by words reduce the consequences he finds to general rules, called *theorems* or *aphorisms*, that is, he can reason or reckon, not only in number, but in all other things whereof one may be added unto or subtracted from another.

7. But this privilege is allayed by another; and that is by the privilege of absurdity, to which no living creature is subject, but men only. And of men, those are of all most subject to it that profess philosophy. For it is most true that Cicero saith of them somewhere[1] that there can be nothing so absurd but may be found in the books of philosophers. And the reason is manifest. For there is not one of them that begins his ratiocination from the definitions or explications of the names they are to use, which is a method that hath been used only in geometry, whose conclusions have thereby been made indisputable.

8. The first cause of absurd conclusions I ascribe to the want of method,[2] in that they begin not their ratiocination from definitions, that is, from settled significations of their words, as if they could cast account without knowing the value of the numeral words, *one*, *two*, and *three*. Causes of absurdity. 1.

9. And whereas all bodies enter into account upon divers considerations (which I have mentioned in the precedent chapter), these considerations being diversely named, divers absurdities proceed from the confusion and unfit connexion of their names into assertions. And therefore

10. The second cause of absurd assertions, I ascribe to the giving of names of *bodies* to *accidents*, or of *accidents* to *bodies*; as they do that say, *faith is infused* or *inspired*, when nothing can be *poured* or *breathed* into anything, but body,[3] and that *extension* is *body*; that *phantasms* are *spirits*, etc. 2.

11. The third I ascribe to the giving of the names of the *accidents* of *bodies without us* to the *accidents* of our 3.

---

1   *De divinatione II, 119.*
2   For Hobbes, like Descartes and some other early modern thinkers, the key to science is the right method. See also 7.4.
3   Other Protestant thinkers mocked similarly inappropriate language used to explain Christian theological concepts, notably the English Calvinist William Twisse (1578-1646).

own bodies, as they do that say, the *colour is in the body; the sound is in the air*, etc.[1]

4. 12. The fourth, to the giving of the names of *bodies* to *names*, or *speeches*; as they do that say that *there be things universal*; that *a living creature is genus* or *a general thing*, etc.

5. 13. The fifth, to the giving of the names of *accidents* to *names* and *speeches*; as they do that say, *the nature of a thing is its definition*; *a man's command is his will*; and the like.

6. 14. The sixth, to the use of metaphors, tropes, and other rhetorical figures, instead of words proper. For though it be lawful to say, for example, in common speech, *the way goeth or leadeth hither or thither; the proverb says this or that* (whereas ways cannot go, nor proverbs speak); yet in reckoning and seeking of truth such speeches are not to be admitted.

7. 15. The seventh, to names that signify nothing, but are
[21] taken up and learned by rote from the Schools, as *hypostatical, transubstantiate, consubstantiate, eternal-now*, and the like canting of Schoolmen.

16. To him that can avoid these things, it is not easy to fall into any absurdity, unless it be by the length of an account; wherein he may perhaps forget what went before. For all men by nature reason alike, and well, when they have good principles. For who is so stupid as both to mistake in geometry and also to persist in it when another detects his error to him?

Science. 17. By this it appears that reason is not, as sense and memory, born with us, nor gotten by experience only, as prudence is, but attained by industry: first in apt imposing of names, and secondly by getting a good and orderly method in proceeding from the elements, which are names, to assertions made by connexion of one of them to another, and so to syllogisms, which are the connexions of one assertion to another, till we come to a knowledge of all the consequences of names appertaining to the subject in hand; and that is it, men call SCIENCE. And whereas sense and memory are but knowledge of fact, which is a thing past and irrevocable, *science* is the knowledge of consequences, and dependence of one fact upon another, by which, out of that we can presently do, we

---

1 See also 1.4.

know how to do something else when we will or the like another time, because when we see how anything comes about, upon what causes, and by what manner, when the like causes come into our power, we see how to make it produce the like effects.

18. Children therefore are not endued with reason at all, till they have attained the use of speech, but are called reasonable creatures for the possibility apparent of having the use of reason in time to come. And the most part of men, though they have the use of reasoning a little way, as in numbering to some degree, yet it serves them to little use in common life, in which they govern themselves, some better, some worse, according to their differences of experience, quickness of memory, and inclinations to several ends, but specially according to good or evil fortune and the errors of one another. For as for *science* or certain rules of their actions, they are so far from it that they know not what it is. Geometry they have thought conjuring. But for other sciences, they who have not been taught the beginnings and some progress in them, that they may see how they be acquired and generated, are in this point like children, that having no thought of generation, are made believe by the women that their brothers and sisters are not born, but found in the garden.

19. But yet they that have no *science* are in better and nobler condition with their natural prudence than men that by misreasoning, or by trusting them that reason wrong, fall upon false and absurd general rules. For ignorance of causes and of rules does not set men so far out of their way as relying on false rules, and taking for causes of what they aspire to those that are not so, but rather causes of the contrary.

20. To conclude, the light of human minds is perspicuous words, but by exact definitions first snuffed and [22] purged from ambiguity; *reason* is the *pace*; increase of *science*, the way; and the benefit of mankind, the *end*. And, on the contrary, metaphors, and senseless and ambiguous words are like *ignes fatui*;[1] and reasoning upon them is wandering amongst innumerable absurdities; and their end, contention and sedition, or contempt.

---

1 Literally, foolish fires. Something deceptive in experience.

21. As much experience is *prudence*, so is much science *sapience*. For though we usually have one name of wisdom for them both; yet the Latins did always distinguish between *prudentia* and *sapientia*, ascribing the former to experience, the latter to science. But to make their difference appear more clearly, let us suppose one man endued with an excellent natural use and dexterity in handling his arms, and another to have added to that dexterity an acquired science of where he can offend or be offended by his adversary in every possible posture or guard. The ability of the former would be to the ability of the latter, as prudence to sapience; both useful, but the latter infallible. But they that, trusting only to the authority of books, follow the blind blindly, are like him that, trusting to the false rules of a master of fence, ventures presumptuously upon an adversary that either kills or disgraces him.

22. The signs of science are some, certain and infallible, some, uncertain. Certain, when he that pretendeth the science of anything can teach the same; that is to say, demonstrate the truth thereof perspicuously to another; uncertain, when only some particular events answer to his pretence and upon many occasions prove so as he says they must. Signs of prudence are all uncertain, because to observe by experience and remember all circumstances that may alter the success is impossible. But in any business, whereof a man has not infallible science to proceed by, to forsake his own natural judgement and be guided by general sentences [opinions] read in authors and subject to many exceptions is a sign of folly, and generally scorned by the name of pedantry. And even of those men themselves that in councils of the commonwealth love to show their reading of politics and history, very few do it in their domestic affairs where their particular interest is concerned, having prudence enough for their private affairs; but in public they study more the reputation of their own wit than the success of another's business.

Chapter VI

Of the Interiour Beginnings of Voluntary Motions, Commonly Called the Passions, and the Speeches by Which they are Expressed

1. There be in animals two sorts of *motions* peculiar to them: one called *vital*, begun in generation, and continued without interruption through their whole life, such as are the course of the blood, the pulse, the breathing, the concoction, nutrition, excretion, etc.; to which motions there needs no help of imagination; the other is *animal motion*, otherwise called *voluntary motion*; as to *go*, to *speak*, to *move* any of our limbs, in such manner as is first fancied in our minds. That sense is motion in the organs and interior parts of man's body, caused by the action of the things we see, hear, etc., and that fancy is but the relics of the same motion, remaining after sense, has been already said in the first and second chapters. And because *going*, *speaking*, and the like voluntary motions depend always upon a precedent thought of *whither*, *which way*, and *what*, it is evident that the imagination is the first internal beginning of all voluntary motion. And although unstudied men do not conceive any motion at all to be there where the thing moved is invisible or the space it is moved in is (for the shortness of it) insensible; yet that doth not hinder but that such motions are. For let a space be never so little, that which is moved over a greater space, whereof that little one is part, must first be moved over that. These small beginnings of motion within the body of man, before they appear in walking, speaking, striking, and other visible actions, are commonly called ENDEAVOUR.[1]

2. This endeavour, when it is toward something which causes it, is called APPETITE or DESIRE, the latter being the general name, and the other oftentimes restrained to signify the desire of food, namely *hunger* and *thirst*. And when the endeavour is fromward something, it is gener-

Motion vital and animal.

Endeavour.

Appetite. Desire.

Hunger. Thirst. Aversion.

---

1 In animals, to try is to endeavor. In *De Corpore*, Hobbes says, endeavor (*conatus*) is a motion smaller than can be measured; it is motion "through the length of a point" or "in an instant of time" (15.2).

ally called AVERSION.[1] These words *appetite* and *aversion* we have from the *Latins*; and they both of them signify the motions, one of approaching, the other of retiring. So also do the Greek words for the same, which are *hormē* and *aphormē*. For Nature itself does often press upon men those truths which afterwards, when they look for somewhat beyond Nature, they stumble at. For the Schools find in mere appetite to go or move, no actual motion at all; but because some motion they must acknowledge, they call it metaphorical motion, which is but an absurd speech; for though words may be called metaphorical, bodies and motions cannot.

Love. Hate.

[24]

3. That which men desire they are said to LOVE, and to HATE those things for which they have aversion. So that desire and love are the same thing, save that by desire, we signify the absence of the object; by love, most commonly the presence of the same. So also by aversion, we signify the absence; and by hate, the presence of the object.

4. Of appetites and aversions, some are born with men; as appetite of food, appetite of excretion, and exoneration (which may also and more properly be called aversions, from somewhat they feel in their bodies), and some other appetites, not many. The rest, which are appetites of particular things, proceed from experience and trial of their effects upon themselves or other men. For of things we know not at all or believe not to be, we can have no further desire than to taste and try. But aversion we have for things, not only which we know have hurt us, but also that we do not know whether they will hurt us, or not.

Contempt.

5. Those things which we neither desire nor hate, we are said to *contemn*: CONTEMPT being nothing else but an immobility or contumacy of the heart in resisting the action of certain things, and proceeding from that the heart is already moved otherwise by other more potent objects or from want of experience of them.

6. And because the constitution of a man's body is in continual mutation, it is impossible that all the same things should always cause in him the same appetites and

---

1 Hobbes's goal in this chapter is to analyze or break down many seemingly irreducible and nonmaterialistic concepts into material components: complex motions of small bodies that move large bodies toward or away from something.

aversions; much less can all men consent in the desire of almost any one and the same object.

7. But whatsoever is the object of any man's appetite or desire, that is it which he for his part calleth *good*; and the object of his hate and aversion, *evil*; and of his contempt, *vile* and *inconsiderable*. For these words of *good, evil*, and *contemptible* are ever used with relation to the person that useth them, there being nothing simply and absolutely so, nor any common rule of good and evil to be taken from the nature of the objects themselves,[1] but from the person of the man (where there is no commonwealth) or (in a commonwealth) from the person that representeth it, or from an arbitrator or judge whom men disagreeing shall by consent set up and make his sentence the rule thereof.

Good.
Evil.

8. The Latin tongue has two words whose significations approach to those of good and evil, but are not precisely the same; and those are *pulchrum* and *turpe*. Whereof the former signifies that which by some apparent signs promiseth good, and the latter that which promiseth evil. But in our tongue we have not so general names to express them by. But for *pulchrum* we say, in some things, *fair*; in others, *beautiful*, or *handsome*, or *gallant*, or *honourable*, or *comely*, or *amiable*; and for *turpe*, *foul, deformed, ugly, base, nauseous*, and the like, as the subject shall require; all which words, in their proper places, signify nothing else but the *mien* or countenance that promiseth good and evil. So that of good there be three kinds: good in the promise, that is *pulchrum*; good in effect, as the end desired, which is called *jucundum, delightful*; and good as the means, which is called *utile, profitable*; and as many of evil: for evil in promise is that they call *turpe*; evil in effect and end is *molestum, unpleasant, troublesome*; and evil in the means, *inutile, unprofitable, hurtful*.

Pulchrum.
Turpe.

Delightful.
Profitable.

[25] Unpleasant.
Unprofitable.

9. As in sense that which is really within us is (as I have said before) only motion, caused by the action of external objects (but in appearance to the sight, light and colour; to the ear, sound; to the nostril, odour, etc.); so when the action of the same object is continued from the eyes, ears, and other organs to the heart, the real effect there

---

1 What is good and evil is determined by each person only when there are no laws. Under a government, what is good or evil is determined by the commands of the sovereign, i.e., what he desires. See also 6.57.

is nothing but motion or endeavour, which consisteth in appetite or aversion to or from the object moving. But the appearance or sense of that motion is that we either call DELIGHT or TROUBLE OF MIND.

10. This motion, which is called appetite and for the appearance of it *delight* and *pleasure*, seemeth to be a corroboration of vital motion and a help thereunto; and therefore such things as caused delight were not improperly called *jucunda* (*à juvando*) from helping or fortifying; and the contrary, *molesta*, *offensive*, from hindering and troubling the motion vital.

11. *Pleasure* therefore (or delight) is the appearance or sense of good; and *molestation* or *displeasure*, the appearance or sense of evil. And consequently all appetite, desire, and love is accompanied with some delight more or less; and all hatred and aversion with more or less displeasure and offence.

12. Of pleasures or delights, some arise from the sense of an object present; and those may be called *pleasures of sense* (the word *sensual*, as it is used by those only that condemn them, having no place till there be laws). Of this kind are all onerations and exonerations of the body, as also all that is pleasant, in the *sight, hearing, smell, taste,* or *touch*. Others arise from the expectation that proceeds from foresight of the end or consequence of things, whether those things in the sense please or displease; and these are *pleasures of the mind* of him that draweth in those consequences, and are generally called JOY. In the like manner, displeasures are some in the sense and called PAIN; others, in the expectation of consequences and are called GRIEF.

13. These simple passions called *appetite, desire, love, aversion, hate, joy,* and *grief,* have their names for divers considerations diversified. As first, when they one succeed another, they are diversely called from the opinion men have of the likelihood of attaining what they desire. Secondly, from the object loved or hated. Thirdly, from the consideration of many of them together. Fourthly, from the alteration[1] or succession itself.

14. For *appetite* with an opinion of attaining is called HOPE.

Delight.
Displeasure.
Pleasure.

Offence.

Pleasures of sense.

Pleasures of the mind. Joy.

Pain. Grief.

Hope.

---

1 This should probably be "alternation."

15. The same, without such opinion, DESPAIR.

16. *Aversion*, with opinion of *hurt* from the object, FEAR.

17. The same, with hope of avoiding that hurt by resistance, COURAGE.

18. Sudden *courage*, ANGER.

19. Constant *hope*, CONFIDENCE of ourselves.

20. Constant *despair*, DIFFIDENCE of ourselves.

21. *Anger* for great hurt done to another, when we conceive the same to be done by injury, INDIGNATION.

22. *Desire* of good to another, BENEVOLENCE, GOOD WILL, CHARITY. If to man generally, GOOD NATURE.

23. *Desire* of riches, COVETOUSNESS, a name used always in signification of blame, because men contending for them are displeased with one another's attaining them; though the desire in itself be to be blamed, or allowed, according to the means by which those riches are sought.

24. Desire of office or precedence, AMBITION, a name used also in the worse sense, for the reason before mentioned.

25. *Desire* of things that conduce but a little to our ends, and fear of things that are but of little hindrance, PUSILLANIMITY.

26. *Contempt* of little helps and hindrances, MAGNANIMITY.

27. *Magnanimity* in danger of death or wounds, VALOUR, FORTITUDE.

28. *Magnanimity* in the use of riches, LIBERALITY.

29. *Pusillanimity*, in the same, WRETCHEDNESS, MISERABLENESS, or PARSIMONY, as it is liked or disliked.

30. *Love* of persons for society, KINDNESS.

31. *Love* of persons for pleasing the sense only, NATURAL LUST.

32. *Love* of the same, acquired from rumination, that is, imagination of pleasure past, LUXURY.

33. *Love* of one singularly, with desire to be singularly beloved, THE PASSION OF LOVE. The same, with fear that the love is not mutual, JEALOUSY.

34. *Desire* by doing hurt to another to make him condemn some fact of his own, REVENGEFULNESS.

35. *Desire* to know why and how, CURIOSITY, such as is in no living creature but *man*; so that man is distinguished, not only by his reason, but also by this singular

Despair.
Fear.
Courage.
Anger.
Confidence.
Diffidence.
[26] Indignation.
Benevolence.
Covetousness.
Ambition.
Pusillanimity.
Magnaminity.
Valour.
Liberality.
Miserableness.
Kindness.
Natural lust.
Luxury.
The passion of love. Jealousy.
Revengefulness.
Curiosity.

passion from other *animals*, in whom the appetite of food and other pleasures of sense by predominance take away the care of knowing causes, which is a lust of the mind, that by a perseverance of delight in the continual and indefatigable generation of knowledge exceedeth the short vehemence of any carnal pleasure.

Religion.
Superstition.
True religion.

36. *Fear* of power invisible,[1] feigned[2] by the mind, or imagined from tales publicly allowed, RELIGION; not allowed, SUPERSTITION.[3] And when the power imagined is truly such as we imagine, TRUE RELIGION.

Panic. Terror.

37. *Fear* without the apprehension of why or what, PANIC TERROR, called so from the fables that make Pan[4] the author of them; whereas in truth there is always in him that so feareth first some apprehension of the cause, though the rest run away by example, every one supposing his fellow to know why. And therefore this passion happens to none but in a throng or multitude of people.

Admiration.

38. *Joy* from apprehension of novelty, ADMIRATION; proper to man because it excites the appetite of knowing the cause.

[27]
Glory.

39. *Joy* arising from imagination of a man's own power and ability is that exultation of the mind which is called GLORYING; which, if grounded upon the experience of his own former actions, is the same with *confidence*; but if grounded on the flattery of others or only supposed by himself for delight in the consequences of it, is called

Vain-glory.

VAIN-GLORY; which name is properly given, because a well-grounded *confidence* begetteth attempt, whereas the supposing of power does not and is therefore rightly called *vain*.

Dejection.

40. *Grief* from opinion of want of power is called DEJECTION of mind.

41. The *vain-glory* which consisteth in the feigning or supposing of abilities in ourselves, which we know are not, is most incident to young men and nourished by the

---

1 See also 11.26 and 12.6.
2 "Feigned" usually means "falsely invented" but it may mean simply "composed." See, e.g., 16.2.
3 It follows that a superstition (something not allowed) might be true religion.
4 Pan is the Greek god of flocks and generally all things rural. The word "panic" comes from the story that Pan liked to frighten travelers.

histories or fictions of gallant persons, and is corrected oftentimes by age and employment.

42. *Sudden glory* is the passion which maketh those *grimaces* called LAUGHTER, and is caused either by some sudden act of their own that pleaseth them or by the apprehension of some deformed thing in another, by comparison whereof they suddenly applaud themselves. And it is incident most to them that are conscious of the fewest abilities in themselves, who are forced to keep themselves in their own favour by observing the imperfections of other men. And therefore much laughter at the defects of others is a sign of pusillanimity. For of great minds one of the proper works is to help and free others from scorn, and compare themselves only with the most able. Sudden glory.
Laughter.

43. On the contrary, *sudden dejection* is the passion that causeth WEEPING, and is caused by such accidents as suddenly take away some vehement hope or some prop of their power; and they are most subject to it that rely principally on helps external, such as are women and children. Therefore, some weep for the loss of friends, others for their unkindness, others for the sudden stop made to their thoughts of revenge by reconciliation. But in all cases both laughter and weeping are sudden motions, custom taking them both away. For no man laughs at old jests, or weeps for an old calamity. Sudden dejection. Weeping.

44. *Grief* for the discovery of some defect of ability is SHAME or the passion that discovereth itself in blushing, and consisteth in the apprehension of something dishonourable, and in young men is a sign of the love of good reputation, and commendable; in old men it is a sign of the same, but because it comes too late, not commendable. Shame.
Blushing.

45. The *contempt* of good reputation is called IMPUDENCE. Imprudence.

46. *Grief* for the calamity of another is PITY, and ariseth from the imagination that the like calamity may befall himself. And therefore is called also compassion, and in the phrase of this present time a fellow-feeling. And therefore for calamity arriving from great wickedness, the best men have the least pity; and for the same calamity those have least pity that think themselves least obnoxious [susceptible] to the same. Pity.

47. *Contempt* or little sense of the calamity of others is that which men call CRUELTY, proceeding from security [28] Cruelty.

of their own fortune. For, that any man should take pleasure in other men's great harms, without other end of his own, I do not conceive it possible.

48. *Grief* for the success of a competitor in wealth, honour, or other good, if it be joined with endeavour to enforce our own abilities to equal or exceed him, is called EMULATION; but joined with endeavour to supplant or hinder a competitor, ENVY.

Emulation.
Envy.

49. When in the mind of man appetites and aversions, hopes and fears concerning one and the same thing arise alternately, and divers good and evil consequences of the doing or omitting the thing propounded come successively into our thoughts, so that sometimes we have an appetite to it, sometimes an aversion from it, sometimes hope to be able to do it, sometimes despair or fear to attempt it, the whole sum of desires, aversions, hopes and fears, continued till the thing be either done or thought impossible, is that we call DELIBERATION.

Deliberation.

50. Therefore of things past there is no *deliberation*, because manifestly impossible to be changed, nor of things known to be impossible, or thought so, because men know or think such deliberation vain. But of things impossible, which we think possible, we may deliberate, not knowing it is in vain. And it is called *deliberation*; because it is a putting an end to the *liberty* we had of doing or omitting according to our own appetite or aversion.

51. This alternate succession of appetites, aversions, hopes and fears is no less in other living creatures than in man; and therefore beasts also deliberate.

52. Every *deliberation* is then said to *end* when that whereof they deliberate is either done or thought impossible, because till then we retain the liberty of doing or omitting, according to our appetite or aversion.

53. In *deliberation*, the last appetite, or aversion, immediately adhering to the action or to the omission thereof, is that we call the WILL, the act (not the faculty) of *willing*.[1] And beasts that have *deliberation* must necessarily also have *will*. The definition of the *will*, given commonly

The will.

---

1 Hobbes is a compatibilist. He believes that freedom is compatible with determinism, the doctrine that every event (including every human action) is caused by or determined by earlier events. He believes that human beings are free (when they are caused by a desire or appetite), but acts of will are not.

by the Schools, that it is a *rational appetite*, is not good. For if it were, then could there be no voluntary act against reason. For a *voluntary act* is that which proceedeth from the *will* and no other. But if instead of a rational appetite, we shall say an appetite resulting from a precedent deliberation, then the definition is the same that I have given here. *Will*, therefore, *is the last appetite in deliberating*. And though we say in common discourse a man had a will once to do a thing that nevertheless he forbore to do; yet that is properly but an inclination, which makes no action voluntary, because the action depends not of it, but of the last inclination or appetite. For if the intervenient appetites make any action voluntary, then by the same reason all intervenient aversions should make the same action involuntary; and so one and the same action should be both voluntary and involuntary.

54. By this it is manifest that not only actions that [29] have their beginning from covetousness, ambition, lust, or other appetites to the thing propounded, but also those that have their beginning from aversion or fear of those consequences that follow the omission are *voluntary actions*.

55. The forms of speech by which the passions are Forms of speech expressed are partly the same and partly different from in passion. those by which we express our thoughts. And first generally all passions may be expressed *indicatively*; as, *I love, I fear, I joy, I deliberate, I will, I command*; but some of them have particular expressions by themselves, which nevertheless are not affirmations, unless it be when they serve to make other inferences besides that of the passion they proceed from. Deliberation is expressed *subjunctively*, which is a speech proper to signify suppositions with their consequences, as, *If this be done, then this will follow*, and differs not from the language of reasoning, save that reasoning is in general words, but deliberation for the most part is of particulars. The language of desire and aversion is *imperative*, as, *Do this, forbear that*; which when the party is obliged to do or forbear is *command*; otherwise *prayer*, or else *counsel*. The language of vain-glory, of indignation, pity and revengefulness, *optative*; but of the desire to know, there is a peculiar expression called *interrogative*; as, *what is it, when shall it, how is it done*, and *why so*? Other language of the passions I find none: for cursing,

swearing, reviling, and the like do not signify as speech, but as the actions of a tongue accustomed.

56. These forms of speech, I say, are expressions or voluntary significations of our passions; but certain signs they be not, because they may be used arbitrarily, whether they that use them have such passions or not. The best signs of passions present are either in the countenance, motions of the body, actions, and ends, or aims which we otherwise know the man to have.

57. And because in deliberation the appetites and aversions are raised by foresight of the good and evil consequences and sequels of the action whereof we deliberate, the good or evil effect thereof dependeth on the foresight of a long chain of consequences, of which very seldom any man is able to see to the end. But for so far as a man seeth, if the good in those consequences be greater than the evil, the whole chain is that which writers call *apparent* or *seeming good*. And contrarily, when the evil exceedeth the good, the whole is *apparent* or *seeming evil*; so that he who hath by experience or reason the greatest and surest prospect of consequences deliberates best himself, and is able, when he will, to give the best counsel unto others.

Good and evil apparent.

58. *Continual success* in obtaining those things which a man from time to time desireth, that is to say, continual prospering, is that men call FELICITY; I mean the felicity of this life. For there is no such thing as perpetual tranquillity of mind while we live here, because life itself is but motion and can never be without desire, nor without fear no more than without sense.[1] What kind of felicity God hath ordained to them that devoutly honour him a man shall no sooner know than enjoy, being joys that now are as incomprehensible as the word of Schoolmen, *beatifical vision*, is unintelligible.

Felicity.

[30]

59. The form of speech whereby men signify their opinion of the goodness of anything is PRAISE. That whereby they signify the power and greatness of anything is MAGNIFYING. And that whereby they signify the opinion they have of a man's felicity is by the Greeks called *makarismos*, for which we have no name in our tongue. And thus much is sufficient for the present purpose to have been said of the PASSIONS.

Praise.

Magnification.

makarismos.

---

1   See 11.1.

Chapter VII

Of the Ends or Resolutions of Discourse

1. Of all *discourse* governed by desire of knowledge, there is at last an *end*, either by attaining or by giving over. And in the chain of discourse, wheresoever it be interrupted, there is an end for that time.

2. If the discourse be merely mental, it consisteth of thoughts that the thing will be and will not be, or that it has been and has not been, alternately. So that wheresoever you break off the chain of a man's discourse, you leave him in a presumption of *it will be*, or *it will not be*; or *it has been*, or *has not been*. All which is *opinion*. And that which is alternate appetite, in deliberating concerning good and evil, the same is alternate opinion in the enquiry of the truth of *past* and *future*. And as the last appetite in deliberation is called the *will*, so the last opinion in search of the truth of past and future is called the JUDGEMENT or *resolute* and *final sentence* of him that *discourseth*. And as the whole chain of appetites alternate in the question of good or bad is called *deliberation*; so the whole chain of opinions alternate in the question of true or false is called DOUBT.

Judgement, or sentence final.

Doubt.

3. No discourse whatsoever can end in absolute knowledge of fact, past or to come. For, as for the knowledge of fact, it is originally sense, and ever after memory. And for the knowledge of consequence, which I have said before is called science, it is not absolute, but conditional. No man can know by discourse that this or that is, has been, or will be, which is to know absolutely; but only that if this be, that is; if this has been, [then] that has been; if this shall be, [then] that shall be; which is to know conditionally; and that not the consequence of one thing to another, but of one name of a thing to another name of the same thing.

4. And therefore, when the discourse is put into speech and begins with the definitions of words and proceeds by connexion of the same into general affirmations and of these again into syllogisms, the end or last sum is called the conclusion, and the thought of the mind by it signified is that conditional knowledge or knowledge of the consequence of words, which is commonly called

[31]

Science

Opinion.

Conscience.

Belief. Faith.

SCIENCE.[1] But if the first ground of such discourse be not definitions or if the definitions be not rightly joined together into syllogisms, then the end or conclusion is again OPINION, namely of the truth of somewhat said, though sometimes in absurd and senseless words, without possibility of being understood. When two or more men know of one and the same fact, they are said to be CONSCIOUS of it one to another; which is as much as to know it together. And because such are fittest witnesses of the facts of one another or of a third, it was and ever will be reputed a very evil act for any man to speak against his *conscience* or to corrupt or force another so to do, insomuch that the plea of conscience has been always hearkened unto very diligently in all times. Afterwards, men made use of the same word metaphorically for the knowledge of their own secret facts and secret thoughts; and therefore it is rhetorically said that the conscience is a thousand witnesses. And last of all, men vehemently in love with their own new opinions (though never so absurd) and obstinately bent to maintain them gave those their opinions also that reverenced name of conscience, as if they would have it seem unlawful to change or speak against them, and so pretend to know they are true, when they know at most but that they think so.

5. When a man's discourse beginneth not at definitions, it beginneth either at some other contemplation of his own, and then it is still called opinion; or it beginneth at some saying of another, of whose ability to know the truth and of whose honesty in not deceiving, he doubteth not; and then the discourse is not so much concerning the thing as the person; and the resolution is called BELIEF and FAITH; *faith in* the man, *belief* both *of* the man and *of* the truth of what he says. So that in belief are two opinions, one of the saying of the man, the other of his virtue.[2] To *have faith in*, or *trust to*, or *believe a man*, signify the same thing, namely, an opinion of the veracity

---

1 See 5.17.
2 Hobbes might have said that belief or faith consists of three things. Consider this: "Ava believes that Beth is honest." (1) The word "believes" expresses the psychological state that Ava is in. (Hobbes does not mention this element.) (2) The words "that Beth is honest" express the content of the belief, that is, what is believed. (3) Ava has that belief because of her trust or

of the man; but to *believe what is said* signifieth only an opinion of the truth of the saying. But we are to observe that this phrase, *I believe in*, as also the Latin, *credo in*, and the Greek, *pisteuō eis*, are never used but in the writings of divines. Instead of them, in other writings are put: *I believe him*, *I trust him*, *I have faith in him*, *I rely on him*; and in Latin, *credo illi*; *fido illi*, and in Greek, *pisteuō autōi*, and this singularity of the ecclesiastic use of the word hath raised many disputes about the right object of the Christian faith.

6. But *by believing in*, as it is in the Creed, is meant, not trust in the person, but confession and acknowledgement of the doctrine. For not only Christians, but all manner of men do so believe in God as to hold all for truth they hear him say, whether they understand it or not, which is all the faith and trust can possibly be had in any person whatsoever; but they do not all believe the doctrine of the Creed.

7. From whence we may infer that when we believe [32] any saying, whatsoever it be, to be true, from arguments taken, not from the thing itself or from the principles of natural reason, but from the authority and good opinion we have of him that hath said it; then is the speaker or person we believe in or trust in and whose word we take, the object of our faith; and the honour done in believing is done to him only. And consequently, when we believe that the Scriptures are the word of God, having no immediate revelation from God himself, our belief, faith, and trust is in the Church, whose word we take and acquiesce therein. And they that believe that which a prophet relates unto them in the name of God, take the word of the prophet, do honour to him, and in him trust and believe, touching the truth of what he relateth, whether he be a true or a false prophet.[1] And so it is also with all other history. For if I should not believe all that is written by historians of the glorious acts of Alexander or Caesar, I do not think the ghost of Alexander or Caesar had any just cause to be offended or anybody else but the historian. If Livy say the gods made once a cow speak and

---

faith in the person who told her that Beth is honest. This third element of belief is usually implicit and not explicit.

1 See also chapter 36.

we believe it not, we distrust not God therein, but Livy.[1] So that it is evident that whatsoever we believe, upon no other reason than what is drawn from authority of men only and their writings, whether they be sent from God or not, is faith in men only.[2]

Chapter VIII

Of the Virtues Commonly Called Intellectual; and their Contrary Defects

Intellectual virtue, defined.

1. Virtue generally in all sorts of subjects is somewhat that is valued for eminence and consisteth in comparison. For if all things were equally in all men, nothing would be prized. And by *virtues* INTELLECTUAL are always understood such abilities of the mind as men praise, value, and desire should be in themselves, and go commonly under the name of a *good wit*; though the same word, WIT, be used also to distinguish one certain ability from the rest.

Wit, natural, or acquired.

2. These *virtues* are of two sorts, *natural* and *acquired*. By natural, I mean not that which a man hath from his birth; for that is nothing else but sense, wherein men differ so little one from another and from brute beasts, as it is not to be reckoned amongst virtues. But I mean that *wit* which is gotten by use only and experience, without method, culture, or instruction. This NATURAL WIT consisteth principally in two things, *celerity of imagining*

Natural wit.

---

1   Livy (59 BCE-17 CE) was a Roman historian. Here is the passage Hobbes is referring to: "Prodigies were reported that year [177 BCE]: in the territory of Crustumerium they say that a bird, called *sangualis*, cut a sacred stone with its beak, that in Campania a cow spoke, that at Syracuse a brazen heifer was approached and impregnated by a wild bull which had strayed from its herd.... [T]he cow was consigned to maintenance at the expense of the state" (*Livy*, tr. Evan T. Sage and Alfred C. Schlesinger [Cambridge, MA: Harvard UP, 1938], p. 223). See also 32.5 and 42.46.

2   Christians, Jews, and Muslims think that they have faith in God because they believe on the basis of the Bible or the Koran. In fact, Hobbes thinks that they have faith in the person who recommended the book to them: parent or clergyman or some other trusted person.

(that is, swift succession of one thought to another) and *steady direction* to some approved end. On the contrary, a slow imagination maketh that defect or fault of the mind, which is commonly called Dullness, *stupidity*, and sometimes by other names that signify slowness of motion or difficulty to be moved.

3. And this difference of quickness is caused by the difference of men's passions, that love and dislike, some one thing, some another; and therefore some men's thoughts run one way, some another, and are held to and observe differently the things that pass through their imagination. And whereas in this succession of men's thoughts there is nothing to observe in the things they think on but either in what they be *like one another* or in what they be *unlike* or *what they serve for* or *how they serve to such a purpose,* those that observe their similitudes, in case they be such as are but rarely observed by others, are said to have a *good wit*; by which, in this occasion, is meant a *good fancy.* But they that observe their differences and dissimilitudes, which is called *distinguishing* and *discerning* and *judging* between thing and thing, in case such discerning be not easy, are said to have a good judgement; and particularly in matter of conversation and business, wherein times, places, and persons are to be discerned, this virtue is called Discretion. The former, that is, fancy without the help of judgement, is not commended as a virtue; but the latter, which is judgement and discretion is commended for itself, without the help of fancy. Besides the discretion of times, places, and persons necessary to a good fancy, there is required also an often application of his thoughts to their end, that is to say, to some use to be made of them. This done, he that hath this virtue will be easily fitted with similitudes that will please, not only by illustration of his discourse and adorning it with new and apt metaphors, but also by the rarity of their invention. But without steadiness and direction to some end, a great fancy is one kind of madness, such as they have that entering into any discourse are snatched from their purpose by everything that comes in their thought into so many and so long digressions and parentheses that they utterly lose themselves; which kind of folly I know no particular name for; but the cause of it is sometimes want of experience, whereby that seemeth to a man new and rare which

Good wit, or fancy.

Good judgement.

Discretion.

doth not so to others, sometimes pusillanimity, by which that seems great to him which other men think a trifle, and whatsoever is new or great and therefore thought fit to be told withdraws a man by degrees from the intended way of his discourse.

4. In a good poem, whether it be *epic* or *dramatic*, as also in *sonnets*, *epigrams*, and other pieces, both judgement and fancy are required, but the fancy must be more eminent, because they please for the extravagancy, but ought not to displease by indiscretion.

5. In a good history, the judgement must be eminent, because the goodness consisteth in the method, in the truth, and in the choice of the actions that are most profitable to be known. Fancy has no place, but only in adorning the style.

6. In orations of praise and in invectives, the fancy is predominant, because the design is not truth, but to honour or dishonour, which is done by noble or by vile comparisons. The judgement does but suggest what circumstances make an action laudable or culpable.

[34]   7. In hortatives and pleadings, as truth or disguise serveth best to the design in hand, so is the judgement or the fancy most required.

8. In demonstration, in counsel, and all rigorous search of truth, judgement does all, except sometimes the understanding have need to be opened by some apt similitude, and then there is so much use of fancy. But for metaphors, they are in this case utterly excluded. For seeing they openly profess deceit, to admit them into counsel or reasoning were manifest folly.

9. And in any discourse whatsoever, if the defect of discretion be apparent, how extravagant soever the fancy be, the whole discourse will be taken for a sign of want of wit; and so will it never when the discretion is manifest, though the fancy be never so ordinary.

10. The secret thoughts of a man run over all things holy, profane, clean, obscene, grave, and light, without shame or blame; which verbal discourse cannot do farther than the judgement shall approve of the time, place, and persons. An anatomist or physician may speak or write his judgement of unclean things, because it is not to please, but profit; but for another man to write his extravagant and pleasant fancies of the same is as if a man, from being

tumbled into the dirt, should come and present himself before good company. And it is the want of discretion that makes the difference. Again, in professed remissness of mind and familiar company, a man may play with the sounds and equivocal significations of words, and that many times with encounters of extraordinary fancy; but in a sermon or in public or before persons unknown or whom we ought to reverence, there is no jingling of words that will not be accounted folly; and the difference is only in the want of discretion. So that where wit is wanting, it is not fancy that is wanting, but discretion. Judgement, therefore, without fancy is wit, but fancy without judgement, not.

11. When the thoughts of a man that has a design in hand, running over a multitude of things, observes how they conduce to that design or what design they may conduce unto, if his observations be such as are not easy or usual, this wit of his is called PRUDENCE, and dependeth on much experience and memory of the like things and their consequences heretofore. In which there is not so much difference of men as there is in their fancies and judgements, because the experience of men equal in age is not much unequal as to the quantity, but lies in different occasions, every one having his private designs. To govern well a family and a kingdom are not different degrees of prudence but different sorts of business, no more than to draw a picture in little or as great or greater than the life are different degrees of art. A plain husbandman is more prudent in affairs of his own house than a Privy Counsellor in the affairs of another man. *Prudence.*

12. To prudence, if you add the use of unjust or dishonest means, such as usually are prompted to men by fear or want, you have that crooked wisdom which is called CRAFT, which is a sign of pusillanimity. For magnanimity is contempt of unjust or dishonest helps. And that which the Latins call *versutia* (translated into English, *shifting*) and is a putting off of a present danger or incommodity by engaging into a greater, as when a man robs one to pay another, is but a shorter-sighted craft, called *versutia*, from *versura*, which signifies taking money at usury for the present payment of interest. *Craft.* [35]

13. As for *acquired wit* (I mean acquired by method and instruction), there is none but reason, which is grounded *Acquired wit.*

on the right use of speech and produceth the sciences. But of reason and science, I have already spoken in the fifth and sixth chapters.

14. The causes of this difference of wits are in the passions; and the difference of passions proceedeth partly from the different constitution of the body and partly from different education. For if the difference proceeded from the temper of the brain and the organs of sense, either exterior or interior, there would be no less difference of men in their sight, hearing, or other senses than in their fancies and discretions. It proceeds, therefore, from the passions, which are different, not only from the difference of men's complexions, but also from their difference of customs and education.

15. The passions that most of all cause the differences of wit are principally the more or less desire of power, of riches, of knowledge, and of honour. All which may be reduced to the first, that is, desire of power. For riches, knowledge and honour are but several sorts of power.

16. And therefore, a man who has no great passion for any of these things, but is as men term it indifferent; though he may be so far a good man as to be free from giving offence; yet he cannot possibly have either a great fancy or much judgement. For the thoughts are to the desires as scouts and spies to range abroad and find the way to the things desired; all steadiness of the mind's motion and all quickness of the same proceeding from thence. For as to have no desire is to be dead, so to have weak passions is dullness; and to have passions indifferently for everything, GIDDINESS and *distraction*; and to have stronger and more vehement passions for anything than is ordinarily seen in others is that which men call MADNESS.

17. Whereof there be almost as many kinds as of the passions themselves. Sometimes the extraordinary and extravagant passion proceedeth from the evil constitution of the organs of the body or harm done them; and sometimes the hurt and indisposition of the organs is caused by the vehemence or long continuance of the passion. But in both cases the madness is of one and the same nature.

18. The passion whose violence or continuance maketh madness is either great *vain-glory*, which is commonly called *pride* and *self-conceit*, or great *dejection* of mind.

Giddiness.

Madness.

19. Pride subjecteth a man to anger, the excess where- Rage.
of is the madness called RAGE and FURY. And thus it
comes to pass that excessive desire of revenge, when it [36]
becomes habitual, hurteth the organs and becomes rage;
that excessive love with jealousy becomes also rage; excessive opinion of a man's own self for divine inspiration,
for wisdom, learning, form, and the like, becomes distraction and giddiness; the same, joined with envy, rage;
vehement opinion of the truth of anything, contradicted
by others, rage.

20. Dejection subjects a man to causeless fears, which Melancholy.
is a madness commonly called MELANCHOLY, apparent
also in divers manners, as in haunting of solitudes and
graves, in superstitious behaviour and in fearing some
one, some another, particular thing. In sum, all passions
that produce strange and unusual behaviour are called
by the general name of madness. But of the several kinds
of madness, he that would take the pains might enroll a
legion. And if the excesses be madness, there is no doubt
but the passions themselves, when they tend to evil, are
degrees of the same.

21. For example, though the effect of folly in them that
are possessed of an opinion of being inspired be not visible always in one man by any very extravagant action that
proceedeth from such passion; yet when many of them
conspire together, the rage of the whole multitude is visible enough. For what argument of madness can there be
greater than to clamour, strike, and throw stones at our
best friends? Yet this is somewhat less than such a multitude will do. For they will clamour, fight against, and
destroy those by whom all their lifetime before they have
been protected and secured from injury. And if this be
madness in the multitude, it is the same in every particular man. For as in the midst of the sea, though a man perceive no sound of that part of the water next him, yet he is
well assured that part contributes as much to the roaring
of the sea as any other part of the same quantity; so also,
though we perceive no great unquietness in one or two
men, yet we may be well assured that their singular passions are parts of the seditious roaring of a troubled nation. And [even] if there were nothing else that bewrayed
[revealed] their madness, yet that very arrogating such inspiration to themselves is argument enough. If some man

in Bedlam[1] should entertain you with sober discourse, and you desire in taking leave to know what he were that you might another time requite his civility, and he should tell you he were God the Father, I think you need expect no extravagant action for argument of his madness.

22. This opinion of inspiration, called commonly, private spirit, begins very often from some lucky finding of an error generally held by others; and not knowing or not remembering by what conduct of reason they came to so singular a truth, as they think it, though it be many times an untruth they light on, they presently admire themselves as being in the special grace of God Almighty, who hath revealed the same to them supernaturally by his Spirit.

23. Again, that madness is nothing else but too much appearing passion may be gathered out of the effects of wine, which are the same with those of the evil disposition of the organs. For the variety of behaviour in men that have drunk too much is the same with that of madmen, some of them raging, others loving, others laughing, all extravagantly, but according to their several domineering passions. For the effect of the wine does but remove dissimulation and take from them the sight of the deformity of their passions. For (I believe) the most sober men, when they walk alone without care and employment of the mind, would be unwilling [that] the vanity and extravagance of their thoughts at that time should be publicly seen; which is a confession that passions unguided are for the most part mere madness.

[37]

24. The opinions of the world, both in ancient and later ages, concerning the cause of madness have been two. Some, deriving them from the passions, some, from demons[2] or spirits, either good or bad, which they thought might enter into a man, possess him, and move his organs in such strange and uncouth manner as madmen use to do. The former sort, therefore, called such men, madmen; but the latter called them sometimes *demoniacs* (that is, possessed with spirits), sometimes *energumeni* (that is, agitated or moved with spirits); and now in Italy

---

1 Bedlam was an asylum in London for the mentally ill.
2 "Demon" is related etymologically to the Greek word *daimōn*, but for the ancient Greeks demons were not evil spirits. See also 12.16, 34.15, 34.18, 36.2.

they are called not only *pazzi*, madmen, but also *spiritati*, men possessed.

25. There was once a great conflux of people in Abdera, a city of the Greeks, at the acting of the tragedy of Andromeda,[1] upon an extreme hot day; whereupon a great many of the spectators, falling into fevers, had this accident from the heat and from the tragedy together that they did nothing but pronounce iambics with the names of Perseus and Andromeda; which, together with the fever, was cured by the coming on of winter; and this madness was thought to proceed from the passion imprinted by the tragedy. Likewise there reigned a fit of madness in another Grecian city which seized only the young maidens and caused many of them to hang themselves. This was by most then thought an act of the devil. But one that suspected that contempt of life in them might proceed from some passion of the mind and supposing they did not contemn also their honour, gave counsel to the magistrates to strip such as so hanged themselves and let them hang out naked. This, the story says, cured that madness. But on the other side, the same Grecians did often ascribe madness to the operation of the Eumenides or Furies, and sometimes of Ceres, Phoebus, and other gods; so much did men attribute to phantasms as to think them aerial living bodies and generally to call them spirits. And as the Romans in this held the same opinion with the Greeks, so also did the Jews, for they called madmen prophets, or (according as they thought the spirits good or bad) demoniacs; and some of them called both prophets and demoniacs madmen; and some called the same man both demoniac and madman. But for the Gentiles, it is no wonder, because diseases and health, vices and virtues, and many natural accidents were with them termed and worshipped as demons. So that a man was to understand by demon, as well (sometimes) an ague, as a devil. But for the Jews to have such opinion is somewhat strange. For [38] neither Moses nor Abraham pretended to prophesy by possession of a spirit, but from the voice of God or by a vision or dream; nor is there anything in his law, moral or

---

1   In Greek mythology, Andromeda was to be sacrificed to a
    sea monster but was saved by Perseus. Euripides wrote a play
    Andromeda (412 BCE), now lost.

ceremonial, by which they were taught there was any such enthusiasm or any possession. When God is said (Num. 11:25) to take from the spirit that was in Moses and give to the seventy elders, the spirit of God (taking it for the substance of God) is not divided. The Scriptures, by the Spirit of God in man, mean a man's spirit, inclined to godliness. And where it is said, *Whom I have filled with the spirit of wisdom to make garments for Aaron* (Exod. 28:3), is not meant a spirit put into them that can make garments, but the wisdom of their own spirits in that kind of work. In the like sense, the spirit of man, when it produceth unclean actions, is ordinarily called an unclean spirit; and so other spirits [are called], though not always, yet as often as the virtue or vice, so styled, is extraordinary and eminent. Neither did the other prophets of the Old Testament pretend enthusiasm or that God spoke in them, but to them by voice, vision, or dream; and the *burden of the Lord* was not possession, but command. How then could the Jews fall into this opinion of possession? I can imagine no reason but that which is common to all men, namely, the want of curiosity to search natural causes and their placing felicity in the acquisition of the gross pleasures of the senses and the things that most immediately conduce thereto. For they that see any strange and unusual ability or defect in a man's mind, unless they see withal from what cause it may probably proceed, can hardly think it natural; and if not natural, they must needs think it supernatural; and then what can it be, but that either God or the Devil is in him? And hence it came to pass, when our Saviour (Mark 3:21) was compassed about with the multitude, those of the house doubted he was mad and went out to hold him; but the Scribes said he had Beelzebub, and that was it by which he cast out devils, as if the greater madman had awed the lesser. And that some said, *He hath a devil and is mad*, whereas others, holding him for a prophet, said, *These are not the words of one that hath a devil* (John 10:20). So in the Old Testament he that came to anoint Jehu was a Prophet; but some of the company asked Jehu, *What came that madman for?* (2 Kings 9:11). So that, in sum, it is manifest that whosoever behaved himself in extraordinary manner was thought by the Jews to be possessed either with a good or evil spirit, except by the Sadducees, who erred so far on the other hand as not to believe there were at all any spirits (which is very near to direct atheism), and thereby perhaps the more provoked others to term such men demoniacs rather than madmen.

26. But why then does our Saviour proceed in the curing of them, as if they were possessed and not as if they were mad? To which I can give no other kind of answer but that which is given to those that urge the Scripture in like manner against the opinion of the motion of the earth. The Scripture was written to show unto men the kingdom of God and to prepare their minds to become his obedient subjects, leaving the world and the philosophy thereof to the disputation of men for the exercising of their natural reason. Whether the earth's or sun's motion make the day and night, or whether the exorbitant actions of men proceed from passion or from the Devil (so [long as] we worship him not), it is all one as to our obedience and subjection to God Almighty; which is the thing for which the Scripture was written. As for that our Saviour speaketh to the disease as to a person, it is the usual phrase of all that cure by words only, as Christ did (and enchanters pretend to do, whether they speak to a devil or not). For is not Christ also said (Matt. 8:26) to have rebuked the winds? Is not he said also (Luke 4:39) to rebuke a fever? Yet this does not argue that a fever is a devil. And whereas many of those devils are said to confess Christ, it is not necessary to interpret those places otherwise than that those madmen confessed him. And whereas our Saviour (Matt. 12:43) speaketh of an unclean spirit, that having gone out of a man wandereth through dry places, seeking rest and finding none, and returning into the same man with seven other spirits worse than himself, it is manifestly a parable, alluding to a man that, after a little endeavour to quit his lusts, is vanquished by the strength of them and becomes seven times worse than he was. So that I see nothing at all in the Scripture that requireth a belief that demoniacs were any other thing but madmen.

27. There is yet another fault in the discourses of some men, which may also be numbered amongst the sorts of madness, namely, that abuse of words whereof I have spoken before in the fifth chapter by the name of absurdity. And that is when men speak such words as,

[39]

Insignificant speech.

put together, have in them no signification at all, but are fallen upon by some through misunderstanding of the words they have received and repeat by rote, by others from intention to deceive by obscurity. And this is incident to none but those that converse in questions of matters incomprehensible, as the Schoolmen, or in questions of abstruse philosophy. The common sort of men seldom speak insignificantly and are therefore, by those other egregious persons, counted idiots. But to be assured their words are without anything correspondent to them in the mind, there would need some examples; which if any man require, let him take a Schoolman into his hands and see if he can translate any one chapter concerning any difficult point, as the Trinity, the Deity, the nature of Christ, transubstantiation, free will, etc., into any of the modern tongues, so as to make the same intelligible, or into any tolerable Latin, such as they were acquainted withal that lived when the Latin tongue was vulgar. What is the meaning of these words: *The first cause does not necessarily inflow anything into the second, by force of the essential subordination of the second causes, by which it may help it to work?* They are the translation of the title of the sixth chapter of *Suarez'*[1] first book, *Of the Concourse, Motion, and Help of God.* When men write whole volumes of such stuff, are they not mad or intend to make others so? And particularly in the question of transubstantiation, where

[40] after certain words spoken they that say the white*ness*, round*ness*, magni*tude*, quali*ty*, corruptibili*ty*, all which are incorporeal, etc., go out of the wafer into the body of our blessed Saviour, do they not make those *nesses*, *tudes*, and *ties* to be so many spirits possessing his body? For by spirits they mean always things that being incorporeal are nevertheless movable from one place to another. So that this kind of absurdity may rightly be numbered amongst the many sorts of madness, and all the time that guided by clear thoughts of their worldly lust they forbear disputing or writing thus, but lucid intervals. And thus much of the virtues and defects intellectual.

---

1 Francisco Suarez, a Spanish Jesuit theologian and critic of Protestantism, was also known for his complex scholastic theories. Hobbes is referring to Suarez's *De Concursu, Motione, et Auxilio Dei* (II.1.6).

Chapter IX

Of the Several Subjects of Knowledge

1. There are of KNOWLEDGE two kinds, whereof one is *knowledge of fact*; the other *knowledge of the consequence of one affirmation to another.* The former is nothing else but sense and memory and is *absolute* knowledge, as when we see a fact doing, or remember it done; and this is the knowledge required in a witness. The latter is called *science* and is *conditional*, as when we know that: *if the figure shown be a circle, then any straight line through the centre shall divide it into two equal parts.* And this is the knowledge required in a philosopher, that is to say, of him that pretends to reasoning.

2. The register of knowledge of fact is called *history*, whereof there be two sorts; one called *natural history*; which is the history of such facts or effects of nature as have no dependence on man's *will*, such as are the histories of metals, plants, animals, regions, and the like. The other is *civil history*, which is the history of the voluntary actions of men in commonwealths.

3. The registers of science are such books as contain the *demonstrations* of consequences of one affirmation to another; and are commonly called *books of philosophy*; whereof the sorts are many, according to the diversity of the matter, and may be divided in such manner as I have divided them in the following table.[1]

---

1   As the table indicates, there are two basic parts of science: that of natural bodies (physics) and that of artificial bodies (politics). But Hobbes's complete system of science consists of three parts: *De Corpore* (*Of Body*), *De Homine* (*Of Man*), and *De Cive* (*Of the Citizen*). Human beings belong to natural science because they are bodies; insofar as they are parts of an artificial body, the civil state, they should be treated under politics. Notice that ethics and the science of just and unjust belong to natural, not civil, philosophy. Also notice the absence of theology from the table because it is not a science.

SCIENCE,
that is,
knowledge of
consequences;
which is
called also
PHILOSOPHY.

Consequences
from accidents
of bodies
natural; which
is called
NATURAL
PHILOSOPHY.

PHYSICS, or
conse-
quences
from
qualities.

Consequences from accidents ....
common to all bodies natural;
which are *quantity*, and *motion*.

Consequences from qualities
of bodies transient, such as
sometimes appear, sometimes
vanish, ...

Consequences
from qualities
of the *stars*.

Consequences
of qualities
from *liquid*
bodies that
fill the space
between the
stars; such as
are the *air*,
or substance
ethereal.

Consequences
from qualities
of bodies
permanent.

Consequences
from qualities
of bodies
terrestrial.

Consequences
from accidents
of politic bodies;
which is called
POLITICS,
and CIVIL
PHILOSOPHY.

1. Of consequences from the institution of COM-
MONWEALTHS, to the *rights*, and *duties* of the *body
politic*, or *sovereign*.

2. Of consequences from the same, to the *duty*
and *right* of the *subjects*.

Consequences from quantity, and motion indeterminate; which, being the principles or first foundation of philosophy, is called *Philosophia Prima.* — PHILOSOPHIA PRIMA

Consequences from motion, and quantity determined.

- Consequences from quantity, and motion determined.
  - By Figure ⎫ *Mathematics.*
  - By Number ⎭
    - GEOMETRY
    - ARITHMETIC

- Consequences from motion, and quantity of bodies in *special.*
  - Consequences from the motion and quantity of the great parts of the world, as the *earth* and *stars,* — *Cosmography*
    - ASTRONOMY
    - GEOGRAPHY
  - Consequences from motion of special kinds, and figures of body, — *Mechanics,* doctrine of *weight.*
    - *Science of*
    - ENGINEERS
    - ARCHITECTURE
    - NAVIGATION

.... METEOROLOGY

Consequences from the *light* of the stars. Out of this, and the motion of the sun, is made the science of .... SCIOGRAPHY

Consequences from the influence of the stars .... ASTROLOGY

Consequences from parts of the earth that are *without sense.*
- Consequences from qualities of *minerals*, as *stones, metals, etc.*
- Consequences from the qualities of *vegetables.*

Consequences from the qualities of animals.
- Conse-quences from qualities of *animals in general.*
  - Consequences from *vision* ....OPTICS
  - Consequences from *sounds* ....MUSIC
  - Consequences from the *rest of the senses.*
- Conse-quences from quali-ties of *men in special.*
  - Consequences from *passions of men* ....ETHICS
  - Consequences from speech,
    - In *magnifying, vilifying, etc.* ⎫ ....POETRY
    - In *persuading,* ....RHETORIC
    - In *reasoning,* ....LOGIC
    - In *contracting,* ....*The Science of* JUST and UNJUST

Chapter X

Of Power, Worth, Dignity, Honour, and Worthiness

1. The power of a man (to take it universally) is his present means to obtain some future apparent good and is either *original*[1] or *instrumental*.

2. *Natural power* is the eminence of the faculties of body or mind, as extraordinary strength, form, prudence, arts, eloquence, liberality, nobility. *Instrumental* are those powers which acquired by these or by fortune are means and instruments to acquire more, as riches, reputation, friends, and the secret working of God, which men call good luck. For the nature of power is in this point like to fame, increasing as it proceeds, or like the motion of heavy bodies, which, the further they go, make still the more haste.

3. The greatest of human powers is that which is compounded of the powers of most men, united by consent, in one person, natural or civil, that has the use of all their powers depending on his will, such as is the power of a commonwealth; or depending on the wills of each particular, such as is the power of a faction or of divers factions leagued. Therefore to have servants is power; to have friends is power; for they are strengths united.

4. Also, riches joined with liberality is power, because it procureth friends and servants; without liberality, not so, because in this case they defend not, but expose men to envy, as a prey.

5. Reputation of power is power, because it draweth with it the adherence of those that need protection.

6. So is reputation of love of a man's country called popularity, for the same reason.

7. Also, what quality soever maketh a man beloved or feared of many, or the reputation of such quality, is power, because it is a means to have the assistance and service of many.

8. Good success is power, because it maketh reputation of wisdom or good fortune, which makes men either fear him or rely on him.

---

1 Hobbes probably should have written "natural" here. See 10.2.

9. Affability of men already in power is increase of power, because it gaineth love.

10. Reputation of prudence in the conduct of peace or war is power, because to prudent men we commit the government of ourselves more willingly than to others.

11. Nobility is power, not in all places, but only in those commonwealths where it has privileges; for in such privileges consisteth their power.

12. Eloquence is power, because it is seeming prudence.

13. Form is power, because being a promise of good, it recommendeth men to the favour of women and [42] strangers.

14. The sciences are small power, because not eminent, and therefore not acknowledged in any man; nor are at all, but in a few, and in them, but of a few things. For science is of that nature, as none can understand it to be, but such as in a good measure have attained it.

15. Arts of public use, as fortification, making of engines, and other instruments of war, because they confer to defence and victory, are power; and though the true mother of them be science, namely, the mathematics, yet, because they are brought into the light by the hand of the artificer, they be esteemed (the midwife passing with the vulgar for the mother) as his issue.

16. The *value* or WORTH of a man is, as of all other   Worth. things, his price, that is to say, so much as would be given for the use of his power and therefore is not absolute, but a thing dependent on the need and judgement of another. An able conductor of soldiers is of great price in time of war present or imminent but in peace not so. A learned and uncorrupt judge is much worth in time of peace, but not so much in war. And as in other things, so in men, not the seller, but the buyer determines the price. For let a man, as most men do, rate themselves at the highest value they can; yet their true value is no more than it is esteemed by others.

17. The manifestation of the value we set on one another is that which is commonly called honouring and dishonouring. To value a man at a high rate is to *honour* him, at a low rate is to *dishonour* him. But high and low in this case is to be understood by comparison to the rate that each man setteth on himself.

18. The public worth of a man, which is the value set on him by the commonwealth, is that which men commonly call DIGNITY. And this value of him by the commonwealth is understood by offices of command, judicature, public employment; or by names and titles introduced for distinction of such value.

Dignity.

19. To pray to another for aid of any kind is *to* HONOUR, because a sign we have an opinion he has power to help; and the more difficult the aid is, the more is the honour.

To honour and dishonour.

20. To obey is to honour, because no man obeys them who they think have no power to help or hurt them. And consequently to disobey is to *dishonour*.

21. To give great gifts to a man is to honour him, because it is buying of protection and acknowledging of power. To give little gifts is to dishonour, because it is but alms and signifies an opinion of the need of small helps.

22. To be sedulous in promoting another's good [and] also to flatter is to honour, as a sign we seek his protection or aid. To neglect is to dishonour.

23. To give way or place to another in any commodity is to honour, being a confession of greater power. To arrogate is to dishonour.

24. To show any sign of love or fear of another is honour, for both to love and to fear is to value. To contemn, or less to love or fear than he expects, is to dishonour, for it is undervaluing.

[43]

25. To praise, magnify, or call happy is to honour, because nothing but goodness, power, and felicity is valued. To revile, mock, or pity is to dishonour.

26. To speak to another with consideration, to appear before him with decency and humility is to honour him, as signs of fear to offend. To speak to him rashly, to do anything before him obscenely, slovenly, impudently is to dishonour.

27. To believe, to trust, to rely on another is to honour him, [a] sign of opinion of his virtue and power. To distrust or not believe is to dishonour.

28. To hearken to a man's counsel or discourse of what kind soever is to honour, as a sign we think him wise or eloquent or witty. To sleep or go forth or talk the while is to dishonour.

29. To do those things to another which he takes for signs of honour or which the law or custom makes so is to

honour, because in approving the honour done by others, he acknowledgeth the power which others acknowledge. To refuse to do them is to dishonour.

30. To agree with in opinion is to honour, as being a sign of approving his judgement and wisdom. To dissent is dishonour and an upbraiding of error, and, if the dissent be in many things, of folly.

31. To imitate is to honour, for it is vehemently to approve. To imitate one's enemy is to dishonour.

32. To honour those another honours is to honour him, as a sign of approbation of his judgement. To honour his enemies is to dishonour him.

33. To employ in counsel or in actions of difficulty is to honour, as a sign of opinion of his wisdom or other power. To deny employment in the same cases to those that seek it is to dishonour.

34. All these ways of honouring are natural, and as well within as without commonwealths. But in commonwealths where he or they that have the supreme authority can make whatsoever they please to stand for signs of honour, there be other honours.

35. A sovereign doth honour a subject with whatsoever title or office or employment or action that he himself will have taken for a sign of his will to honour him.

36. The king of Persia honoured Mordecai when he appointed [that] he should be conducted through the streets in the king's garment upon one of the king's horses with a crown on his head and a prince before him, proclaiming, *Thus shall it be done to him that the king will honour.*[1] And yet another king of Persia or the same another time to one that demanded for some great service to wear one of the king's robes, gave him leave so to do; but with this addition, that he should wear it as the king's fool, and then it was dishonour. So that of civil honour the fountain is in the person of the commonwealth and dependeth on the will of the sovereign and is therefore temporary and called *civil honour*, such as are magistracy, [44] offices, titles, and in some places coats and scutcheons painted; and men honour such as have them, as having so many signs of favour in the commonwealth, which favour is power.

---

1 See Esth. 1:1-12.

37. *Honourable* is whatsoever possession, action, or quality is an argument and sign of power.

38. And therefore to be honoured, loved, or feared of many is honourable, as arguments of power. To be honoured of few or none, dishonourable.

39. Dominion and victory is honourable because acquired by power; and servitude, for need or fear, is dishonourable.

40. Good fortune (if lasting) honourable, as a sign of the favour of God. Ill fortune and losses, dishonourable. Riches are honourable, for they are power. Poverty, dishonourable. Magnanimity, liberality, hope, courage, [and] confidence are honourable; for they proceed from the conscience of power. Pusillanimity, parsimony, fear, diffidence, are dishonourable.

41. Timely resolution or determination of what a man is to do is honourable, as being the contempt of small difficulties and dangers. And irresolution dishonourable, as a sign of too much valuing of little impediments and little advantages, for when a man has weighed things as long as the time permits and resolves not, the difference of weight is but little; and therefore if he resolve not, he overvalues little things, which is pusillanimity.[1]

42. All actions and speeches that proceed or seem to proceed from much experience, science, discretion, or wit are honourable, for all these are powers. Actions or words that proceed from error, ignorance, or folly, dishonourable.

43. Gravity, as far forth as it seems to proceed from a mind employed on something else, is honourable, because employment is a sign of power. But if it seem to proceed from a purpose to appear grave, it is dishonourable. For the gravity of the former is like the steadiness of a ship laden with merchandise, but of the latter the steadiness of a ship ballasted with sand and other trash.

44. To be conspicuous, that is to say, to be known, for wealth, office, great actions, or any eminent good is honourable, as a sign of the power for which he is conspicuous. On the contrary, obscurity is dishonourable.

45. To be descended from conspicuous parents is honourable, because they the more easily attain the aids and

---

1 See 6.25.

friends of their ancestors. On the contrary, to be descended from obscure parentage is dishonourable.

46. Actions proceeding from equity, joined with loss, are honourable, as signs of magnanimity, for magnanimity is a sign of power. On the contrary, craft, shifting, [and] neglect of equity is dishonourable.

47. Covetousness of great riches and ambition of great honours are honourable, as signs of power to obtain them. Covetousness and ambition of little gains or preferments is dishonourable.

48. Nor does it alter the case of honour whether an action (so it be great and difficult and consequently a sign of much power) be just or unjust, for honour consisteth only in the opinion of power. Therefore, the ancient heathen did not think they dishonoured but greatly honoured the gods, when they introduced them in their poems committing rapes, thefts, and other great, but unjust or unclean acts, insomuch as nothing is so much celebrated in Jupiter as his adulteries, nor in Mercury as his frauds and thefts, of whose praises in a hymn of Homer the greatest is this, that being born in the morning, he had invented music at noon and before night stolen away the cattle of Apollo from his herdsmen. [45]

49. Also amongst men, till there were constituted great commonwealths, it was thought no dishonour to be a pirate or a highway thief, but rather a lawful trade, not only amongst the Greeks, but also amongst all other nations, as is manifest by the histories of ancient time. And at this day, in this part of the world, private duels are and always will be honourable, though unlawful, till such time as there shall be honour ordained for them that refuse and ignominy for them that make the challenge. For duels also are many times effects of courage, and the ground of courage is always strength or skill, which are power, though for the most part they be effects of rash speaking and of the fear of dishonour in one or both the combatants, who, engaged by rashness, are driven into the lists to avoid disgrace.

50. Scutcheons and coats of arms hereditary, where they have any eminent privileges, are honourable; otherwise not; for their power consisteth either in such privileges or in riches or some such thing as is equally honoured in other men. This kind of honour, commonly

Coats of arms.

called gentry, has been derived from the ancient Germans. For there never was any such thing known where the German customs were unknown. Nor is it now anywhere in use where the Germans have not inhabited. The ancient Greek commanders, when they went to war, had their shields painted with such devices as they pleased, insomuch as an unpainted buckler was a sign of poverty and of a common soldier; but they transmitted not the inheritance of them. The Romans transmitted the marks of their families; but they were the images, not the devices of their ancestors. Amongst the people of Asia, Africa, and America, there is not, nor was ever, any such thing. The Germans only had that custom, from whom it has been derived into England, France, Spain and Italy, when in great numbers they either aided the Romans or made their own conquests in these western parts of the world.

51. For Germany, being anciently, as all other countries in their beginnings, divided amongst an infinite number of little lords or masters of families that continually had wars one with another, those masters or lords, principally to the end [that] they might, when they were covered with arms, be known by their followers, and partly for ornament, both painted their armor or their scutcheon or coat with the picture of some beast or other [46] thing and also put some eminent and visible mark upon the crest of their helmets. And this ornament both of the arms and crest descended by inheritance to their children to the eldest pure and to the rest with some note of diversity, such as the old master, that is to say in Dutch, the *Here-alt*, thought fit. But when many such families, joined together, made a greater monarchy, this duty of the herald to distinguish scutcheons was made a private office apart. And the issue of these lords is the great and ancient gentry, which for the most part bear living creatures noted for courage and rapine, or castles, battlements, belts, weapons, bars, palisades, and other notes of war; nothing being then in honour, but virtue military. Afterwards, not only kings but popular commonwealths gave divers manners of scutcheons to such as went forth to the war, or returned from it, for encouragement or recompense to their service. All which, by an observing reader, may be found

in such ancient histories, Greek and Latin, as make mention of the German nation and manners in their times.[1]

52. Titles of honour, such as are duke, count, marquis, and baron, are honourable, as signifying the value set upon them by the sovereign power of the commonwealth; which titles were in old time titles of office and command derived some from the Romans, some from the Germans and French. Dukes, in Latin, *duces*, being generals in war; counts, *comites*, such as bore the general company out of friendship, and were left to govern and defend places conquered and pacified; marquises, *marchiones*, were counts that governed the marches or bounds of the Empire. Which titles of duke, count, and marquis came into the Empire about the time of Constantine the Great[2] from the customs of the German *militia*. But baron seems to have been a title of the Gauls and signifies a great man, such as were the kings' or princes' men whom they employed in war about their persons, and seems to be derived from *vir*, to *ber*, and *bar*, that signified the same in the language of the Gauls that *vir* [signified] in Latin, and thence to *bero* and *baro*, so that such men were called *berones*, and after *barones*; and (in Spanish) *varones*. But he that would know more, particularly the original of titles of honour, may find it, as I have done this, in Mr. Selden's most excellent treatise of that subject.[3] In process of time these offices of honour, by occasion of trouble and for reasons of good and peaceable government, were turned into mere titles, serving for the most part to distinguish the precedence, place, and order of subjects in the commonwealth; and men were made dukes, counts, marquises, and barons of places, wherein they had neither possession nor command, and other titles also were devised to the same end.

---

1   See Hobbes's translation of Thucydides, *History of the Peloponnesian War* 1.5-6.
2   Flavius Constantinus (274-337), Roman emperor who made Christianity the state religion. He was praised by John Fox in his *Book of Martyrs* (English version, 1563), and Hobbes was similarly approving.
3   John Selden, *Titles of Honour* (1614). Selden (1584-1654) was a friend of Hobbes during the early 1650s but they may have met at Great Tew in the 1630s.

53. WORTHINESS is a thing different from the worth or value of a man and also from his merit or desert, and consisteth in a particular power or ability for that whereof he is said to be worthy; which particular ability is usually named FITNESS or *aptitude*.

54. For he is worthiest to be a commander, to be a judge, or to have any other charge, that is best fitted with the qualities required to the well discharging of it, and worthiest of riches that has the qualities most requisite for the well using of them, any of which qualities being absent, one may nevertheless be a worthy man and valuable for something else. Again, a man may be worthy of riches, office, and employment that nevertheless can plead no right to have it before another, and therefore cannot be said to merit or deserve it. For merit presupposeth a right and that the thing deserved is due by promise, of which I shall say more hereafter when I shall speak of contracts.

Chapter XI

Of the Difference of Manners

1. By MANNERS, I mean not here decency of behaviour, as how one man should salute another, or how a man should wash his mouth, or pick his teeth before company, and such other points of the *small morals*, but those qualities of mankind that concern their living together in peace and unity.[1] To which end we are to consider that the felicity of this life consisteth not in the repose of a mind satisfied. For there is no such *finis ultimus* (utmost aim) nor *summum bonum* (greatest good) as is spoken of in the books of the old moral philosophers. Nor can a man any more live whose desires are at an end than he whose senses and imaginations are at a stand.[2] Felicity is a continual progress of the desire from one object to another, the attaining of the former being still but the way to the latter. The cause whereof is that the object of

---

1 By "manners" Hobbes does not mean etiquette but ethics.
2 In ancient Greek philosophy, to have a desire was a kind of imperfection, because it meant that one lacked (wanted) the thing desired. For Hobbes, desire is a necessary condition of life. See also 6.58.

man's desire is not to enjoy once only and for one instant of time, but to assure forever the way of his future desire. And therefore the voluntary actions and inclinations of all men tend not only to the procuring, but also to the assuring of a contented life; and [they] differ only in the way, which ariseth partly from the diversity of passions in divers men, and partly from the difference of the knowledge or opinion each one has of the causes which produce the effect desired.

2. So that in the first place, I put for a general inclination of all mankind a perpetual and restless desire of power after power that ceaseth only in death. And the cause of this is not always that a man hopes for a more intensive delight than he has already attained to, or that he cannot be content with a moderate power, but because he cannot assure the power and means to live well, which he hath present, without the acquisition of more. And from hence it is that kings, whose power is greatest, turn their endeavours to the assuring it at home by laws or abroad by wars; and when that is done, there succeedeth a new desire: in some, of fame from new conquest, in others, of ease and sensual pleasure, in others, of admiration or being flattered for excellence in some art or other ability of the mind. *A restless desire of power in all men.*

3. Competition of riches, honour, command, or other power inclineth to contention, enmity, and war, because the way of one competitor to the attaining of his desire is to kill, subdue, supplant, or repel the other. Particularly, competition of praise inclineth to a reverence of antiquity. For men contend with the living, not with the dead, to these ascribing more than due, that they may obscure the glory of the other. *Love of contention from competition. [48]*

4. Desire of ease and sensual delight disposeth men to obey a common power, because by such desires a man doth abandon the protection [that] might be hoped for from his own industry and labour. Fear of death and wounds disposeth to the same and for the same reason. On the contrary, needy men and hardy, not contented with their present condition, as also all men that are ambitious of military command, are inclined to continue the causes of war and to stir up trouble and sedition; for there is no honour military but by war, nor any such hope to mend an ill game as by causing a new shuffle. *Desire of ease.*

And from
love of arts.

Love of virtue
from love of
praise.

Hate from
difficulty of
requiting great
benefits.

And from
conscience of
deserving to
be hated. [49]

5. Desire of knowledge and arts of peace inclineth men to obey a common power; for such desire containeth a desire of leisure and consequently [a desire of] protection from some other power than their own.

6. Desire of praise disposeth to laudable actions, such as please them whose judgement they value; for of those men whom we contemn, we contemn also the praises. Desire of fame after death does the same. And though after death there be no sense of the praise given us on earth, as being joys that are either swallowed up in the unspeakable joys of heaven or extinguished in the extreme torments of hell; yet is not such fame vain, because men have a present delight therein from the foresight of it and of the benefit that may redound thereby to their posterity, which though they now see not, yet they imagine; and anything that is pleasure in the sense the same also is pleasure in the imagination.

7. To have received from one to whom we think ourselves equal greater benefits than there is hope to requite disposeth to counterfeit love; but really [it disposeth to] secret hatred, and puts a man into the estate of a desperate debtor, that in declining the sight of his creditor, tacitly wishes him there where he might never see him more. For benefits oblige, and obligation is thraldom; and unrequitable obligation, perpetual thraldom, which is to one's equal, hateful. But to have received benefits from one whom we acknowledge for superior inclines to love, because the obligation is no new depression; and cheerful acceptation (which men call *gratitude*) is such an honour done to the obliger as is taken generally for retribution. Also to receive benefits, though from an equal or inferior, as long as there is hope of requital, disposeth to love; for in the intention of the receiver the obligation is of aid and service mutual; from whence proceedeth an emulation of who shall exceed in benefiting, the most noble and profitable contention possible, wherein the victor is pleased with his victory, and the other revenged by confessing it.

8. To have done more hurt to a man than he can or is willing to expiate inclineth the doer to hate the sufferer. For he must expect revenge or forgiveness, both which are hateful.

9. Fear of oppression disposeth a man to anticipate or to seek aid by society; for there is no other way by which a man can secure his life and liberty.

Promptness to hurt from fear.

10. Men that distrust their own subtlety are in tumult and sedition better disposed for victory than they that suppose themselves wise or crafty. For these love to consult, the other (fearing to be circumvented) to strike first. And in sedition, men being always in the precincts of battle, to hold together and use all advantages of force is a better stratagem than any that can proceed from subtlety of wit.

And from distrust of their own wit.

11. Vain-glorious men, such as without being conscious to themselves of great sufficiency, delight in supposing themselves gallant men, are inclined only to ostentation, but not to attempt; because when danger or difficulty appears, they look for nothing but to have their insufficiency discovered.

Vain undertaking from vain-glory.

12. Vain-glorious men, such as estimate their sufficiency by the flattery of other men or the fortune of some precedent action, without assured ground of hope from the true knowledge of themselves, are inclined to rash engaging, and in the approach of danger or difficulty to retire if they can; because not seeing the way of safety they will rather hazard their honour, which may be salved with an excuse, than their lives, for which no salve is sufficient.

13. Men that have a strong opinion of their own wisdom in matter of government are disposed to ambition, because without public employment in counsel or magistracy, the honour of their wisdom is lost. And therefore eloquent speakers are inclined to ambition, for eloquence seemeth wisdom both to themselves and others.

Ambition from opinion of sufficiency.

14. Pusillanimity disposeth men to irresolution and consequently to lose the occasions and fittest opportunities of action. For after men have been in deliberation till the time of action approach, if it be not then manifest what is best to be done, it is a sign [that] the difference of motives the one way and the other are not great; therefore not to resolve then is to lose the occasion by weighing of trifles, which is pusillanimity.

Irresolution from too great valuing of small matters.

15. Frugality (though in poor men a virtue) maketh a man unapt to achieve such actions as require the strength of many men at once; for it weakeneth their endeavour, which is to be nourished and kept in vigour by reward.

Confidence in
others from
ignorance of
the marks of
wisdom and
kindness.

[50] And from
ignorance of
natural causes.

And from
want of
understanding

Adherence to
custom from
ignorance of the

16. Eloquence with flattery disposeth men to confide in them that have it, because the former is seeming wisdom, the latter seeming kindness. Add to them military reputation and it disposeth men to adhere and subject themselves to those men that have them. The two former, having given them caution against danger from him; the latter gives them caution against danger from others.

17. Want of science, that is, ignorance of causes, disposeth or rather constraineth a man to rely on the advice and authority of others. For all men whom the truth concerns, if they rely not on their own, must rely on the opinion of some other whom they think wiser than themselves and see not why he should deceive them.

18. Ignorance of the signification of words, which is want of understanding, disposeth men to take on trust, not only the truth they know not, but also the errors, and which is more, the nonsense of them they trust; for neither error nor nonsense can without a perfect understanding of words be detected.

19. From the same it proceedeth that men give different names to one and the same thing from the difference of their own passions; as they that approve a private opinion call it opinion, but they that mislike it, heresy;[1] and yet heresy signifies no more than private opinion, but has only a greater tincture of choler [anger].

20. From the same also it proceedeth that men cannot distinguish, without study and great understanding, between one action of many men and many actions of one multitude; as for example, between the one action of all the senators of Rome in killing Catiline[2] and the many actions of a number of senators in killing Caesar; and therefore are disposed to take for the action of the people that which is a multitude of actions done by a multitude of men led perhaps by the persuasion of one.[3]

21. Ignorance of the causes and original constitution of right, equity, law, and justice disposeth a man to make custom and example the rule of his actions, in

---

1 See 42.130.
2 Catiline (c. 108-62 BCE), Roman politician who plotted to take over the government, but was arrested through the influence of Cicero.
3 Hobbes may be alluding to the execution of King Charles I (1649) by the members of the Rump Parliament.

such manner as to think that unjust which it hath been nature of right and wrong. the custom to punish, and that just, of the impunity and approbation whereof they can produce an example, or (as the lawyers which only use this false measure of justice barbarously call it) a precedent;[1] like little children that have no other rule of good and evil manners but the correction they receive from their parents and masters, save that children are constant to their rule, whereas men are not so; because grown strong and stubborn, they appeal from custom to reason, and from reason to custom, as it serves their turn, receding from custom when their interest requires it and setting themselves against reason as oft as reason is against them; which is the cause that the doctrine of right and wrong is perpetually disputed both by the pen and the sword, whereas the doctrine of lines and figures is not so, because men care not in that subject what be truth, as a thing that crosses no man's ambition, profit, or lust. For I doubt not but if it had been a thing contrary to any man's right of dominion or to the interest of men that have dominion *that the three angles of a triangle should be equal to two angles of a square*, that doctrine should [would] have been, if not disputed, yet by the burning of all books of geometry, suppressed, as far as he whom it concerned was able.

22. Ignorance of remote causes disposeth men to attribute all events to the causes immediate and instrumental; for these are all the causes they perceive. And hence it comes to pass that in all places, men that are grieved with payments to the public discharge their anger upon the publicans, that is to say, farmers, collectors, and other officers of the public revenue, and adhere to such as find fault with the public government; and thereby, when they have engaged themselves beyond hope of justification, fall also upon the supreme authority for fear of punishment or shame of receiving pardon.

Adherence to private men, from ignorance of the causes of peace.

[51]

23. Ignorance of natural causes disposeth a man to credulity, so as to believe many times impossibilities; for such [men] know nothing to the contrary but that they may be true, being unable to detect the impossibility. And credulity, because men love to be hearkened unto in

Credulity from ignorance of nature.

---

1 Hobbes is criticizing Edward Coke (1552-1634), who claimed the Common Law was independent of the king.

company, disposeth them to lying; so that ignorance itself, without malice, is able to make a man both to believe lies and tell them, and sometimes also to invent them.

Curiosity to know from care of future time.

24. Anxiety for the future time disposeth men to inquire into the causes of things, because the knowledge of them maketh men the better able to order the present to their best advantage.[1]

Natural religion from the same

25. Curiosity or love of the knowledge of causes draws a man from consideration of the effect to seek the cause, and again, the cause of that cause; till of necessity he must come to this thought at last, that there is some cause whereof there is no former cause, but is eternal; which is it men call God. So that it is impossible to make any profound inquiry into natural causes without being inclined thereby to believe there is one God eternal, though they cannot have any idea of him in their mind answerable to his nature.[2] For as a man that is born blind, hearing men talk of warming themselves by the fire and being brought to warm himself by the same, may easily conceive and assure himself there is somewhat there which men call fire and is the cause of the heat he feels, but cannot imagine what it is like nor have an idea of it in his mind such as they have that see it, so also by the visible things of this world and their admirable order, a man may conceive there is a cause of them, which men call God, and yet not have an idea or image of him in his mind.

26. And they that make little or no inquiry into the natural causes of things, yet from the fear that proceeds from the ignorance itself of what it is that hath the power to do them much good or harm, are inclined to suppose and feign unto themselves several kinds of powers invisible; and to stand in awe of their own imaginations; and in time of distress to invoke them; as also in the time of unexpected[3] good success, to give them thanks; making the creatures of their own fancy their gods. By which means it hath come to pass that from the innumerable variety of fancy, men have created in the world innumerable sorts of gods. And this fear of things invisible is the natural seed

---

1 See also 12.5.
2 Humans can know that God exists, but not what his nature is like, because they have no direct or unmediated knowledge of God. See also 3.12 and 12.6.
3 Early printed editions incorrectly have "an expected."

of that which every one in himself calleth religion, and in them that worship or fear that power otherwise than they do, superstition.[1]

27. And this seed of religion, having been observed by many, some of those that have observed it have been inclined thereby to nourish, dress, and form it into laws, and to add to it of their own invention any opinion of the causes of future events by which they thought they should best be able to govern others and make unto themselves the greatest use of their powers.

Chapter XII

Of Religion

1. Seeing there are no signs nor fruit of *religion* but in man only, there is no cause to doubt but that the seed of *religion* is also only in man[2] and consisteth in some peculiar quality or at least in some eminent degree thereof, not to be found in other living creatures.

Religion in man only.

2. And first, it is peculiar to the nature of man to be inquisitive into the causes of the events they see, some more, some less, but all men so much as to be curious in the search of the causes of their own good and evil fortune.

First, from his desire of knowing causes.

3. Secondly, upon the sight of anything that hath a beginning, to think also it had a cause which determined the same to begin then when it did, rather than sooner or later.

From the consideration of the beginning of things.

4. Thirdly, whereas there is no other felicity of beasts but the enjoying of their quotidian food, ease, and lusts; as having little or no foresight of the time to come for want of observation and memory of the order, consequence, and dependence of the things they see; man observeth how one event hath been produced by another and remembereth in them antecedence and consequence, and when he cannot assure himself of the true causes of things (for the causes of good and evil fortune for the most part are invisible), he supposes causes of them, either such as

From his observation of the sequel of things.

---

1 See 6.36 and 12.6.
2 The seed of religion is the fear of things invisible. See 11.26.

his own fancy suggesteth, or trusteth to the authority of other men such as he thinks to be his friends and wiser than himself.

The natural cause of religion, the anxiety of the time to come.

5. The two first make anxiety. For being assured that there be causes of all things that have arrived hitherto or shall arrive hereafter, it is impossible for a man, who continually endeavoureth to secure himself against the evil he fears, and procure the good he desireth, not to be in a perpetual solicitude of the time to come; so that every man, especially those that are over-provident, are in an estate like to that of Prometheus. For as Prometheus (which, interpreted, is *the prudent man*) was bound to the hill Caucasus, a place of large prospect, where an eagle, feeding on his liver, devoured in the day as much as was repaired in the night, so that man, which looks too far before him in the care of future time, hath his heart all the day long gnawed on by fear of death, poverty, or other calamity, and has no repose, nor pause of his anxiety, but in sleep.[1]

Which makes them fear the power of invisible things.

6. This perpetual fear, always accompanying mankind in the ignorance of causes, as it were in the dark, must needs have for object something. And therefore when there is nothing to be seen, there is nothing to accuse either of their good or evil fortune but some *power* or agent *invisible*; in which sense perhaps it was that some of the old poets said that the gods were at first created by human fear, which, spoken of the gods (that is to say, of the many gods of the Gentiles), is very true. But the acknowledging of one God, eternal, infinite, and omnipotent, may more easily be derived from the desire men have to know the causes of natural bodies and their several virtues and operations than from the fear of what was to befall them in time to come. For he that from any effect he seeth come to pass should reason to the next and immediate cause thereof, and from thence to the cause of that cause, and plunge himself profoundly in the pursuit of causes, shall at last come to this, that there must be (as even the heathen philosophers confessed) one First Mover, that is, a first and an eternal cause of all things, which is that which men mean by the name of God; and all this without thought of their fortune, the solicitude whereof

[53]

---

1 Cf. Francis Bacon on Prometheus in *Wisdom of the Ancients* (1619), pp. 119–44.

both inclines to fear and hinders them from the search of the causes of other things, and thereby gives occasion of feigning of as many gods as there be men that feign them.

7. And for the matter or substance of the invisible agents, so fancied, they could not by natural cogitation fall upon any other concept but that it was the same with that of the soul of man; and that the soul of man was of the same substance with that which appeareth in a dream to one that sleepeth, or in a looking-glass to one that is awake; which, men not knowing that such apparitions are nothing else but creatures of the fancy, think to be real and external substances and therefore call them ghosts, as the Latins called them *imagines* [images] and *umbrae* [shadows]; and [men] thought them spirits (that is, thin aerial bodies), and those invisible agents which they feared, to be like them, save that they appear and vanish when they please. But the opinion that such spirits were incorporeal or immaterial could never enter into the mind of any man by nature, because though men may put together words of contradictory signification, as *spirit* and *incorporeal*; yet they can never have the imagination of anything answering to them; and therefore, men that by their own meditation arrive to the acknowledgement of one infinite, omnipotent, and eternal God choose rather to confess he is incomprehensible and above their understanding than to define his nature by · *spirit incorporeal*,[1] and then confess their definition to be unintelligible; or if they give him such a title, it is not *dogmatically* with intention to make the Divine Nature understood, but *piously*, to honour him with attributes of significations as remote as they can from the grossness of bodies visible.

And suppose them incorporeal.

8. Then, for the way by which they think these invisible agents wrought their effects, that is to say, what immediate causes they used in bringing things to pass, men that know not what it is that we call *causing* (that is, almost all men) have no other rule to guess by but by observing and remembering what they have seen to precede the like effect at some other time or times before, without seeing between the antecedent and subsequent event any dependence or connexion at all; and therefore from the

But know not the way how they effect anything.

1   See 3.12.

like things past, they expect the like things to come, and hope for good or evil luck superstitiously from things that have no part at all in the causing of it; as the Athenians did for their Lepanto demand another Phormio, the Pompeian faction for their war in Africa another Scipio,[1] and others have done in divers other occasions since. In like manner they attribute their fortune to a stander by, to a lucky or unlucky place, to words spoken, especially if the name of God be amongst them; as charming, and conjuring (the liturgy of witches), insomuch as to believe they have power to turn a stone into bread, bread into a man, or anything into anything.

9. Thirdly, for the worship which naturally men exhibit to powers invisible, it can be no other but such expressions of their reverence as they would use towards men: gifts, petitions, thanks, submission of body, considerate addresses, sober behaviour, premeditated words, swearing (that is, assuring one another of their promises) by invoking them. Beyond that, reason suggesteth nothing but leaves them either to rest there, or for further ceremonies, to rely on those they believe to be wiser than themselves.

10. Lastly, concerning how these invisible powers declare to men the things which shall hereafter come to pass, especially concerning their good or evil fortune in general, or good or ill success in any particular undertaking, men are naturally at a stand; save that using [being inclined] to conjecture of the time to come by the time past, they are very apt, not only to take casual things, after one or two encounters, for prognostics of the like encounter ever after, but also to believe the like prognostics from other men of whom they have once conceived a good opinion.

11. And in these four things, opinion of ghosts, ignorance of second causes, devotion towards what men fear, and taking of things casual for prognostics, consisteth the natural seed of *religion*; which, by reason of the different fancies, judgements, and passions of several men, hath grown up into ceremonies so different, that those which are used by one man are for the most part ridiculous to another.

[54]

But honour them as they honour men.

And attribute to them all extraordinary events.

Four things, natural seeds of religion.

---

1 See Thucydides, *History of the Peloponnesian War* iii.7; and Plutarch, *Lives*, "Cato the Younger."

12. For these seeds have received culture from two sorts of men. One sort have been they that have nourished and ordered them, according to their own invention. The other have done it by God's commandment and direction. But both sorts have done it with a purpose to make those men that relied on them the more apt to obedience, laws, peace, charity, and civil society. So that the religion of the former sort is a part of human politics and teacheth part of the duty which earthly kings require of their subjects. And the religion of the latter sort is divine politics and containeth precepts to those that have yielded themselves subjects in the kingdom of God. Of the former sort were all the founders of commonwealths and the lawgivers of the Gentiles, of the latter sort were Abraham, Moses, and our blessed Saviour, by whom have been derived unto us the laws of the kingdom of God.

13. And for that part of religion which consisteth in opinions concerning the nature of powers invisible, there is almost nothing that has a name that has not been esteemed amongst the Gentiles in one place or another [as] a god or devil, or by their poets feigned to be animated, inhabited, or possessed by some spirit or other.

14. The unformed matter of the world was a god by the name of Chaos.

15. The heaven, the ocean, the planets, the fire, the earth, the winds, were so many gods.

16. Men, women, a bird, a crocodile, a calf, a dog, a snake, an onion, a leek, [were] deified. Besides that, they filled almost all places with spirits called *demons*;[1] the plains with Pan and Panises or Satyrs, the woods with Fauns and Nymphs, the sea with Tritons and other Nymphs, every river and fountain with a ghost of his name and with Nymphs, every house with its *Lares* or familiars, every man with his *Genius*; [they filled] hell with ghosts and spiritual officers, as Charon, Cerberus, and the Furies, and in the night time, all places with *larvae*, *lemures*, ghosts of men deceased, and a whole kingdom of fairies and bugbears. They have also ascribed divinity and built temples to mere accidents and qualities; such as are time, night, day, peace, concord, love, contention, virtue, honour, health, rust, fever, and the like, which

---

1   See also 8.25, 34.15, 34.18, and 36.2.

when they prayed for or against, they prayed to as if there were ghosts of those names hanging over their heads and letting fall or withholding that good or evil for or against which they prayed. They invoked also their own wit by the name of Muses, their own ignorance by the name of Fortune, their own lust by the name of Cupid, their own rage by the name Furies, their own privy members by the name of Priapus, and attributed their pollutions to *incubi* and *succubae*, insomuch as there was nothing which a poet could introduce as a person in his poem which they did not make either a *god* or a *devil*.[1]

17. The same authors of the religion of the Gentiles, observing the second ground for religion, which is men's ignorance of causes and thereby their aptness to attribute their fortune to causes on which there was no dependence at all apparent, took occasion to obtrude on their ignorance, instead of second causes, a kind of second and ministerial gods, ascribing the cause of fecundity to Venus, the cause of arts to Apollo, of subtlety and craft to Mercury, of tempests and storms to Aeolus, and of other effects to other gods, insomuch as there was amongst the heathen almost as great variety of gods as of business.

18. And to the worship which naturally men conceived fit to be used towards their gods, namely, oblations, prayers, thanks, and the rest formerly named, the same legislators of the Gentiles have added their images both in picture and sculpture, that the more ignorant sort (that is to say, the most part or generality of the people), thinking the gods for whose representation they were made were really included and as it were housed within them, might so much the more stand in fear of them; and [the legislators of the Gentiles] endowed them with lands and houses and officers and revenues set apart from all other human uses, that is, consecrated, made holy to those their idols; as caverns, groves, [56] woods, mountains, and whole islands; and have attributed to them, not only the shapes, some of men, some of beasts, some of monsters, but also the faculties and passions of men and beasts; as sense, speech, sex, lust, generation, and this not only by mixing one with another to

---

1 See also 38.6, 44.3, 45.33, and 45.38.

propagate the kind of gods, but also by mixing with men and women to beget mongrel gods and but inmates of heaven, as Bacchus, Hercules, and others; besides [also] anger, revenge, and other passions of living creatures and the actions proceeding from them, as fraud, theft, adultery, sodomy, and any vice that may be taken for an effect of power or a cause of pleasure, and all such vices as amongst men are taken to be against law rather than against honour.

19. Lastly, to the prognostics of time to come, which are naturally but conjectures upon the experience of time past, and supernaturally, divine revelation, the same authors of the religion of the Gentiles, partly upon pretended experience, partly upon pretended revelation, have added innumerable other superstitious ways of divination; and [they] made men believe they should find their fortunes sometimes in the ambiguous or senseless answers of the priests at Delphi, Delos, Ammon, and other famous oracles, which answers were made ambiguous by design, to own the event both ways, or absurd by the intoxicating vapour of the place, which is very frequent in sulphurous caverns; sometimes [the authors of the religion of the Gentiles made men believe they should find their fortunes] in the leaves of the Sibyls, of whose prophecies (like those perhaps of Nostradamus;[1] for the fragments now extant seem to be the invention of later times) there were some books in reputation in the time of the Roman republic; sometimes in the insignificant speeches of madmen, supposed to be possessed with a divine spirit, which possession they called enthusiasm; and these kinds of foretelling events were accounted theomancy or prophecy. Sometimes [they made men believe they should find their fortunes] in the aspect of the stars at their nativity, which was called horoscopy and esteemed a part of judiciary astrology; sometimes in their own hopes and fears, called *thumomancy* or *presage*; sometimes in the prediction of witches that pretended conference with the dead, which is called necromancy, conjuring, and witchcraft, and is but juggling

---

1 Michel de Nostredame (1503-66), French physician, whose obscure prognostications in his *Prophecies* are still believed by some people today.

and confederate knavery; sometimes in the casual flight or feeding of birds, called augury; sometimes in the entrails of a sacrificed beast, which was *aruspicina*; sometimes in dreams; sometimes in croaking of ravens or chattering of birds; sometimes in the lineaments of the face, which was called metoposcopy, or by palmistry in the lines of the hand; sometimes in casual words called *omina*; sometimes in monsters or unusual accidents, as eclipses, comets, rare meteors, earthquakes, inundations, uncouth births, and the like, which they called *portenta* and *ostenta*, because they thought them to portend or foreshow some great calamity to come; [and] sometimes in mere lottery, as cross and pile, counting holes in a sieve, dipping of verses in Homer and Virgil, and innumerable other such vain conceits. So easy are men to be drawn to believe anything from such men as have gotten credit with them, and [who] can with gentleness and dexterity take hold of their fear and ignorance.

[57] The designs of the authors of the religion of the heathen.

20. And therefore the first founders and legislators of commonwealths amongst the Gentiles, whose ends were only to keep the people in obedience and peace, have in all places taken care first to imprint in their minds a belief that those precepts which they gave concerning religion might not be thought to proceed from their own device, but from the dictates of some god or other spirit, or else that they themselves were of a higher nature than mere mortals, [in order] that their laws might the more easily be received; so Numa Pompilius pretended to receive the ceremonies he instituted amongst the Romans from the nymph Egeria, and the first king and founder of the kingdom of Peru pretended himself and his wife to be the children of the sun; and Mahomet,[1] to set up his new religion, pretended to have conferences with the Holy Ghost in form of a dove. Secondly, they have had a care to make it believed that the same things were displeasing to the gods which were forbidden by the laws. Thirdly, to prescribe ceremonies, supplications, sacrifices, and festivals by which they were to believe the anger of the gods might be appeased; and that ill success in war, great contagions of sickness, earthquakes, and each man's private misery

---

1 Muhammed (570-632), founder of Islam and author of the *Koran*, which was dictated to him by the angel Gabriel.

came from the anger of the gods, and their anger from the neglect of their worship or the forgetting or mistaking some point of the ceremonies required. And though amongst the ancient Romans men were not forbidden to deny that which in the poets is written of the pains and pleasures after this life, which divers of great authority and gravity in that state have in their harangues openly derided; yet that belief was always more cherished than the contrary.

21. And by these and such other institutions, they obtained in order to their end (which was the peace of the commonwealth) that the common people in their misfortunes, laying the fault on neglect or error in their ceremonies or on their own disobedience to the laws, were the less apt to mutiny against their governors. And being entertained with the pomp and pastime of festivals and public games made in honour of the gods, [the common people] needed nothing else but bread to keep them from discontent, murmuring, and commotion against the state. And therefore the Romans, that had conquered the greatest part of the then known world, made no scruple of tolerating any religion whatsoever in the city of Rome itself, unless it had something in it that could not consist with their civil government; nor do we read that any religion was there forbidden but that of the Jews, who (being the peculiar kingdom of God) thought it unlawful to acknowledge subjection to any mortal king or state whatsoever. And thus you see how the religion of the Gentiles was a part of their policy.

22. But where God himself by supernatural revelation planted religion, there he also made to himself a peculiar kingdom and gave laws, not only of behaviour towards himself, but also towards one another; and thereby in the kingdom of God the policy and laws civil are a part of religion; and therefore the distinction of temporal and spiritual domination hath there no place. It is true that God is king of all the earth; yet may he be king of a peculiar and chosen nation. For there is no more incongruity therein than that he that hath the general command of the whole army should have withal a peculiar regiment or company of his own. God is king of all the earth by his power, but of his chosen people, he is king by covenant. But to speak more largely of the kingdom of God, both

The true religion and the laws of God's kingdom the same.

[58]

by nature and covenant, I have in the following discourse assigned another place.

23. From the propagation of religion, it is not hard to understand the causes of the resolution of the same into its first seeds or principles, which are only an opinion of a deity and powers invisible and supernatural, that can never be so abolished out of human nature but that new religions may again be made to spring out of them by the culture of such men as for such purpose are in reputation.

24. For seeing all formed religion is founded at first upon the faith which a multitude hath in some one person, whom they believe not only to be a wise man and to labour to procure their happiness, but also to be a holy man to whom God himself vouchsafeth to declare his will supernaturally; it followeth necessarily, when they that have the government of religion shall come to have either the wisdom of those men, their sincerity, or their love suspected, or that they shall be unable to show any probable token of divine revelation, that the religion which they desire to uphold must be suspected likewise and (without the fear of the civil sword) contradicted and rejected.

Enjoining belief of impossibilities.

25. That which taketh away the reputation of wisdom in him that formeth a religion or addeth to it when it is already formed is the enjoining of a belief of contradictories; for both parts of a contradiction cannot possibly be true; and therefore to enjoin the belief of them is an argument of ignorance, which detects the author in that, and discredits him in all things else he shall propound as from revelation supernatural; which revelation a man may indeed have of many things above, but of nothing against natural reason.

Doing contrary to the religion they establish.

26. That which taketh away the reputation of sincerity is the doing or saying of such things as appear to be signs that what they require other men to believe is not believed by themselves; all which doings or sayings are therefore called scandalous because they be stumblingblocks that make men to fall in the way of religion, as injustice, cruelty, profaneness, avarice, and luxury. For

---

1 Hobbes should also have mentioned chapter 31, as Edwin Curley pointed out in his edition of *Leviathan* (Indianapolis: Hackett Publishing Company, 1994).

who can believe that he that doth ordinarily such actions, as proceed from any of these roots, believeth there is any such invisible power to be feared as he affrighteth other men withal for lesser faults?

27. That which taketh away the reputation of love is the being detected of private ends, as when the belief they require of others conduceth or seemeth to conduce to the acquiring of dominion, riches, dignity, or secure pleasure [59] to themselves only or specially. For that which men reap benefit by to themselves they are thought to do for their own sakes, and not for love of others.

28. Lastly, the testimony that men can render of divine calling can be no other than the operation of miracles, or true prophecy (which also is a miracle), or extraordinary felicity. And therefore, to those points of religion which have been received from them that did such miracles, those that are added by such, as approve not their calling by some miracle, obtain no greater belief than what the custom and laws of the places in which they be educated have wrought into them. For as in natural things, men of judgement require natural signs and arguments; so in supernatural things they require signs supernatural (which are miracles) before they consent inwardly and from their hearts. Want of the testimony of miracles.

29. All which causes of the weakening of men's faith do manifestly appear in the examples following. First, we have the example of the children of Israel, who when Moses, that had approved his calling to them by miracles and by the happy conduct of them out of Egypt, was absent but forty days, revolted from the worship of the true God recommended to them by him, and setting up a golden calf for their god, relapsed into the idolatry of the Egyptians from whom they had been so lately delivered. And again, after Moses, Aaron, Joshua, and that generation which had seen the great works of God in Israel were dead, another generation arose and served Baal. So that miracles failing, faith also failed. Exod. 32:1-2.

Judg. 2:11.

30. Again, when the sons of Samuel, being constituted by their father Judges in Beer-sheba, received bribes and judged unjustly, the people of Israel refused any more to have God to be their king in other manner than he was king of other people, and therefore cried out to Samuel to choose them a king after the manner of the nations. 1 Sam. 8:3.

So that justice failing, faith also failed, insomuch as they deposed their God from reigning over them.

31. And whereas in the planting of Christian religion the oracles ceased in all parts of the Roman Empire, and the number of Christians increased wonderfully every day and in every place by the preaching of the Apostles and Evangelists, a great part of that success may reasonably be attributed to the contempt into which the priests of the Gentiles of that time had brought themselves by their uncleanness, avarice, and juggling between princes. Also the religion of the Church of Rome was partly for the same cause abolished in England and many other parts of Christendom, insomuch as the failing of virtue in the pastors maketh faith fail in the people; and partly from bringing of the philosophy and doctrine of Aristotle into religion by the Schoolmen; from whence there arose so many contradictions and absurdities as brought the clergy into a reputation both of ignorance and of fraudulent intention, and inclined people to revolt from them, either against the will of their own princes, as in France and Holland, or with their will, as in England.

[60] 32. Lastly, amongst the points by the Church of Rome declared necessary for salvation, there be so many manifestly to the advantage of the Pope and of his spiritual subjects residing in the territories of other Christian princes, that were it not for the mutual emulation of those princes, they might without war or trouble exclude all foreign authority as easily as it has been excluded in England. For who is there that does not see to whose benefit it conduceth to have it believed that a king hath not his authority from Christ unless a bishop crown him? That a king, if he be a priest, cannot marry? That whether a prince be born in lawful marriage or not must be judged by authority from Rome? That subjects may be freed from their allegiance if by the court of Rome the king be judged a heretic? That a king, as Childeric[1] of France, may be deposed by a Pope, as Pope Zachary, for no cause, and his kingdom given to one of his subjects? That the clergy and regulars, in what country soever,

---

1 Childeric, last of the Merovingian kings in France, was deposed in 751 by Pepin, the Mayor of the Palace. Pope Zachary [Zacharias] held that the deposition was permissible. In 1651 editions of *Leviathan*, Childeric's name is spelled "Chilperique."

shall be exempt from the jurisdiction of their king in cases criminal? Or who does not see to whose profit redound the fees of private Masses [Eucharistic celebrations] and the vales of purgatory,[1] with other signs of private interest enough to mortify the most lively faith, if (as I said) the civil magistrate and custom did not more sustain it than any opinion they have of the sanctity, wisdom, or probity of their teachers? So that I may attribute all the changes of religion in the world to one and the same cause, and that is unpleasing priests; and those not only amongst catholics, but even in that Church that hath presumed most of reformation.[2]

Chapter XIII

Of the Natural Condition of Mankind as Concerning their Felicity and Misery

1. Nature hath made men so equal in the faculties of body and mind, as that, though there be found one man sometimes manifestly stronger in body or of quicker mind than another, yet when all is reckoned together, the difference between man and man is not so considerable as that one man can thereupon claim to himself any benefit to which another may not pretend as well as he. For as to the strength of body, the weakest has strength enough to kill the strongest, either by secret machination or by confederacy with others that are in the same danger with himself.

Men by nature equal.

2. And as to the faculties of the mind, setting aside the arts grounded upon words, and especially that skill of proceeding upon general and infallible rules, called science, which very few have and but in few things, as being not a native faculty born with us, nor attained, as prudence, while we look after somewhat else, I find yet a greater equality amongst men than that of strength. For prudence is but experience, which equal time equally bestows on all men in those things they equally apply

[61]

---

1 See also 12.42, 43.14, 43.17, 44.16, 44.30-40, 46.21, 46.27, and 47.14.
2 Edward Hyde, the earl of Clarendon, thought that Hobbes was referring to the Church of England. Most commentators think he was referring to the Presbyterian Church.

themselves unto. That which may perhaps make such equality incredible is but a vain conceit of one's own wisdom, which almost all men think they have in a greater degree than the vulgar, that is, than all men but themselves and a few others, whom by fame or for concurring with themselves, they approve. For such is the nature of men that howsoever they may acknowledge many others to be more witty or more eloquent or more learned, they will hardly believe there be many so wise as themselves; for they see their own wit at hand and other men's at a distance. But this proveth rather that men are in that point equal, than unequal. For there is not ordinarily a greater sign of the equal distribution of anything than that every man is contented with his share.

From equality proceeds diffidence. 3. From this equality of ability ariseth equality of hope in the attaining of our ends. And therefore if any two men desire the same thing, which nevertheless they cannot both enjoy, they become enemies; and in the way to their end (which is principally their own conservation, and sometimes their delectation only) endeavour to destroy or subdue one another. And from hence it comes to pass that where an invader hath no more to fear than another man's single power, if one plant, sow, build, or possess a convenient seat, others may probably be expected to come prepared with forces united to dispossess and deprive him, not only of the fruit of his labour, but also of his life or liberty. And the invader again is in the like danger of another.

From diffidence war. 4. And from this diffidence of one another, there is no way for any man to secure himself so reasonable as [by] anticipation, that is, by force or wiles to master the persons of all men he can so long till he see no other power great enough to endanger him; and this is no more than his own conservation requireth, and is generally allowed. Also, because there be some that, taking pleasure in contemplating their own power in the acts of conquest, which they pursue farther than their security requires; if others that otherwise would be glad to be at ease within modest bounds should not by invasion increase their power, [then] they would not be able, long time, by standing only on their defence, to subsist. And by consequence, such augmentation of dominion over men being necessary to a man's conservation, it ought to be allowed him.

5. Again, men have no pleasure (but on the contrary a great deal of grief) in keeping company where there is no power able to overawe them all. For every man looketh that his companion should value him at the same rate he sets upon himself, and upon all signs of contempt or undervaluing naturally endeavours, as far as he dares (which amongst them that have no common power to keep them in quiet is far enough to make them destroy each other), to extort a greater value from his contemners, by damage; and from others, by the example.

6. So that in the nature of man, we find three principal causes of quarrel. First, competition; secondly, diffidence; thirdly, glory.

7. The first maketh men invade for gain; the second, for safety; and the third, for reputation. The first use violence to make themselves masters of other men's persons, wives, children, and cattle; the second, to defend them; the third, for trifles, as a word, a smile, a different opinion, and any other sign of undervalue, either direct in their persons or by reflection in their kindred, their friends, their nation, their profession, or their name. [62]

8. Hereby it is manifest that during the time men live without a common power to keep them all in awe, they are in that condition which is called war; and such a war as is of every man against every man. For WAR consisteth not in battle only, or the act of fighting, but in a tract of time, wherein the will to contend by battle is sufficiently known; and therefore the notion of *time* is to be considered in the nature of war, as it is in the nature of weather. For as the nature of foul weather lieth not in a shower or two of rain, but in an inclination thereto of many days together, so the nature of war consisteth not in actual fighting, but in the known disposition thereto during all the time there is no assurance to the contrary. All other time is PEACE. Out of civil states there is always war of every one against every one.

9. Whatsoever therefore is consequent to a time of war, where every man is enemy to every man, the same is consequent to the time wherein men live without other security than what their own strength and their own invention shall furnish them withal. In such condition there is no place for industry, because the fruit thereof is uncertain; and consequently no culture of the earth; no navigation, nor use of the commodities that may be imported by sea; The incommodities of such a war.

no commodious building; no instruments of moving and removing such things as require much force; no knowledge of the face of the earth; no account of time; no arts; no letters; no society; and which is worst of all, continual fear, and danger of violent death; and the life of man, solitary, poor, nasty, brutish, and short.

10. It may seem strange to some man that has not well weighed these things that nature should thus dissociate and render men apt to invade and destroy one another; and he may therefore, not trusting to this inference, made from the passions, desire perhaps to have the same confirmed by experience. Let him therefore consider with himself; when taking a journey, he arms himself and seeks to go well accompanied; when going to sleep, he locks his doors; when even in his house he locks his chests; and this when he knows there be laws and public officers, armed to revenge all injuries shall be done him; what opinion he has of his fellow subjects, when he rides armed; of his fellow citizens, when he locks his doors; and of his children, and servants, when he locks his chests. Does he not there as much accuse mankind by his actions as I do by my words? But neither of us accuse man's nature in it. The desires and other passions of man are in themselves no sin. No more are the actions that proceed from those passions till they know a law that forbids them; which, till laws be made, they cannot know; nor can any law be made till they have agreed upon the person that shall make it.

[63]　　11. It may peradventure be thought there was never such a time nor condition of war as this; and I believe it was never generally so, over all the world; but there are many places where they live so now. For the savage people in many places of America, except the government of small families, the concord whereof dependeth on natural lust, have no government at all, and live at this day in that brutish manner, as I said before. Howsoever, it may be perceived what manner of life there would be, where there were no common power to fear, by the manner of life which men that have formerly lived under a peaceful government use to degenerate into in a civil war.

12. But though there had never been any time wherein particular men were in a condition of war one against another; yet in all times kings and persons of sovereign

authority, because of their independency, are in continual jealousies, and in the state and posture of gladiators, having their weapons pointing and their eyes fixed on one another, that is, their forts, garrisons, and guns upon the frontiers of their kingdoms, and continual spies upon their neighbours, which is a posture of war. But because they uphold thereby the industry of their subjects, there does not follow from it that misery which accompanies the liberty of particular men.

13. To this war of every man against every man, this also is consequent; that nothing can be unjust. The notions of right and wrong, justice and injustice, have there no place. Where there is no common power, there is no law; where no law, no injustice.[1] Force and fraud are in war the two cardinal virtues. Justice and injustice are none of the faculties neither of the body nor mind. If they were, they might be in a man that were alone in the world, as well as his senses and passions. They are qualities that relate to men in society, not in solitude. It is consequent also to the same condition that there be no propriety, no dominion, no *mine* and *thine* distinct; but only that to be every man's that he can get, and for so long as he can keep it. And thus much for the ill condition which man by mere nature is actually placed in; though with a possibility to come out of it, consisting partly in the passions, partly in his reason. *In such a war nothing is unjust.*

14. The passions that incline men to peace are fear of death,[2] desire of such things as are necessary to commodious living, and a hope by their industry to obtain them. And reason suggesteth convenient articles of peace upon which men may be drawn to agreement. These articles are they which otherwise are called the laws of nature, whereof I shall speak more particularly in the two following chapters. *The passions that incline men to peace.*

---

1 Cf. 14.7 and 15.2.
2 See also 11.4-9 and 27.19

Chapter XIV

Of the First and Second Natural Laws, and of Contracts

Right of nature what.

1. The right of nature, which writers commonly call *jus naturale*, is the liberty each man hath to use his own power as he will himself for the preservation of his own nature; that is to say, of his own life; and consequently, of doing anything which, in his own judgement and reason, he shall conceive to be the aptest means thereunto.

Liberty what.

2. By LIBERTY is understood, according to the proper signification of the word, the absence of external impediments; which impediments may oft take away part of a man's power to do what he would, but cannot hinder him from using the power left him according as his judgement and reason shall dictate to him.[1]

A law of nature what.

3. A LAW OF NATURE (*lex naturalis*) is a precept or general rule,[2] found out by reason, by which a man is forbidden to do that which is destructive of his life, or taketh away the means of preserving the same, and to omit that by which he thinketh it may be best preserved. For though they that speak of this subject use to confound *jus* and *lex*, *right* and *law*; yet they ought to be distinguished, because right consisteth in liberty to do or to forbear; whereas law determineth and bindeth to one of them; so that law and right differ as much as obligation and liberty,[3] which in one and the same matter are inconsistent.[4]

Naturally every man has right to every thing.

4. And because the condition of man (as hath been declared in the precedent chapter) is a condition of war of every one against every one, in which case every one is governed by his own reason, and there is nothing he can make use of that may not be a help unto him in preserving his life against his enemies; it followeth that in such a condition every man has a right to every thing, even to one another's body. And therefore, as long as this natural right of every man to every thing endureth, there can be no security to any man, how strong or wise soever he be, of living out the time which nature ordinarily alloweth men to live. And consequently it is a precept, or general

---

1   See also 21.1.
2   See also 25.1.
3   See also 26.43.
4   Cf. 21.10.

rule of reason *that every man ought to endeavour peace, as far as he has hope of obtaining it; and when he cannot obtain it, that he may seek and use all helps and advantages of war.*[1] The first branch of which rule containeth the first and fundamental law of nature, which is *to seek peace and follow it.* The second, the sum of the right of nature, which is *by all means we can to defend ourselves.*

The fundamental law of nature, to seek peace.

5. From this fundamental law of nature, by which men are commanded to endeavour peace, is derived this second law: *that a man be willing, when others are so too, as far forth as for peace and defence of himself he shall think it necessary, to lay down this right to all things; and be contented with so much liberty against other men as he would allow other men against himself.* For as long as every man holdeth this right of doing anything he liketh, so long are all men in the condition of war. But if other men will not lay down their right, as well as he, then there is no reason for anyone to divest himself of his, for that were to expose himself to prey, which no man is bound to, rather than to dispose himself to peace. This is that law of the gospel: *Whatsoever you require that others should do to you, that do ye to them.*[2] And that law of all men, *quod tibi fieri non vis, alteri ne feceris [What you do not want done to you, do not do to another].*

The second law of nature. Contract and way of peace. [65]

6. To *lay down* a man's *right* to anything is to *divest* himself of the *liberty* of hindering another of the benefit of his own right to the same. For he that renounceth or passeth away his right giveth not to any other man a right which he had not before, because there is nothing to which every man had not right by nature, but only standeth out of his way that he may enjoy his own original right without hindrance from him, not without hindrance from another. So that the effect which redoundeth to one man by another man's defect of right is but so much diminution of impediments to the use of his own right original.

What it is to lay down a right.

---

1   The fundamental precept or general rule consists of two parts: the first part is the first or fundamental law of nature; the second part is the right of nature.

2   Hobbes is wrong about what is "the law of the gospel." The gospel does not require but recommends, "Whatsoever you wish others to do to you, that do ye to them" (Matt. 7:12). At 15.35, Hobbes gives the so-called negative Golden Rule: "*Do not that to another which thou wouldest not have done to thyself.*"

Renouncing a
right what it is.

Transferring
right what.
Obligation.

Duty.
Injustice.

7. Right is laid aside either by simply renouncing it
or by transferring it to another. By *simply* RENOUNCING,
when he cares not to whom the benefit thereof redoundeth. By TRANSFERRING, when he intendeth the benefit
thereof to some certain person or persons. And when a
man hath in either manner abandoned or granted away
his right, then is he said to be OBLIGED or BOUND, not
to hinder those to whom such right is granted, or abandoned, from the benefit of it; and that he *ought*, and it is
DUTY, not to make void that voluntary act of his own; and
that such hindrance is INJUSTICE and INJURY, as being *sine
jure [without right]*; the right being before renounced or
transferred. So that *injury* or *injustice*, in the controversies
of the world, is somewhat like to that which in the dis-
putations of scholars is called *absurdity*. For as it is there
called an absurdity to contradict what one maintained in
the beginning, so in the world it is called injustice and
injury voluntarily to undo that which from the beginning
he had voluntarily done. The way by which a man either
simply renounceth or transferreth his right is a declaration or signification by some voluntary and sufficient sign
or signs that he doth so renounce or transfer or hath so
renounced or transferred the same to him that accepteth
it. And these signs are either words only, or actions only;
or, as it happeneth most often, both words and actions.
And the same are the BONDS, by which men are bound
and obliged, bonds that have their strength, not from
their own nature (for nothing is more easily broken than
a man's word), but from fear of some evil consequence
upon the rupture.

8. Whensoever a man transferreth his right, or renounceth it, it is either in consideration of some right recip-

rocally transferred to himself, or for some other good
he hopeth for thereby. For it is a voluntary act; and of
the voluntary acts of every man, the object is some *good
to himself*. And therefore there be some rights which no
man can be understood by any words, or other signs, to

have abandoned or transferred.[1] As first a man cannot lay
down the right of resisting them that assault him by force
to take away his life, because he cannot be understood to
aim thereby at any good to himself. The same may be said

---

1   See also 14.29.

of wounds, and chains, and imprisonment, both because there is no benefit consequent to such patience as there is to the patience of suffering another to be wounded or imprisoned, as also because a man cannot tell when he seeth men proceed against him by violence whether they intend his death or not. And lastly the motive and end for which this renouncing and transferring of right is introduced is nothing else but the security of a man's person in his life,[1] and in the means of so preserving life as not to be weary of it. And therefore if a man by words, or other signs, seem to despoil himself of the end for which those signs were intended, he is not to be understood as if he meant it, or that it was his will, but that he was ignorant of how such words and actions were to be interpreted.

9. The mutual transferring of right is that which men call CONTRACT.

Contract what.

10. There is difference between transferring of right to the thing, and transferring or tradition, that is, delivery of the thing itself. For the thing may be delivered together with the translation of the right, as in buying and selling with ready money, or exchange of goods or lands; and it may be delivered some time after.

11. Again, one of the contractors may deliver the thing contracted for on his part, and leave the other to perform his part at some determinate time after, and in the meantime be trusted; and then the contract on his part is called PACT or COVENANT; or both parts may contract now to perform hereafter, in which cases he that is to perform in time to come, being trusted, his performance is called *keeping of promise*, or faith, and the failing of performance, if it be voluntary, *violation of faith*.

Covenant what.

12. When the transferring of right is not mutual, but one of the parties transferreth in hope to gain thereby friendship or service from another or from his friends; or in hope to gain the reputation of charity or magnanimity; or to deliver his mind from the pain of compassion; or in hope of reward in heaven; this is not contract, but GIFT, FREE GIFT, GRACE; which words signify one and the same thing.

Free gift.

13. Signs of contract are either *express* or *by inference*. Express are words spoken with understanding of what

Signs of contract express.

---

1 See also 14.20.

they signify; and such words are either of the time *present* or *past*, as, *I give, I grant, I have given, I have granted, I will that this be yours*; or of the future, as, *I will give, I will grant*, which words of the future are called PROMISE.

Signs of contract by inference. [67]

14. Signs by inference are sometimes the consequence of words, sometimes the consequence of silence, sometimes the consequence of actions, sometimes the consequence of forbearing an action; and generally a sign by inference, of any contract, is whatsoever sufficiently argues the will of the contractor.

Free gift passeth by words of the present or past.

15. Words alone, if they be of the time to come, and contain a bare promise, are an insufficient sign of a free gift and therefore not obligatory. For if they be of the time to come, as, *tomorrow I will give*, they are a sign I have not given yet, and consequently that my right is not transferred, but remaineth till I transfer it by some other act. But if the words be of the time present or past, as, *I have given*, or *do give to be delivered tomorrow*, then is my tomorrow's right given away today; and that by the virtue of the words, though there were no other argument of my will. And there is a great difference in the signification of these words, *volo hoc tuum esse cras*, and *cras dabo*; that is, between *I will that this be thine tomorrow*, and, *I will give it thee tomorrow*, for the word *I will*, in the former manner of speech, signifies an act of the will present; but in the latter, it signifies a promise of an act of the will to come; and therefore the former words, being of the present, transfer a future right; the latter, that be of the future, transfer nothing. But if there be other signs of the will to transfer a right besides words, then, though the gift be free, yet may the right be understood to pass by words of the future, as [for example] if a man propound a prize to him that comes first to the end of a race, the gift is free; and though the words be of the future, yet the right passeth, for if he would not have his words so be understood, he should not have let them run.

Signs of contract are words both of the past, present, and future.

16. In contracts the right passeth, not only where the words are of the time present or past, but also where they are of the future, because all contract is mutual translation or change of right; and therefore he that promiseth only, because he hath already received the benefit for which he promiseth, is to be understood as if he intended the right should pass; for unless he had been content to

have his words so understood, the other would not have performed his part first. And for that cause, in buying and selling, and other acts of contract, a promise is equivalent to a covenant, and therefore obligatory.

17. He that performeth first in the case of a contract is said to MERIT that which he is to receive by the performance of the other, and he hath it as *due*. Also when a prize is propounded to many, which is to be given to him only that winneth, or money is thrown amongst many to be enjoyed by them that catch it, though this be a free gift; yet so to win or so to catch is to *merit*, and to have it as DUE. For the right is transferred in the propounding of the prize and in throwing down the money, though it be not determined to whom, but by the event of the contention. But there is between these two sorts of merit this difference, that in contract I merit by virtue of my own power and the contractor's need, but in this case of free gift I am enabled to merit only by the benignity [kindness] of the giver; in contract I merit at the contractor's hand that he should depart with [relinquish] his right; in this case of gift, I merit not that the giver should part with his right, but that when he has parted with it, it should be mine rather than another's. And this I think to be the meaning of that distinction of the Schools between *meritum congrui* and *meritum condigni*. For God Almighty, having promised paradise to those men (hoodwinked with carnal desires) that can walk through this world according to the precepts and limits prescribed by him, they say he that shall so walk shall merit paradise *ex congruo [from its appropriateness]*. But because no man can demand a right to it by his own righteousness, or any other power in himself, but by the free grace of God only, they say no man can merit paradise *ex condigno [from being deserved]*. This, I say, I think is the meaning of that distinction; but because disputers do not agree upon the signification of their own terms of art longer than it serves their turn, I will not affirm anything of their meaning; only this I say; when a gift is given indefinitely, as a prize to be contended for, he that winneth meriteth, and may claim the prize as due.

18. If a covenant be made wherein neither of the parties perform presently but trust one another, in the condition of mere nature (which is a condition of war of every

Merit what.

[68]

Covenants of mutual trust, when invalid.

man against every man), [then] upon any reasonable suspicion, it is void;[1] but if there be a common power set over them both, with right and force sufficient to compel performance, it is not void. For he that performeth first has no assurance the other will perform after, because the bonds of words are too weak to bridle men's ambition, avarice, anger, and other passions, without the fear of some coercive power; which in the condition of mere nature [the state of nature], where all men are equal, and judges of the justness of their own fears, cannot possibly be supposed. And therefore he which performeth first does but betray himself to his enemy, contrary to the right he can never abandon of defending his life and means of living.

19. But in a civil estate, where there is a power set up to constrain those that would otherwise violate their faith, that fear is no more reasonable; and for that cause, he which by the covenant is to perform first is obliged so to do.

20. The cause of fear, which maketh such a covenant invalid, must be always something arising after the covenant made, as some new fact or other sign of the will not to perform, else it cannot make the covenant void. For that which could not hinder a man from promising ought not to be admitted as a hindrance of performing.

Right to the end, containeth right to the means.

21. He that transferreth any right transferreth the means of enjoying it, as far as lieth in his power. As he that selleth land is understood to transfer the herbage and whatsoever grows upon it; nor can he that sells a mill turn away the stream that drives it. And they that give to a man the right of government in sovereignty are understood to give him the right of levying money to maintain soldiers, and of appointing magistrates for the administration of justice.

No covenant with beasts.
[69]

22. To make covenants with brute beasts is impossible, because not understanding our speech, they understand not, nor accept of any translation of right, nor can translate any right to another; and without mutual acceptation, there is no covenant.

Nor with God without special revelation.

23. To make covenant with God is impossible but by mediation of such as God speaketh to either by revelation

---

1 See 15.3.

supernatural or by his lieutenants that govern under him and in his name; for otherwise we know not whether our covenants be accepted or not. And therefore they that vow anything contrary to any law of nature, vow in vain, as being a thing unjust to pay such vow. And if it be a thing commanded by the law of nature, it is not the vow, but the law that binds them.

24. The matter or subject of a covenant is always something that falleth under deliberation; for to covenant is an act of the will, that is to say, an act, and the last act, of deliberation, and is therefore always understood to be something to come, and which is judged possible for him that covenanteth to perform.

No covenant, but of possible and future.

25. And therefore, to promise that which is known to be impossible is no covenant. But if that prove impossible afterwards, which before was thought possible, the covenant is valid and bindeth, though not to the thing itself, yet to the value; or, if that also be impossible, to the unfeigned endeavour of performing as much as is possible, for to more no man can be obliged.

26. Men are freed of their covenants two ways, by performing or by being forgiven. For performance is the natural end of obligation, and forgiveness the restitution of liberty, as being a retransferring of that right in which the obligation consisted.

Covenants, how made void.

27. Covenants entered into by fear, in the condition of mere nature, are obligatory.[1] For example, if I covenant to pay a ransom or service for my life to an enemy, I am bound by it. For it is a contract, wherein one receiveth the benefit of life, the other is to receive money or service for it; and consequently, where no other law (as in the condition of mere nature) forbiddeth the performance, the covenant is valid. Therefore prisoners of war, if trusted with the payment of their ransom, are obliged to pay it; and if a weaker prince make a disadvantageous peace with a stronger, for fear, he is bound to keep it, unless (as hath been said before) there ariseth some new and just cause of fear to renew the war. And even in commonwealths, if I be forced to redeem myself from a thief by promising him money, I am bound to pay it, till the civil law discharge me. For whatsoever I may lawfully do without obligation,

Covenants extorted by fear are valid.

---

1 See also 21.3.

the same I may lawfully covenant to do through fear; and what I lawfully covenant, I cannot lawfully break.[1]

The former covenant to one makes void the later to another.

28. A former covenant makes void a later. For a man that hath passed away his right to one man today hath it not to pass tomorrow to another; and therefore the later promise passeth no right, but is null.

A man's covenant not to defend himself is void. [70]

29. A covenant not to defend myself from force, by force, is always void. For (as I have shown before)[2] no man can transfer or lay down his right to save himself from death, wounds, and imprisonment, the avoiding whereof is the only end of laying down any right; and therefore the promise of not resisting force, in no covenant transferreth any right, nor is obliging. For though a man may covenant thus, *unless I do so, or so, kill me*; he cannot covenant thus, *unless I do so, or so, I will not resist you when you come to kill me*. For man by nature chooseth the lesser evil, which is danger of death in resisting, rather than the greater, which is certain and present death in not resisting. And this is granted to be true by all men in that they lead criminals to execution and prison with armed men, notwithstanding that such criminals have consented to the law by which they are condemned.

No man obliged to accuse himself.

30. A covenant to accuse oneself, without assurance of pardon, is likewise invalid. For in the condition of nature where every man is judge, there is no place for accusation; and in the civil state the accusation is followed with punishment, which, being force, a man is not obliged not to resist. The same is also true of the accusation of those by whose condemnation a man falls into misery, as of a father, wife, or benefactor. For the testimony of such an accuser, if it be not willingly given, is presumed to be corrupted by nature, and therefore not to be received; and where a man's testimony is not to be credited, he is not bound to give it. Also accusations upon torture are not to be reputed as testimonies. For torture is to be used but as means of conjecture and light in the further examination and search of truth; and what is in that case confessed tendeth to the ease of him that is tortured, not to the informing of the torturers, and therefore ought not to have the credit of a sufficient testimony; for whether he deliver

---

1 Cf. 20.2.
2 14.8.

himself by true or false accusation, he does it by the right of preserving his own life.

31. The force of words being (as I have formerly noted) too weak to hold men to the performance of their covenants, there are in man's nature but two imaginable helps to strengthen it. And those are either a fear of the consequence of breaking their word or a glory or pride in appearing not to need to break it. This latter is a generosity too rarely found to be presumed on, especially in the pursuers of wealth, command, or sensual pleasure, which are the greatest part of mankind. The passion to be reckoned upon is fear; whereof there be two very general objects: one, the power of spirits invisible; the other, the power of those men they shall therein offend. Of these two, though the former be the greater power; yet the fear of the latter is commonly the greater fear. The fear of the former is in every man his own religion, which hath place in the nature of man before civil society. The latter hath not so, at least not place enough to keep men to their promises, because in the condition of mere nature, the inequality of power is not discerned, but by the event of battle. So that before the time of civil society, or in the interruption thereof by war, there is nothing can strengthen a covenant of peace agreed on against the temptations of avarice, ambition, lust, or other strong desire, but the fear of that invisible power which they every one worship as God, and fear as a revenger of their perfidy. All therefore that can be done between two men not subject to civil power is to put one another to swear by the God he feareth; which *swearing*, or OATH, is a *form of speech, added to a promise, by which he that promiseth signifieth that unless he perform he renounceth the mercy of his God, or calleth to him for vengeance on himself.* Such was the heathen form, *Let Jupiter kill me else, as I kill this beast.* So is our form, *I shall do thus, and thus, so help me God.* And this, with the rites and ceremonies which every one useth in his own religion, that the fear of breaking faith might be the greater.

32. By this it appears that an oath taken according to any other form or rite than his that sweareth is in vain and no oath; and that there is no swearing by anything which the swearer thinks not God. For though men have sometimes used to swear by their kings, for fear, or flattery; yet they would have it thereby understood they attributed to

them divine honour. And that swearing unnecessarily by God is but profaning of his name; and swearing by other things, as men do in common discourse, is not swearing, but an impious custom, gotten by too much vehemence of talking.

An oath adds nothing to the obligations.

33. It appears also that the oath adds nothing to the obligation. For a covenant, if lawful, binds in the sight of God, without the oath, as much as with it; if unlawful, bindeth not at all, though it be confirmed with an oath.

Chapter XV

Of Other Laws of Nature

The third law of nature.

1. From that law of nature by which we are obliged to transfer to another such rights as, being retained, hinder the peace of mankind, there followeth a third, which is this; *that men perform their covenants made*; without which, covenants are in vain and but empty words; and the right of all men to all things remaining, we are still in the condition of war.

Justice and injustice what.

2. And in this law of nature consisteth the fountain and original of JUSTICE. For where no covenant hath preceded, there hath no right been transferred;[1] and every man has right to everything; and consequently, no action can be unjust. But when a covenant is made, then to break it is *unjust* and the definition of INJUSTICE is no other than *the not performance of covenant*. And whatsoever is not unjust is *just*.[2]

Justice and propriety begin with the constitution of the commonwealth.

3. But because covenants of mutual trust, where there is a fear of not performance on either part (as hath been said in the former chapter),[3] are invalid, though the original of justice be the making of covenants; yet injustice actually there can be none till the cause of such fear be

---

1 Hobbes seems to have forgotten that rights can be transferred by gift, and this involves no covenant. See 14.12.
2 "Just" and "unjust" are normally contraries, not contradictories. However, Hobbes defines "just" in such a way that it becomes the contradictory of "unjust." Taking his definitions strictly, anyone in the state of nature who makes no covenants is just, because he is not unjust.
3 14.18.

taken away; which, while men are in the natural condition of war, cannot be done. Therefore before the names of *just* and *unjust* can have place, there must be some coercive power to compel men equally to the performance of their covenants by the terror of some punishment greater than the benefit they expect by the breach of their covenant, and to make good that propriety which by mutual contract men acquire in recompense of the universal right they abandon; and such power there is none before the erection of a commonwealth. And this is also to be gathered out of the ordinary definition of justice in the Schools, for they say that *justice is the constant will of giving to every man his own.* And therefore where there is no *own*, that is, no propriety [property], there is no injustice; and where there is no coercive power erected, that is, where there is no commonwealth, there is no propriety, all men having right to all things; therefore where there is no commonwealth, there nothing is unjust. So that the nature of justice consisteth in keeping of valid covenants; but the validity of covenants begins not but with the constitution of a civil power sufficient to compel men to keep them; and then it is also that propriety begins. [72]

4. The fool hath said in his heart, there is no such thing as justice; and sometimes also with his tongue, seriously alleging that every man's conservation and contentment being committed to his own care, there could be no reason why every man might not do what he thought conduced thereunto; and therefore also to make or not make, keep or not keep covenants was not against reason when it conduced to one's benefit. He does not therein deny that there be covenants; and that they are sometimes broken, sometimes kept; and that such breach of them may be called injustice, and the observance of them justice; but he questioneth whether injustice, taking away the fear of God (for the same fool hath said in his heart there is no God), not sometimes stand with that reason which dictateth to every man his own good; and particularly then, when it conduceth to such a benefit as shall put a man in a condition to neglect not only the dispraise and revilings, but also the power of other men. The kingdom of God is gotten by violence; but what if it could be gotten by unjust violence? Were it against reason so to get it, when it is impossible to receive hurt by it? And if it be not against

Justice not contrary to reason.

reason, it is not against justice; or else justice is not to be approved for good. From such reasoning as this, successful wickedness hath obtained the name of virtue; and some that in all other things have disallowed the violation of faith, yet have allowed it when it is for the getting of a kingdom. And the heathen that believed that Saturn was deposed by his son Jupiter believed nevertheless the same Jupiter to be the avenger of injustice, somewhat like to a piece of law in Coke's[1] *Commentaries on Littleton*, where he says, if the right heir of the crown be attainted of treason, yet the crown shall descend to him, and *eo instante* the attainder be void; from which instances a man will be very prone to infer that when the heir apparent of a kingdom shall kill him that is in possession, though his father, you may call it injustice or by what other name you will; yet it can never be against reason, seeing all the voluntary actions of men tend to the benefit of themselves; and those actions are most reasonable that conduce most to their ends. This specious [plausible] reasoning is nevertheless false.

[73]

5. For the question is not of promises mutual, where there is no security of performance on either side, as when there is no civil power erected over the parties promising; for such promises are no covenants; but either where one of the parties has performed already or where there is a power to make him perform, there is the question whether it be against reason, that is, against the benefit of the other to perform or not. And I say it is not against reason. For the manifestation [justification] whereof we are to consider, first, that when a man doth a thing, which notwithstanding anything [that] can be foreseen and reckoned on, tendeth to his own destruction, howsoever some accident, which he could not expect, arriving, may turn it to his benefit; yet such events do not make it reasonably or wisely done. Secondly, that in a condition of war, wherein every man to every man, for want of a common power to keep them all in awe, is an enemy, there is no man can hope by his own strength or wit to

---

1 Edward Coke was England's leading theorist of the common law. His views sometimes put him into conflict with King James I and later Charles I. His commentaries on the *Tenures of Sir Thomas Littleton* (c. 1422-81), an English jurist, are among his most famous works.

defend himself from destruction without the help of confederates, where every one expects the same defence by the confederation that any one else does; and therefore he which declares he thinks it reason to deceive those that help him can in reason expect no other means of safety than what can be had from his own single power. He, therefore, that breaketh his covenant and consequently declareth that he thinks he may with reason do so, cannot be received into any society that unite themselves for peace and defence but by the error of them that receive him; nor when he is received be retained in it without seeing the danger of their error; which errors a man cannot reasonably reckon upon as the means of his security; and therefore if he be left or cast out of society, he perisheth; and if he live in society, it is by the errors of other men, which he could not foresee nor reckon upon, and consequently against the reason of his preservation; and so, as all[1] men that contribute not to his destruction forbear him only out of ignorance of what is good for themselves.

6. As for the instance of gaining the secure and perpetual felicity of heaven by any way, it is frivolous; there being but one way imaginable, and that is not breaking, but keeping of covenant.

7. And for the other instance of attaining sovereignty by rebellion, it is manifest that, though the event follow; yet because it cannot reasonably be expected, but rather the contrary, and because, by gaining it so, others are taught to gain the same in like manner, the attempt thereof is against reason. Justice therefore, that is to say, keeping of covenant, is a rule of reason by which we are forbidden to do anything destructive to our life, and consequently a law of nature.

8. There be some that proceed further and will not have the law of nature to be those rules which conduce to the preservation of man's life on earth, but to the attaining of an eternal felicity after death, to which [felicity] they think the breach of covenant may conduce and consequently be just and reasonable; such are they that think it a work of merit to kill or depose or rebel against the [74] sovereign power constituted over them by their own consent. But because there is no natural knowledge of man's

---

1 As many.

estate after death, much less of the reward that is then to be given to breach of faith, but only a belief grounded upon other men's saying that they know it supernaturally or that they know those that knew them that knew others that knew it supernaturally, breach of faith cannot be called a precept of reason or nature.

Covenants not discharged by the vice of the person to whom they are made.

9. Others, that allow for a law of nature the keeping of faith, do nevertheless make exception of certain persons, as heretics, and such as use not to perform their covenant to others; and this also is against reason. For if any fault of a man be sufficient to discharge our covenant made, the same ought in reason to have been sufficient to have hindered the making of it.

Justice of men, & justice of actions what.

10. The names of *just* and *unjust*, when they are attributed to men, signify one thing, and, when they are attributed to actions, another. When they are attributed to men, they signify conformity or inconformity of manners to reason. But when they are attributed to action they signify the conformity or inconformity to reason, not of manners, or manner of life, but of particular actions. A just man therefore is he that taketh all the care he can that his actions may be all just; and an unjust man is he that neglecteth it. And such men are more often in our language styled by the names of righteous and unrighteous than just and unjust though the meaning be the same.[1] Therefore a righteous man does not lose that title by one or a few unjust actions that proceed from sudden passion or mistake of things or persons; nor does an unrighteous man lose his character for such actions as he does or forbears to do for fear, because his will is not framed by the justice, but by the apparent benefit of what he is to do. That which gives to human actions the relish of justice is a certain nobleness or gallantness of courage, rarely found, by which a man scorns to be beholding for the contentment of his life to fraud or breach of promise. This justice of the manners is that which is meant where justice is called a virtue; and injustice, a vice.

11. But the justice of actions denominates men, not just, but *guiltless*; and the injustice of the same (which is also called injury) gives them but the name of *guilty*.

---

1 See also 43.20; cf. 42.96.

12. Again, the injustice of manners is the disposition or aptitude to do injury, and is injustice before it proceed to act and without supposing any individual person injured. But the injustice of an action (that is to say, injury) supposeth an individual person injured; namely him to whom the covenant was made; and therefore many times the injury is received by one man when the damage redoundeth to another. As when the master commandeth his servant to give money to a stranger; if it be not done, the injury is done to the master, whom he had before covenanted to obey; but the damage redoundeth to the stranger, to whom he had no obligation, and therefore could not injure him. And so also in commonwealths private men may remit to one another their debts, but not robberies or other violences, whereby they are endamaged, because the detaining of debt is an injury to themselves, but robbery and violence are injuries to the person of the commonwealth. *(Injustice of manners and injustice of actions.[1])*

[75]

13. Whatsoever is done to a man, conformable to his own will signified to the doer, is not injury to him. For if he that doeth it hath not passed away his original right to do what he please by some antecedent covenant, there is no breach of covenant, and therefore no injury done him. And if he have, then his will to have it done, being signified, is a release of that covenant, and so again there is no injury done him. *(Nothing done to a man by his own consent can be injury.)*

14. Justice of actions is by writers divided into *commutative* and *distributive*; and the former they say consisteth in proportion arithmetical; the latter in proportion geometrical.[2] Commutative, therefore, they place in the equality of value of the things contracted for; and distributive, in the distribution of equal benefit to men of equal merit. As if it were injustice to sell dearer than we buy, or to give more to a man than he merits. The value of all things contracted for is measured by the appetite of the contractors, and therefore the just value is that which they be contented to give. And merit (besides that which is by covenant, where the performance on one part meriteth the performance of the other part, and falls under justice *(Justice commutative and distributive.)*

---

1 Most printed editions have the obviously incorrect "Justice … and justice."
2 Cf. Aristotle, *Nichomachean Ethics*, Book V.

commutative, not distributive) is not due by justice, but is rewarded of grace only.[1] And therefore this distinction, in the sense wherein it useth to be expounded, is not right. To speak properly, commutative justice is the justice of a contractor; that is, a performance of covenant in buying and selling, hiring and letting to hire, lending and borrowing, exchanging, bartering, and other acts of contract.

15. And distributive justice [is] the justice of an arbitrator, that is to say, the act of defining what is just. Wherein, being trusted by them that make him arbitrator, if he perform his trust, he is said to distribute to every man his own; and this is indeed just distribution, and may be called, though improperly, distributive justice, but more properly equity, which also is a law of nature, as shall be shown in due place.

16. As justice dependeth on antecedent covenant, so does GRATITUDE depend on antecedent grace, that is to say, antecedent free gift, and is the fourth law of nature, which may be conceived in this form: *that a man which receiveth benefit from another of mere grace endeavour that he which giveth it have no reasonable cause to repent him of his good will.* For no man giveth but with intention of good to himself, because gift is voluntary; and of all voluntary acts, the object is to every man his own good; of which [object], if men see [that] they shall be frustrated, there will be no beginning of benevolence or trust, nor consequently of mutual help, nor of reconciliation of one man to another; and therefore they are to remain still in the condition of *war*, which is contrary to the first and fundamental law of nature which commandeth men to *seek*

peace. The breach of this law is called *ingratitude* and hath the same relation to grace that injustice hath to obligation by covenant.

17. A fifth law of nature is COMPLAISANCE; that is to say, *that every man strive to accommodate himself to the rest.* For the understanding whereof we may consider that there is in men's aptness to society a diversity of nature, rising from their diversity of affections, not unlike to that we see in stones brought together for building of an edifice. For as that stone which by the asperity and irregularity of figure takes more room from others than itself fills, and

---

1 See 14.17.

for hardness cannot be easily made plain, and thereby hindereth the building, is by the builders cast away as unprofitable and troublesome; so also, a man that by asperity of nature will strive to retain those things which to himself are superfluous and to others necessary, and for the stubbornness of his passions cannot be corrected, is to be left or cast out of society as cumbersome thereunto. For seeing every man, not only by right, but also by necessity of nature, is supposed to endeavour all he can to obtain that which is necessary for his conservation, he that shall oppose himself against it for things superfluous is guilty of the war that thereupon is to follow, and therefore doth that which is contrary to the fundamental law of nature, which commandeth *to seek peace.* The observers of this law may be called SOCIABLE (the Latins call them *commodi*); the contrary, *stubborn, insociable, froward* [obstinate], *intractable.*

18. A sixth law of nature is this: *that upon caution of the future time, a man ought to pardon the offences past of them that, repenting, desire it.* For PARDON is nothing but granting of peace, which though granted to them that persevere in their hostility, be not peace, but fear; yet not granted to them that give caution of the future time is sign of an aversion to peace and therefore contrary to the law of nature.

> The sixth, facility to pardon.

19. A seventh is, *that in revenges* (that is, retribution of evil for evil), *men look not at the greatness of the evil past, but the greatness of the good to follow.* Whereby we are forbidden to inflict punishment with any other design than for correction of the offender or direction of others. For this law is consequent to the next before it, that commandeth pardon upon security of the future time. Besides, revenge without respect to the example and profit to come is a triumph or glorying in the hurt of another, tending to no end (for the end is always somewhat to come); and glorying to no end is vain-glory and contrary to reason; and to hurt without reason tendeth to the introduction of war, which is against the law of nature, and is commonly styled by the name of *cruelty.*

> The seventh, that in revenges men respect on the future good

20. And because all signs of hatred or contempt provoke to fight, insomuch as most men choose rather to hazard their life than not to be revenged, we may in the eighth place, for a law of nature, set down this precept;

> The eighth, against contumely.

that no man by deed, word, countenance, or gesture, declare hatred or contempt of another. The breach of which law is commonly called *contumely*.

The ninth, against pride.

[77]

21. The question who is the better man has no place in the condition of mere nature, where (as has been shown before) all men are equal. The inequality that now is has been introduced by the laws civil. I know that Aristotle in the first book of his *Politics*, for a foundation of his doctrine, maketh men by nature, some more worthy to command, meaning the wiser sort, such as he thought himself to be for his philosophy; others to serve, meaning those that had strong bodies, but were not philosophers as he, as [if] master and servant were not introduced by consent of men, but by difference of wit; which is not only against reason, but also against experience. For there are very few so foolish that had not rather govern themselves than be governed by others; nor when the wise, in their own conceit, contend by force with them who distrust their own wisdom, do they always, or often, or almost at any time, get the victory. If nature therefore have made men equal, that equality is to be acknowledged; or if nature have made men unequal, yet because men that think themselves equal will not enter into conditions of peace, but upon equal terms, such equality must be admitted. And therefore for the ninth law of nature, I put this, *that every man acknowledge another for his equal by nature.* The breach of this precept is *pride*.

The tenth, against arrogance.

22. On this law dependeth another, *that at the entrance into conditions of peace, no man require to reserve to himself any right which he is not content should be reserved to every one of the rest.* As it is necessary for all men that seek peace to lay down certain rights of nature, that is to say, not to have liberty to do all they list, so is it necessary for man's life to retain some, as right to govern their own bodies, enjoy air, water, motion, ways to go from place to place, and all things else without which a man cannot live or not live well. If in this case, at the making of peace, men require for themselves that which they would not have to be granted to others, they do contrary to the precedent law that commandeth the acknowledgement of natural equality, and therefore also against the law of nature. The observers of this law are those we call *modest*, and the breakers *arrogant* men. The

Greeks call the violation of this law *pleonexia*, that is, a desire of more than their share.

23. Also, if *a man he trusted to judge between man and man*, it is a precept of the law of nature *that he deal equally between them.* For without that, the controversies of men cannot be determined but by war. He therefore that is partial in judgement doth what in him lies to deter men from the use of judges and arbitrators, and consequently (against the fundamental law of nature) is the cause of war.

The eleventh, equity.

24. The observance of this law, from the equal distribution to each man of that which in reason belongeth to him, is called EQUITY, and (as I have said before) distributive justice; the violation, *acception of persons, prosōpolēpsia.*

25. And from this followeth another law: *that such things as cannot be divided be enjoyed in common, if it can be; and if the quantity of the thing permit, without stint; otherwise proportionably to the number of them that have right.* For otherwise the distribution is unequal, and contrary to equity.

The twelfth, equal use of things common.

26. But some things there be that can neither be divided nor enjoyed in common. Then, the law of nature which prescribeth equity requireth, *that the entire right, or else (making the use alternate) the first possession, be determined by lot.* For equal distribution is of the law of nature; and other means of equal distribution cannot be imagined.

[78] The thirteenth, of lot.

27. Of *lots* there be two sorts, *arbitrary* and *natural*. Arbitrary is that which is agreed on by the competitors; natural is either *primogeniture* (which the Greek calls *klēronomia*, which signifies, *given by lot*) or *first seizure*.

The fourteenth, of primogeniture, and first seizing.

28. And therefore those things which cannot be enjoyed in common, nor divided, ought to be adjudged to the first possessor; and in some cases to the first born, as acquired by lot.

29. It is also a law of nature, *that all men that mediate peace be allowed safe conduct.* For the law that commandeth peace, as the *end*, commandeth intercession, as the *means*; and to intercession the means is safe conduct.

The fifteenth, of mediators.

30. And because, though men be never so willing to observe these laws, there may nevertheless arise questions concerning a man's action; first, whether it were done or not done; secondly, if done, whether against the law or not against the law; the former whereof is called

The sixteenth, of submission to arbitrement.

a question *of fact*, the latter a question *of right*; therefore unless the parties to the question covenant mutually to stand to the sentence of another, they are as far from peace as ever. This other, to whose sentence they submit, is called an ARBITRATOR. And therefore it is of the law of nature *that they that are at controversy submit their right to the judgement of an arbitrator.*

The seventeenth, no man is his own judge.

31. And seeing every man is presumed to do all things in order to his own benefit, no man is a fit arbitrator in his own cause; and if he were never so fit, yet equity allowing to each party equal benefit, if one be admitted to be judge, the other is to be admitted also; and so the controversy, that is, the cause of war, remains, against the law of nature.

The eighteenth, no man is to be judge that has in him a natural cause of partiality.

32. For the same reason no man in any cause ought to be received for arbitrator to whom greater profit or honour or pleasure apparently ariseth out of the victory of one party than of the other, for he hath taken (though an unavoidable bribe, yet) a bribe; and no man can be obliged to trust him. And thus also the controversy and the condition of war remaineth, contrary to the law of nature.

The nineteenth, of witnesses.

33. And in a controversy of *fact*, the judge being to give no more credit to one than to the other, if there be no other arguments, must give credit to a third; or to a third and fourth; or more; for else the question is undecided, and left to force, contrary to the law of nature.

34. These are the laws of nature, dictating peace, for a means of the conservation of men in multitudes; and which only concern the doctrine of civil society. There be other things tending to the destruction of particular men, as drunkenness, and all other parts of intemperance, which may therefore also be reckoned amongst those things which the law of nature hath forbidden, but are not necessary to be mentioned, nor are pertinent enough to this place.

[79]

A rule by which the laws of nature may easily be examined.

35. And though this may seem too subtle a deduction of the laws of nature to be taken notice of by all men, whereof the most part are too busy in getting food, and the rest too negligent to understand; yet to leave all men inexcusable, they have been contracted into one easy sum, intelligible even to the meanest capacity; and that is: *Do not that to another which thou wouldest not have done*

to thyself; which showeth him that he has no more to do in learning the laws of nature, but, when weighing the actions of other men with his own they seem too heavy, to put them into the other part of the balance and his own into their place, that his own passions and self-love may add nothing to the weight; and then there is none of these laws of nature that will not appear unto him very reasonable.[1]

36. The laws of nature oblige *in foro interno*, that is to say, they bind to a desire they should take place;[2] but *in foro externo*, that is, to the putting them in act, not always. For he that should be modest and tractable, and perform all he promises in such time and place where no man else should do so, should but make himself a prey to others, and procure his own certain ruin, contrary to the ground of all laws of nature which tend to nature's preservation. And again, he that having sufficient security that others shall observe the same laws towards him, observes them not himself, seeketh not peace, but war, and consequently the destruction of his nature by violence.

The laws of nature oblige in conscience always, but in effect then only when there is security.

37. And whatsoever laws bind *in foro interno* may be broken, not only by a fact contrary to the law, but also by a fact according to it, in case a man think it contrary. For though his action in this case be according to the law, yet his purpose was against the law; which, where the obligation is *in foro interno*, is a breach.

38. The laws of nature are immutable and eternal, for injustice, ingratitude, arrogance, pride, iniquity, acception of persons, and the rest can never be made lawful. For it can never be that war shall preserve life, and peace destroy it.

The laws of nature are eternal;

39. The same laws, because they oblige only to a desire and endeavour (I mean an unfeigned and constant endeavour), are easy to be observed. For in that they require nothing but endeavour, he that endeavoureth their performance fulfilleth them; and he that fulfilleth the law is just.

And yet easy.

40. And the science of them is the true and only moral philosophy. For moral philosophy is nothing else but

The science of these laws is

---

1 See also 27.4 and 27.23.
2 See also 30.30 and 43.20. *In foro interno* means "in the internal court," i.e., conscience.

the science of what is *good* and *evil* in the conversation [interactions] and society of mankind. *Good* and *evil* are names that signify our appetites and aversions, which in different tempers, customs, and doctrines of men are different; and divers men differ not only in their judgement on the senses of what is pleasant and unpleasant to the taste, smell, hearing, touch, and sight; but also of what is conformable or disagreeable to reason in the actions of common life. Nay, the same man, in divers times, differs from himself; and one time praiseth, that is, calleth *good*, [80] what another time he dispraiseth, and calleth *evil*. From whence arise disputes, controversies, and at last war. And therefore so long as a man is in the condition of mere nature (which is a condition of war), private appetite is the measure of good and evil; and consequently all men agree on this, that peace is good, and therefore also the way or means of peace, which (as I have shown before) are *justice, gratitude, modesty, equity, mercy*, and the rest of the laws of nature, are good; that is to say, *moral virtues*; and their contrary *vices*, evil. Now the science of virtue and vice is moral philosophy; and therefore the true doctrine of the laws of nature is the true moral philosophy. But the writers of moral philosophy, though they acknowledge the same virtues and vices; yet, not seeing wherein consisted their goodness, nor that they come to be praised as the means of peaceable, sociable, and comfortable living, place them in a mediocrity of passions, as if not the cause, but the degree of daring, made fortitude, or not the cause, but the quantity of a gift, made liberality.

41. These dictates of reason men use to call by the name of laws, but improperly; for they are but conclusions or theorems concerning what conduceth to the conservation and defence of themselves; whereas law, properly, is the word of him that by right hath command over others. But yet if we consider the same theorems as delivered in the word of God that by right commandeth all things, then are they properly called *laws*.

Chapter XVI

Of Persons, Authors, and Things Personated

1. A person is he *whose words or actions are considered, either as his own, or as representing the words or actions of another man, or of any other thing to whom they are attributed, whether truly or by fiction.*[1]

A person what.

2. When they are considered as his own, then is he called a *natural person*; and when they are considered as representing the words and actions of another, then is he a *feigned* or *artificial* person.

Person natural, and artificial.

3. The word person is Latin, instead whereof the Greeks have *prosōpon*, which signifies the *face*, as *persona* in Latin signifies the *disguise* or *outward appearance* of a man, counterfeited on the stage; and sometimes more particularly that part of it which disguiseth the face, as a mask or vizard; and from the stage hath been translated to any represener of speech and action, as well in tribunals as theatres. So that a *person* is the same that an *actor* is, both on the stage and in common conversation; and to *personate* is to *act* or *represent* himself or another; and he that acteth another is said to bear his person or act in his name (in which sense Cicero useth it where he says, *Unus sustineo tres personas: mei, adversarii, et judicis*; I bear three persons: my own, my adversary's, and the judge's), and is called in divers occasions, diversely, as a *represener*, or *representative*, a *lieutenant*, a *vicar*, an *attorney*, a *deputy*, a *procurator*, an *actor*, and the like.

The word person whence.

[81]

4. Of persons artificial, some[2] have their words and actions *owned* by those whom they represent. And then the person is the *actor*; and he that owneth his words and actions is the AUTHOR, in which case the actor acteth by authority. For that which in speaking of goods and possessions is called an *owner*, and in Latin *dominus*, in Greek *kurios*, speaking of actions, is called author. And as the right of possession is called dominion, so the right of doing any action is called AUTHORITY and sometimes *warrant*. So that by authority is always understood a right of

Actor, author.

Authority

---

1 See also 23.2; cf. 42.3.
2 Cf. 16.9.

doing any act; and *done by authority*, done by commission
or license from him whose right it is.

Covenants by
authority bind
the author.
5. From hence it followeth that when the actor maketh
a covenant by authority, he bindeth thereby the author no
less than if he had made it himself, and no less subjecteth
him to all the consequences of the same. And therefore all
that hath been said formerly (Chapter 14) of the nature of
covenants between man and man in their natural capacity
is true also when they are made by their actors, representers, or procurators, that have authority from them, so far
forth as is in their commission, but no further.

6. And therefore he that maketh a covenant with the
actor, or representer, not knowing the authority he [the
actor] hath, doth it at his own peril. For no man is obliged
by a covenant whereof he is not author, nor consequently
by a covenant made against or beside the authority he
gave.

But not the
actor.
7. When the actor doth anything against the law of nature by command of the author, if he be obliged by former
covenant to obey him, not he, but the author breaketh the
law of nature, for though the action be against the law
of nature, yet it is not his; but, contrarily, to refuse to do
it is against the law of nature that forbiddeth breach of
covenant.

The authority is
to be shown.
8. And he that maketh a covenant with the author
by mediation of the actor, not knowing what authority
he hath, but only takes his word, in case such authority be not made manifest unto him upon demand, is no
longer obliged; for the covenant made with the author is
not valid without his counter-assurance. But if he that so
covenanteth knew beforehand he was to expect no other
assurance than the actor's word, then is the covenant
valid, because the actor in this case maketh himself the
author. And therefore, as when the authority is evident,
the covenant obligeth the author, not the actor, so when
the authority is feigned, it obligeth the actor only, there
being no author but himself.

Things person-
ated, inanimate.
9. There are few things that are incapable of being
represented by fiction. Inanimate things, as a church, a
hospital, a bridge, may be personated by a rector, master,
or overseer. But things inanimate cannot be authors, nor
therefore give authority to their actors. Yet the actors may
[82] have authority to procure their maintenance, given them

by those that are owners or governors of those things. And therefore such things cannot be personated before there be some state of civil government.

10. Likewise children, fools, and madmen that have no use of reason may be personated by guardians or curators, but can be no authors during that time of any action done by them, longer than (when they shall recover the use of reason) they shall judge the same reasonable. Yet during the folly he that hath right of governing them may give authority to the guardian. But this again has no place but in a state civil, because before such estate there is no dominion of persons.

Irrational.

11. An idol or mere figment of the brain may be personated, as were the gods of the heathen, which, by such officers as the state appointed, were personated and held possessions and other goods and rights, which men from time to time dedicated and consecrated unto them. But idols cannot be authors; for an idol is nothing. The authority proceeded from the state; and therefore before introduction of civil government the gods of the heathen could not be personated.

False gods.

12. The true God may be personated. As he was, first, by Moses, who governed the Israelites (that were not his, but God's people), not in his own name (with *hoc dicit Moses* [*thus Moses says*], but in God's name, with (*hoc dicit Dominus* [*thus the Lord says*]). Secondly, by the Son of Man, his own son, our blessed Saviour Jesus Christ, that came to reduce the Jews and induce all nations into the kingdom of his Father; not as of himself, but as sent from his Father. And thirdly, by the Holy Ghost or Comforter, speaking and working in the Apostles; which Holy Ghost was a Comforter that came not of himself, but was sent and proceeded from them both on the day of the Pentecost.

The true God.

13. A multitude of men are made *one* person when they are by one man, or one person, represented, so that it be done[1] with the consent of every one of that multitude in particular. For it is the *unity* of the represented, that maketh the person *one*. And it is the representer that beareth the person, and but

A multitude of men, how one person.

---

1 Read: "in such a way that it is accomplished." See 18.1 and 18.5.

one person; and *unity* cannot otherwise be understood in multitude.

Every one is author.

14. And because the multitude naturally is not *one*, but *many*, they cannot be understood for one, but many authors, of everything their representative saith or doth in their name, every man giving their common representer authority from himself in particular, and owning all the actions the representer doth, in case they give him authority without stint; otherwise, when they limit him in what, and [in] how far, he shall represent them, none of them owneth more than they gave him commission to act.

An actor may be many men made one by plurality of voices.

[83]

15. And if the representative consist of many men, the voice of the greater number must be considered as the voice of them all. For if the lesser number pronounce (for example) in the affirmative, and the greater in the negative, there will be negatives more than enough to destroy the affirmatives; and thereby the excess of negatives, standing uncontradicted, are the only voice the representative hath.

Representatives, when the number is even, unprofitable.

16. And a representative of even number, especially when the number is not great, whereby the contradictory voices are oftentimes equal, is therefore oftentimes mute and incapable of action. Yet in some cases contradictory voices, equal in number, may determine a question, as [for example] in condemning or absolving, equality of votes, even in that they condemn not, do absolve, but not on the contrary condemn, in that they absolve not. For when a cause is heard, not to condemn is to absolve; but on the contrary to say that not absolving is condemning is not true. The like it is in deliberation of executing presently or deferring till another time; for when the voices are equal, the not decreeing execution is a decree of dilation.

Negative voice.

17. Or if the number be odd, as three or more men or assemblies, whereof every one has, by a negative voice, authority to take away the effect of all the affirmative voices of the rest, this number is no representative; by the diversity of opinions and interests of men, it becomes oftentimes, and in cases of the greatest consequence, a mute person and unapt, as for many things else, so for the government of a multitude, especially in time of war.[1]

---

1 Hobbes gives additional reasons for preferring monarchy at 19.4-13.

18. Of authors there be two sorts. The first simply so called, which I have before defined to be him that owneth the action of another simply. The second is he that owneth an action or covenant of another conditionally; that is to say, he undertaketh to do it, if the other doth it not, at or before a certain time. And these authors conditional are generally called SURETIES, in Latin, *fidejussores* and *sponsores*; and particularly for debt, *praedes*; and for appearance before a judge or magistrate, *vades*.

THE SECOND PART

OF COMMONWEALTH

Chapter XVII

Of the Causes, Generation, and Definition of a Commonwealth

1. The final cause, end, or design of men (who naturally love liberty, and dominion over others) in the introduction of that restraint upon themselves (in which we see them live in commonwealths) is the foresight of their own preservation and of a more contented life thereby, that is to say, of getting themselves out from that miserable condition of war which is necessarily consequent (as hath been shown) to the natural passions of men, when there is no visible power to keep them in awe and tie them by fear of punishment to the performance of their covenants[1] and observation of those laws of nature set down in the fourteenth and fifteenth chapters.

The end of commonwealth, particular security.

Chap 13.

2. For the laws of nature (as *justice, equity, modesty, mercy,* and, in sum, *doing to others as we would be done to*) of themselves, without the terror of some power to cause them to be observed, are contrary to our natural passions that carry us to partiality, pride, revenge, and the like. And covenants without the sword are but words and of no strength to secure a man at all.[2] Therefore, notwithstanding the laws of nature (which every one hath then kept, when he has the will to keep them when he can do it safely),[3] if there be no power erected or not great enough for our security, every man will and may lawfully rely on his own strength and art for caution against all other men. And in all places, where men have lived by small families, to rob and spoil one another has been a trade, and so far from being reputed against the law of nature, that the greater spoils they gained, the greater was their

Which is not to be had from the law of nature.

---

1 See also 14.19 and 15.3.
2 See also 14.31 and 18.4.
3 See 15.36-37.

honour; and men observed no other laws therein but the laws of honour, that is, to abstain from cruelty, leaving to men their lives and instruments of husbandry. And as small families did then, so now do cities and kingdoms, which are but greater families[1] (for their own security), enlarge their dominions upon all pretences of danger and fear of invasion or assistance that may be given to invaders, [and] endeavour as much as they can to subdue or weaken their neighbours by open force and secret arts, for want of other caution, justly, and are remembered for it in after ages with honour.

Nor from the conjunction of a few men or families. [86]

3. Nor is it the joining together of a small number of men that gives them this security, because in small numbers, small additions on the one side or the other make the advantage of strength so great as is sufficient to carry the victory, and therefore gives encouragement to an invasion. The multitude sufficient to confide in for our security is not determined by any certain number, but by comparison with the enemy we fear, and is then sufficient when the odds of the enemy is not of so visible and conspicuous moment to determine the event of war, as to move him to attempt.

Nor from a great multitude, unless directed by one judgement.

4. And be there never so great a multitude, yet if their actions be directed according to their particular judgements and particular appetites, they can expect thereby no defence nor protection, neither against a common enemy nor against the injuries of one another. For being distracted in opinions concerning the best use and application of their strength, they do not help but hinder one another; and [they] reduce their strength, by mutual opposition, to nothing, whereby they are easily not only subdued by a very few that agree together, but also, when there is no common enemy, they make war upon each other for their particular interests. For if we could suppose a great multitude of men to consent in the observation of justice and other laws of nature, without a common power to keep them all in awe, we might as well suppose all mankind to do the same; and then there neither would

---

1 Cf. 17.5 and 20.15. When a family is big enough to withstand raids from others and when the members have covenanted to make one or more members the sovereign, then a family is a commonwealth and not otherwise.

be nor need to be any civil government or commonwealth at all, because there would be peace without subjection.

5. Nor is it enough for the security which men desire should last all the time of their life, that they be governed and directed by one judgement for a limited time, as in one battle or one war. For though they obtain a victory by their unanimous endeavour against a foreign enemy; yet afterwards, when either they have no common enemy, or he that by one part is held for an enemy is by another part held for a friend, they must needs by the difference of their interests dissolve and fall again into a war amongst themselves.

And that continually.

6. It is true that certain living creatures, as bees and ants, live sociably one with another (which are therefore by Aristotle numbered amongst political creatures), and yet have no other direction than their particular judgements and appetites, nor [do they have] speech, whereby one of them can signify to another what he thinks expedient for the common benefit; and therefore some man may perhaps desire to know why mankind cannot do the same. To which I answer,

Why certain creatures without reason or speech do nevertheless live in society, without any coercive power.

7. First, that men are continually in competition for honour and dignity, which these creatures are not; and consequently amongst men there ariseth on that ground envy and hatred and finally war; but amongst these not so.

8. Secondly, that amongst these creatures the common good differeth not from the private; and being by nature inclined to their private, they procure thereby the common benefit. But man, whose joy consisteth in comparing himself with other men, can relish nothing but what is eminent.

9. Thirdly, that these creatures, having not, as man, the use of reason, do not see, nor think they see, any fault in the administration of their common business; whereas amongst men there are very many that think themselves wiser and abler to govern the public better than the rest; and these strive to reform and innovate, one this way, another that way, and thereby bring it into distraction and civil war.

[87]

10. Fourthly, that these creatures, though they have some use of voice in making known to one another their desires and other affections; yet they want that art of words by which some men can represent to others that

which is good in the likeness of evil and evil in the likeness of good, and augment or diminish the apparent greatness of good and evil, discontenting men and troubling their peace at their pleasure.

11. Fifthly, irrational creatures cannot distinguish between *injury* and *damage*; and therefore as long as they be at ease, they are not offended with their fellows; whereas man is then most troublesome when he is most at ease; then it is that he loves to show his wisdom, and control the actions of them that govern the commonwealth.

12. Lastly, the agreement of these creatures is natural; that of men is by covenant only, which is artificial; and therefore it is no wonder if there be somewhat else required, besides covenant, to make their agreement constant and lasting, which is a common power to keep them in awe and to direct their actions to the common benefit.

The generation of a commonwealth.

13. The only way to erect such a common power as may be able to defend them from the invasion of foreigners and the injuries of one another, and thereby to secure them in such sort as that by their own industry and by the fruits of the earth they may nourish themselves and live contentedly, is to confer all their power and strength[1] upon one man or upon one assembly of men, that may reduce all their wills by plurality of voices unto one will; which is as much as to say, to appoint one man or assembly of men to bear their person; and every one to own and acknowledge himself to be author of whatsoever he that so beareth their person shall act or cause to be acted in those things which concern the common peace and safety; and therein to submit their wills, every one to his will, and their judgements to his judgement. This is more than consent or concord; it is a real unity of them all in one and the same person, made by covenant of every man with every man in such manner as if every man should say to every man, *I authorize and give up my right of governing myself, to this man,*[2] *or to this assembly of men, on this condition: that thou give up thy right to him,*

---

1 If citizens confer all of their power and strength on the sovereign, it would appear that they would have none left for themselves. Cf. 14.6.

2 Authorizing someone to exercise one's right, which does not involve giving up that right, does not seem to be consistent with giving up that right.

and authorize all his actions in like manner.[1] This done, the multitude so united in one person is called a COMMON-WEALTH; in Latin, CIVITAS. This is the generation of that great LEVIATHAN,[2] or rather, to speak more reverently, of that *mortal god* to which we owe, under the *immortal God*, our peace and defence. For by this authority, given him by every particular man in the commonwealth, he hath the use of so much power and strength conferred on him that, by terror thereof, he is enabled to conform[3] the wills of them all to peace at home and mutual aid against their enemies abroad. And in him consisteth the essence of the commonwealth, which, to define it, is *one person, of whose acts a great multitude, by mutual covenants one with another, have made themselves every one the author, to the end he may use the strength and means of them all as he shall think expedient for their peace and common defence.*

[88]

The definition of a commonwealth.

14. And he that carryeth this person is called SOVEREIGN, and said to have *sovereign power*; and every one besides, his SUBJECT.

Sovereign, and subject, what.

15. The attaining to this sovereign power is by two ways. One, by natural force, as when a man maketh his children to submit themselves and their children to his government, as being able to destroy them if they refuse, or [as when a man] by war subdueth his enemies to his will, giving them their lives on that condition. The other is when men agree amongst themselves to submit to some man, or assembly of men, voluntarily, on confidence to be protected by him against all others. This latter may be called a political commonwealth or commonwealth by *institution*, and the former [may be called] a commonwealth by *acquisition*. And first, I shall speak of a commonwealth by institution.

---

1 See also 14.8, 18.1, 20.13, and 21.10
2 See, e.g., Job 41, Ps. 74.15-17, and Is. 27.1. In the Bible, Leviathan, sometimes pictured as a whale and sometimes as a crocodile, is a principle of chaos and an enemy of God, whom God defeats. For Hobbes, Leviathan saves people from the state of nature. At 28.27, Hobbes quotes the book of Job, which says at 41:34 that Leviathan is "king of all the children of pride." Christian theologians often identified pride as the principal cause of sin.
3 Many editions have "conform" and there is some textual support for "form." But "conform" makes more sense.

Chapter XVIII

Of the Rights of Sovereigns by Institution

1. A *commonwealth* is said to be *instituted* when a *multitude* of men do agree and *covenant, every one with every one,* that to whatsoever *man* or *assembly of men* shall be given by the major part the *right* to *present*[1] the person of them all, that is to say, to be their *representative,* every one, as well he that *voted for it* as he that *voted against it,* shall *authorize* all the actions[2] and judgements of that man, or assembly of men, in the same manner as if they were his own, to the end to live peaceably amongst themselves and be protected against other men.[3]

2. From this institution of a commonwealth are derived all the *rights* and *faculties* of him or them, on whom the sovereign power is conferred by the consent of the people assembled.[4]

3. First, because they covenant, it is to be understood they are not obliged by former covenant to anything repugnant hereunto. And consequently they that have already instituted a commonwealth, being thereby bound by covenant to own the actions and judgements

---

1 To present one's person is presumably to bear that person. But perhaps Hobbes should have used "represent."

2 This seems to be hyperbolic. If a subject authorizes all of the sovereign's actions, then he would authorize the sovereign's killing or punishing of him, even though no one can ever lay down his right of self-preservation. Hobbes sometimes says that a criminal punishes himself because he has authorized all of his sovereign's actions (18.3; cf. 20.3).

3 See also 22.9. Hobbes gives the impression that there are two stages to instituting a commonwealth. First, people agree to have a vote on the kind of commonwealth, and then they vote on who will be the sovereign. In his *The Elements of Law, Natural and Politic* (1640), Hobbes said that democracy is the first kind of commonwealth (although it is the least stable). What Hobbes says in *Leviathan* may be a remnant of that doctrine. See also 18.5 and *De Cive,* chapter 7.

4 The sovereign is the artificial person who governs his subjects. The sovereign is a single human being in a monarchy. In an aristocracy, the sovereign is the group of people who rule. In a democracy, the sovereign is the entire citizenry, considered as a unity, not in the multiplicity of each subject.

of one, cannot lawfully make a new covenant amongst themselves to be obedient to any other, in anything whatsoever, without his permission. And therefore, they that are subjects to a monarch cannot without his leave cast off monarchy and return to the confusion of a disunited multitude nor transfer their person from him that beareth it to another man or other assembly of men;[1] for they are bound, every man to every man, to own and be reputed author of all that he that already is their sovereign shall do and judge fit to be done; so that any one man dissenting, all the rest should break their covenant made to that man, which is injustice; and they have also every man given the sovereignty to him that beareth their person; and therefore if they depose him, they take from him that which is his own, and so again it is injustice. Besides, if he that attempteth to depose his sovereign be killed or punished by him for such attempt, he is author of his own punishment, as being, by the institution, author of all his sovereign shall do;[2] and because it is injustice for a man to do anything for which he may be punished by his own authority, he is also upon that title unjust. And whereas some men have pretended for their disobedience to their sovereign a new covenant, made, not with men but with God, this also is unjust; for there is no covenant with God but by mediation of somebody that representeth God's person, which none doth but God's lieutenant who hath the sovereignty under God. But this pretence of covenant with God is so evident a lie, even in the pretenders' own consciences, that it is not only an act of an unjust, but also of a vile and unmanly disposition.

[89]

4. Secondly, because the right of bearing the person of them all is given to him [whom] they make sovereign by covenant only of one to another and not of him to any of them, there can happen no breach of covenant on the part of the sovereign; and consequently none of his subjects, by any pretence of forfeiture, can be freed from his subjection. That he which is made sovereign maketh no

2. Sovereign power cannot be forfeited.

---

1 Hobbes is probably criticizing the Scots, who in the National Covenant (1638) made a covenant that appeared to supersede one that Hobbes thought they already had with the king, and criticizing the English who, with the Scots, did the same in the Solemn League and Covenant (1643).

2 See also 18.5.

covenant with his subjects before hand is manifest,[1] because either he must make it with the whole multitude, as one party to the covenant, or he must make a several covenant with every man. With the whole, as one party, it is impossible, because as yet they are not one person; and if he make so many several covenants as there be men, those covenants after he hath the sovereignty are void, because what act soever can be pretended by any one of them for breach thereof is the act both of himself and of all the rest, because done in the person and by the right of every one of them in particular.[2] Besides, if any one or more of them pretend [allege] a breach of the covenant made by the sovereign at his institution, and others or one other of his subjects or himself alone pretend there was no such breach, [then] there is in this case no judge to decide the controversy; it returns therefore to the sword again, and every man recovereth the right of protecting himself by his own strength, contrary to the design they had in the institution. It is therefore in vain to grant sovereignty by way of precedent covenant. The opinion that any monarch receiveth his power by covenant, that is to say, on condition, proceedeth from want of understanding this easy truth: that covenants being but words and breath, have no force to oblige, contain, constrain, or protect any man, but what it has from the public sword,[3] that is, from the untied hands of that man or assembly of men that hath the
[90] sovereignty, and whose actions are avouched by them all and performed by the strength of them all in him united. But when an assembly of men is made sovereign, then no man imagineth any such covenant to have passed in the institution; for no man is so dull as to say, for example, the people of Rome made a covenant with the Romans to hold the sovereignty on such or such conditions, which not performed, the Romans might lawfully depose the Roman people. That men see not the reason to be alike in a monarchy and in a popular government proceedeth from

---

1 King James I wrote, "I deny any such contract to be made [between the king and the people]" ("The Trew Law of Free Monarchies" [1598]).

2 If a sovereign "makes" a covenant with a subject and "breaks" it, the subject himself nullifies it because the sovereign acts for the subject.

3 See also 14.31 and 17.2.

the ambition of some that are kinder to the government of an assembly, whereof they may hope to participate, than of monarchy, which they despair to enjoy.

5. Thirdly, because the major part hath by consenting voices declared a sovereign, he that dissented must now consent with the rest, that is, be contented to avow all the actions he shall do, or else justly be destroyed by the rest.[1] For if he voluntarily entered into the congregation of them that were assembled, [then] he sufficiently declared thereby his will and therefore tacitly covenanted to stand to what the major part should ordain; and therefore if he refuse to stand thereto or [he] make protestation against any of their decrees, [then] he does contrary to his covenant and therefore unjustly. And whether he be of the congregation or not and whether his consent be asked or not, he must either submit to their decrees or be left in the condition of war he was in before, wherein he might without injustice be destroyed by any man whatsoever.

6. Fourthly, because every subject is by this institution author of all the actions and judgements of the sovereign instituted,[2] it follows that whatsoever he doth can be no injury to any of his subjects nor ought he to be by any of them accused of injustice. For he that doth anything by authority from another doth therein no injury to him by whose authority he acteth; but by this institution of a commonwealth every particular man is author of all the sovereign doth; and consequently he that complaineth of injury from his sovereign complaineth of that whereof he himself is author; and therefore [he] ought not to accuse any man but himself, no, nor himself, of injury, because to do injury to oneself is impossible. It is true that they that have sovereign power may commit iniquity, but not injustice or injury[3] in the proper signification.

7. Fifthly, and consequently to that which was said last, no man that hath sovereign power can justly be put to death or otherwise in any manner by his subjects

3. No man can without injustice protest against the institution of the sovereign declared by the major part.

4. The sovereign's actions cannot be justly accused by the subject.

5. Whatsoever the sovereign doth is

---

1   See also 18.1.

2   See 16.14.

3   Hobbes is playing on the etymology of the Latin word for "right," *jus* (genitive *juris*). Injustice and injury is what is done without *jus*, because the wrongdoer has laid down or given up his *jus*. Iniquity is merely harm done; the word comes from the Latin *in* + *aequus*: not equal.

punished. For seeing every subject is author of the actions of his sovereign, he punisheth another for the actions committed by himself.

6. The sovereign
is judge of what
is necessary for
the peace and
defence of his-
subjects.

8. And because the end of this institution is the peace and defence of them all, and whosoever has right to the end has right to the means,[1] it belonged of right to whatsoever man or assembly that hath the sovereignty to be judge both of the means of peace and defence and also of the hindrances and disturbances of the same; and to do whatsoever he shall think necessary to be done, both beforehand, for the preserving of peace and security, by prevention of discord at home and hostility from abroad; and when peace and security are lost, for the recovery of the same. And therefore,

And judge of
what doctrines
are fit to be
taught them.

9. Sixthly, it is annexed to the sovereignty to be judge of what opinions and doctrines are averse, and what [opinions and doctrines are] conducing to peace; and consequently on what occasions, how far, and what men are to be trusted withal in speaking to multitudes of people, and who shall examine the doctrines of all books before they be published. For the actions of men proceed from their opinions, and in the well governing of opinions consisteth the well governing of men's actions in order to their peace and concord. And though in matter of doctrine nothing ought to be regarded but the truth; yet this is not repugnant to regulating of the same by peace. For doctrine repugnant to peace can no more be true than peace and concord can be against the law of nature. It is true that in a commonwealth, where by the negligence or unskillfulness of governors and teachers false doctrines are by time generally received, the contrary truths may be generally offensive. Yet the most sudden and rough bustling in of a new truth that [there] can be does never break the peace, but only sometimes awake the war. For those men that are so remissly governed that they dare take up arms to defend or introduce an opinion are still in war; and their condition not peace, but only a cessation of arms for fear of one another; and they live, as it were, in the precincts of battle continually. It belongeth therefore to him that hath the sovereign power to be judge, or constitute all

---

1 See 14.21.

judges of opinions and doctrines, as a thing necessary to peace, thereby to prevent discord and civil war.

10. Seventhly, is annexed to the sovereignty the whole power of prescribing the rules whereby every man may know what goods he may enjoy and what actions he may do without being molested by any of his fellow subjects; and this is it men call *propriety [property]*. For before constitution of sovereign power, as hath already been shown, all men had right to all things,[1] which necessarily causeth war; and therefore this propriety, being necessary to peace and depending on sovereign power, is the act of that power, in order to the public peace. These rules of propriety (or *meum* and *tuum*) and of *good, evil, lawful,* and *unlawful* in the actions of subjects are the civil laws,[2] that is to say, the laws of each commonwealth in particular; though the name of civil law be now restrained to the ancient civil laws of the city of Rome, which being the head of a great part of the world, her laws at that time were in these parts the civil law.

7. The right of making rules; whereby the subjects may every man know what is so his own, as no other subject can without injustice take it from him.

11. Eighthly, is annexed to the sovereignty the right of judicature, that is to say, of hearing and deciding all controversies which may arise concerning law, either civil or natural, or concerning fact. For without the decision of controversies there is no protection of one subject against the injuries of another, the laws concerning *meum* and *tuum* are in vain, and to every man remaineth, from the natural and necessary appetite of his own conservation, the right of protecting himself by his private strength, which is the condition of war and contrary to the end for which every commonwealth is instituted.

8. To him also belongeth the right of judicature and decision of controversy.

[92]

12. Ninthly, is annexed to the sovereignty the right of making war and peace with other nations and commonwealths, that is to say, of judging when it is for the public good, and how great forces are to be assembled, armed, and paid for that end, and to levy money upon the subjects to defray the expenses thereof. For the power by which the people are to be defended consisteth in their armies and the strength of an army in the union of their strength under one command; which command the sovereign instituted therefore hath, because the command

9. And of making war, and peace, as he shall think best.

---

1 See 14.4.
2 See also 26.3, 26.8, and 29.6.

of the *militia*, without other institution, maketh him that hath it sovereign. And therefore, whosoever is made general of an army, he that hath the sovereign power is always generalissimo.

10. And of choosing all counsellors and ministers, both of peace and war.

13. Tenthly, is annexed to the sovereignty the choosing of all counsellors, ministers, magistrates, and officers, both in peace and war. For seeing the sovereign is charged with the end, which is the common peace and defence, he is understood to have power to use such means as he shall think most fit for his discharge.

11. And of rewarding and punishing, and that (where no former law hath determined the measure of it) arbitrarily.

14. Eleventhly, to the sovereign is committed the power of rewarding with riches or honour and of punishing with corporal or pecuniary punishment or with ignominy [disgrace], every subject according to the law he hath formerly made; or if there be no law made, according as he shall judge most to conduce to the encouraging of men to serve the commonwealth or deterring of them from doing disservice to the same.

12. And of honour and order.

15. Lastly, considering what values men are naturally apt to set upon themselves, what respect they look for from others, and how little they value other men, from whence continually arise amongst them emulation, quarrels, factions, and at last war, to the destroying of one another and diminution of their strength against a common enemy, it is necessary that there be laws of honour and a public rate of the worth of such men as have deserved or are able to deserve well of the commonwealth, and that there be force in the hands of some or other to put those laws in execution. But it hath already been shown that not only the whole militia or forces of the commonwealth, but also the judicature of all controversies is annexed to the sovereignty. To the sovereign therefore it belongeth also to give titles of honour and to appoint what order of place and dignity each man shall hold and what signs of respect in public or private meetings they shall give to one another.

These rights are indivisible.

16. These are the rights which make the essence of sovereignty and which are the marks whereby a man may discern in what man or assembly of men the sovereign power is placed and resideth. For these are incommunicable and inseparable. The power to coin money, to dispose of the estate and persons of infant heirs, to have preemption in markets, and all other statute prerogatives

may be transferred by the sovereign, and yet the power to protect his subjects be retained. But if he transfer the militia, he retains the judicature in vain, for want of execution of the laws; or if he grant away the power of raising money, the militia is in vain; or if he give away the government of doctrines, men will be frighted into rebellion with the fear of spirits. And so if we consider any one of the said rights, we shall presently see that the holding of all the rest will produce no effect in the conservation of peace and justice, the end for which all commonwealths are instituted. And this division is it whereof it is said, *A kingdom divided in itself cannot stand*; for unless this division precede, division into opposite armies can never happen. If there had not first been an opinion received of the greatest part of England that these powers were divided between the King and the Lords and the House of Commons, the people had never been divided and fallen into this Civil War, first between those that disagreed in politics and after between the dissenters about the liberty of religion; which have so instructed men in this point of sovereign right that there be few now (in England) that do not see that these rights are inseparable and will be so generally acknowledged at the next return of peace; and so [they will] continue [to see this] till their miseries are forgotten; and [then] no longer, except[1] the vulgar be better taught than they have hitherto been.[2]

17. And because they are essential and inseparable rights, it follows necessarily that in whatsoever words any of them seem to be granted away, yet if the sovereign power itself be not in direct terms renounced and the name of sovereign no more given by the grantees to him that grants them, [then] the grant is void;[3] for when he has granted all he can, if we grant back the sovereignty, all is restored, as inseparably annexed thereunto.

And can by no grant pass away without direct renouncing of the sovereign power.

18. This great authority being indivisible and inseparably annexed to the sovereignty, there is little ground for the opinion of them that say of sovereign kings, though they be *singulis majores*, of greater power than every one of their subjects; yet they be *universis minores*, of less power

The power and honour of subjects vanisheth in the presence of the power sovereign.

---

1 Unless.
2 Better teaching would include teaching *Leviathan*, according to Hobbes. Cf. 30.14.
3 Cf. 14.8.

than them all together. For if by *all together* they mean not the collective body as one person, then *all together* and *every one* signify the same and the speech is absurd. But if by *all together* they understand them as one person (which person the sovereign bears), then the power of all together is the same with the sovereign's power and so again the speech is absurd, which absurdity they see well enough when the sovereignty is in an assembly of the people; but in a monarch they see it not, and yet the power of sovereignty is the same in whomsoever it be placed.

19. And as the power, so also the honour of the sovereign ought to be greater than that of any or all the subjects. For in the sovereignty is the fountain of honour. The dignities of lord, earl, duke, and prince are his creatures. As in the presence of the master the servants are equal and without any honour at all, so are the subjects in the presence of the sovereign. And though they shine some more, some less, when they are out of his sight; yet in his presence they shine no more than the stars in presence of the sun.

[94] Sovereign power not so hurtful as the want of it, and the hurt proceeds for the greatest part from not submitting readily to a less.

20. But a man may here object that the condition of subjects is very miserable, as being obnoxious [liable] to the lusts and other irregular passions of him or them that have so unlimited a power in their hands. And commonly they that live under a monarch think it the fault of monarchy; and they that live under the government of democracy or other sovereign assembly attribute all the inconvenience to that form of commonwealth; whereas the power in all forms, if they be perfect enough to protect them, is the same; [they are] not considering that the estate of man can never be without some incommodity or other, and that the greatest [incommodity] that in any form of government can possibly happen to the people in general is scarce sensible in respect of the miseries and horrible calamities that accompany a civil war or that dissolute condition of masterless men without subjection to laws and a coercive power to tie their hands from rapine and revenge; nor [are they] considering that the greatest pressure [burden] of sovereign governors proceedeth not from any delight or profit they can expect in the damage or weakening of their subjects (in whose vigour consisteth their own strength and glory), but in the restiveness of themselves that, unwillingly contributing to their own

defence, make it necessary for their governors to draw from them what they can in time of peace, [in order] that they may have means on any emergent occasion or sudden need to resist or take advantage on their enemies. For all men are by nature provided of notable multiplying glasses (that is their passions and self-love) through which every little payment appeareth a great grievance, but are destitute of those prospective glasses (namely moral and civil science) to see afar off the miseries that hang over them and cannot without such payments be avoided.

Chapter XIX

Of the Several Kinds of Commonwealth by Institution, and of Succession to the Sovereign Power

1. The difference of commonwealths consisteth in the difference of the sovereign or the person representative of all and every one of the multitude. And because the sovereignty is either in one man or in an assembly of more than one, and into that assembly either every man hath right to enter or not every one, but certain men distinguished from the rest; it is manifest there can be but three kinds of commonwealth. For the representative must needs be one man or more; and if more, then it is the assembly of all, or but of a part. When the representative is one man, then is the commonwealth a MONARCHY; when an assembly of all that will come together, then it is a DEMOCRACY or popular commonwealth; when an assembly of a part only, then it is called an ARISTOCRACY. Other kind of commonwealth there can be none; for either one, or more, or all, must have the sovereign power (which I have shown to be indivisible) entire. The different forms of commonwealths but three.

2. There be other names of government in the histories and books of policy, as *tyranny* and *oligarchy*; but they are not the names of other forms of government, but of the same forms misliked. For they that are discontented under *monarchy* call it *tyranny*[1] and they that are displeased with *aristocracy* call it *oligarchy*; so also, they which find [95] Tyranny and oligarchy, but different names of monarchy, and aristocracy.

---

1   See also 46.35 and "Review and Conclusion," 9.

themselves grieved under a *democracy* call it *anarchy*,[1] which signifies want of government; and yet I think no man believes that want of government is any new kind of government; nor by the same reason ought they to believe that the government is of one kind when they like it and another when they mislike it or are oppressed by the governors.

Subordinate
representatives
dangerous.

3. It is manifest that men who are in absolute liberty may, if they please, give authority to one man to represent them every one, as well as give such authority to any assembly of men whatsoever; and consequently [they] may subject themselves, if they think good, to a monarch as absolutely as to any other representative. Therefore, where there is already erected a sovereign power, there can be no other representative of the same people, but only to certain particular ends by the sovereign limited. For that were to erect two sovereigns and every man to have his person represented by two actors that, by opposing one another, must needs divide that power which (if men will live in peace) is indivisible, and thereby reduce the multitude into the condition of war, contrary to the end for which all sovereignty is instituted.[2] And therefore as it is absurd to think that a sovereign assembly, inviting the people of their dominion to send up their deputies with power to make known their advice or desires, should therefore hold such deputies, rather than themselves, for the absolute representative of the people, so it is absurd also to think the same in a monarchy. And I know not how this so manifest a truth should of late be so little observed, that in a monarchy he that had the sov-

---

1 The word "tyranny" means monarchy but has a negative connotation. "Oligarchy" means aristocracy but has a negative connotation. "Anarchy" means democracy but has a negative connotation, according to Hobbes. Almost everyone else, all those who think there is a difference between a good government and a bad government, would claim that "tyranny" does not mean the same thing as "monarchy," and so on.

2 Hobbes thinks that genuine separation of powers, as the United States claims for its government, leads to civil war. He was thinking in particular of the English Civil Wars (1642-49), which pitted the king and his followers against a majority of the parliament and their followers.

ereignty from a descent of six hundred years,[1] was alone called sovereign, had the title of Majesty from every one of his subjects, and was unquestionably taken by them for their king, was notwithstanding never considered as their representative, that name ["representative"] without contradiction passing for the title of those men which at his command were sent up by the people to carry their petitions and give him, if he permitted it, their advice.[2] Which may serve as an admonition for those that are the true and absolute representative of a people to instruct men in the nature of that office, and to take heed how they admit of any other general representation upon any occasion whatsoever, if they mean to discharge the trust committed to them.

4. The difference between these three kinds of commonwealth consisteth not in the difference of power,[3] but in the difference of convenience or aptitude to produce the peace and security of the people, which end they were instituted. And to compare monarchy with the other two, we may observe, first, that whosoever beareth the person of the people or is one of that assembly that bears it beareth also his own natural person.[4] And though he be careful in his politic person to procure the common interest; yet he is more, or no less, careful to procure the private good of himself, his family, kindred and friends; and for the most part, if the public interest chance to cross the private, he prefers the private, for the passions of men are commonly more potent than their reason. From whence it follows that where the public and private interest are most closely united, there is the public most advanced. Now in monarchy the private interest is the same with the public. The riches, power, and honour of a monarch arise only from the riches, strength, and reputa-

Comparison of monarchy, with sovereign assemblies.

[96]

---

1   The Stuart monarchs traced their lineage back to William I (the Conqueror), who conquered England in 1066.
2   Hobbes believed that Parliament had no political power independent of the monarch. He thought it was a purely advisory body, as the French word *parler*, from which the English word "parliament" comes, suggests: to talk.
3   All three forms of government are equally sovereign. But Hobbes thinks that monarchy is the most stable form of government, democracy the least.
4   Cf. 23.2.

tion of his subjects. For no king can be rich nor glorious nor secure, whose subjects are either poor or contemptible or too weak through want or dissension to maintain a war against their enemies; whereas in a democracy or aristocracy, the public prosperity confers not so much to the private fortune of one that is corrupt or ambitious, as doth many times a perfidious advice, a treacherous action, or a civil war.

5. Secondly, that a monarch receiveth counsel of whom, when, and where he pleaseth; and consequently may hear the opinion of men versed in the matter about which he deliberates, of what rank or quality soever, and as long before the time of action and with as much secrecy as he will. But when a sovereign assembly has need of counsel, none are admitted but such as have a right thereto from the beginning, which for the most part are of those who have been versed more in the acquisition of wealth than of knowledge and are to give their advice in long discourses which may, and do commonly, excite men to action, but not govern them in it. For the *understanding* is by the flame of the passions never enlightened, but dazzled; nor is there any place or time wherein an assembly can receive counsel with secrecy, because of their own multitude.

6. Thirdly, that the resolutions of a monarch are subject to no other inconstancy than that of human nature; but in assemblies, besides that of nature, there ariseth an inconstancy from the number. For the absence of a few that would have the resolution, once taken, continue firm (which [absence] may happen by security, negligence, or private impediments), or the diligent appearance of a few of the contrary opinion undoes today all that was concluded yesterday.

7. Fourthly, that a monarch cannot disagree with himself out of envy or interest, but an assembly may, and that to such a height as may produce a civil war.

8. Fifthly, that in monarchy there is this inconvenience: that any subject, by the power of one man, for the enriching of a favourite or flatterer, may be deprived of all he possesseth, which I confess is a great and inevitable inconvenience. But the same may as well happen where the sovereign power is in an assembly; for their power is the same, and they are as subject to evil counsel and

to be seduced by orators as a monarch by flatterers; and becoming one another's flatterers, serve one another's covetousness and ambition by turns. And whereas the favourites of monarchs are few and they have none else to advance but their own kindred, the favourites of an assembly are many, and the kindred much more numerous than of any monarch. Besides, there is no favourite of a monarch which cannot as well succour his friends as hurt his enemies; but orators, that is to say favourites of sovereign assemblies, though they have great power to hurt, have little to save. For to accuse requires less eloquence (such is man's nature) than to excuse; and condemnation, than absolution, more resembles justice. [97]

9. Sixthly, that it is an inconvenience in monarchy that the sovereignty may descend upon an infant or one that cannot discern between good and evil, and [the inconvenience] consisteth in this, that the use of his power must be in the hand of another man or of some assembly of men, which are to govern by his right and in his name as curators and protectors of his person and authority. But to say there is inconvenience in putting the use of the sovereign power into the hand of a man or an assembly of men is to say that all government is more inconvenient than confusion and civil war. And therefore all the danger that can be pretended must arise from the contention of those that, for an office of so great honour and profit, may become competitors. To make it appear that this inconvenience proceedeth not from that form of government we call monarchy, we are to consider that the precedent monarch hath appointed who shall have the tuition of his infant successor, either expressly by testament or tacitly by not controlling the custom in that case received; and then such inconvenience, if it happen, is to be attributed not to the monarchy, but to the ambition and injustice of the subjects, which in all kinds of government where the people are not well instructed in their duty and the rights of sovereignty, is the same. Or else[1] the precedent monarch hath not at all taken order for such tuition; and then the law of nature hath provided this sufficient rule, that the tuition shall be in him that hath by nature most interest in the preservation of the authority of the infant,

---

1   In case.

and to whom least benefit can accrue by his death or diminution. For seeing every man by nature seeketh his own benefit and promotion, to put an infant into the power of those that can promote themselves by his destruction or damage is not tuition but treachery. So that[1] sufficient provision being taken against all just quarrel about the government under a child, if any contention arise to the disturbance of the public peace, it is not to be attributed to the form of monarchy but to the ambition of subjects and ignorance of their duty. On the other side, there is no great commonwealth, the sovereignty whereof is in a great assembly, which is not, as to consultations of peace and war and making of laws, in the same condition as if the government were in a child. For as a child wants[2] the judgement to dissent from counsel given him and is thereby necessitated to take the advice of them or him to whom he is committed; so an assembly wanteth the liberty to dissent from the counsel of the major part, be it good or bad. And as a child has need of a tutor or protector to preserve his person and authority, so also in great commonwealths the sovereign assembly, in all great dangers and troubles, have need of *custodes libertatis*, that is, of dictators or protectors of their authority, which are as much as temporary monarchs to whom for a time they may commit the entire exercise of their power; and have (at the end of that time) been oftener deprived thereof than infant kings by their protectors, regents, or any other tutors.

[98]

10. Though the kinds of sovereignty be, as I have now shown, but three; that is to say, monarchy, where one man has it; or democracy, where the general assembly of subjects hath it; or aristocracy, where it is in an assembly of certain persons nominated or otherwise distinguished from the rest; yet he that shall consider the particular commonwealths that have been and are in the world will not perhaps easily reduce them to three, and may thereby be inclined to think there be other forms arising from these mingled together. As for example elective kingdoms, where kings have the sovereign power put into their hands for a time, or kingdoms wherein the king hath

---

1   Assuming that.
2   Lacks.

a power limited, which governments are nevertheless by most writers called monarchy. Likewise if a popular or aristocratical commonwealth subdue an enemy's country and govern the same by a president, procurator, or other magistrate, this may seem perhaps, at first sight, to be a democratical or aristocratical government. But it is not so. For elective kings are not sovereigns, but ministers of the sovereign;[1] nor limited kings sovereigns, but ministers of them that have the sovereign power; nor are those provinces which are in subjection to a democracy or aristocracy of another commonwealth democratically or aristocratically governed, but monarchically.[2]

11. And first, concerning an elective king whose power is limited to his life, as it is in many places of Christendom at this day, or to certain years or months, as the dictator's power amongst the Romans, if he have right to appoint his successor he is no more elective but hereditary. But if he have no power to elect his successor, then there is some other man or assembly known, which after his decease may elect a new; or else the commonwealth dieth and dissolveth with him, and returneth to the condition of war. If it be known who have the power to give the sovereignty after his death, it is known also that the sovereignty was in them before; for none have right to give that which they have not right to possess, and keep to themselves, if they think good. But if there be none that can give the sovereignty after the decease of him that was first elected, then has he power, nay he is obliged by the law of nature, to provide, by establishing his successor, to keep to those that had trusted him with the government from relapsing into the miserable condition of civil war. And consequently he was, when elected, a sovereign absolute.

12. Secondly, that king whose power is limited is not superior to him or them that have the power to limit it;

---

1 Cf. 23.2.
2 A government may appear to be of one form but really be of another. Constitutional monarchies, such as the United Kingdom and Canada, are not monarchies at all, but representative democracies. When a province, such as first-century Palestine, is ruled by a foreign conqueror, such as Rome, the form of government is monarchy. The sovereign of Palestine is "the people of Rome," considered as a monarch. See also 19.13.

and he that is not superior is not supreme, that is to say, not sovereign. The sovereignty therefore was always in that assembly which had the right to limit him, and by consequence the government [was] not monarchy, but either democracy or aristocracy, as of old time in Sparta, where the kings had a privilege to lead their armies, but the sovereignty was in the Ephori.[1]

13. Thirdly, whereas heretofore the Roman people governed the land of Judea, for example, by a president; yet was not Judea therefore a democracy, because they were not governed by any assembly into which any of them had right to enter, nor by an aristocracy, because they were not governed by any assembly into which any man could enter by their election; but they were governed by one person, which though as to the people of Rome was an assembly of the people, or democracy; yet as to the people of Judea, which had no right at all of participating in the government, was a monarch. For though where the people are governed by an assembly chosen by themselves out of their own number, the government is called a democracy or aristocracy; yet when they are governed by an assembly not of their own choosing, it is a monarchy, not of one man over another man, but of one people over another people.

Of the right of succession.

14. Of all these forms of government, the matter being mortal, so that not only monarchs but also whole assemblies die, it is necessary for the conservation of the peace of men that as there was order taken for an artificial man, so there be order also taken for an artificial eternity of life, without which men that are governed by an assembly should return into the condition of war in every age, and they that are governed by one man as soon as their governor dieth. This artificial eternity is that which men call the right of *succession*.

15. There is no perfect form of government, where the disposing of the succession is not in the present sovereign. For if it be in any other particular man or private assembly, it is in a person subject, and may be assumed by the sovereign at his pleasure; and consequently the

---

1 The Ephori were five senior government officials, elected annually, who, among other things, supervised the two kings of Sparta. *Ephori* in Greek means "overseers."

right is in himself. And if it be in no particular man, but left to a new choice, then is the commonwealth dissolved, and the right is in him that can get it, contrary to the intention of them that did institute the commonwealth for their perpetual, and not temporary, security.

16. In a democracy, the whole assembly cannot fail unless the multitude that are to be governed fail. And therefore questions of the right of succession have in that form of government no place at all.

17. In an aristocracy, when any of the assembly dieth, the election of another into his room belonged to the assembly, as the sovereign, to whom belonged the choosing of all counsellors and officers. For that which the representative doth as actor, every one of the subjects doth as author.[1] And though the sovereign assembly may give power to others to elect new men for supply of their court; yet it is still by their authority that the election is made; and by the same it may (when the public shall require it) be recalled.

18. The greatest difficulty about the right of succession is in monarchy; and the difficulty ariseth from this, that at first sight it is not manifest who is to appoint the successor nor many times who it is whom he hath appointed. For in both these cases there is required a more exact ratiocination than every man is accustomed to use. As to the question who shall appoint the successor of a monarch that hath the sovereign authority, that is to say, who shall determine of the right of inheritance (for elective kings and princes have not the sovereign power in propriety, but in use only),[2] we are to consider that either he that is in possession has right to dispose of the succession or else that right is again in the dissolved multitude. For the death of him that hath the sovereign power in propriety leaves the multitude without any sovereign at all, that is, without any representative in whom they should be united and be capable of doing any one action at all.[3] And therefore they are incapable of election of any new monarch, every man having equal right to submit himself to such as he thinks best able to protect him, or,

[100] The present monarch hath right to dispose of the succession.

---

1 Cf. 16.14, 18.1, 18.3, and 18.6.
2 See 19.10-12.
3 Cf. 16.13.

if he can, protect himself by his own sword, which is a return to confusion and to the condition of a war of every man against every man, contrary to the end for which monarchy had its first institution. Therefore it is manifest that by the institution of monarchy the disposing of the successor is always left to the judgement and will of the present possessor.

19. And for the question (which may arise sometimes), *who it is that the monarch in possession hath designed to the succession and inheritance of his power*, it is determined by his express words and testament, or by other tacit signs sufficient.[1]

Succession passeth by express words.

20. By express words or testament, when it is declared by him in his lifetime, *viva voce*, or by writing, as the first emperors of Rome declared who should be their heirs. For the word *heir* does not of itself imply the children or nearest kindred of a man, but whomsoever a man shall any way declare he would have to succeed him in his estate. If therefore a monarch declare expressly that such a man shall be his heir, either by word or writing, then is that man immediately after the decease of his predecessor invested in the right of being monarch.

Or, by not controlling a custom.

21. But where testament and express words are wanting, other natural signs of the will are to be followed, whereof the one is custom. And therefore where the custom is that the next of kindred absolutely succeedeth, there also the next of kindred hath right to the succession; for that, if the will of him that was in possession had been otherwise, he might easily have declared the same in his lifetime. And likewise where the custom is that the next of the male kindred succeedeth, there also the right of succession is in the next of the kindred male, for the same reason. And so it is if the custom were to advance the female. For whatsoever custom a man may by a word control and does not, it is a natural sign he would have that custom stand.

Or, by presumption of natural affection. [101]

22. But where neither custom nor testament hath preceded, there it is to be understood: first, that a monarch's will is that the government remain monarchical, because he hath approved that government in himself. Secondly, that a child of his own, male or female, be preferred before

---

1 See 19.19.

any other, because men are presumed to be more inclined by nature to advance their own children than the children of other men; and of their own, rather a male than a female, because men are naturally fitter than women for actions of labour and danger. Thirdly, where his own issue faileth, rather a brother than a stranger, and so still the nearer in blood rather than the more remote, because it is always presumed that the nearer of kin is the nearer in affection, and it is evident that a man receives always, by reflection, the most honour from the greatness of his nearest kindred.

23. But if it be lawful for a monarch to dispose of the succession by words of contract or testament, men may perhaps object a great inconvenience; for he may sell or give his right of governing to a stranger, which, because strangers (that is, men not used to live under the same government, nor speaking the same language) do commonly undervalue one another, may turn to the oppression of his subjects, which is indeed a great inconvenience; but it [the oppression] proceedeth not necessarily from the subjection to a stranger's government, but from the unskillfulness of the governors ignorant of the true rules of politics. And therefore the Romans, when they had subdued many nations, to make their government digestible were wont to take away that grievance as much as they thought necessary by giving sometimes to whole nations, and sometimes to principal men of every nation they conquered, not only the privileges but also the name of Romans, and took many of them into the Senate and offices of charge, even in the Roman city. And this was it our most wise king, King James, aimed at in endeavouring the union of his two realms of England and Scotland.[1] Which, if he could have obtained, had in all likelihood prevented the civil wars which make both those kingdoms, at this present, miserable. It is not therefore any injury to the people for a monarch to dispose of the succession by will, though by the fault of many princes it hath been sometimes found inconvenient. Of the lawfulness of it, this also is an argument: that whatsoever inconvenience

To dispose of the succession, though to a king of another nation, not unlawful.

---

1   James I and VI was separately king of Scotland (hence I) and king of England and Wales (VI). His attempt to unite the two realms failed, and union was achieved only in 1707 by the Act of Union.

can arrive by giving a kingdom to a stranger may arrive also by so marrying with strangers, as the right of succession may descend upon them; yet this by all men is accounted lawful.

Chapter XX

Of Dominion Paternal and Despotical

A commonwealth by acquisition.

1. A commonwealth *by acquisition* is that where the sovereign power is acquired by force; and it is acquired by force when men singly, or many together by plurality of voices, for fear of death or bonds, do authorize all the actions of that man or assembly that hath their lives and liberty in his power.

[102]

Wherein different from a commonwealth by institution.

2. And this kind of dominion or sovereignty differeth from sovereignty by institution only in this, that men who choose their sovereign do it for fear of one another and not of him whom they institute; but in this case, they subject themselves to him they are afraid of. In both cases they do it for fear; which is to be noted by them that hold all such covenants, as proceed from fear of death or violence, void; which, if it were true, no man in any kind of commonwealth could be obliged to obedience.[1] It is true that in a commonwealth once instituted or acquired, promises proceeding from fear of death or violence are no covenants nor obliging when the thing promised is contrary to the laws; but the reason is not because it was made upon fear, but because he that promiseth hath no right in the thing promised. Also, when he may lawfully perform and doth not, it is not the invalidity of the covenant that absolveth him, but the sentence of the sovereign. Otherwise, whensoever a man lawfully promiseth, he unlawfully breaketh; but when the sovereign, who is the actor, acquitteth him, then he is acquitted by him that extorted the promise, as by the author of such absolution.[2]

The rights of sovereignty the same in both.

3. But the rights and consequences of sovereignty are the same in both. His power cannot without his consent be transferred to another; he cannot forfeit it; he cannot be

---

1 Cf. 13.14, 14.27.
2 Cf. 16.14.

accused by any of his subjects of injury; he cannot be punished by them; he is judge of what is necessary for peace and judge of doctrines; he is sole legislator and supreme judge of controversies and of the times and occasions of war and peace; to him it belongeth to choose magistrates, counselors, commanders, and all other officers and ministers, and to determine of rewards and punishments, honour and order. The reasons whereof are the same which are alleged in the precedent chapter for the same rights and consequences of sovereignty by institution.

4. Dominion is acquired two ways, by generation and by conquest. The right of dominion by generation is that which the parent hath over his children and is called PATERNAL. And is not so derived from the generation, as if therefore the parent had dominion over his child because he begat him, but from the child's consent, either express or by other sufficient arguments declared. For as to the generation, God hath ordained to man a helper, and there be always two that are equally parents; the dominion therefore over the child should belong equally to both and he be equally subject to both, which is impossible; for no man can obey two masters. And whereas some have attributed the dominion to the man only, as being of the more excellent sex, they misreckon in it. For there is not always that difference of strength or prudence between the man and the woman as that the right can be determined without war. In commonwealths this controversy is decided by the civil law; and for the most part (but not always) the sentence is in favour of the father,[1] because for the most part commonwealths have been erected by the fathers, not by the mothers of families. But the question lieth now in the state of mere nature where there are supposed no laws of matrimony, no laws for the education of children but the law of nature and the natural inclination of the sexes, one to another, and to their children. In this condition of mere nature either the parents between themselves dispose of the dominion over the child by contract or do not dispose thereof at all. If they dispose thereof, the right passeth according to the contract. We find in history that the Amazons contracted with the men of the neighbouring countries, to whom

Dominion paternal how attained. Not by generation, but by contract;

[103]

---

1 See also 22.26.

they had recourse for issue, that the issue male should be sent back, but the female remain with themselves; so that the dominion of the females was in the mother.

Or education;   5. If there be no contract, the dominion is in the mother. For in the condition of mere nature, where there are no matrimonial laws, it cannot be known who is the father unless it be declared by the mother; and therefore the right of dominion over the child dependeth on her will, and is consequently hers.[1] Again, seeing the infant is first in the power of the mother, so as she may either nourish or expose it, if she nourish it, it oweth its life to the mother, and is therefore obliged to obey her rather than any other; and by consequence the dominion over it is hers. But if she expose it, and another find and nourish it, dominion is in him that nourisheth it. For it ought to obey him by whom it is preserved, because preservation of life being the end for which one man becomes subject to another, every man is supposed to promise obedience to him in whose power it is to save or destroy him.

Or precedent subjection of one of the parents to the other.   6. If the mother be the father's subject, the child is in the father's power; and if the father be the mother's subject (as when a sovereign queen marrieth one of her subjects), the child is subject to the mother, because the father also is her subject.

7. If a man and a woman, monarchs of two several kingdoms, have a child, and contract concerning who shall have the dominion of him, the right of the dominion passeth by the contract. If they contract not, the dominion followeth the dominion of the place of his residence. For the sovereign of each country hath dominion over all that reside therein.

8. He that hath the dominion over the child hath dominion also over the children of the child, and over their children's children. For he that hath dominion over the person of a man hath dominion over all that is his, without which dominion were but a title without the effect.[2]

The right of succession followeth the rules of the right of possession.   9. The right of succession to paternal dominion proceedeth in the same manner as doth the right of succession to monarchy, of which I have already sufficiently spoken in the precedent chapter.

---

1 Cf. 19.18, 19.21.
2 See also 24.7.

10. Dominion acquired by conquest or victory in war is that which some writers call DESPOTICAL from [Greek] *Despotēs*, which signifieth a *lord* or *master* and is the dominion of the master over his servant. And this dominion is then acquired to the victor when the vanquished, to avoid the present stroke of death, covenanteth either in express words or by other sufficient signs of the will that so long as his life and the liberty of his body is allowed him, the victor shall have the use thereof at his pleasure. And after such covenant[1] made, the vanquished is a SERVANT, and not before; for by the word *servant* (whether it be derived from *servire*, to serve, or from *servare*, to save, which I leave to grammarians to dispute) is not meant a captive, which is kept in prison or bonds, till the owner of him that took him or bought him of one that did, shall consider what to do with him; for such men, commonly called slaves, have no obligation at all, but may break their bonds or the prison and kill or carry away captive their master, justly; but one that, being taken, hath corporal liberty allowed him, and upon promise not to run away nor to do violence to his master, is trusted by him.

Despotical dominion how attained.

[104]

11. It is not therefore the victory that giveth the right of dominion over the vanquished, but his own covenant. Nor is he obliged because he is conquered, that is to say, beaten and taken or put to flight, but because he cometh in and submitteth to the victor; nor is the victor obliged by an enemy's rendering himself, without promise of life, to spare him for this his yielding to discretion, which obliges not the victor longer than in his own discretion he shall think fit.

Not by the victory, but by the consent of the vanquished.

12. And that which men do when they demand, as it is now called, *quarter* (which the Greeks called *Zōgria*, *taking alive*) is to evade the present fury of the victor by submission and to compound for their life with ransom or service; and therefore he that hath quarter hath not his life given, but deferred till further deliberation; for it is not a yielding on condition of life, but to discretion. And then only is his life in security, and his service due, when the victor hath trusted him with his corporal liberty. For slaves that work in prisons or fetters do it not of duty, but to avoid the cruelty of their task-masters.

---

1 Cf. 18.4.

13. The master of the servant is master also of all he hath and may exact the use thereof; that is to say, of his goods, of his labour, of his servants, and of his children, as often as he shall think fit. For he holdeth his life of his master by the covenant of obedience, that is, of owning and authorizing whatsoever the master shall do. And in case the master, if he refuse, kill him or cast him into bonds, or otherwise punish him for his disobedience, he is himself the author of the same and cannot accuse him of injury.[1]

14. In sum, the rights and consequences of both *paternal* and *despotical* dominion are the very same with those of a sovereign by institution, and for the same reasons, which reasons are set down in the precedent chapter. So that for a man that is monarch of divers nations, he hath in one the sovereignty by institution of the people assembled, and in another by conquest, that is, by the submission of each particular to avoid death or bonds, to demand of one nation more than of the other, from the title of conquest, as being a conquered nation, is an act of [105] ignorance of the rights of sovereignty. For the sovereign is absolute over both alike or else there is no sovereignty at all; and so [in the latter case] every man may lawfully protect himself, if he can, with his own sword, which is the condition of war.

Difference between a family and a kingdom.
15. By this it appears that a great family, if it be not part of some commonwealth, is of itself, as to the rights of sovereignty, a little monarchy, whether that family consist of a man and his children, or of a man and his servants, or of a man and his children and servants together, wherein the father or master is the sovereign. But yet a family is not properly a commonwealth unless it be of that power by its own number or by other opportunities,[2] as not to be subdued without the hazard of war. For where a number of men are manifestly too weak to defend themselves united, every one may use his own reason in time of danger to save his own life either by flight or by submission to the enemy, as he shall think best; in the same manner as a very small company of soldiers, surprised by an army, may cast down their arms and demand quarter

---

1 See 18.3.
2 See also 17.2.

or run away rather than be put to the sword. And thus much shall suffice concerning what I find by speculation and deduction of sovereign rights, from the nature, need, and designs of men in erecting of commonwealths and putting themselves under monarchs or assemblies entrusted with power enough for their protection.

16. Let us now consider what the Scripture teacheth in the same point. To Moses the children of Israel say thus: *Speak thou to us, and we will hear thee; but let not God speak to us, lest we die.* This is absolute obedience to Moses. Concerning the right of kings, God himself, by the mouth of Samuel, saith, *This shall be the right of the king you will have to reign over you. He shall take your sons, and set them to drive his chariots and to be his horsemen, and to run before his chariots, and gather in his harvest, and to make his engines of war, and instruments of his chariots; and [he] shall take your daughters to make perfumes, to be his cooks, and bakers. He shall take your fields, your vineyards, and your olive-yards, and give them to his servants. He shall take the tithe of your corn and wine, and give it to the men of his chamber, and to his other servants. He shall take your man-servants, and your maidservants, and the choice of your youth, and employ them in his business. He shall take the tithe of your flocks; and you shall be his servants.* This is absolute power, and summed up in the last words, *you shall be his servants.*[1] Again, when the people heard what power their king was to have; yet they consented thereto, and say thus: *We will be as all other nations, and our king shall judge our causes, and go before us, to conduct our wars.* Here is confirmed the right that sovereigns have, both to the *militia* and to all *judicature*, in which is contained as absolute power as one man can possibly transfer to another. Again, the prayer of King Solomon to God was this: *Give to thy servant understanding, to judge thy people, and to discern between good and evil.* It belonged therefore to the sovereign to be *judge* and to prescribe the rules of *discerning good and evil,* which rules are laws;[2] and therefore in him is the legislative power. Saul sought the life of David; yet when it was in his power to slay Saul, and his servants would have done it, David

The rights of monarchy from Scripture. Exod. 20:19.

1 Sam. 8:11-17.

1 Sam. 8:19-20.

1 Kings 3:9.

[106]

---

1   It is ironic that Hobbes uses this passage to support absolute sovereignty since the passage clearly is warning the Israelites against establishing a monarchy.

2   See also 18.10, 29.6, 46.11, and 46.32.

forbade them, saying, *God forbid I should do such an act against my Lord, the anointed of God.* For obedience of servants St. Paul saith, *Servants obey your masters in all things*; and *Children obey your parents in all things.* There is simple obedience in those that are subject to paternal or despotical dominion. Again, *The scribes and Pharisees sit in Moses' chair, and therefore all that they shall bid you observe, that observe and do.* There again is simple obedience. And St. Paul, *Warn them that they subject themselves to princes, and to those that are in authority, and obey them.* This obedience is also simple. Lastly, our Saviour himself acknowledges that men ought to pay such taxes as are by kings imposed where he says, *Give to Caesar that which is Caesar's* and paid such taxes himself. And [our Saviour acknowledges] that the king's word is sufficient to take anything from any subject, when there is need; and that the king is judge of that need; for he himself, as king of the Jews,[1] commanded his Disciples to take the ass and ass's colt to carry him into Jerusalem, saying, *Go into the village over against you, and you shall find a she ass tied, and her colt with her; untie them, and bring them to me. And if any man ask you, what you mean by it, say the Lord hath need of them; and they will let them go.* They will not ask whether his necessity be a sufficient title nor whether he be judge of that necessity, but acquiesce in the will of the Lord.

17. To these places may be added also that of Genesis, *You shall be as gods, knowing good and evil.* And, *Who told thee that thou wast naked? Hast thou eaten of the tree, of which I commanded thee thou shouldest not eat?* [Gen. 3:11]. For the cognizance or judicature of good and evil being forbidden by the name of the fruit of the tree of knowledge, as a trial of Adam's obedience, the devil [in order] to inflame the ambition of the woman, to whom that fruit already seemed beautiful, told her that by tasting it they should be as gods, knowing good and evil.[2] Whereupon having both eaten, they did indeed take upon them God's office, which is judicature of good and evil, but acquired no new ability to distinguish between them aright. And whereas it is said that having eaten, they saw they were naked, no man hath so interpreted that place as if they

1 Sam. 24:9.

Col. 3:20.
Col. 3:22.

Matt. 23:2-3.

Titus 3:2.

Matt. 21:2-3.

Gen. 3:5.

---

1 Usually Hobbes claims that Jesus was not a king; cf. 42.3-4.
2 See also 15.40, 35.3, 38.2, and 44.14.

had been formerly blind and saw not their own skins; the meaning is plain that it was then they first judged their nakedness (wherein it was God's will to create them) to be uncomely, and by being ashamed did tacitly censure God himself. And thereupon God saith, *Hast thou eaten,* etc., as if he should say, doest thou that owest me obedience take upon thee to judge of my commandments? Whereby it is clearly, though allegorically, signified that the commands of them that have the right to command are not by their subjects to be censured nor disputed.

18. So that it appeareth plainly, to my understanding, both from reason and Scripture, that the sovereign power, whether placed in one man, as in monarchy, or in one assembly of men, as in popular and aristocratical commonwealths, is as great as possibly men can be imagined to make it. And though of so unlimited a power men may fancy many evil consequences; yet the consequences of the want of it, which is perpetual war of every man against his neighbour, are much worse.[1] The condition of man in this life shall never be without inconveniences; but there happeneth in no commonwealth any great inconvenience but what proceeds from the subjects' disobedience and breach of those covenants from which the commonwealth hath its being. And whosoever thinking sovereign power too great will seek to make it less must subject himself to the power that can limit it, that is to say, to a greater.

Sovereign power ought in all commonwealths to be absolute. [107]

19. The greatest objection is that of the practice when men ask where and when such power has by subjects been acknowledged. But one may ask them again, when or where has there been a kingdom long free from sedition and civil war? In those nations whose commonwealths have been long-lived and not been destroyed but by foreign war, the subjects never did dispute of the sovereign power. But howsoever, an argument from the practice of men that have not sifted to the bottom and with exact reason weighed the causes and nature of commonwealths, and suffer daily those miseries that proceed

---

1 King James I wrote, "For a king cannot be imagined to be so unruly and tyrannous, but the commonwealth will be kept in better order, notwithstanding thereof by him than it can be by his way-taking.... [I]t is better to live in a commonwealth where nothing is lawful, than [a commonwealth] where all things are lawful to all men" ("The Trew Law of Free Monarchies").

from the ignorance thereof, is invalid. For though in all places of the world men should lay the foundation of their houses on the sand, it could not thence be inferred that so it ought to be. The skill of making and maintaining commonwealths consisteth in certain rules, as doth arithmetic and geometry, not, as tennis play, on practice only; which rules neither poor men have the leisure, nor men that have had the leisure have hitherto had the curiosity or the method, to find out.

Chapter XXI

Of the Liberty of Subjects

Liberty, what. 1. LIBERTY or FREEDOM signifieth properly the absence of opposition (by opposition I mean external impediments of motion) and may be applied no less to irrational and inanimate creatures than to rational. For whatsoever is so tied or environed, as it cannot move but within a certain space, which space is determined by the opposition of some external body, we say it hath not liberty to go further. And so of all living creatures, whilst they are imprisoned or restrained with walls or chains, and of the water, whilst it is kept in by banks or vessels that otherwise would spread itself into a larger space, we use to say they are not at liberty to move in such manner as without those external impediments they would. But when the impediment of motion is in the constitution of the thing itself, we use not to say it wants the liberty, but the power, to move, as when a stone lieth still or a man is fastened to his bed by sickness.[1]

[108] What it is to be free. 2. And according to this proper and generally received meaning of the word, a FREEMAN *is he that, in those things which by his strength and wit he is able to do, is not hindered to do what he has a will to.* But when the words *free* and *liberty* are applied to anything but *bodies*, they are abused; for that which is not subject to motion is not subject to impediment; and therefore, when it is said, for example,

---

1 Liberty or freedom relates to the absence of *external* impediments to motion. Power relates to the *internal* constitution of a thing that makes it able to do things.

the way is free, no liberty of the way is signified, but of those that walk in it without stop. And when we say a gift is free, there is not meant any liberty of the gift, but of the giver that was not bound by any law or covenant to give it. So when we *speak freely*, it is not the liberty of voice or pronunciation, but of the man whom no law hath obliged to speak otherwise than he did. Lastly, from the use of the words *free will*, no liberty can be inferred of the will, desire, or inclination, but the liberty of the man, which consisteth in this, that he finds no stop in doing what he has the will, desire, or inclination to do.[1]

3. Fear and liberty are consistent, as when a man throweth his goods into the sea for *fear* the ship should sink, he doth it nevertheless very willingly,[2] and may refuse to do it if he will; it is therefore the action of one that was *free*; so a man sometimes pays his debt only for *fear* of imprisonment, which, because no body hindered him from detaining, was the action of a man at *liberty*. And generally all actions which men do in common-wealths for *fear* of the law are actions which the doers had *liberty* to omit.[3]

Fear and liberty consistent.

4. *Liberty* and *necessity* are consistent, as in the water that hath not only *liberty* but a *necessity* of descending by the channel; so likewise [liberty and necessity are consistent] in the actions which men voluntarily do, which (because they proceed from their will) proceed from *liberty*; and yet because every act of man's will and every desire and inclination proceedeth from some cause and that from another cause; which causes in a continual chain (whose first link [is] in the hand of God, the first of all causes) proceed from *necessity*.[4] So that to him that could see the connexion of those causes, the *necessity* of all men's voluntary actions would appear manifest. And therefore God, that seeth and disposeth all things, seeth

Liberty and necessity consistent.

---

1 The term "free will" is incoherent because freedom applies only to bodies. A will is the last desire a body has before it acts; that is, it is the desire that causes the motion (see 6.53).
2 Cf. Aristotle, *Nicomachean Ethics* 3.1.
3 Hobbes needs freedom to be consistent with fear, because fear motivates people to institute a sovereign. See 13.14, 14.27, and 20.2.
4 Liberty is absence of external impediments. Necessity is the result of a cause.

also that the *liberty* of man in doing what he will is accompanied with the *necessity* of doing that which God will and no more nor less. For though men may do many things which God does not command nor is therefore author of them;[1] yet they can have no passion nor appetite to anything of which appetite God's will is not the cause. And did not his will assure the *necessity* of man's will, and consequently of all that on man's will dependeth, the *liberty* of men would be a contradiction and impediment to the omnipotence and *liberty* of God. And this shall suffice, as to the matter in hand, of that natural *liberty*, which only is properly called *liberty*.

Artificial bonds, or covenants.

[109]

5. But as men, for the attaining of peace and conservation of themselves thereby, have made an artificial man, which we call a commonwealth, so also have they made artificial chains, called *civil laws*,[2] which they themselves by mutual covenants have fastened at one end to the lips of that man or assembly to whom they have given the sovereign power and at the other to their own ears. These bonds, in their own nature but weak, may nevertheless be made to hold by the danger, though not by the difficulty, of breaking them.

Liberty of subjects consisteth in liberty from covenants.

6. In relation to these bonds only it is that I am to speak now of the *liberty of subjects*. For seeing there is no commonwealth in the world wherein there be rules enough set down for the regulating of all the actions and words of men (as being a thing impossible); it followeth necessarily that in all kinds of actions by the laws pretermitted,[3] men have the liberty of doing what their own reasons shall suggest for the most profitable to themselves. For if we take liberty in the proper sense, for corporal liberty, that is to say, freedom from chains and prison, it were very absurd for men to clamour as they do for the liberty they so manifestly enjoy. Again, if we take liberty for an exemption from laws, it is no less absurd for men to demand

---

1 Hobbes agrees with Calvin that God is the cause of sin. Many of Hobbes's contemporaries did not like the fine line he drew between the fact that God is the cause of everything, but not the author of everything because he does not command people to sin.

2 See 26.3.

3 Liberty is what is left over after the sovereign has issued all of his laws or commands. See also 21.18.

as they do that liberty by which all other men may be masters of their lives. And yet as absurd as it is, this is it they demand, not knowing that the laws are of no power to protect them without a sword in the hands of a man or men to cause those laws to be put in execution. The liberty of a subject lieth therefore only in those things which, in regulating their actions, the sovereign hath pretermitted, such as is the liberty to buy, and sell, and otherwise contract with one another, to choose their own abode, their own diet, their own trade of life, and institute their children as they themselves think fit, and the like.

7. Nevertheless we are not to understand that by such liberty the sovereign power of life and death is either abolished or limited. For it has been already shown[1] that nothing the sovereign representative can do to a subject, on what pretence soever, can properly be called injustice or injury, because every subject is author of every act the sovereign doth, so that he [the sovereign] never wanteth right to any thing, otherwise than as he himself is the subject of God and bound thereby to observe the laws of nature.[2] And therefore it may and doth often happen in commonwealths that a subject may be put to death by the command of the sovereign power and yet neither do the other wrong, as when Jephthah caused his daughter to be sacrificed; in which, and the like cases, he that so dieth had liberty to do the action for which he is nevertheless, without injury, put to death.[3] And the same holdeth also in a sovereign prince that putteth to death an innocent subject. For though the action be against the law of nature, as being contrary to equity (as was the killing of Uriah by David); yet it was not an injury to Uriah, but to God.[4] Not to Uriah, because the right to do what he pleased was given him [David] by Uriah himself; and yet to God, because David was God's subject and prohibited all iniquity by the law of nature; which distinction David

Liberty of the subject consistent with the unlimited power of the sovereign.

---

1 See 18.6.
2 See also 22.7 and 29.9.
3 Hobbes's point has nothing to do with the actual moral of the story of Jephthah, namely that one should be careful about what one promises. See Judg. 11:29-40.
4 King David committed adultery with Bathsheba, the wife of his soldier Uriah. Afraid that Uriah would discover the fact, David sent Uriah into the front line of battle to be killed (2 Sam.11).

himself, when he repented the fact, evidently confirmed, saying, *To thee only have I sinned.* In the same manner the people of Athens, when they banished the most potent of their commonwealth for ten years, thought they committed no injustice; and yet they never questioned what crime he had done, but what hurt he would do; nay, they commanded the banishment of they knew not whom; and every citizen bringing his oyster shell into the market place, written with the name of him he desired should be banished, without at all accusing him, sometimes banished an Aristides, for his reputation of justice, and sometimes a scurrilous jester, as Hyperbolus, to make a jest of it. And yet a man cannot say the sovereign people of Athens wanted right to banish them, or an Athenian the liberty to jest, or to be just.

8. The liberty whereof there is so frequent and honourable mention in the histories and philosophy of the ancient Greeks and Romans and in the writings and discourse of those that from them have received all their learning in the politics is not the liberty of particular men, but the liberty of the commonwealth,[1] which [liberty] is the same with that which every man then should have if there were no civil laws nor commonwealth at all. And the effects of it also be the same. For as amongst masterless men there is perpetual war of every man against his neighbour, no inheritance to transmit to the son nor to expect from the father, no propriety of goods or lands, no security, but a full and absolute liberty in every particular man, so in states and commonwealths not dependent on one another every commonwealth (not every man) has an absolute liberty to do what it shall judge (that is to say, what that man or assembly that representeth it shall judge) most conducing to their benefit. But withal they live in the condition of a perpetual war and upon the confines of battle, with their frontiers armed and cannons planted against their neighbours round about. The Athenians and Romans were free, that is, free commonwealths; not that any particular men had the liberty to resist their own representative, but that their representative had the liberty to resist, or invade, other people. There is

The liberty which writers praise, is the liberty of sovereigns; not of private men.

---

1 Hobbes is criticizing the neo-Roman or republican theory of government in 21.8-15.

192 PART II: OF COMMONWEALTH

written on the turrets of the city of Luca in great characters at this day the word LIBERTAS; yet no man can thence infer that a particular man has more liberty or immunity from the service of the commonwealth there than in Constantinople. Whether a commonwealth be monarchical or popular, the freedom is still the same.

9. But it is an easy thing for men to be deceived by the specious name of liberty and (for want of judgement to distinguish) mistake that for their private inheritance and birthright which is the right of the public only. And when the same error is confirmed by the authority of men in reputation for their writings on this subject, it is no wonder if it produce sedition and change of government. In these western parts of the world, we are made to receive our opinions concerning the institution and rights of commonwealths from Aristotle, Cicero, and other men, Greeks and Romans,[1] that, living under popular [nonmonarchical] states, derived those rights not from the principles of nature, but transcribed them into their books out of the practice of their own commonwealths, which [111] were popular, as the grammarians describe the rules of language out of the practice of the time or the rules of poetry out of the poems of Homer and Virgil. And because the Athenians were taught (to keep them from desire of changing their government) that they were freemen, and all that lived under monarchy were slaves, therefore Aristotle puts it down in his *Politics, In democracy, LIBERTY is to be supposed; for it is commonly held that no man is FREE in any other government* (Bk. VI: Ch.2). And as Aristotle, so Cicero and other writers have grounded their civil doctrine on the opinions of the Romans, who were taught to hate monarchy, at first by them that, having deposed their sovereign, shared amongst them the sovereignty of Rome, and afterwards by their successors. And by reading of these Greek and Latin authors, men from their childhood have gotten a habit, under a false show of liberty, of favouring tumults, and of licentious [people] controlling the actions of their sovereigns, and again of controlling those controllers, with the effusion of so much blood as I think I may truly say there was never anything so dearly

---

1 See also 29.14.

bought as these western parts have bought the learning of the Greek and Latin tongues.

10. To come now to the particulars of the true liberty of a subject, that is to say, what are the things which, though commanded by the sovereign, he may nevertheless without injustice refuse to do, we are to consider what rights we pass away when we make a commonwealth, or, which is all one, what liberty we deny ourselves by owning all the actions, without exception, of the man or assembly we make our sovereign. For in the act of our *submission* consisteth both our *obligation* and our *liberty*, which must therefore be inferred by arguments taken from thence; there being no obligation on any man which ariseth not from some act of his own;[1] for all men equally are by nature free. And because such arguments must either be drawn from the express words, *I authorize all his actions*, or from the intention of him that submitteth himself to his power (which intention is to be understood by the end for which he so submitteth), the obligation and liberty of the subject is to be derived either from those words or others equivalent, or else from the end of the institution of sovereignty; namely, the peace of the subjects within themselves and their defence against a common enemy.[2]

11. First therefore, seeing sovereignty by institution is by covenant of every one to every one, and sovereignty by acquisition by covenants of the vanquished to the victor or child to the parent, it is manifest that every subject has liberty in all those things the right whereof cannot by covenant be transferred. I have shown before, in the fourteenth chapter, that covenants not to defend a man's own body are void. Therefore,

12. If the sovereign command a man, though justly condemned, to kill, wound, or maim himself, or not to resist those that assault him, or to abstain from the use of food, air, medicine, or any other thing without which he cannot live; yet hath that man the liberty to disobey.

---

1 See 21.5-6.
2 Hobbes is emphasizing his theory of authorization in this and the following paragraphs and suppressing his theory of alienation. See 17.13. He is claiming here that authorization preserves the complete liberty of a subject and that political obligation arises from the subject's intention in entering a civil state. See 21.15, 21.17, and 21.21.

13. If a man be interrogated by the sovereign or his authority, concerning a crime done by himself, [then] he is not bound (without assurance of pardon) to confess it, because no man, as I have shown in the same chapter,[1] can be obliged by covenant to accuse himself.

14. Again, the consent of a subject to sovereign power is contained in these words, *I authorize, or take upon me, all his actions*, in which there is no restriction at all of his own former natural liberty; for by allowing him to *kill me*, I am not bound to kill myself when he commands me.[2] It is one thing to say, *Kill me, or my fellow, if you please*, another thing to say, *I will kill myself, or my fellow*.[3] It followeth, therefore, that

15. No man is bound by the words themselves either to kill himself or any other man; and consequently, that the obligation a man may sometimes have, upon the command of the sovereign, to execute any dangerous or dishonourable office, dependeth not on the words of our submission, but on the intention, which is to be understood by the end thereof. When therefore our refusal to obey frustrates the end for which the sovereignty was ordained, then there is no liberty to refuse; otherwise, there is.[4]

16. Upon this ground a man that is commanded as a soldier to fight against the enemy, though his sovereign have right enough to punish his refusal with death, may nevertheless in many cases refuse without injustice, as when he substituteth a sufficient soldier in his place; for in this case he deserteth not the service of the commonwealth. And there is allowance to be made for natural timorousness, not only to women (of whom no such dangerous duty is expected) but also to men of feminine courage. When armies fight, there is on one side or both

Nor to warfare, unless they voluntarily undertake it.

---

1 See 14.30.
2 Authorization of the sovereign's actions does not impose an obligation on the subject to let the sovereign kill him. So if the sovereign tried to "command" a subject to kill himself, the subject would be under no obligation to do so.
3 The sentence "Kill me, or my fellow, if you please" imposes no obligation on me to kill myself or my fellow. The sentence "I will kill myself, or my fellow" would impose an obligation on me (in virtue of the future tense) if it were possible for a person to lay down his right to self-preservation. But it is not.
4 See 21.10 and 21.17.

a running away; yet when they do it not out of treachery, but fear, they are not esteemed to do it unjustly, but dishonourably. For the same reason to avoid battle is not injustice but cowardice. But he that enrolleth himself a soldier, or taketh impressed money, taketh away the excuse of a timorous nature and is obliged, not only to go to the battle, but also not to run from it without his captain's leave. And when the defence of the commonwealth requireth at once the help of all that are able to bear arms, every one is obliged, because otherwise the institution of the commonwealth, which they have not the purpose or courage to preserve, was in vain.

17. To resist the sword of the commonwealth in defence of another man, guilty or innocent, no man hath liberty, because such liberty takes away from the sovereign the means of protecting us and is therefore destructive of the very essence of government. But in case a great many men together have already resisted the sovereign power unjustly or committed some capital crime for which every one of them expecteth death, whether have they [the guilty] not the liberty then to join together, and assist, and defend one another? Certainly they have; for they [113] but defend their lives, which the guilty man may as well do as the innocent. There was indeed injustice in the first breach of their duty; their bearing of arms subsequent to it, though it be to maintain what they have done, is no new unjust act. And if it be only to defend their persons, it is not unjust at all. But the offer of pardon taketh from them to whom it is offered the plea of self-defence, and maketh their perseverance in assisting or defending the rest unlawful.

The greatest
liberty of sub-
jects, dependeth
on the silence of
the law.
18. As for other liberties, they depend on the silence of the law. In cases where the sovereign has prescribed no rule, there the subject hath the liberty to do or forbear, according to his own discretion. And therefore such liberty is in some places more and in some less, and in some times more, in other times less, according as they that have the sovereignty shall think most convenient. As for example, there was a time when in England a man might enter into his own land (and dispossess such as wrongfully possessed it) by force. But in after times that liberty of forcible entry was taken away by a statute made (by the king) in parliament. And in some places of the world

men have the liberty of many wives; in other places, such liberty is not allowed.

19. If a subject have a controversy with his sovereign of debt, or of right of possession of lands or goods, or concerning any service required at his hands, or concerning any penalty, corporal or pecuniary, grounded on a precedent law, he hath the same liberty to sue for his right as if it were against a subject, and before such judges as are appointed by the sovereign. For seeing the sovereign demandeth by force of a former law and not by virtue of his power, he declareth thereby that he requireth no more than shall appear to be due by that law. The suit therefore is not contrary to the will of the sovereign, and consequently the subject hath the liberty to demand the hearing of his cause, and sentence according to that law. But if he demand or take anything by pretence of his power, there lieth, in that case, no action of law; for all that is done by him in virtue of his power is done by the authority of every subject, and consequently, he that brings an action against the sovereign brings it against himself.

20. If a monarch or sovereign assembly grant a liberty to all or any of his subjects, which grant standing, he is disabled to provide for their safety, [then] the grant is void, unless he directly renounce or transfer the sovereignty to another. For in that he might openly (if it had been his will) and in plain terms have renounced or transferred it and did not, it is to be understood it was not his will, but that the grant proceeded from ignorance of the repugnancy between such a liberty and the sovereign power;[1] and therefore the sovereignty is still retained, and consequently all those powers which are necessary to the exercising thereof, such as are the power of war and peace, of judicature, of appointing officers and counsellors, of levying money, and the rest named in the eighteenth chapter.

21. The obligation of subjects to the sovereign is understood to last as long [as] and no longer than the power lasteth by which he is able to protect them. For the right men have by nature to protect themselves, when none else can protect them, can by no covenant be relinquished.[2] The sovereignty is the soul of the commonwealth, which,

[114] In what cases subjects are absolved of their obedience to their sovereign.

---

1 See 18.7.
2 See also "Review and Conclusion," 7.

once departed from the body, the members do no more receive their motion from it. The end of obedience is protection, which, wheresoever a man seeth it either in his own or in another's sword, nature applieth his obedience to it and his endeavour to maintain it. And though sovereignty, in the intention of them that make it, be immortal; yet is it in its own nature not only subject to violent death by foreign war, but also through the ignorance and passions of men, it hath in it from the very institution many seeds of a natural mortality, by intestine discord.

In case of captivity.

22. If a subject be taken prisoner in war or his person or his means of life be within the guards of the enemy, and hath his life and corporal liberty given him on condition to be subject to the victor, [then] he hath liberty to accept the condition; and, having accepted it, is the subject of him that took him, because he had no other way to preserve himself. The case is the same if he be detained on the same terms in a foreign country. But if a man be held in prison or bonds or is not trusted with the liberty of his body, he cannot be understood to be bound by covenant to subjection, and therefore may, if he can, make his escape by any means whatsoever.[1]

In case the sovereign cast off the government from himself and his heirs.

23. If a monarch shall relinquish the sovereignty, both for himself and his heirs, his subjects return to the absolute liberty of nature, because, though nature may declare who are his sons and who are the nearest of his kin; yet it dependeth on his own will, as hath been said in the precedent chapter,[2] who shall be his heir. If therefore he will have no heir, there is no sovereignty, nor subjection. The case is the same if he die without known kindred and without declaration of his heir. For then there can no heir be known, and consequently no subjection be due.

In case of banishment.

24. If the sovereign banish his subject, [then] during the banishment he is not subject. But he that is sent on a message or hath leave to travel is still subject, but it is by contract between sovereigns, not by virtue of the covenant of subjection. For whosoever entereth into another's dominion is subject to all the laws thereof, unless he have a privilege by the amity of the sovereigns or by special license.

---

1 See 20.10.
2 See 19.18-22.

25. If a monarch subdued by war render himself subject to the victor, his subjects are delivered from their former obligation and become obliged to the victor. But if he be held prisoner or have not the liberty of his own body, he is not understood to have given away the right of sovereignty; and therefore his subjects are obliged to yield obedience to the magistrates formerly placed, governing not in their own name, but in his. For, his right remaining, the question is only of the administration, that is to say, of the magistrates and officers, which if he have not means to name, he is supposed to approve those which he himself had formerly appointed.

In case the sovereign render himself subject to another.

[115]

Chapter XXII

Of Systems Subject, Political and Private

1. Having spoken of the generation, form, and power of a commonwealth, I am in order to speak next of the parts thereof. And first of systems, which resemble the similar parts or muscles of a body natural. By SYSTEMS I understand any numbers of men joined in one interest or one business. Of which some are *regular* and some *irregular*. *Regular* are those where one man or assembly of men is constituted representative of the whole number. All other are *irregular*.

The divers sorts of systems of people

2. Of regular, some are *absolute* and *independent*, subject to none but their own representative; such are only commonwealths, of which I have spoken already in the five last precedent chapters. Others are *dependent*, that is to say, subordinate to some sovereign power, to which every one, as also their representative, is *subject*.

3. Of systems subordinate, some are *political* and some *private*. *Political* (otherwise called *bodies politic* and *persons in law*) are those which are made by authority from the sovereign power of the commonwealth. *Private* are those which are constituted by subjects amongst themselves or by authority from a stranger. For no authority derived from foreign power, within the dominion of another, is public there, but private.

4. And of private systems, some are *lawful*, some *unlawful*; *lawful* are those which are allowed by the

commonwealth; all other are *unlawful*. *Irregular* systems are those which, having no representative, consist only in concourse of people, which if not forbidden by the commonwealth nor made on evil design (such as are conflux of people to markets, or shows, or any other harmless end) are lawful. But when the intention is evil or (if the number be considerable) unknown, they are unlawful.

In all bodies politic the power of the representative is limited.

5. In bodies politic, the power of the representative is always limited; and that which prescribeth the limits thereof is the power sovereign. For power unlimited is absolute sovereignty. And the sovereign in every commonwealth is the absolute representative of all the subjects; and therefore no other can be representative of any part of them but so far forth as he shall give leave; and to give leave to a body politic of subjects to have an absolute representative, to all intents and purposes were to abandon the government of so much of the commonwealth, and to divide the dominion, contrary to their peace and defence, which the sovereign cannot be understood to do by any grant that does not plainly and directly discharge them of their subjection.[1] For consequences of words are not the signs of his will, when other consequences are signs of the contrary, but rather signs of error and misreckoning to which all mankind is too prone.

[116]

6. The bounds of that power which is given to the representative of a body politic are to be taken notice of from two things. One is their writ or letters from the sovereign; the other is the law of the commonwealth.

By letters patents.

7. For though in the institution or acquisition of a commonwealth, which is independent, there needs no writing, because the power of the representative has there no other bounds but such as are set out by the unwritten law of nature;[2] yet in subordinate bodies there are such diversities of limitation necessary concerning their businesses, times, and places, as can neither be remembered without letters nor taken notice of unless such letters be patent, that they may be read to them, and withal sealed or testified with the seals or other permanent signs of the authority sovereign.

And the laws.

8. And because such limitation is not always easy or perhaps possible to be described in writing, the ordinary

---

1 Cf. 21.20.
2 See also 21.7 and 29.9.

laws common to all subjects must determine what the representative may lawfully do in all cases where the letters themselves are silent. And therefore

9. In a body politic, if the representative be one man, whatsoever he does in the person of the body which is not warranted in his letters nor by the laws is his own act and not the act of the body, nor of any other member thereof besides himself; because further than his letters or the laws limit, he representeth no man's person but his own. But what he does according to these is the act of every one; for of the act of the sovereign every one is author, because he is their representative unlimited; and the act of him that recedes not from the letters of the sovereign is the act of the sovereign, and therefore every member of the body is author of it.

When the representative is one man, his unwarranted acts are his own only.

10. But if the representative be an assembly, whatsoever that assembly shall decree, not warranted by their letters or the laws, is the act of the assembly or body politic; and [it is] the act of every one by whose vote the decree was made, but not the act of any man that being present voted to the contrary, nor of any man absent, unless he voted it by procuration [proxy]. It is the act of the assembly because voted by the major part; and if it be a crime, [then] the assembly may be punished as far forth as it is capable, as by dissolution or forfeiture of their letters (which is to such artificial and fictitious bodies, capital); or, if the assembly have a common stock wherein none of the innocent members have propriety, [then they may be punished] by pecuniary mulct [fine]. For from corporal penalties nature hath exempted all bodies politic. But they that gave not their vote are therefore innocent, because the assembly cannot represent any man in things unwarranted by their letters, and consequently are not involved in their votes.

When it is an assembly, it is the act of them that assented only.

11. If the person of the body politic, being in one man, borrow money of a stranger, that is, of one that is not of the same body (for no letters need limit borrowing, seeing it is left to men's own inclinations to limit lending), the debt is the representative's. For if he should have authority from his letters to make the members pay what he borroweth, he should have by consequence the sovereignty of them; and therefore the grant [of authority][1]

When the representative is one man, if he borrow money, or owe it, by contract, he is liable only, the members not.

[117]

---

1 See 22.5.

were either void, as proceeding from error, commonly incident to human nature, and an insufficient sign of the will of the granter; or if it be avowed by him, then is the representer sovereign, and falleth not under the present question, which is only of bodies subordinate. No member therefore is obliged to pay the debt so borrowed but the representative himself, because he that lendeth it, being a stranger to the letters and to the qualification of the body, understandeth those only for his debtors that are engaged; and seeing the representer can engage himself, and none else, has him only for debtor, who must therefore pay him out of the common stock, if there be any, or, if there be none, out of his own estate.

12. If he come into debt by contract or mulct, the case is the same.

When it is an assembly, they only are liable that have assented.

13. But when the representative is an assembly and the debt to a stranger, all they, and only they, are responsible for the debt that gave their votes to the borrowing of it or to the contract that made it due or to the fact for which the mulct was imposed, because every one of those in voting did engage himself for the payment; for he that is author of the borrowing is obliged to the payment, even of the whole debt, though when paid by any one, he be discharged.

If the debt be to one of the assembly, the body only is obliged.

14. But if the debt be [owed] to one of the assembly, the assembly only is obliged to the payment out of their common stock (if they have any); for having liberty of vote, if he [the lender] vote [that] the money shall be borrowed, [then] he votes it shall be paid; if he vote it shall not be borrowed or [he] be absent [when the vote was made]; yet because in lending he voteth the borrowing, he contradicteth his former vote and is obliged by the latter, and becomes both borrower and lender, and consequently cannot demand payment from any particular man, but from the common treasury only; which failing, he hath no remedy nor complaint but against himself, that being privy to the acts of the assembly, and to their means to pay, and not being enforced, did nevertheless through his own folly lend his money.

Protestation against the decrees of bodies politic

15. It is manifest by this that in bodies politic subordinate and subject to a sovereign power, it is sometimes not only lawful but expedient for a particular man to make open protestation against the decrees of the representative

assembly and cause their dissent to be registered, or to take witness of it, because otherwise they may be obliged to pay debts contracted and be responsible for crimes committed by other men. But in a sovereign assembly that liberty is taken away, both because he that protesteth there denies their sovereignty and also because whatsoever is commanded by the sovereign power is as to the subject (though not so always in the sight of God) justified by the command; for of such command every subject is the author.

sometimes lawful, but against sovereign power never.

16. The variety of bodies politic is almost infinite; for they are not only distinguished by the several affairs for which they are constituted, wherein there is an unspeakable diversity, but also by the times, places, and numbers, subject to many limitations. And as to their affairs, some are ordained for government; as first, the government of a province may be committed to an assembly of men, wherein all resolutions shall depend on the votes of the major part; and then this assembly is a body politic, and their power limited by commission. This word *province* signifies a charge or care of business, which he whose it is committeth to another man to be administered for and under him; and therefore when in one commonwealth there be divers countries that have their laws distinct one from another or are far distant in place, the administration of the government being committed to divers persons, those countries where the sovereign is not resident, but governs by commission, are called provinces. But of the government of a province by an assembly residing in the province itself there be few examples. The Romans, who had the sovereignty of many provinces; yet governed them always by presidents and praetors and not by assemblies, as they governed the city of Rome and territories adjacent.[1] In like manner, when there were colonies sent from England to plant Virginia,[2] and Sommer-islands [the Bermudas], though the government of them here were committed to assemblies in London; yet did those assemblies never commit [entrust] the government under them to any assembly there, but did

Bodies politic for government of a province, colony, or town. [118]

---

1 Cf. 19.13.
2 Hobbes had owned one share of stock in the Virginia Company, a gift from his employer, the earl of Devonshire.

to each plantation send one governor; for though every man, where he can be present by nature, desires to participate of government; yet where they cannot be present, they are by nature also inclined to commit the government of their common interest rather to a monarchical, than a popular, form of government; which is also evident in those men that have great private estates, who, when they are unwilling to take the pains of administering the business that belongs to them, choose rather to trust one servant than an assembly either of their friends or servants. But howsoever it be in fact; yet we may suppose the government of a province or colony committed to an assembly; and when it is, that which in this place I have to say is this: that whatsoever debt is by that assembly contracted, or whatsoever unlawful act is decreed, is the act only of those that assented, and not of any that dissented or were absent, for the reasons before alleged. Also that an assembly residing out of the bounds of that colony whereof they have the government cannot execute any power over the persons or goods of any of the colony, to seize on them for debt or other duty in any place without the colony itself, as having no jurisdiction nor authority elsewhere, but are left to the remedy which the law of the place alloweth them. And though the assembly have right to impose mulct upon any of their members that shall break the laws they make; yet out of the colony itself they have no right to execute the same. And that which is said here of the rights of an assembly for the government of a province or a colony is applicable also to an assembly for the government of a town, a university, or a college, or a church, or for any other government over the persons of men.

[119]   17. And generally, in all bodies politic, if any particular member conceive himself injured by the body itself, the cognizance of his cause belonged to the sovereign and those the sovereign hath ordained for judges[1] in such causes or shall ordain for that particular cause, and not to the body itself. For the whole body is in this case his fellow subject, which in a sovereign assembly, is otherwise; for there, if the sovereign be not judge, though in his own cause, there can be no judge at all.

---

1   See 23.7.

18. In a body politic, for the well ordering of foreign traffic, the most commodious representative is an assembly of all the members, that is to say, such a one as every one that adventureth his money may be present at all the deliberations and resolutions of the body, if they will themselves. For proof whereof we are to consider the end for which men that are merchants, and may buy and sell, export and import their merchandise according to their own discretions, do nevertheless bind themselves up in one corporation. It is true there be few merchants that with the merchandise they buy at home can freight a ship to export it, or with that they buy abroad to bring it home; and [they] have therefore need to join together in one society, where every man may either participate of the gain according to the proportion of his adventure, or take his own and sell what he transports or imports at such prices as he thinks fit. But this is no body politic, there being no common representative to oblige them to any other law than that which is common to all other subjects. The end of their incorporating is to make their gain the greater, which is done two ways, by sole buying and sole selling, both at home and abroad. So that to grant to a company of merchants to be a corporation or body politic is to grant them a double monopoly, whereof one is to be sole buyers, another to be sole sellers. For when there is a company incorporate for any particular foreign country, they only export the commodities vendible in that country, which is sole buying at home and sole selling abroad. For at home there is but one buyer and abroad but one that selleth, both which is gainful to the merchant, because thereby they buy at home at lower and sell abroad at higher rates; and abroad there is but one buyer of foreign merchandise and but one that sells them at home, both which again are gainful to the adventurers.

19. Of this double monopoly one part is disadvantageous to the people at home, the other to foreigners. For at home by their sole exportation they set what price they please on the husbandry and handiworks of the people, and by the sole importation what price they please on all foreign commodities the people have need of, both which are ill for the people. On the contrary, by the sole selling of the native commodities abroad and sole buying the foreign commodities upon the place, they raise the

price of those and abate the price of these, to the disadvantage of the foreigner; for where but one selleth the merchandise is the dearer and where but one buyeth, the cheaper; such corporations therefore are no other than monopolies, though they would be very profitable for a commonwealth, if being bound up into one body in foreign markets they were [nevertheless] at liberty at home, every man to buy and sell at what price he could.

20. The end then of these bodies of merchants, being not a common benefit to the whole body (which have in this case no common stock, but what is deducted out of the particular adventures for building, buying, victualling [supplying food] and manning of ships), but the particular gain of every adventurer, it is reason that every one be acquainted with the employment of his own, that is, that every one be of the assembly that shall have the power to order the same and be acquainted with their accounts. And therefore the representative of such a body must be an assembly, where every member of the body may be present at the consultations, if he will.

21. If a body politic of merchants contract a debt to a stranger by the act of their representative assembly, every member is liable by himself for the whole.[1] For a stranger can take no notice of their private laws, but considereth them as so many particular men, obliged every one to the whole payment till payment made by one dischargeth all the rest; but if the debt be to one of the company, the creditor is debtor for the whole to himself, and cannot therefore demand his debt, but only from the common stock, if there be any.

22. If the commonwealth impose a tax upon the body, it is understood to be laid upon every member proportionably to his particular adventure in the company. For there is in this case no other common stock, but what is made of their particular adventures.

23. If a mulct [fine] be laid upon the body for some unlawful act, they only are liable by whose votes the act was decreed or by whose assistance it was executed;[2] for in none of the rest is there any other crime but being of the body, which if a crime (because the body was

---

1 Cf. 22.11.
2 Cf. 22.10.

ordained by the authority of the commonwealth) is not his.

24. If one of the members be indebted to the body, he may be sued by the body, but his goods cannot be taken nor his person imprisoned by the authority of the body, but only by authority of the commonwealth; for if they can do it by their own authority, they can by their own authority give judgement that the debt is due, which is as much as to be judge in their own cause.

25. These bodies made for the government of men or of traffic be either perpetual or for a time prescribed by writing. But there be bodies also whose times are limited, and that only by the nature of their business. For example, if a sovereign monarch or a sovereign assembly shall think fit to give command to the towns and other several parts of their territory to send to him their deputies to inform him of the condition and necessities of the subjects, or to advise with him for the making of good laws, or for any other cause, as with one person representing the whole country, [then] such deputies, having a place and time of meeting assigned them, are there and at that time a body politic, representing every subject of that dominion; but it is only for such matters as shall be propounded unto them by that man or assembly, that by the sovereign authority sent for them; and when it shall be declared that nothing more shall be propounded nor debated by them, the body is dissolved. For if they were the absolute representative of the people, then were it the sovereign assembly; and so there would be two sovereign assemblies or two sovereigns over the same people, which cannot consist [be consistent] with their peace. And therefore where there is once a sovereignty, there can be no absolute representation of the people but by it. And for the limits of how far such a body shall represent the whole people, they are set forth in the writing by which they were sent for. For the people cannot choose their deputies to other intent than is in the writing directed to them from their sovereign expressed.

26. Private bodies regular and lawful are those that are constituted without letters or other written authority, saving the laws common to all other subjects. And because they be united in one person representative, they are held for regular, such as are all families in which the father

A body politic
for counsel to
be given to the
sovereign.

[121]

A regular private
body, lawful, as a
family.

or master ordereth the whole family. For he obligeth his children and servants as far as the law permitteth, though not further, because none of them are bound to obedience in those actions which the law hath forbidden to be done. In all other actions during the time they are under domestic government, they are subject to their fathers and masters as to their immediate sovereigns. For the father and master being before the institution of commonwealth absolute sovereigns in their own families, they lose afterward no more of their authority than the law of the commonwealth taketh from them.

Private bodies regular, but unlawful. 27. Private bodies regular, but unlawful, are those that unite themselves into one person representative without any public authority at all, such as are the corporations of beggars, thieves and gipsies, the better to order their trade of begging and stealing; and [such as] the corporations of men that by authority from any foreign person unite themselves in another's dominion for the easier propagation of doctrines and for making a party against the power of the commonwealth.

Systems irregular, such as are private leagues. 28. Irregular systems, in their nature but leagues, or sometimes mere concourse of people,[1] without union to any particular design, nor[2] obligation of one to another, but proceeding only from a similitude of wills and inclinations, become lawful or unlawful according to the lawfulness or unlawfulness of every particular man's design therein; and his design is to be understood by the occasion.

29. The leagues of subjects (because leagues are commonly made for mutual defence) are in a commonwealth (which is no more than a league of all the subjects together) for the most part unnecessary and savour of unlawful design and are for that cause unlawful, and go commonly by the name of factions or conspiracies. For a league being a connexion of men by covenants, if there be no power given to any one man or assembly (as in the condition of mere nature) to compel them to performance, is so long only valid as there ariseth no just cause of distrust;[3] and therefore leagues between commonwealths,

[122]

---

1 See 22.33.
2 Some editions have "not by" and others just "by."
3 See 14.18.

over whom there is no human power established to keep them all in awe, are not only lawful but also profitable for the time they last. But leagues of the subjects of one and the same commonwealth, where every one may obtain his right by means of the sovereign power, are unnecessary to the maintaining of peace and justice, and, in case the design of them be evil or unknown to the commonwealth, unlawful. For all uniting of strength by private men is, if for evil intent, unjust; if for intent unknown, dangerous to the public and unjustly concealed.

30. If the sovereign power be in a great assembly and [if] a number of men [who are] part of the assembly, without authority, consult a part to contrive the guidance of the rest, this is a faction or conspiracy unlawful, as being a fraudulent seducing of the assembly for their particular interest. But if he whose private interest is to be debated and judged in the assembly make as many friends as he can, in him it is no injustice, because in this case he is no part of the assembly. And though he hire such friends with money (unless there be an express law against it); yet it is not injustice. For sometimes (as men's manners are) justice cannot be had without money, and every man may think his own cause just till it be heard and judged. Secret cabals.

31. In all commonwealths, if private men entertain more servants than the government of his estate and lawful employment he has for them requires, it is faction, and unlawful. For having the protection of the commonwealth, he needeth not the defence of private force. And whereas in nations not thoroughly civilized, several numerous families have lived in continual hostility and invaded one another with private force; yet it is evident enough that they have done unjustly, or else that they had no commonwealth. Feuds of private families.

32. And as factions for kindred, so also factions for government of religion, as of Papists, Protestants, etc., or of state, as patricians and plebeians of old time in Rome and of aristocraticals and democraticals of old time in Greece, are unjust, as being contrary to the peace and safety of the people and a taking of the sword out of the hand of the sovereign. Factions for government.

33. Concourse of people is an irregular system, the lawfulness or unlawfulness whereof dependeth on the occasion and on the number of them that are assembled.

If the occasion be lawful and manifest, the concourse is lawful, as the usual meeting of men at church or at a public show, in usual numbers; for if the numbers be extraordinarily great, the occasion is not evident, and consequently he that cannot render a particular and good account of his being amongst them is to be judged conscious of an unlawful and tumultuous design. It may be [123] lawful for a thousand men to join in a petition to be delivered to a judge or magistrate; yet if a thousand men come to present it, it is a tumultuous assembly, because there needs but one or two for that purpose. But in such cases as these it is not a set number that makes the assembly unlawful, but such a number as the present officers are not able to suppress and bring to justice.

34. When an unusual number of men assemble against a man whom they accuse, the assembly is an unlawful tumult, because they may deliver their accusation to the magistrate by a few or by one man. Such was the case of St. Paul at Ephesus, where Demetrius and a great number of other men brought two of Paul's companions before the magistrate, saying with one voice, *Great is Diana of the Ephesians*, which was their way of demanding justice against them for teaching the people such doctrine as was against their religion and trade. The occasion here, considering the laws of that people, was just; yet was their assembly judged unlawful, and the magistrate reprehended them for it in these words, *If Demetrius and the other workmen can accuse any man of any thing, there be pleas, and deputies; let them accuse one another. And if you have any other thing to demand, your case may be judged in an assembly lawfully called. For we are in danger to be accused for this day's sedition, because there is no cause by which any Acts 19:40. man can render any reason of this concourse of people.* Where he calleth an assembly whereof men can give no just account, a sedition, and such as they could not answer for. And this is all I shall say concerning *systems* and assemblies of people, which may be compared, as I said [in the Introduction], to the similar parts of man's body, such as be lawful to the muscles, such as are unlawful to wens [tumors], biles, and apostems [a large, deep abscess] engendered by the unnatural conflux of evil humours.

Chapter XXIII

Of the Public Ministers of Sovereign Power

1. In the last chapter I have spoken of the similar parts of a commonwealth; in this I shall speak of the parts organical, which are public ministers.

2. A PUBLIC MINISTER is he that by the sovereign, whether a monarch or an assembly, is employed in any affairs with authority to represent in that employment the person of the commonwealth.[1] And whereas every man or assembly that hath sovereignty representeth two persons, or (as the more common phrase is) has two capacities, one natural and another politic (as a monarch hath the person not only of the commonwealth but also of a man, and a sovereign assembly hath the person not only of the commonwealth but also of the assembly),[2] they that be servants to them in their natural capacity are not public ministers, but those only that serve them in the administration of the public business. And therefore neither ushers nor sergeants nor other officers that wait on the assembly for no other purpose but for the commodity of the men assembled in an aristocracy or democracy, nor stewards, chamberlains, cofferers, or any other officers of the household of a monarch, are public ministers in a monarchy.

Public minister, who.

[124]

3. Of public ministers, some have charge committed to them of a general administration, either of the whole dominion or of a part thereof. Of the whole, as to a protector or regent may be committed by the predecessor of an infant king during his minority the whole administration of his kingdom. In which case, every subject is so far obliged to obedience as the ordinances he shall make and the commands he shall give be in the king's name, and not inconsistent with his sovereign power. Of a part or province, as when either a monarch or a sovereign assembly shall give the general charge thereof to a governor, lieutenant, prefect, or viceroy, and in this case also

Ministers for the general administration.

---

1 Cf. 16.3 and 17.14.
2 The doctrine of the king's two bodies was well established in seventeenth-century England. The regicides claimed that they were executing the man Charles Stuart, not the king of England.

every one of that province is obliged to all he shall do in the name of the sovereign and that is not incompatible with the sovereign's right. For such protectors, viceroys, and governors have no other right but what depends on the sovereign's will; and no commission that can be given them can be interpreted for a declaration of the will to transfer the sovereignty without express and perspicuous words to that purpose.[1] And this kind of public ministers resembleth the nerves and tendons that move the several limbs of a body natural.

For special administration, as for economy. 4. Others have special administration, that is to say, charges of some special business either at home or abroad; as at home, first, for the economy of a commonwealth, they that have authority concerning the *treasure*, as tributes, impositions, rents, fines, or whatsoever public revenue, to collect, receive, issue, or take the accounts thereof, are public ministers; ministers, because they serve the person representative and can do nothing against his command nor without his authority; public, because they serve him in his political capacity.

5. Secondly, they that have authority concerning the *militia* to have the custody of arms, forts, ports, to levy, pay, or conduct soldiers, or to provide for any necessary thing for the use of war either by land or sea, are public ministers. But a soldier without command, though he fight for the commonwealth, does not therefore represent the person of it, because there is none to represent it to. For every one that hath command represents it to them only whom he commandeth.

For instruction of the people. 6. They also that have authority to teach or to enable others to teach the people their duty to the sovereign power and instruct them in the knowledge of what is just and unjust, thereby to render them more apt to live in godliness and in peace amongst themselves and resist the public enemy, are public ministers; ministers, in that they do it not by their own authority but by another's; and public, because they do it (or should do it) by no authority but that of the sovereign. The monarch or the sovereign assembly only hath immediate authority from God to teach and instruct the people, and no man but the sovereign receiveth his power *Dei gratia* simply, that

[125]

---

1 See 21.20 and 22.5.

is to say from the favour of none but God;[1] all other receive theirs from the favour and providence of God and their sovereigns, as in a monarchy *Dei gratia et regis* or *Dei providentia et voluntate regis*.

7. They also to whom jurisdiction is given are public ministers. For in their seats of justice they represent the person of the sovereign; and their sentence is his sentence; for as hath been before declared,[2] all judicature is essentially annexed to the sovereignty, and therefore all other judges are but ministers of him or them that have the sovereign power. And as controversies are of two sorts, namely of *fact* and of *law*, so are judgements, some of fact, some of law; and consequently in the same controversy there may be two judges, one of fact, another of law. *For judicature.*

8. And in both these controversies, there may arise a controversy between the party judged and the judge, which, because they be both subjects to the sovereign, ought in equity to be judged by men agreed on by consent of both, for no man can be judge in his own cause.[3] But the sovereign is already agreed on for judge by them both, and is therefore either to hear the cause and determine it himself or appoint for judge such as they shall both agree on. And this agreement is then understood to be made between them divers ways; as first, if the defendant be allowed to except against such of his judges whose interest maketh him suspect them (for as to the complainant, he hath already chosen his own judge), those which he excepteth not against are judges he himself agrees on. Secondly, if he appeal to any other judge, he can appeal no further, for his appeal is his choice. Thirdly, if he appeal to the sovereign himself, and he by himself or by delegates which the parties shall agree on give sentence, that sentence is final; for the defendant is judged by his own judges, that is to say, by himself.

9. These properties of just and rational judicature considered, I cannot forbear to observe the excellent constitution of the courts of justice established both for common

---

1 Hobbes is using the language of the theory of the divine right of kings here even though it does not fit his theory, according to which sovereigns are instituted by their subjects.
2 See 18.11.
3 See 15.31.

and also for public pleas in England. By common pleas I mean those where both the complainant and defendant are subjects, and by public (which are also called pleas of the crown) those where the complainant is the sovereign. For whereas there were two orders of men, whereof one was lords, the other commons, the lords had this privilege, to have for judges in all capital crimes none but lords, and of them, as many as would be present; which being ever acknowledged as a privilege of favour, their judges were none but such as they had themselves desired. And in all controversies every subject (as also in civil controversies the lords) had for judges men of the country where the matter in controversy lay, against which he might make his exceptions, till at last twelve men without exception [126] being agreed on, they were judged by those twelve. So that having his own judges, there could be nothing alleged by the party why the sentence should not be final. These public persons, with authority from the sovereign power either to instruct or judge the people, are such members of the commonwealth as may fitly be compared to the organs of voice in a body natural.

For execution.   10. Public ministers are also all those that have authority from the sovereign to procure the execution of judgements given, to publish the sovereign's commands, to suppress tumults, to apprehend and imprison malefactors, and other acts tending to the conservation of the peace. For every act they do by such authority is the act of the commonwealth, and their service [is] answerable to that of the hands in a body natural.

11. Public ministers abroad are those that represent the person of their own sovereign to foreign states. Such are ambassadors, messengers, agents, and heralds sent by public authority and on public business.

12. But such as are sent by authority only of some private party of a troubled state, though they be received, are neither public nor private ministers of the commonwealth, because none of their actions have the commonwealth for author. Likewise, an ambassador, sent from a prince to congratulate, condole, or to assist at a solemnity, though the authority be public; yet because the business is private and belonging to him in his natural capacity, is a private person. Also if a man be sent into another country, secretly to explore their counsels and strength,

though both the authority and the business be public; yet because there is none to take notice of any person in him but his own, he is but a private minister, but yet a minister of the commonwealth, and may be compared to an eye in the body natural. And those that are appointed to receive the petitions or other informations of the people[1] and are, as it were, the public ear, are public ministers and represent their sovereign in that office.

13. Neither a councillor (nor a council of state, if we consider it with no authority of judicature or command, but only of giving advice to the sovereign when it is required or of offering it when it is not required) is a public person. For the advice is addressed to the sovereign only, whose person cannot in his own presence be represented to him by another. But a body of counsellors are never without some other authority, either of judicature or of immediate administration. As in a monarchy, they represent the monarch in delivering his commands to the public ministers. In a democracy, the council or senate propounds the result of their deliberations to the people as a council; but when they appoint judges, or hear causes, or give audience to ambassadors, it is in the quality of a minister of the people. And in an aristocracy the council of state is the sovereign assembly itself and gives counsel to none but themselves.

Councillors without other employment than to advise are not public ministers.

Chapter XXIV

Of the Nutrition and Procreation of a Commonwealth

1. The NUTRITION of a commonwealth consisteth in the plenty and distribution of materials conducing to life: in concoction (or preparation), and (when concocted) in the conveyance of it by convenient conduits to the public use.

2. As for the plenty of matter, it is a thing limited by nature to those commodities which from (the two breasts of our common mother) land and sea, God usually either freely giveth or for labour selleth to mankind.

3. For the matter of this nutriment, consisting in animals, vegetables, and minerals, God hath freely laid them

The nourishment of a commonwealth consisteth in the commodities of sea and land:

---

1 Cf. 22.25.

before us in or near to the face of the earth, so as there needeth no more but the labour and industry of receiving them. Insomuch as plenty dependeth (next to God's favour) merely on the labour and industry of men.

4. This matter, commonly called commodities, is partly *native* and partly *foreign*; *native*, that which is to be had within the territory of the commonwealth; *foreign*, that which is imported from without. And because there is no territory under the dominion of one commonwealth (except it be of very vast extent) that produceth all things needful for the maintenance and motion of the whole body, and few that produce not something more than necessary, the superfluous commodities to be had within become no more superfluous, but supply these wants at home by importation of that which may be had abroad, either by exchange or by just war or by labour; for a man's labour also is a commodity exchangeable for benefit as well as any other thing; and there have been commonwealths that, having no more territory than hath served them for habitation, have nevertheless not only maintained but also increased their power, partly by the labour of trading from one place to another, and partly by selling the manufactures, whereof the materials were brought in from other places.

And the right distribution of them. 5. The distribution of the materials of this nourishment is the constitution of *mine* and *thine* and *his*, that is to say in one word, *propriety [property]*, and belongeth in all kinds of commonwealth to the sovereign power.[1] For where there is no commonwealth there is, as hath been already shown, a perpetual war of every man against his neighbour, and therefore everything is his that getteth it and keepeth it by force, which is neither *propriety* nor *community*, but *uncertainty*. Which is so evident that even Cicero, a passionate defender of liberty, in a public pleading

---

1 Hobbes seems to be taking the republican theorists of the 1640s (and earlier) head on. The republicans, that is, those inspired by certain ancient authors, especially Roman ones such as Cicero and Livy, claimed that if citizens did not have an absolute right in their property, then they were servants or slaves. Hobbes says that subjects do not have such a right and they are servants of the sovereign (chapter 20). See 18.10 and also Quentin Skinner, "John Milton and the Politics of Slavery," *Prose Studies* 23 (2000): 1-23.

attributeth all propriety to the law civil; *Let the civil law,* saith he, *be once abandoned, or but negligently guarded (not to say oppressed), and there is nothing that any man can be* [128] *sure to receive from his ancestor, or leave to his children.* And again, *Take away the civil law, and no man knows what is his own, and what another man's.*[1] Seeing therefore the introduction of propriety is an effect of commonwealth, which can do nothing but by the person that represents it, it is the act only of the sovereign and consisteth in the laws, which none can make that have not the sovereign power. And this they well knew of old, who called that *nomos* (that is to say, *distribution*) which we call law, and defined justice, by *distributing* to every man *his own.*[2]

6. In this distribution, the first law is for division of the land itself, wherein the sovereign assigneth to every man a portion according as he, and not according as any subject or any number of them, shall judge agreeable to equity and the common good. The children of Israel were a commonwealth in the wilderness, but wanted the commodities of the earth till they were masters of the Land of Promise, which afterward was divided amongst them not by their own discretion but by the discretion of Eleazar the priest and Joshua their general; who when there were twelve tribes, making them thirteen by subdivision of the tribe of Joseph, made nevertheless but twelve portions of the land and ordained for the tribe of Levi no land, but assigned them the tenth part of the whole fruits, which division was therefore arbitrary. And though a people coming into possession of a land by war do not always exterminate the ancient inhabitants, as did the Jews, but leave to many or most or all of them their estates; yet it is manifest they hold them afterwards as of the victor's distribution, as the people of England held all theirs of William the Conqueror.

All private estates of land proceed originally from the arbitrary distribution of the sovereign.

7. From whence we may collect that the propriety which a subject hath in his lands consisteth in a right to exclude all other subjects from the use of them, and not to exclude their sovereign, be it an assembly or a monarch. For seeing the sovereign, that is to say, the commonwealth (whose person he representeth), is understood to

Propriety of a subject excludes not the dominion of the sovereign, but only of another subject.

---

1 Cicero, *De Caecina* XXV, sections 73 and 70, respectively.
2 Cf. 15.3 and 15.14-15.

do nothing but in order to the common peace and security, this distribution of lands is to be understood as done in order to the same; and consequently, whatsoever distribution he[1] shall make in prejudice thereof is contrary to the will of every subject that committed his peace and safety to his discretion and conscience, and therefore by the will of every one of them is to be reputed void. It is true that a sovereign monarch, or the greater part of a sovereign assembly, may ordain the doing of many things in pursuit of their passions, contrary to their own consciences, which is a breach of trust and of the law of nature; but this is not enough to authorise any subject either to make war upon or so much as to accuse of injustice or any way to speak evil of their sovereign, because they have authorised all his actions, and in bestowing the sovereign power made them their own.[2] But in what cases the commands of sovereigns are contrary to equity and the law of nature is to be considered hereafter in another place.

The public is not to be dieted. [129]   8. In the distribution of land, the commonwealth itself may be conceived to have a portion and possess and improve the same by their representative; and [it may be conceived] that such portion may be made sufficient to sustain the whole expense to the common peace and defence necessarily required; which were very true, if there could be any representative conceived free from human passions and infirmities. But the nature of men being as it is, the setting forth of public land or of any certain revenue for the commonwealth is in vain and tendeth to the dissolution of government, to the condition of mere nature and war, as soon as ever the sovereign power falleth into the hands of a monarch or of an assembly that are either too negligent of money or too hazardous in engaging the public stock into long or costly war. Commonwealths can endure no diet; for seeing their expense is not limited

---

1   A manuscript version of *Leviathan* has "another" at this place. We follow all the early printed editions.

2   In *Eikonoklastes* (1649), John Milton writes that Charles I had aspired to make all Britain "ty'd and chain'd to the conscience, judgement, and reason of one Man" and thereby to put his subjects "into the condition of Slaves" (quoted from Skinner, "John Milton and the Politics of Slavery," p.12). See also 18.1 and 21.10.

by their own appetite but by external accidents and the appetites of their neighbours, the public riches cannot be limited by other limits than those which the emergent occasions shall require. And whereas in England there were, by the Conqueror, divers lands reserved to his own use (besides forests and chases, either for his recreation or for preservation of woods), and divers services reserved on the land he gave his subjects; yet it seems they were not reserved for his maintenance in his public but in his natural capacity; for he and his successors did, for all that, lay arbitrary taxes on all subjects' land when they judged it necessary. Or if those public lands and services were ordained as a sufficient maintenance of the commonwealth, it was contrary to the scope of the institution, being (as it appeared by those ensuing taxes) insufficient and (as it appears by the late small revenue of the Crown) subject to alienation and diminution. It is therefore in vain to assign a portion to the commonwealth, which may sell or give it away, and does sell and give it away when it is done by their representative.

9. As the distribution of lands at home, so also to assign in what places and for what commodities the subject shall traffic abroad belongeth to the sovereign. For if it did belong to private persons to use their own discretion therein, some of them would be drawn for gain, both to furnish the enemy with means to hurt the commonwealth and hurt it themselves by importing such things as, pleasing men's appetites, be nevertheless noxious or at least unprofitable to them. And therefore it belongeth to the commonwealth (that is, to the sovereign only) to approve or disapprove both of the places and matter of foreign traffic. *The places and matter of traffic depend, as their distribution, on the sovereign.*

10. Further, seeing it is not enough to the sustentation of a commonwealth that every man have a propriety in a portion of land or in some few commodities, or a natural property in some useful art, and that there is no art in the world but is necessary either for the being or well-being almost of every particular man, it is necessary that men distribute that which they can spare and transfer their propriety therein mutually one to another by exchange and mutual contract. And therefore it belongeth to the commonwealth (that is to say, to the sovereign) to appoint in what manner all kinds of contract between subjects (as *The laws of transferring propriety belong also to the sovereign.*

[130]

buying, selling, exchanging, borrowing, lending, letting, and taking to hire) are to be made, and by what words and signs they shall be understood for valid. And for the matter and distribution of the nourishment to the several members of the commonwealth, thus much, considering the model of the whole work, is sufficient.

Money the
blood of a
commonwealth.

11. By concoction, I understand the reducing of all commodities which are not presently consumed, but reserved for nourishment in time to come, to something of equal value, and withal so portable as not to hinder the motion of men from place to place, to the end a man may have in what place soever such nourishment as the place affordeth. And this is nothing else but gold, and silver, and money. For gold and silver, being, as it happens, almost in all countries of the world highly valued, is a commodious measure of the value of all things else between nations; and money, of what matter soever coined by the sovereign of a commonwealth, is a sufficient measure of the value of all things else between the subjects of that commonwealth. By the means of which measures all commodities, movable and immovable, are made to accompany a man to all places of his resort within and without the place of his ordinary residence; and the same passeth from man to man within the commonwealth and goes round about, nourishing (as it passeth) every part thereof, in so much as this concoction is as it were the sanguification of the commonwealth; for natural blood is in like manner made of the fruits of the earth, and circulating, nourisheth by the way every member of the body of man.

12. And because silver and gold have their value from the matter itself, they have first this privilege, that the value of them cannot be altered by the power of one nor of a few commonwealths, as being a common measure of the commodities of all places. But base money may easily be enhanced or abased. Secondly, they have the privilege to make commonwealths move and stretch out their arms, when need is, into foreign countries, and supply not only private subjects that travel but also whole armies with provision. But that coin which is not considerable for the matter, but for the stamp of the place, being unable to endure change of air, hath its effect at home only, where also it is subject to the change of laws and thereby to have

the value diminished to the prejudice many times of those that have it.

13. The conduits and ways by which it is conveyed to the public use are of two sorts: one, that conveyeth it to the public coffers; the other, that issueth the same out again for public payments. Of the first sort are collectors, receivers, and treasurers; of the second are the treasurers again and the officers appointed for payment of several public or private ministers. And in this also the artificial man maintains his resemblance with the natural, whose veins receiving the blood from the several parts of the body carry it to the heart, where being made vital, the heart by the arteries sends it out again to enliven and enable for motion all the members of the same.[1]

14. The procreation or children of a commonwealth are those we call *plantations* or *colonies*, which are numbers of men sent out from the commonwealth under a conductor or governor to inhabit a foreign country either formerly void of inhabitants or made void then by war. And when a colony is settled, they are either a commonwealth of themselves, discharged of their subjection to their sovereign that sent them (as hath been done by many commonwealths of ancient time), in which case the commonwealth from which they went was called their metropolis or mother, and requires no more of them than fathers require of the children whom they emancipate and make free from their domestic government, which is honour and friendship, or else they remain united to their metropolis, as were the colonies of the people of Rome; and then they are no commonwealths themselves, but provinces,[2] and parts of the commonwealth that sent them. So that the right of colonies, saving honour and league with their metropolis, dependeth wholly on their license or letters, by which their sovereign authorized them to plant.

The conduits and way of money to the public use.

[131]

The children of a commonwealth [are] colonies.

---

1 Hobbes's friend William Harvey had discovered the way blood circulates in the body and explained it in *De Motu Cordis et Sanguinis* (1628). Hobbes is showing off his scientific knowledge.

2 See 22.16.

Chapter XXV

Of Counsel

1. How fallacious it is to judge of the nature of things by the ordinary and inconstant use of words appeareth in nothing more than in the confusion of counsels and commands, arising from the imperative manner of speaking in them both, and in many other occasions besides. For the words *do this* are the words not only of him that commandeth, but also of him that giveth counsel and of him that exhorteth; and yet there are but few that see not that these are very different things or that cannot distinguish between them when they perceive who it is that speaketh and to whom the speech is directed and upon what occasion. But finding those phrases in men's writings and being not able or not willing to enter into a consideration of the circumstances, they mistake sometimes the precepts of counsellors for the precepts[1] of them that command, and sometimes the contrary, according as it best agreeth with the conclusions they would infer or the actions they approve. To avoid which mistakes and render to those terms of commanding, counselling, and exhorting, their proper and distinct significations, I define them thus.

2. COMMAND is where a man saith, *Do this* or *Do not this*, without expecting other reason than the will of him that says it.[2] From this it followeth manifestly that he that commandeth pretendeth thereby his own benefit; for the reason of his command is his own will only, and the proper object of every man's will is some good to himself.[3]

---

1 A precept is a sentence that guides action. Hobbes talks about two kinds of precepts: counsels or commands (or laws). See also 14.3 and 26.2.

2 See also 26.44.

3 According to Hobbes, an imperative sentence is used as a command when the speaker intends the addressee's action to benefit himself, the speaker, rather than the addressee. In the next paragraph, he says that an imperative sentence is used as advice ("counsel") when the speaker intends the addressee to benefit from his own action. It is not clear what Hobbes would say about the cases in which a parent says to her child, "Eat your carrots," or a sergeant during combat says to his soldiers, "Get down!" See also 25.4, 25.9, and 25.10.

3. COUNSEL is where a man saith, *Do* or *Do not this*, and deduceth his reasons from the benefit that arriveth by it to him to whom he saith it. And from this it is evident that he that giveth counsel pretendeth only (whatsoever he intendeth) the good of him to whom he giveth it.[1]

4. Therefore between counsel and command, one great difference is that command is directed to a man's own benefit and counsel to the benefit of another man. And from this ariseth another difference, that a man may be obliged to do what he is commanded, as when he hath covenanted to obey: but he cannot be obliged to do as he is counselled, because the hurt of not following it is his own; or if he should covenant to follow it, then is the counsel turned into the nature of a command. A third difference between them is that no man can pretend a right to be of another man's counsel, because he is not to pretend benefit by it to himself; but to demand right to counsel another argues a will to know his designs or to gain some other good to himself, which, as I said before, is of every man's will the proper object.

5. This also is incident to the nature of counsel, that whatsoever it be, he that asketh it cannot in equity[2] accuse or punish it; for to ask counsel of another is to permit him to give such counsel as he shall think best; and consequently, he that giveth counsel to his sovereign (whether a monarch or an assembly) when he asketh it, cannot in equity be punished for it,[3] whether the same be conformable to the opinion of the most or not, so it be to the proposition in debate. For if the sense of the assembly can be taken notice of, before the debate be ended, they should neither ask nor take any further counsel; for the sense of the assembly is the resolution of the debate and end of all deliberation. And generally he that demandeth counsel is author of it and therefore cannot punish it; and what the sovereign cannot, no man else can.[4] But if one

---

1 See also 42.45, 42.101, and 42.104-9.
2 See 15.23.
3 The king's counselors sometimes were punished for the advice they gave. Hobbes is defending counselors against the actual practice of kings.
4 Hobbes may be giving a belated defense of Lord Strafford (Thomas Wentworth, 1593-1641), who was executed by a bill of attainder in Parliament for doing the king's business.

subject giveth counsel to another to do anything contrary to the laws, whether that counsel proceed from evil intention or from ignorance only, it is punishable by the commonwealth, because ignorance of the law is no good excuse,[1] where every man is bound to take notice of the laws to which he is subject.

Exhortation and
dehortation,
what.

6. EXHORTATION and DEHORTATION is counsel, accompanied with signs in him that giveth it of vehement desire to have it followed, or, to say it more briefly, counsel vehemently pressed. For he that exhorteth doth not deduce the consequences of what he adviseth to be done and tie himself therein to the rigour of true reasoning, but encourages him he counselleth to action, as he that dehorteth deterreth him from it. And therefore they have in their speeches a regard to the common passions and opinions of men in deducing their reasons, and [they] make use of similitudes, metaphors, examples, and other tools of oratory, to persuade their hearers of the utility, honour, or justice of following their advice.

[133]   7. From whence may be inferred, first, that exhortation and dehortation is directed to the good of him that giveth the counsel, not of him that asketh it, which is contrary to the duty of a counsellor, who, by the definition of counsel, ought to regard, not his own benefit, but his whom he adviseth. And that he directeth his counsel to his own benefit is manifest enough by the long and vehement urging or by the artificial giving thereof, which being not required of him and consequently proceeding from his own occasions, is directed principally to his own benefit and but accidentally to the good of him that is counselled, or not at all.

8. Secondly, that the use of exhortation and dehortation lieth only where a man is to speak to a multitude, because when the speech is addressed to one, he may interrupt him and examine his reasons more rigorously than can be done in a multitude, which are too many to enter into dispute and dialogue with him that speaketh indifferently to them all at once.

9. Thirdly, that they that exhort and dehort, where they are required to give counsel, are corrupt counsellors and, as it were, bribed by their own interest. For

---

1   See 27.5.

though the counsel they give be never so good; yet he that gives it is no more a good counsellor than he that giveth a just sentence for a reward is a just judge. But where a man may lawfully command, as a father in his family or a leader in an army, his exhortations and dehortations are not only lawful, but also necessary and laudable; but when they are no more counsels, but commands, which when they are for execution of sour [disagreeable] labour, sometimes necessity and always humanity requireth to be sweetened in the delivery by encouragement and in the tune and phrase of counsel, rather than in harsher language of command.

10. Examples of the difference between command and counsel we may take from the forms of speech that express them in Holy Scripture. *Have no other Gods but me; Make to thyself no graven image; Take not God's name in vain; Sanctify the Sabbath; Honour thy parents; Kill not; Steal not, etc.* are commands, because the reason for which we are to obey them is drawn from the will of God our King,[1] whom we are obliged to obey. But these words, *Sell all thou hast; give it to the poor; and follow me*, are counsel, because the reason for which we are to do so is drawn from our own benefit, which is this; that we shall have *treasure in Heaven.* These words, *Go into the village over against you, and you shall find an ass tied, and her colt; loose her, and bring her to me*, are a command;[2] for the reason of their fact is drawn from the will of their master; but these words, *Repent, and be baptized in the name of Jesus*, are counsel, because the reason why we should so do tendeth not to any benefit of God Almighty, who shall still be King in what manner soever we rebel, but of ourselves, who have no other means of avoiding the punishment hanging over us for our sins.

11. As the difference of counsel from command hath been now deduced from the nature of counsel, consisting in a deducing of the benefit or hurt that may arise to him that is to be counselled by the necessary or probable consequences of the action he propoundeth; so may also the

Differences of fit and unfit counsellors.
[134]

---

1 Hobbes's view differs from the usual one according to which God's commands are for our own benefit. Also against the usual view, Hobbes claims that the precepts of Jesus are counsels, i.e., precepts for our benefit.
2 Cf. 20.16.

differences between apt and inept counsellors be derived from the same. For experience, being but memory of the consequences of like actions formerly observed, and counsel but the speech whereby that experience is made known to another, the virtues and defects of counsel are the same with the virtues and defects intellectual; and to the person of a commonwealth, his counsellors serve him in the place of memory and mental discourse. But with this resemblance of the commonwealth to a natural man, there is one dissimilitude joined of great importance, which is that a natural man receiveth his experience from the natural objects of sense, which work upon him without passion or interest of their own; whereas they that give counsel to the representative person of a commonwealth may have, and have often, their particular ends and passions that render their counsels always suspected, and many times unfaithful. And therefore we may set down for the first condition of a good counsellor, *that his ends and interest be not inconsistent with the ends and interest of him he counselleth.*

12. Secondly, because the office of a counsellor, when an action comes into deliberation, is to make manifest the consequences of it in such manner as he that is counselled may be truly and evidently informed, he ought to propound his advice in such form of speech as may make the truth most evidently appear, that is to say, with as firm ratiocination, as significant and proper language and as briefly as the evidence will permit. And therefore *rash and unevident inferences* (such as are fetched only from examples or authority of books and are not arguments of what is good or evil, but witnesses of fact or of opinion), *obscure, confused, and ambiguous expressions, also all metaphorical speeches tending to the stirring up of passion* (because such reasoning and such expressions are useful only to deceive or to lead him we counsel towards other ends than his own), *are repugnant to the office of a counsellor.*

13. Thirdly, because the ability of counselling proceedeth from experience and long study and no man is presumed to have experience in all those things that to the administration of a great commonwealth are necessary to be known, *no man is presumed to be a good counsellor but in such business as he hath not only been much versed in,*

but hath also much meditated on and considered. For seeing the business of a commonwealth is this, to preserve the people in peace at home and defend them against foreign invasion, we shall find it requires great knowledge of the disposition of mankind, of the rights of government, and of the nature of equity, law, justice, and honour, not to be attained without study; and of the strength, commodities, places, both of their own country and their neighbours', as also of the inclinations and designs of all nations that may [in] any way annoy them. And this is not attained to without much experience. Of which things, not only the whole sum, but every one of the particulars requires [135] the age and observation of a man in years and of more than ordinary study. The wit required for counsel, as I have said before (Chapter 8), is judgement. And the differences of men in that point come from different education, of some, to one kind of study or business, and of others, to another. When for the doing of anything there be infallible rules (as in engines and edifices, the rules of geometry), all the experience of the world cannot equal his counsel that has learned or found out the rule. And when there is no such rule, he that hath most experience in that particular kind of business has therein the best judgement and is the best counsellor.

14. Fourthly, to be able to give counsel to a commonwealth in a business that hath reference to another commonwealth, *it is necessary to be acquainted with the intelligences and letters that come from thence and with all the records of treaties and other transactions of state* between them, which none can do but such as the representative shall think fit. By which we may see that they who are not called to counsel can have no good counsel in such cases to obtrude.

15. Fifthly, supposing the number of counsellors equal, a man is better counselled by hearing them apart than in an assembly, and that for many causes. First, in hearing them apart, you have the advice of every man; but in an assembly many of them deliver their advice with aye or no or with their hands or feet, not moved by their own sense, but by the eloquence of another, or for fear of displeasing some that have spoken or the whole by contradiction, or for fear of appearing duller in apprehension than those that have applauded the contrary

opinion. Secondly, in an assembly of many there cannot choose but be some interests are contrary to that of the public; and these their interests make passionate, and passion eloquent, and eloquence draws others into the same advice. For the passions of men, which asunder are moderate, as the heat of one brand, in assembly are like many brands that inflame one another (especially when they blow one another with orations) to the setting of the commonwealth on fire, under pretence of counselling it. Thirdly, in hearing every man apart, one may examine, when there is need, the truth or probability of his reasons and of the grounds of the advice he gives, by frequent interruptions and objections; which cannot be done in an assembly, where in every difficult question a man is rather astonied [bewildered] and dazzled with the variety of discourse upon it, than informed of the course he ought to take. Besides, there cannot be an assembly of many, called together for advice, wherein there be not some that have the ambition to be thought eloquent and also learned in the politics; and [they] give not their advice with care of the business propounded, but of the applause of their motley orations, made of the divers coloured threads or shreds of authors; which is an impertinence, at least, that takes away the time of serious consultation and in the secret way of counselling apart is easily avoided. Fourthly, in deliberations that ought to be kept secret, whereof there be many occasions in public business, the counsels of many and especially in assemblies, are dangerous; and therefore great [large] assemblies are necessitated to commit such affairs to lesser numbers and of such persons as are most versed in them and in whose fidelity they have most confidence.

[136]

16. To conclude, who is there that so far approves the taking of counsel from a great assembly of counsellors, that wisheth for or would accept of their pains, when there is a question of marrying his children, disposing of his lands, governing his household, or managing his private estate, especially if there be amongst them such as wish not his prosperity? A man that doth his business by the help of many prudent counsellors, with every one consulting apart in his proper element, does it best, as he that useth able seconds at tennis play, placed in their proper stations. He does next best that useth his own

judgement only, as he that has no second at all. But he that is carried up and down to his business in a framed counsel, which cannot move but by the plurality of consenting opinions, the execution whereof is commonly, out of envy or interest, retarded by the part dissenting, does it worst of all, and like one that is carried to the ball, though by good players; yet in a wheelbarrow or other frame, heavy of itself, and retarded also by the inconcurrent [conflicting] judgements and endeavours of them that drive it, and so much the more, as they be more that set their hands to it, and most of all, when there is one or more amongst them that desire to have him lose. And though it be true that many eyes see more than one; yet it is not to be understood of many counsellors, but then only when the final resolution is in one man. Otherwise, because many eyes see the same thing in divers lines and are apt to look asquint towards their private benefit, they that desire not to miss their mark, though they look about with two eyes, yet they never aim but with one; and therefore no great popular commonwealth was ever kept up, but either by a foreign enemy that united them, or by the reputation of some one eminent man amongst them, or by the secret counsel of a few, or by the mutual fear of equal factions, and not by the open consultations of the assembly. And as for very little commonwealths, be they popular or monarchical, there is no human wisdom can uphold them longer than the jealousy lasteth of their potent neighbours.

Chapter XXVI

Of Civil Laws

1. By CIVIL LAWS, I understand the laws that men are therefore bound to observe because they are members, not of this or that commonwealth in particular, but of a commonwealth. For the knowledge of particular laws belongeth to them that profess the study of the laws of their several countries; but the knowledge of civil law in general to any man. The ancient law of Rome was called their *civil law* from the word *civitas*, which signifies a commonwealth; and those countries which, having been

Civil law, what.

[137]

under the Roman Empire and governed by that law, retain still such part thereof as they think fit, call that part the civil law to distinguish it from the rest of their own civil laws.[1] But that is not it I intend to speak of here, my design being not to show what is law here and there, but what is law, as Plato, Aristotle, Cicero, and divers others have done, without taking upon them the profession of the study of the law.

2. And first it is manifest that law in general is not counsel, but command, nor a command of any man to any man, but only of him whose command is addressed to one formerly obliged to obey him. And as for civil law, it addeth only the name of the person commanding, which is *persona civitatis*, the person of the commonwealth.

3. Which considered, I define civil law in this manner. CIVIL LAW *is to every subject those rules which the commonwealth hath commanded him (by word, writing, or other sufficient sign of the will) to make use of, for the distinction of right and wrong, that is to say, of what is contrary and what is not contrary to the rule.*

4. In which definition there is nothing that is not at first sight evident. For every man seeth that some laws are addressed to all the subjects in general, some to particular provinces, some to particular vocations, and some to particular men; and are therefore laws to every of those to whom the command is directed, and to none else. As also, [every man seeth] that laws are the rules of just and unjust, nothing being reputed unjust that is not contrary to some law. Likewise, that none can make laws but the commonwealth, because our subjection is to the commonwealth only; and that commands are to be signified by sufficient signs, because a man knows not otherwise how to obey them. And therefore, whatsoever can from this definition by necessary consequence be deduced, ought to be acknowledged for truth. Now I deduce from it this that followeth.

1. The sovereign is legislator.
5. The legislator in all commonwealths is only the sovereign, be he one man, as in a monarchy, or one assembly of men, as in a democracy or aristocracy. For the legislator is he that maketh the law. And the commonwealth only prescribes and commandeth the observation of those rules

---

1 See also 18.10.

which we call law; therefore the commonwealth is the legislator. But the commonwealth is no person, nor has capacity to do anything, but by the representative, that is, the sovereign; and therefore the sovereign is the sole legislator.[1] For the same reason, none can abrogate a law made, but the sovereign, because a law is not abrogated but by another law that forbiddeth it to be put in execution.

6. The sovereign of a commonwealth, be it an assembly or one man, is not subject to the civil laws. For having power to make and repeal laws, he may, when he pleaseth, free himself from that subjection by repealing those laws that trouble him and making of new, and consequently he was free before. For he is free that can be free when he will; nor is it possible for any person to be bound to himself, because he that can bind can release; and therefore he that is bound to himself only is not bound.

2. And not subject to civil law. [138]

7. When long use obtaineth the authority of a law, it is not the length of time that maketh the authority,[2] but the will of the sovereign signified by his silence (for silence is sometimes an argument of consent); and it is no longer law, than the sovereign shall be silent therein. And therefore if the sovereign shall have a question of right grounded, not upon his present will, but upon the laws formerly made, the length of time shall bring no prejudice to his right; but the question shall be judged by equity. For many unjust actions and unjust sentences go uncontrolled a longer time than any man can remember. And our lawyers account no customs law but such as are reasonable, and that evil customs are to be abolished; but the judgement of what is reasonable and of what is to be abolished, belonged to him that maketh the law, which is the sovereign assembly or monarch.

3. Use, a law not by virtue of time, but of the sovereign's consent.

8. The law of nature and the civil law contain each other and are of equal extent.[3] For the laws of nature,

4. The law of nature and the

---

1 Since England had been a monarchy prior to 1649, Hobbes thought that parliament had no part in the sovereignty and that the belief that it did contributed to the English Civil War. See also 24.5 and 31.38.

2 Hobbes is probably criticizing Edward Coke, the great advocate of common law. Hobbes criticized his views at more length in *Dialogue Between a Philosopher and a Student of the Common Law* (1681). See also 19.21

3 See *De Cive* 14.9-10 for a further discussion of this point.

which consist in equity, justice, gratitude, and other moral virtues on these depending, in the condition of mere nature (as I have said before in the end of the fifteenth Chapter), are not properly laws, but qualities that dispose men to peace and to obedience.[1] When a commonwealth is once settled, then are they actually laws, and not before, as being then the commands of the commonealth; and therefore also civil laws; for it is the sovereign power that obliges men to obey them. For in the differences of private men, to declare what is equity, what is justice, and what is moral virtue, and to make them binding, there is need of the ordinances of sovereign power; and punishments to be ordained for such as shall break them, which ordinances are therefore part of the civil law. The law of nature therefore is a part of the civil law in all commonwealths of the world. Reciprocally also, the civil law is a part of the dictates of nature. For justice, that is to say, performance of covenant and giving to every man his own, is a dictate of the law of nature. But every subject in a commonwealth hath covenanted to obey the civil law; either one with another, as when they assemble to make a common representative, or with the representative itself one by one when, subdued by the sword, they promise obedience that they may receive life; and therefore obedience to the civil law is part also of the law of nature. Civil and natural law are not different kinds, but different parts of law, whereof one part, being written, is called civil, the other unwritten, natural. But the right of nature, that is, the natural liberty of man, may by the civil law be abridged and restrained, nay, the end of making laws is no other but such restraint, without which there cannot possibly be any peace. And law was brought into the

world for nothing else but to limit the natural liberty of particular men in such manner as they might not hurt, but assist one another, and join together against a common enemy.

5. Provincial
laws are not
made by custom,
but by the sovereign power.

9. If the sovereign of one commonwealth subdue a people that have lived under other written laws and afterwards govern them by the same laws by which they were governed before; yet those laws are the civil laws of

---

1 This sentence is strong evidence that the laws of nature are not genuine laws.

the victor and not of the vanquished commonwealth. For the legislator is he, not by whose authority the laws were first made, but by whose authority they now continue to be laws. And therefore where there be divers provinces within the dominion of a commonwealth and in those provinces diversity of laws, which commonly are called the customs of each several province, we are not to understand that such customs have their force only from length of time, but that they were anciently laws written or otherwise made known for the constitutions and statutes of their sovereigns, and are now laws, not by virtue of the prescription of time, but by the constitutions of their present sovereigns.[1] But if an unwritten law in all the provinces of a dominion shall be generally observed and no iniquity appear in the use thereof, that law can be no other but a law of nature, equally obliging all mankind.

10. Seeing then all laws, written and unwritten, have their authority and force from the will of the commonwealth, that is to say, from the will of the representative, which in a monarchy is the monarch and in other commonwealths the sovereign assembly, a man may wonder from whence proceed such opinions as are found in the books of lawyers of eminence in several commonwealths, directly or by consequence making the legislative power depend on private men or subordinate judges. As for example, *that the common law hath no controller but the parliament*, which is true only where a parliament has the sovereign power and cannot be assembled nor dissolved, but by their own discretion.[2] For if there be a right in any else to dissolve them, there is a right also to control them and consequently to control their controllings. And if there be no such right, then the controller of laws is not *parlamentum*, but *rex in parlamento* [the king in parliament]. And where a parliament is sovereign, if it should assemble never so many or so wise men from the countries subject to them for whatsoever cause; yet there is no man will believe that such an assembly hath thereby acquired to themselves a legislative power. *Item* [also], that the two arms of a commonwealth are *force and justice*,

6. Some foolish opinions of lawyers concerning the making of laws.

---

1 See also 26.7.
2 The English parliament was assembled at the command of the monarch and dissolved at his command.

the first whereof is in the king, the other deposited in the hands of the parliament.[1] As if a commonwealth could consist where the force were in any hand which justice had not the authority to command and govern.

7.   11. That law can never be against reason, our lawyers are agreed, and that not the letter (that is, every construction of it), but that which is according to the intention of the legislator is the law.[2] And it is true; but the doubt is of whose reason it is that shall be received for law. It is not

[140] meant of any private reason; for then there would be as much contradiction in the laws as there is in the Schools;

Sir Edw. Coke upon Littleton, lib. 2, ch. 6, fol. 97, b. nor yet, as Sir Edward Coke makes it, an *artificial perfection of reason, gotten by long study, observation, and experience,* as his was. For it is possible long study may increase and confirm erroneous sentences; and where men build on false grounds, the more they build, the greater is the ruin; and of those that study and observe with equal time and diligence, the reasons and resolutions are and must remain discordant; and therefore it is not that *juris prudentia* or wisdom of subordinate judges, but the reason of this our artificial man the commonwealth and his command that maketh law; and the commonwealth being in their representative but one person, there cannot easily arise any contradiction in the laws; and when there doth [arise contradiction], the same reason is able, by interpretation or alteration, to take it away. In all courts of justice, the sovereign (which is the person of the commonwealth) is he that judgeth; the subordinate judge ought to have regard to the reason which moved his sovereign to make such law, that his sentence may be according thereunto, which then is his sovereign's sentence;[3] otherwise it is his own, and an unjust one.

8. Law made, if not also made known, is no law. 12. From this, that the law is a command, and a command consisteth in declaration or manifestation of the will of him that commandeth by voice, writing, or some other sufficient argument of the same, we may understand that

---

1 Hobbes is criticizing various actions by parliament in the early 1640s. For example, parliament organized a military force independent of the king.

2 What Hobbes gives with the first clause, "the law can never be against reason," he effectively takes back with the last, "that which is according to the intention of the legislator is the law."

3 See 23.7.

the command of the commonwealth is law only to those that have means to take notice of it. Over natural fools, children, or madmen[1] there is no law, no more than over brute beasts; nor are they capable of the title of just or unjust, because they had never power to make any covenant or to understand the consequences thereof, and consequently never took upon them to authorise the actions of any sovereign, as they must do that make to themselves a commonwealth. And as those from whom nature or accident hath taken away the notice of all laws in general, so also every man, from whom any accident not proceeding from his own default, hath taken away the means to take notice of any particular law, is excused if he observe it not; and to speak properly, that law is no law to him. It is therefore necessary to consider in this place what arguments and signs be sufficient for the knowledge of what is the law, that is to say, what is the will of the sovereign, as well in monarchies as in other forms of government.

13. And first, if it be a law that obliges all the subjects without exception and is not written nor otherwise published in such places as they may take notice thereof, it is a law of nature. For whatever men are to take knowledge of for law, not upon other men's words, but every one from his own reason, must be such as is agreeable to the reason of all men; which no law can be, but the law of nature. The laws of nature therefore need not any publishing nor proclamation, as being contained in this one sentence, approved by all the world, *Do not that to another which thou thinkest unreasonable to be done by another to thyself.*[2]

14. Secondly, if it be a law that obliges only some condition of men or one particular man and be not written nor published by word, then also it is a law of nature and known by the same arguments and signs that distinguish those in such a condition from other subjects. For whatsoever law is not written or some way published by him that makes it law can be known no way but by the reason of him that is to obey it; and is therefore also a law not only civil, but natural. For example, if the sovereign employ a public minister, without written instructions what

Unwritten laws are all of them laws of nature.

[141]

---

1 See also 16.10 and 27.23.
2 See 15.35.

to do, [then] he is obliged to take for instructions the dictates of reason, as [for example] if he make a judge, the judge is to take notice that his sentence ought to be according to the reason of his sovereign[1] (which being always understood to be equity), he is bound to it by the law of nature; or if an ambassador, he is (in all things not contained in his written instructions), to take for instruction that which reason dictates to be most conducing to his sovereign's interest, and so of all other ministers of the sovereignty, public and private. All which instructions of natural reason may be comprehended under one name of *fidelity*, which is a branch of natural justice.

15. The law of nature excepted, it belonged to the essence of all other laws to be made known to every man that shall be obliged to obey them, either by word or writing or some other act known to proceed from the sovereign authority. For the will of another cannot be understood but by his own word or act or by conjecture taken from his scope and purpose, which in the person of the commonwealth is to be supposed always consonant to equity and reason. And in ancient time, before letters were in common use, the laws were many times put into verse, [in order] that the rude people, taking pleasure in singing or reciting them, might the more easily retain them in memory. And for the same reason Solomon adviseth a man to bind the Ten Commandments upon his ten fingers. And for the Law which Moses gave to the people of Israel at the renewing of the Covenant, he biddeth them to teach it their children by discoursing of it both at home and upon the way at going to bed and at rising from bed; and to write it upon the posts and doors of their houses and to assemble the people, man, woman, and child, to hear it read.

Prov. 7:3.
Deut. 11:19.

Deut. 31:12.

Nothing is law where the legislator cannot be known.

16. Nor is it enough the law be written and published, but also that there be manifest signs that it proceedeth from the will of the sovereign. For private men, when they have or think they have force enough to secure their unjust designs and convoy them safely to their ambitious ends, may publish for laws what they please, without or against the legislative authority. There is therefore requisite not only a declaration of the law, but also sufficient

---

1 See 26.11.

signs of the author and authority.[1] The author or legislator is supposed in every commonwealth to be evident, because he is the sovereign, who, having been constituted by the consent of every one, is supposed by every one to be sufficiently known. And though the ignorance and security of men be such, for the most part, as that when the [142] memory of the first constitution of their commonwealth is worn out, they do not consider by whose power they use to be defended against their enemies and to have their industry protected and to be righted when injury is done them; yet because no man that considers can make question of it, no excuse can be derived from the ignorance of where the sovereignty is placed. And it is a dictate of natural reason and consequently an evident law of nature that no man ought to weaken that power, the protection whereof he hath himself demanded or wittingly received against others. Therefore of who is sovereign, no man but by his own fault (whatsoever evil men suggest), can make any doubt. The difficulty consisteth in the evidence of the authority derived from him,[2] the removing whereof dependeth on the knowledge of the public registers, public counsels, public ministers, and public seals, by which all laws are sufficiently verified; verified, I say, not authorised; for the verification is but the testimony and record, not the authority of the law, which consisteth in the command of the sovereign only.

Difference between verifying and authorising.

17. If therefore a man have a question of injury, depending on the law of nature, that is to say, on common equity, the sentence of the judge, that by commission hath authority to take cognizance of such causes, is a sufficient verification of the law of nature in that individual case. For though the advice of one that professeth the study of the law be useful for the avoiding of contention; yet it is but advice; it is the judge must tell men what is law, upon the hearing of the controversy.

The law verified by the subordinate judge.

18. But when the question is of injury or crime upon a written law, every man by recourse to the registers by himself or others may, if he will, be sufficiently informed, before he do such injury or commit the crime, whether

By the public registers.

---

1 In traditional terms, this is the requirement that a law must be promulgated.
2 See 16.4.

it be an injury or not; nay, he ought to do so; for when a man doubts whether the act he goeth about be just or unjust, and may inform himself if he will, the doing is unlawful. In like manner, he that supposeth himself injured in a case determined by the written law, which he may by himself or others see and consider; if he complain before he consults with the law, he does unjustly, and bewrayeth a disposition rather to vex other men than to demand his own right.

By letters patent and by public seal.

19. If the question be of obedience to a public officer, to have seen his commission (with the public seal) and heard it read, or to have had the means to be informed of it, if a man would, is a sufficient verification of his authority.[1] For every man is obliged to do his best endeavour to inform himself of all written laws that may concern his own future actions.

The interpretation of the law dependeth on the sovereign power.

[143]

20. The legislator [being] known, and the laws either by writing or by the light of nature sufficiently published, there wanteth yet another very material circumstance to make them obligatory. For it is not the letter, but the intendment or meaning, that is to say, the authentic interpretation of the law (which is the sense of the legislator), in which the nature of the law consisteth;[2] and therefore the interpretation of all laws dependeth on the authority sovereign; and the interpreters can be none but those which the sovereign, to whom only the subject oweth obedience, shall appoint. For else, by the craft of an interpreter, the law may be made to bear a sense contrary to that of the sovereign, by which means the interpreter becomes the legislator.

All laws need interpretation.

21. All laws, written and unwritten, have need of interpretation. The unwritten law of nature, though it be easy to such as without partiality and passion make use of their natural reason[3] and therefore leaves the violators thereof without excuse; yet considering there be very few, perhaps none, that in some cases are not blinded by self-love or some other passion, it is now become of all laws the most obscure and has consequently the greatest need of able interpreters. The written laws, if they be

---

1   See also 16.8.
2   See 26.11.
3   Cf. 15.39.

short, are easily misinterpreted, from the divers significations of a word or two; if long, they be more obscure
by the divers significations of many words, insomuch as
no written law, delivered in few or many words, can be
well understood without a perfect understanding of the
final causes for which the law was made, the knowledge
of which final causes is in the legislator. To him therefore there cannot be any knot in the law insoluble either
by finding out the ends to undo it by or else by making
what ends he will (as Alexander did with his sword in the
Gordian knot[1]) by the legislative power; which no other
interpreter can do.

22. The interpretation of the laws of nature in a commonwealth dependeth not on the books of moral philosophy. The authority of writers without the authority of the
commonwealth maketh not their opinions law, be they
never so true. That which I have written in this treatise
concerning the moral virtues and of their necessity for the
procuring and maintaining peace, though it be evident
truth, is not therefore presently law, but because in all
commonwealths in the world it is part of the civil law. For
though it be naturally reasonable; yet it is by the sovereign
power that it is law; otherwise, it were a great error to call
the laws of nature unwritten law, whereof we see so many
volumes published and in them so many contradictions
of one another and of themselves.

The authentical interpretation of law is not that of writers.

23. The interpretation of the law of nature is the sentence of the judge constituted by the sovereign authority
to hear and determine such controversies as depend thereon, and consisteth in the application of the law to the
present case. For in the act of judicature the judge doth
no more but consider whether the demand of the party be
consonant to natural reason and equity; and the sentence
he giveth is therefore the interpretation of the law of nature; which interpretation is authentic, not because it is
his private sentence, but because he giveth it by authority
of the sovereign, whereby it becomes the sovereign's sentence; which is law for that time to the parties pleading.

The interpreter of the law is the judge giving sentence viva voce [orally] in every particular case.

---

1 According to legend, whoever untied the Gordian knot would
rule Asia. Supposedly, Alexander the Great "untied" the knot
by cutting it with his sword. He went on to capture much of
Asia.

24. But because there is no judge subordinate nor sovereign but may err in a judgement of equity, if afterward in another like case he find it more consonant to equity to give a contrary sentence, he is obliged to do it. No man's error becomes his own law nor obliges him to persist in it. Neither, for the same reason, becomes it a law to other judges, though sworn to follow it. For though a wrong sentence given by authority of the sovereign, if he know and allow it, in such laws as are mutable, be a constitution of a new law in cases in which every little circumstance is the same; yet in laws immutable, such as are the laws of nature, they are no laws to the same or other judges in the like cases for ever after. Princes succeed one another; and one judge passeth, another cometh; nay, heaven and earth shall pass; but not one tittle of the law of nature shall pass; for it is the eternal law of God.[1] Therefore all the sentences of precedent judges that have ever been cannot all together make a law contrary to natural equity. Nor any examples of former judges can warrant an unreasonable sentence or discharge the present judge of the trouble of studying what is equity (in the case he is to judge) from the principles of his own natural reason. For example sake, it is against the law of nature to punish the innocent; and innocent is he that acquitteth himself judicially and is acknowledged for innocent by the judge. Put the case now that a man is accused of a capital crime, and seeing the power and malice of some enemy and the frequent corruption and partiality of judges, runneth away for fear of the event and afterwards is taken and brought to a legal trial and maketh it sufficiently appear he was not guilty of the crime, and being thereof acquitted is nevertheless condemned to lose his goods; this is a manifest condemnation of the innocent. I say therefore that there is no place in the world where this can be an interpretation of a law of nature or be made a law by the sentences of precedent judges that had done the same. For he that judged it first judged unjustly; and no injustice can be a pattern of judgement to succeeding judges. A written law may forbid innocent men to fly, and they may be punished for flying; but that flying for fear of injury should be taken for presumption of guilt after a man is already absolved

---

1 See 15.38, 15.41, and 42.11.

of the crime judicially is contrary to the nature of a presumption, which hath no place after judgement given. Yet this is set down by a great lawyer[1] for the common law of England: *If a man,* saith he, *that is innocent be accused of felony, and for fear flyeth for the same; albeit he judicially acquitteth himself of the felony; yet if it be found that he fled for the felony, he shall, notwithstanding his innocency, forfeit all his goods, chattels, debts, and duties. For as to the forfeiture of them, the law will admit no proof against the presumption in law, grounded upon his flight.* Here you see *an innocent man, judicially acquitted, notwithstanding his innocency* (when no written law forbade him to fly) after his acquittal, *upon a presumption in law,* condemned to lose all the goods he hath. If the law ground upon his flight a presumption of the fact (which was capital), the sentence ought to have been capital: if the presumption were not of the fact, for what then ought he to lose his goods? This therefore is no law of England;[2] nor is the condemnation grounded upon a presumption of law, but upon the presumption of the judges. It is also against law to say that no proof shall be admitted against a presumption of law. For all judges, sovereign and subordinate, if they refuse to hear proof, refuse to do justice; for though the sentence be just; yet the judges that condemn, without hearing the proofs offered, are unjust judges; and their presumption is but prejudice; which no man ought to bring with him to the seat of justice whatsoever precedent judgements or examples he shall pretend to follow. There be other things of this nature, wherein men's judgements have been perverted by trusting to precedents; but this is enough to show that though the sentence of the judge be a law to the party pleading; yet it is no law to any judge that shall succeed him in that office.

[145]

25. In like manner, when question is of the meaning of written laws, he is not the interpreter of them that writeth a commentary upon them. For commentaries are commonly more subject to cavil than the text, and therefore need other commentaries; and so there will be no end of such interpretation. And therefore unless there be an

---

1 I.e., Edward Coke. See also 15.4.
2 Hobbes is declaring what is the law of England. Recall that he said the law is whatever the sovereign wills it to be (26.7).

interpreter authorised by the sovereign, from which the subordinate judges are not to recede, the interpreter can be no other than the ordinary judges, in the same manner as they are in cases of the unwritten law; and their sentences are to be taken by them that plead for laws in that particular case, but not to bind other judges in like cases to give like judgements. For a judge may err in the interpretation even of written laws; but no error of a subordinate judge can change the law, which is the general sentence of the sovereign.

The difference between the letter and the sentence of the law.

26. In written laws men use to make a difference between the letter and the sentence of the law; and when by the letter is meant whatsoever can be gathered from the bare words, it is well distinguished. For the significations of almost all [words] are either in themselves or in the metaphorical use of them ambiguous, and may be drawn in argument to make many senses; but there is only one sense of the law. But if by the letter be meant the literal sense,[1] then the letter and the sentence or intention of the law is all one. For the literal sense is that which the legislator intended should by the letter of the law be signified. Now the intention of the legislator is always supposed to be equity; for it were a great contumely for a judge to think otherwise of the sovereign. He ought therefore, if the word of the law do not fully authorise a reasonable sentence, to supply it with the law of nature; or if the case be difficult, to respite judgement till he have received more ample authority. For example, a written law ordaineth that he which is thrust out of his house by force shall be restored by force. It happens that a man by negligence leaves his house empty and returning is kept out by force, in which case there is no special law ordained. It is evident that this case is contained in the same law; for else there is no remedy for him at all, which is to be supposed against the intention of the legislator. Again, the word of the law commandeth to judge according to the evidence. A man is accused falsely of a fact which the judge himself saw done by another, and not by him that is accused. In this case neither shall the

[146]

---

1 Traditionally, the literal sense meant the sense intended by the author, not, as it is today, the "dictionary meaning." The literal sense of the law is the sense intended by the sovereign.

letter of the law be followed to the condemnation of the innocent, nor shall the judge give sentence against the evidence of the witnesses, because the letter of the law is to the contrary, but procure of the sovereign that another be made judge and himself witness. So that the incommodity that follows the bare words of a written law may lead him to the intention of the law, whereby to interpret the same the better; though no incommodity can warrant a sentence against the law. For every judge of right and wrong is not judge of what is commodious or incommodious to the commonwealth.

27. The abilities required in a good interpreter of the law, that is to say, in a good judge, are not the same with those of an advocate, namely, the study of the laws. For a judge, as he ought to take notice of the fact from none but the witnesses, so also he ought to take notice of the law from nothing but the statutes and constitutions of the sovereign, alleged in the pleading or declared to him by some that have authority from the sovereign power to declare them; and [the judge] need not take care beforehand what he shall judge; for it shall be given him what he shall say concerning the fact, by witnesses; and what he shall say in point of law, from those that shall in their pleadings show it and by authority interpret it upon the place. The Lords of Parliament in England were judges; and most difficult causes have been heard and determined by them; yet few of them were much versed in the study of the laws, and fewer had made profession of them; and though they consulted with lawyers that were appointed to be present there for that purpose; yet they alone had the authority of giving sentence. In like manner, in the ordinary trials of right, twelve men of the common people are the judges and give sentence, not only of the fact, but of the right; and pronounce simply for the complainant or for the defendant; that is to say, are judges not only of the fact, but also of the right; and in a question of crime, not only determine whether done or not done, but also whether it be *murder, homicide, felony, assault,* and the like, which are determinations of law; but because they are not supposed to know the law of themselves, there is one that hath authority to inform them of it in the particular case they are to judge of. But yet if they judge not according to that he tells them, they are not subject thereby to any

The abilities required in a judge.

penalty, unless it be made appear they did it against their consciences or had been corrupted by reward.

28. The things that make a good judge or good interpreter of the laws are, first, *a right understanding* of that principal law of nature called *equity*, which, depending not on the reading of other men's writings, but on the goodness of a man's own natural reason and meditation, is presumed to be in those most that had most leisure and had the most inclination to meditate thereon. Secondly, *contempt of unnecessary riches and preferments*. Thirdly, *to be able in judgement to divest himself of all fear, anger, hatred, love, and compassion*. Fourthly, and lastly, *patience to hear, diligent attention in hearing, and memory to retain, digest, and apply what he hath heard.*

[147]

Divisions of law.

29. The difference and division of the laws has been made in divers manners, according to the different methods of those men that have written of them. For it is a thing that dependeth not on nature, but on the scope of the writer and is subservient to every man's proper method. In the *Institutions* of Justinian, we find seven sorts of civil laws: The *edicts, constitutions,* and *epistles of the prince,* that is, of the emperor, because the whole power of the people was in him. Like these are the proclamations of the kings of England.

1.

30. *The decrees of the whole people of Rome* (comprehending the Senate), when they were put to the question by the *senate*. These were laws, at first, by the virtue of the sovereign power residing in the people; and such of them as by the emperors were not abrogated remained laws by the authority imperial. For all laws that bind are understood to be laws by his authority that has power to repeal them. Somewhat like to these laws are the Acts of Parliament in England.

2.

31. *The decrees of the common people* (excluding the Senate), when they were put to the question by the *tribune* of the people. For such of them as were not abrogated by the emperors, remained laws by the authority imperial. Like to these were the orders of the House of Commons in England.

3.

32. *Senatus consulta,* the *orders of the senate,* because when the people of Rome grew so numerous as it was inconvenient to assemble them, it was thought fit by the emperor that men should consult the Senate instead of

4.

the people: and these have some resemblance with the Acts of Council.

33. *The edicts of praetors,* and (in some cases) of the aediles,[1] such as are the chief justices in the courts of England. 5.

34. *Responsa prudentium,* which were the sentences and opinions of those lawyers to whom the emperor gave authority to interpret the law, and to give answer to such as in matter of law demanded their advice; which answers the judges in giving judgement were obliged by the constitutions [enactments] of the emperor to observe; and [such answers] should be like the reports of cases judged if other judges be by the law of England bound to observe them. For the judges of the common law of England are not properly judges, but *juris consulti,*[2] of whom the judges, who are either the lords or twelve men of the country, are in point of law to ask advice. 6.

35. Also, *unwritten customs* (which in their own nature are an imitation of law), by the tacit consent of the emperor, in case they be not contrary to the law of nature, are very laws. 7.

36. Another division of laws is into *natural* and *positive.*[3] Natural are those which have been laws from all eternity, and are called not only natural, but also moral laws, consisting in the moral virtues, as justice, equity, and all habits of the mind that conduce to peace and charity, of which I have already spoken in the fourteenth and fifteenth chapters. [148]

37. *Positive* are those which have not been from eternity, but have been made laws by the will of those that have had the sovereign power over others, and are either written or made known to men by some other argument of the will of their legislator.

38. Again, of positive laws some are *human,* some *divine*; and of human positive laws, some are *distributive,* some *penal. Distributive* are those that determine the rights of the subjects, declaring to every man what it is Another division of law.

---

1 Praetors and aediles were two kinds of magistrates of ancient Rome. The praetors held the higher rank.
2 *Juris consulti* means lawyers.
3 If the laws of nature are not genuine laws, then the division of laws into natural and positive is analogous to the division of horses into saw horses and biological horses. See also 15.40.

by which he acquireth and holdeth a propriety in lands or goods, and a right or liberty of action; and these speak to all the subjects. *Penal* are those which declare what penalty shall be inflicted on those that violate the law; and [they] speak to the ministers and officers ordained for execution.[1] For though every one ought to be informed of the punishments ordained beforehand for their transgression, nevertheless the command is not addressed to the delinquent (who cannot be supposed will faithfully punish himself), but to public ministers appointed to see the penalty executed. And these penal laws are for the most part written together with the laws distributive, and are sometimes called judgements. For all laws are general judgements, or sentences of the legislator, as also every particular judgement is a law to him whose case is judged.

Divine positive law how made known to be law. 39. *Divine positive laws* (for natural laws, being eternal and universal, are all divine)[2] are those which, being the commandments of God, not from all eternity, nor universally addressed to all men, but only to a certain people or to certain persons, are declared for such by those whom God hath authorised to declare them. But this authority of man to declare what be these positive laws of God, how can it be known? God may command a man by a supernatural way to deliver laws to other men. But because it is of the essence of law that he who is to be obliged be assured of the authority of him that declareth it, which we cannot naturally take notice to be from God, *how can a man without supernatural revelations be assured of the revelation received by the declarer?* and *how can he be bound to obey them?* For the first question, how a man can be assured of the revelation of another without a revelation particularly to himself, it is evidently impossible; for though a man may be induced to believe such revelation from the miracles they see him do or from seeing the extraordinary sanctity of his life or from seeing the extraordinary wisdom or extraordinary felicity of his actions, all which are marks of God's extraordinary favour; yet they are not assured evidences of special revelation. Miracles are marvellous works; but that which is marvellous to one

---

1 See 23.10.
2 If "natural laws" are laws, then, it seems, the laws of nature are genuine laws. If they are not genuine laws, then God's command does not seem to make something a law.

may not be so to another. Sanctity may be feigned; and the visible felicities of this world are most often the work of God by natural and ordinary causes. And therefore no [149] man can infallibly know by natural reason that another has had a supernatural revelation of God's will, but only a belief; every one, as the signs thereof shall appear greater or lesser, a firmer or a weaker belief.[1]

40. But for the second,[2] how he can be bound to obey them, it is not so hard. For if the law declared be not against the law of nature (which is undoubtedly God's law) and he undertake to obey it, he is bound by his own act; bound I say to obey it, but not bound to believe it;[3] for men's belief and interior cogitations are not subject to the commands, but only to the operation of God, ordinary or extraordinary. Faith of supernatural law is not a fulfilling, but only an assenting to the same and not a duty that we exhibit to God, but a gift which God freely giveth to whom he pleaseth, as also unbelief is not a breach of any of his laws, but a rejection of them all, except the laws natural. But this that I say will be made yet clearer by the examples and testimonies concerning this point in Holy Scripture. The covenant God made with Abraham in a supernatural manner was thus, *This is the covenant which thou shalt observe between me and thee and thy seed after thee.* Abraham's seed had not this revelation, Gen. 17:10 nor were yet in being; yet they are a party to the covenant and bound to obey what Abraham should declare to them for God's law; which they could not be but in virtue of the obedience they owed to their parents, who (if they be subject to no other earthly power, as here in the case of

---

1 Hobbes draws a sharp line between belief and knowledge. People can believe or have faith in some person who claims to have had a revelation from God. But this is never knowledge. Hobbes does not commit himself here about whether the person who purportedly has the revelation knows that he had it. Cf. Chapter 36.

2 This was the second question posed about halfway through 26.39.

3 Hobbes's conventionalist answer—one is required to obey laws about religion commanded by the sovereign, but one is not required to believe them—drove his contemporaries to consternation and has delighted cynics and some atheists since the eighteenth century.

Abraham) have sovereign power over their children and servants.[1] Again, where God saith to Abraham, *In thee shall all nations of the earth be blessed; for I know thou wilt command thy children and thy house after thee to keep the way of the Lord, and to observe righteousness and judgement,* it is manifest the obedience of his family, who had no revelation, depended on their former obligation to obey their sovereign. At Mount Sinai Moses only went up to God; the people were forbidden to approach on pain of death; yet were they bound to obey all that Moses declared to them for God's law. Upon what ground, but on this submission of their own, *Speak thou to us, and we will hear thee; but let not God speak to us, lest we die?* By which two places it sufficiently appeareth that in a commonwealth a subject that has no certain and assured revelation particularly to himself concerning the will of God is to obey for such the command of the commonwealth; for if men were at liberty to take for God's commandments their own dreams and fancies or the dreams and fancies of private men, scarce two men would agree upon what is God's commandment; and yet in respect of them every man would despise the commandments of the commonwealth. I conclude, therefore, that in all things not contrary to the moral law (that is to say, to the law of nature), all subjects are bound to obey that for divine law which is declared to be so by the laws of the commonwealth.[2] Which also is evident to any man's reason; for whatsoever is not against the law of nature may be made law in the name of them that have the sovereign power; there is no reason men should be the less obliged by it when it is propounded in the name of God. Besides, there is no place in the world where men are permitted to pretend other commandments of God than are declared for such by the commonwealth. Christian states punish those that revolt from Christian religion; and all other states, those that set up any religion by them forbidden. For in whatsoever is not regulated by the commonwealth, it is equity (which is the law of nature, and therefore an eternal law of God) that every man equally enjoy his liberty.

[150]

---

1 See 20.5.
2 Hobbes wants to preserve the status quo. Allowing each person to judge what God has revealed is politically destabilizing and hence dangerous.

41. There is also another distinction of laws into *fundamental* and *not fundamental*: but I could never see in any author what a fundamental law signifieth. Nevertheless one may very reasonably distinguish laws in that manner.

Another division of laws.

42. For a fundamental law in every commonwealth is that which, being taken away, the commonwealth faileth and is utterly dissolved, as a building whose foundation is destroyed. And therefore a fundamental law is that by which subjects are bound to uphold whatsoever power is given to the sovereign, whether a monarch or a sovereign assembly, without which the commonwealth cannot stand; such as is the power of war and peace, of judicature, of election of officers, and of doing whatsoever he shall think necessary for the public good. Not fundamental is that, the abrogating whereof draweth not with it the dissolution of the commonwealth; such as are the laws concerning controversies between subject and subject. Thus much of the division of laws.

A fundamental law, what.

43. I find the words *lex civilis* and *jus civile*, that is to say, *law* and *right civil*, promiscuously used for the same thing, even in the most learned authors; which nevertheless ought not to be so. For *right* is liberty, namely that liberty which the civil law leaves us; but *civil law* is an *obligation*, and takes from us the liberty which the law of nature[1] gave us. Nature gave a right to every man to secure himself by his own strength and to invade a suspected neighbour by way of prevention; but the civil law takes away that liberty, in all cases where the protection of the law may be safely stayed for. Insomuch as *lex* and *jus* are as different as *obligation* and *liberty*.[2]

Difference between law and right.

44. Likewise laws and charters are taken promiscuously for the same thing. Yet charters are donations of the sovereign; and not laws, but exemptions from law. The phrase of a law is *jubeo, injungo*; *I command*, and *[I] enjoin*: the phrase of a charter is *dedi, concessi*; *I have given, I have granted*: but what is given or granted to a man is not forced upon him by a law.[3] A law may be made to bind all the subjects of a commonwealth; a liberty or charter

And between a law and a charter.

---

1 Hobbes should have said, "right of nature." In the Latin *Leviathan,* Hobbes correctly wrote that obligation takes away the liberty given by nature. Cf. 14.1.
2 See also 14.3.
3 See also 25.2–5.

is only to one man or some one part of the people. For to say all the people of a commonwealth have liberty in any case whatsoever is to say that, in such case, there hath been no law made; or else, having been made, is now abrogated.

[151]

Chapter XXVII

Of Crimes, Excuses, and Extenuations

Sin what. 1. A SIN is not only a transgression of a law, but also any contempt of the legislator. For such contempt is a breach of all his laws at once, and therefore may consist, not only in the *commission* of a fact or in the speaking of words by the laws forbidden or in the *omission* of what the law commandeth, but also in the intention or purpose to transgress. For the purpose to break the law is some degree of contempt of him to whom it belonged to see it executed. To be delighted in the imagination only of being possessed of another man's goods, servants, or wife, without any intention to take them from him by force or fraud, is no breach of the law that saith, *Thou shalt not covet*; nor is the pleasure a man may have in imagining or dreaming of the death of him from whose life he expecteth nothing but damage and displeasure a sin, but the resolving to put some act in execution that tendeth thereto. For to be pleased in the fiction of that which would please a man if it were real is a passion so adherent to the nature both of man and every other living creature, as to make it a sin were to make sin of being a man. The consideration of this has made me think them too severe, both to themselves and others, that maintain that the first motions of the mind, though checked with the fear of God, be sins. But I confess it is safer to err on that hand than on the other.

A crime, what. 2. A CRIME is a sin consisting in the committing by deed or word of that which the law forbiddeth, or the omission of what it hath commanded. So that every crime is a sin; but not every sin a crime. To intend to steal or kill is a sin, though it never appear in word or fact; for God that seeth the thought of man can lay it to his charge; but till it appear by something done or said, by which the intention may be argued by a human judge, it hath not the name of crime; which distinction the Greeks observed in the word *hamartēma* and *engklēma* or *aitia*; whereof the former (which is translated *sin*) signifieth any swerving from the law whatsoever; but the two latter (which are translated *crime*) signify that sin only whereof one man may accuse another. But of intentions which never appear by any outward act there is no place for human accusation. In like manner the Latins by *peccatum*, which is sin, signify all manner of deviation from the law; but by *crimen* (which word they derive from *cerno*, which signifies *to perceive*) they mean only such sins as may be made appear before a judge, and therefore are not mere intentions.

3. From this relation of sin to the law and of crime to the civil law, may be inferred, first, that where law ceaseth, sin ceaseth.[1] But because the law of nature is eternal, violation of covenants, ingratitude, arrogance, and all facts contrary to any moral virtue can never cease to be sin.[2] Secondly, that the civil law ceasing, crimes cease; for there being no other law remaining but that of nature, there is no place for accusation, every man being his own judge and accused only by his own conscience and cleared by the uprightness of his own intention. When therefore his intention is right, his fact is no sin; if otherwise, his fact is sin, but not crime. Thirdly, that when the sovereign power ceaseth, crime also ceaseth; for where there is no such power, there is no protection to be had from the law; and therefore everyone may protect himself by his own power; for no man in the institution of sovereign power can be supposed to give away the right of preserving his own body, for the safety whereof all sovereignty was ordained. But this is to be understood only of those that have not themselves contributed to the taking away of the

Where no civil law is, there is no crime. [152]

---

1 In the state of nature, considered as having no law of any kind, there can be no sin (and no crime). It is a mistake to think of Adam and Eve as being in the state of nature. They were under God's law, namely, not to eat of the fruit of the tree in the middle of the garden.

2 In the state of nature, considered as regulated by the laws of nature, sin is possible. If the laws of nature are not genuine laws, it would seem that sin would be impossible. Hobbes must be thinking of the laws of nature here as genuine divine laws.

power that protected them; for that was a crime from the beginning.

Ignorance of the law of nature excuseth no man.

4. The source of every crime is some defect of the understanding or some error in reasoning or some sudden force of the passions. Defect in the understanding is *ignorance*; in reasoning, *erroneous opinion*. Again, ignorance is of three sorts: of the *law*, and of the *sovereign*, and of the *penalty*. Ignorance of the law of nature excuseth no man, because every man that hath attained to the use of reason is supposed to know he ought not to do to another what he would not have done to himself. Therefore into what place soever a man shall come, if he do anything contrary to that law, it is a crime. If a man come from the Indies hither and persuade men here to receive a new religion or teach them anything that tendeth to disobedience of the laws of this country, though he be never so well persuaded of the truth of what he teacheth, he commits a crime and may be justly punished for the same, not only because his doctrine is false, but also because he does that which he would not approve in another, namely, that coming from hence, he should endeavour to alter the religion there. But ignorance of the civil law shall excuse a man in a strange country till it be declared to him, because till then no civil law is binding.[1]

Ignorance of the civil law excuseth sometimes.

5. In the like manner, if the civil law of a man's own country be not so sufficiently declared as he may know it if he will, nor the action against the law of nature, [then] the ignorance is a good excuse; in other cases ignorance of the civil law excuseth not.

Ignorance of the sovereign excuseth not.

6. Ignorance of the sovereign power in the place of a man's ordinary residence excuseth him not, because he ought to take notice of the power by which he hath been protected there.

Ignorance of penalty excuseth not.

7. Ignorance of the penalty, where the law is declared, excuseth no man; for in breaking the law, which without a fear of penalty to follow were not a law, but vain words, he undergoeth the penalty though he know not what it is, because whosoever voluntarily doth any action, accepteth all the known consequences of it; but punishment is a known consequence of the violation of the laws in every

[153] commonwealth; which punishment, if it be determined

---

1 See also 26.12 and 26.16.

already by the law, he is subject to that; if not, then is he subject to arbitrary punishment. For it is reason [reasonable] that he which does injury, without other limitation than that of his own will should suffer punishment without other limitation than that of his will whose law is thereby violated.

8. But when a penalty is either annexed to the crime in the law itself or hath been usually inflicted in the like cases, there the delinquent is excused from a greater penalty. For the punishment foreknown, if not great enough to deter men from the action, is an invitement to it, because when men compare the benefit of their injustice with the harm of their punishment, by necessity of nature they choose that which appeareth best for themselves; and therefore when they are punished more than the law had formerly determined or more than others were punished for the same crime, it is the law that tempted and deceiveth them. Punishments declared before the fact excuse from greater punishments after it.

9. No law made after a fact done can make it a crime, because if the fact be against the law of nature, the law was before the fact; and a positive law cannot be taken notice of before it be made and therefore cannot be obligatory. But when the law that forbiddeth a fact is made before the fact be done; yet he that doth the fact is liable to the penalty ordained after, in case no lesser penalty were made known before, neither by writing nor by example, for the reason immediately before alleged. Nothing can be made a crime by a law made after the fact.

10. From defect in reasoning (that is to say, from error), men are prone to violate the laws three ways. First, by presumption of false principles, as when men, from having observed how in all places and in all ages unjust actions have been authorised by the force and victories of those who have committed them; and that, potent men breaking through the cobweb laws of their country, the weaker sort and those that have failed in their enterprises have been esteemed the only criminals, have thereupon taken for principles and grounds of their reasoning *that justice is but a vain word, that whatsoever a man can get by his own industry and hazard is his own, that the practice of all nations cannot be unjust, that examples of former times are good arguments of doing the like again,* and many more of that kind; which being granted, no act in itself can be a crime, but must be made so (not by the law, but) by the False principles of right and wrong causes of crime.

success of them that commit it; and the same fact be virtuous or vicious, as fortune pleaseth; so that what Marius makes a crime, Sylla[1] shall make meritorious, and Caesar (the same laws standing) turn again into a crime, to the perpetual disturbance of the peace of the commonwealth.

11. Secondly, by false teachers that either misinterpret the law of nature, making it thereby repugnant to the law civil, or by teaching for laws such doctrines of their own, or traditions of former times, as are inconsistent with the duty of a subject.

12. Thirdly, by erroneous inferences from true principles; which happens commonly to men that are hasty and precipitate in concluding and resolving what to do; such as are they that have both a great opinion of their own understanding and believe that things of this nature require not time and study, but only common experience and a good natural wit, whereof no man thinks himself unprovided; whereas the knowledge of right and wrong, which is no less difficult, there is no man will pretend to without great and long study.[2] And of those defects in reasoning, there is none that can excuse, though some of them may extenuate, a crime in any man that pretendeth to the administration of his own private business; [it excuses] much less in them that undertake a public charge, because they pretend to the reason upon the want whereof they would ground their excuse.

13. Of the passions that most frequently are the causes of crime, one is vainglory or a foolish overrating of their own worth, as if difference of worth were an effect of their wit or riches or blood or some other natural quality, not depending on the will of those that have the sovereign authority. From whence proceedeth a presumption that the punishments ordained by the laws and extended generally to all subjects ought not to be inflicted on them with the same rigour they are inflicted on poor, obscure,

---

1 Caius Marius (155-86 BCE) and Lucius Cornelius Sulla (138-78 BCE) were Roman generals who competed for power. Sulla defeated Marius and set himself up as dictator.

2 Everyone knows that the knowledge of right and wrong requires great and long study; nonetheless, people think that drawing the right conclusions from the laws requires only common experience and a good natural wit, even though getting this knowledge is as difficult as getting that of right and wrong.

and simple men, comprehended under the name of the *vulgar.*

14. Therefore it happeneth commonly that such as value themselves by the greatness of their wealth adventure on crimes, upon hope of escaping punishment by corrupting public justice or obtaining pardon by money or other rewards.

Presumption of riches.

15. And that such as have multitude of potent kindred and popular men that have gained reputation amongst the multitude take courage to violate the laws from a hope of oppressing the power to whom it belonged to put them in execution.

And friends.

16. And that such as have a great and false opinion of their own wisdom take upon them to reprehend the actions and call in question the authority of them that govern and so to unsettle the laws with their public discourse, as that nothing shall be a crime but what their own designs require should be so. It happeneth also to the same men to be prone to all such crimes as consist in craft and in deceiving of their neighbours, because they think their designs are too subtle to be perceived. These I say are effects of a false presumption of their own wisdom. For of them that are the first movers in the disturbance of commonwealth (which can never happen without a civil war), very few are left alive long enough to see their new designs established; so that the benefit of their crimes redoundeth to posterity and such as would least have wished it; which argues they were not so wise as they thought they were. And those that deceive upon hope of not being observed do commonly deceive themselves (the darkness in which they believe they lie hidden being nothing else but their own blindness), and are no wiser than children that think all hid by hiding their own eyes.

Wisdom.

17. And generally all vainglorious men (unless they be withal timorous) are subject to anger, as being more prone than others to interpret for contempt the ordinary liberty of conversation; and there are few crimes that may not be produced by anger.

[155]

18. As for the passions of hate, lust, ambition, and covetousness, what crimes they are apt to produce is so obvious to every man's experience and understanding, as there needeth nothing to be said of them, saving that they are infirmities so annexed to the nature both

Hatred, lust, ambition, covetousness, causes of crime.

of man and all other living creatures, as that their effects cannot be hindered but by extraordinary use of reason or a constant severity in punishing them. For in those things men hate, they find a continual and unavoidable molestation, whereby either a man's patience must be everlasting or he must be eased by removing the power of that which molesteth him; the former is difficult; the latter is many times impossible without some violation of the law. Ambition and covetousness are passions also that are perpetually incumbent and pressing; whereas reason is not perpetually present to resist them; and therefore whensoever the hope of impunity appears, their effects proceed. And for lust, what it wants in the lasting it hath in the vehemence, which sufficeth to weigh down the apprehension of all easy or uncertain punishments.

Fear sometimes cause of crime, as when the danger is neither present nor corporeal. 19. Of all passions, that which inclineth men least to break the laws is fear.[1] Nay, excepting some generous natures, it is the only thing (when there is appearance of profit or pleasure by breaking the laws) that makes men keep them. And yet in many cases a crime may be committed through fear.

20. For not every fear justifies the action it produceth, but the fear only of corporeal hurt, which we call bodily fear and from which a man cannot see how to be delivered but by the action. A man is assaulted [and] fears present death, from which he sees not how to escape but by wounding him that assaulteth him; if he wound him to death, this is no crime, because no man is supposed at the making of a commonwealth to have abandoned the defence of his life or limbs, where the law cannot arrive time enough to his assistance. But to kill a man because from his actions or his threatenings I may argue he will kill me when he can (seeing I have time and means to demand protection from the sovereign power) is a crime.[2]

---

1 Hobbes could be called the philosopher of fear. See also 11.4-9, 13.14, and 14.31.

2 Hobbes does not discuss intermediate cases, such as when a person knows that his enemy is about to set in motion a complex plan to kill him and that the only way to stop the plan is to kill the enemy before the plan is begun. Another intermediate case is that in which a person knows an enemy will kill him some time in the future and has good reason to believe that the sovereign cannot protect him from that attack.

Again, a man receives words of disgrace or some little injuries (for which they that made the laws had assigned no punishment, nor thought it worthy of a man that hath the use of reason to take notice of) and is afraid unless he revenge it, he shall fall into contempt and consequently be obnoxious to the like injuries from others; and to avoid this, [he] breaks the law and protects himself for the future by the terror of his private revenge. This is a crime; for the hurt is not corporeal, but fantastical, and (though, in this corner of the world, made sensible by a custom not many years since begun, amongst young and vain men) so light as a gallant man and one that is assured of his own courage cannot take notice of. Also a man may stand in fear of spirits, either through his own superstition or through too much credit given to other men that tell him of strange dreams and visions; and thereby be made believe they will hurt him for doing or omitting divers things which, nevertheless, to do or omit is contrary to the laws; and that which is so done or omitted is not to be excused by this fear, but is a crime. For, as I have shown before in the second chapter, dreams be naturally but the fancies remaining in sleep after the impressions our senses had formerly received waking, and when men are by any accident unassured they have slept, seem to be real visions; and therefore he that presumes to break the law upon his own or another's dream or pretended vision, or upon other fancy of the power of invisible spirits than is permitted by the commonwealth, leaveth the law of nature, which is a certain offence, and followeth the imagery of his own or another private man's brain, which he can never know whether it signifieth anything or nothing, nor whether he that tells his dream say true or lie; which if every private man should have leave to do (as they must, by the law of nature, if any one have it), there could no law be made to hold, and so all commonwealth would be dissolved. [156]

21. From these different sources of crimes, it appears already that all crimes are not, as the Stoics of old time maintained,[1] of the same alloy. There is place, not only for EXCUSE, by which that which seemed a crime is proved to be none at all; but also for EXTENUATION, by which the crime, that seemed great, is made less. For though

Crimes not equal.

---

1 See for example, Cicero, *De Finibus* iv. 23 and 28.

all crimes do equally deserve the name of injustice, as all deviation from a straight line is equally crookedness, which the Stoics rightly observed; yet it does not follow that all crimes are equally unjust, no more than that all crooked lines are equally crooked; which the Stoics, not observing, held it as great a crime to kill a hen, against the law, as to kill one's father.

22. That which totally excuseth a fact and takes away from it the nature of a crime can be none but that which, at the same time, taketh away the obligation of the law. For the fact committed once against the law, if he that committed it be obliged to the law, can be no other than a crime.

23. The want of means to know the law totally excuseth; for the law whereof a man has no means to inform himself is not obligatory. But the want of diligence to enquire shall not be considered as a want of means; nor shall any man that pretendeth to reason enough for the government of his own affairs be supposed to want means to know the laws of nature, because they are known by the reason he pretends to; only children and madmen are excused from offences against the law natural.[1]

24. Where a man is captive, or in the power of the enemy (and he is then in the power of the enemy when his person, or his means of living, is so), if it be without his own fault, the obligation of the law ceaseth, because he must obey the enemy or die, and consequently such obedience is no crime; for no man is obliged (when the protection of the law faileth) not to protect himself by the best means he can.

[157] 25. If a man by the terror of present death be compelled to do a fact against the law, he is totally excused, because no law can oblige a man to abandon his own preservation. And supposing such a law were obligatory; yet a man would reason thus: *If I do it not, I die presently; if I do it, I die afterwards; therefore by doing it, there is time of life gained.* Nature therefore compels him to the fact.

26. When a man is destitute of food or other thing necessary for his life and cannot preserve himself any other way but by some fact against the law, as if in a great famine he take the food by force or stealth, which he cannot

---

1 See also 26.12, 27.4, and "Review and Conclusion," 13.

obtain for money nor charity; or in defence of his life, snatch away another man's sword; he is totally excused for the reason next before alleged.

27. Again, facts done against the law by the authority of another are by that authority excused against the author, because no man ought to accuse his own fact in another that is but his instrument;[1] but it is not excused against a third person thereby injured, because in the violation of the law both the author and actor are criminals. From hence it followeth that when that man or assembly that hath the sovereign power commandeth a man to do that which is contrary to a former law, the doing of it is totally excused; for he ought not to condemn it himself, because he is the author; and what cannot justly be condemned by the sovereign cannot justly be punished by any other. Besides, when the sovereign commandeth anything to be done against his own former law, the command, as to that particular fact, is an abrogation of the law.

Excuses against the author.

28. If that man or assembly that hath the sovereign power disclaim any right essential to the sovereignty, whereby there accrueth to the subject any liberty inconsistent with the sovereign power, that is to say, with the very being of a commonwealth; if the subject shall refuse to obey the command in anything, contrary to the liberty granted, [then] this is nevertheless a sin and contrary to the duty of the subject; for he ought to take notice of what is inconsistent with the sovereignty, because it was erected by his own consent and for his own defence, and that such liberty as is inconsistent with it was granted through ignorance of the evil consequence thereof. But if he not only disobey, but also resist a public minister in the execution of it, then it is a crime, because he might have been righted, without any breach of the peace, upon complaint.

29. The degrees of crime are taken on divers scales and measured, first, by the malignity of the source or cause; secondly, by the contagion of the example; thirdly, by the

---

1   In 1640 and earlier, an agent of the monarch could be convicted of doing something that the king had commanded, even though the king could not be. Hobbes may be thinking again of the famous case of Lord Strafford (see p. 223, note 4 above).

mischief of the effect; and fourthly, by the concurrence of times, places, and persons.

30. The same fact done against the law, if it proceed from presumption of strength, riches, or friends to resist those that are to execute the law, is a greater crime than if it proceed from hope of not being discovered or of escape by flight; for presumption of impunity by force is a root from whence springeth at all times and upon all temptations a contempt of all laws; whereas in the latter case the apprehension of danger that makes a man fly renders him more obedient for the future. A crime which we know to be so is greater than the same crime proceeding from a false persuasion that it is lawful; for he that committeth it against his own conscience presumeth on his force or other power, which encourages him to commit the same again, but he that doth it by error, after the error shown him, is conformable to the law.

31. He whose error proceeds from the authority of a teacher or an interpreter of the law publicly authorised is not so faulty as he whose error proceedeth from a peremptory pursuit of his own principles and reasoning; for what is taught by one that teacheth by public authority, the commonwealth teacheth and hath a resemblance of law, till the same authority controlleth it; and in all crimes that contain not in them a denial of the sovereign power nor are against an evident law excuseth totally; whereas he that groundeth his actions on his private judgement ought, according to the rectitude or error thereof, to stand or fall.

32. The same fact, if it have been constantly punished in other men, is a greater crime than if there have been many precedent examples of impunity. For those examples are so many hopes of impunity, given by the sovereign himself; and because he which furnishes a man with such a hope and presumption of mercy, as encourageth him to offend, hath his part in the offence, he cannot reasonably charge the offender with the whole.

33. A crime arising from a sudden passion is not so great as when the same ariseth from long meditation; for in the former case there is a place for extenuation in the common infirmity of human nature; but he that doth it with premeditation has used circumspection and cast his eye on the law, on the punishment, and on the

consequence thereof to human society; all which in committing the crime he hath contemned and postponed to his own appetite. But there is no suddenness of passion sufficient for a total excuse; for all the time between the first knowing of the law and the commission of the fact, shall be taken for a time of deliberation, because he ought, by meditation of the law, to rectify the irregularity of his passions.

34. Where the law is publicly and with assiduity before all the people read and interpreted, a fact done against it is a greater crime than where men are left without such instruction to inquire of it with difficulty, uncertainty, and interruption of their callings, and be informed by private men; for in this case, part of the fault is discharged upon common infirmity; but in the former there is apparent negligence, which is not without some contempt of the sovereign power.

35. Those facts which the law expressly condemneth, but the lawmaker by other manifest signs of his will tacitly approveth, are less crimes than the same facts condemned both by the law and lawmaker. For seeing the will of the lawmaker is a law, there appear in this case two contradictory laws; which would totally excuse, if men were bound to take notice of the sovereign's approbation, by other arguments than are expressed by his command. But because there are punishments consequent, not only to the transgression of his law, but also to the observing of it, he is in part a cause of the transgression and therefore cannot reasonably impute the whole crime to the delinquent. For example, the law condemneth duels; the punishment is made capital; on the contrary part, he that refuseth duel is subject to contempt and scorn, without remedy; and sometimes by the sovereign himself thought unworthy to have any charge or preferment in war; if thereupon he accept duel, considering all men lawfully endeavour to obtain the good opinion of them that have the sovereign power, he ought not in reason to be rigorously punished, seeing part of the fault may be discharged on the punisher; which I say, not as wishing liberty of private revenges or any other kind of disobedience, but a care in governors not to countenance anything obliquely which directly they forbid. The examples of princes, to those that see them, are and ever have been

Tacit approbation of the sovereign extenuates.

[159]

more potent to govern their actions than the laws themselves. And though it be our duty to do, not what they do, but what they say; yet will that duty never be performed till it please God to give men an extraordinary and supernatural grace to follow that precept.

Comparison of crimes from their effect. 36. Again, if we compare crimes by the mischief of their effects; first, the same fact when it redounds to the damage of many is greater than when it redounds to the hurt of few. And therefore when a fact hurteth, not only in the present, but also by example in the future, it is a greater crime than if it hurt only in the present; for the former is a fertile crime and multiplies to the hurt of many; the latter is barren. To maintain doctrines contrary to the religion established in the commonwealth is a greater fault in an authorised preacher than in a private person; so also is it to live profanely, incontinently, or do any irreligious act whatsoever. Likewise in a professor of the law to maintain any point or do any act that tendeth to the weakening of the sovereign power is a greater crime than in another man; also in a man that hath such reputation for wisdom, as that his counsels are followed or his actions imitated by many, his fact against the law is a greater crime than the same fact in another; for such men not only commit crime, but teach it for law to all other men. And generally all crimes are the greater by the scandal they give, that is to say, by becoming stumbling-blocks to the weak, that look not so much upon the way they go in, as upon the light that other men carry before them.

Laesa majestas. 37. Also facts of hostility against the present state of the commonwealth are greater crimes than the same acts done to private men; for the damage extends itself to all; such are the betraying of the strengths or revealing of the secrets of the commonwealth to an enemy; also all attempts upon the representative of the commonwealth, be [160] it a monarch or an assembly; and all endeavours by word or deed to diminish the authority of the same either in the present time or in succession; which crimes the Latins understand by *crimina laesae majestatis*,[1] and consist in design or act contrary to a fundamental law.

Bribery and false testimony. 38. Likewise those crimes which render judgements of no effect are greater crimes than injuries done to one or a

---

1 Latin: crimes against the sovereignty of the state.

few persons; as to receive money to give false judgement or testimony is a greater crime than otherwise to deceive a man of the like or a greater sum, because not only he has wrong that falls by such judgements, but [also] all judgements are rendered useless and occasion ministered to force and private revenges.

39. Also robbery and depeculation [embezzlement] of the public treasury or revenues is a greater crime than the robbing or defrauding of a private man, because to rob the public is to rob many at once. Depeculation.

40. Also the counterfeit usurpation of public minis- try, the counterfeiting of public seals or public coin [is a greater crime] than counterfeiting of a private man's person or his seal, because the fraud thereof extendeth to the damage of many. Counterfeiting authority.

41. Of facts against the law done to private men, the greater crime is that where the damage, in the common opinion of men, is most sensible. And therefore: Crimes against private men compared.

42. To kill against the law is a greater crime than any other injury, life preserved.

43. And to kill with torment, greater than simply to kill.

44. And mutilation of a limb, greater than the spoiling a man of his goods.

45. And the spoiling a man of his goods by terror of death or wounds, than by clandestine surreption [theft].

46. And by clandestine surreption, than by consent fraudulently obtained.

47. And the violation of chastity by force, greater than by flattery.

48. And of a woman married, than of a woman not married.

49. For all these things are commonly so valued, though some men are more, and some less, sensible of the same offence. But the law regardeth not the particular, but the general inclination of mankind.

50. And therefore the offence men take from contume- ly [insult] in words or gesture, when they produce no oth- er harm than the present grief of him that is reproached, hath been neglected in the laws of the Greeks, Romans, and other both ancient and modern commonwealths, supposing the true cause of such grief to consist, not in the contumely (which takes no hold upon men conscious

of their own virtue), but in the pusillanimity [pettiness] of him that is offended by it.

51. Also a crime against a private man is much aggravated by the person, time, and place. For to kill one's parent is a greater crime than to kill another; for the parent ought to have the honour of a sovereign (though he have surrendered his power to the civil law), because he had it [161] originally by nature. And to rob a poor man is a greater crime than to rob a rich man, because it is to the poor a more sensible damage.[1]

52. And a crime committed in the time or place appointed for devotion is greater than if committed at another time or place; for it proceeds from a greater contempt of the law.

53. Many other cases of aggravation and extenuation might be added; but by these I have set down, it is obvious to every man to take the altitude of any other crime proposed.

Public crimes   54. Lastly, because in almost all crimes there is an
what.   injury done, not only to some private men, but also to the commonwealth, the same crime, when the accusation is in the name of the commonwealth, is called a public crime; and when in the name of a private man, a private crime; and the pleas according thereupon called public, *judicia publica*, Pleas of the Crown; or Private Pleas. As in an accusation of murder, if the accuser be a private man, the plea is a private plea; if the accuser be the sovereign, the plea is a public plea.

Chapter XXVIII

Of Punishments and Rewards

The definition of   1. A PUNISHMENT *is an evil inflicted by public authority on*
punishment.   *him that hath done or omitted that which is judged by the same authority to be a transgression of the law, to the end that the will of men may thereby the better be disposed to obedience.*[2]

Right to punish   2. Before I infer anything from this definition, there
whence derived.   is a question to be answered of much importance; which

---

1 This is Hobbes at his best.
2 Cf. 20.13 and 30.23.

is, by what door the right or authority of punishing, in any case, came in. For by that which has been said before, no man is supposed bound by covenant not to resist violence;[1] and consequently it cannot be intended that he gave any right to another to lay violent hands upon his person. In the making of a commonwealth every man giveth away the right of defending another, but not of defending himself.[2] Also he obligeth himself to assist him that hath the sovereignty in the punishing of another, but of himself not. But to covenant to assist the sovereign in doing hurt to another, unless he that so covenanteth have a right to do it himself, is not to give him a right to punish. It is manifest therefore that the right which the commonwealth (that is, he or they that represent it) hath to punish is not grounded on any concession or gift of the subjects.[3] But I have also shown formerly that before the institution of commonwealth, every man had a right to everything and to do whatsoever he thought necessary to his own preservation, subduing, hurting, or killing any man in order thereunto. And this is the foundation of that right of punishing which is exercised in every commonwealth. For the subjects did not give the sovereign that right, but only, in laying down theirs, strengthened him to use his own as he should think fit for the preservation of them all; so that it was not given, but left to him and to him only, and, excepting the limits set him by natural law, as entire as in the condition of mere nature and of war of everyone against his neighbour. [162]

3. From the definition of punishment, I infer, first, that neither private revenges nor injuries of private men can properly be styled punishment, because they proceed not from public authority.[4]

Private injuries and revenges, no punishments:

4. Secondly, that to be neglected and unpreferred by the public favour is not a punishment, because no new

Nor denial of preferment.

---

1 See 14.29.
2 See also 27.20.
3 See also 18.2, 20.1, and 21.14
4 Hobbes is commenting on the concept of punishment. It is part of the concept of punishment that if x is a punishment, then x was administered by a public authority. If someone says, "Ali punished Liston in the fourth round of the boxing match," either the use is metaphorical or the sentence is false. See also 28.22.

evil is thereby on any man inflicted; he is only left in the estate he was in before.

5. Thirdly, that the evil inflicted by public authority, without precedent public condemnation, is not to be styled by the name of punishment, but of a hostile act, because the fact for which a man is punished ought first to be judged by public authority to be a transgression of the law.

6. Fourthly, that the evil inflicted by usurped power and judges without authority from the sovereign is not punishment, but an act of hostility, because the acts of power usurped have not for author the person condemned, and therefore are not acts of public authority.

7. Fifthly, that all evil which is inflicted without intention or possibility of disposing the delinquent or, by his example, other men to obey the laws is not punishment, but an act of hostility, because without such an end no hurt done is contained under that name.

8. Sixthly, whereas to certain actions there be annexed by nature divers hurtful consequences, as when a man in assaulting another is himself slain or wounded or when he falleth into sickness by the doing of some unlawful act; such hurt, though in respect of God, who is the author of nature, it may be said to be inflicted and therefore a punishment divine;[1] yet it is not contained in the name of punishment in respect of men, because it is not inflicted by the authority of man.

9. Seventhly, if the harm inflicted be less than the benefit of contentment that naturally followeth the crime committed, that harm is not within the definition and is rather the price or redemption than the punishment of a crime, because it is of the nature of punishment to have for end the disposing of men to obey the law; which end (if it be less than the benefit of the transgression) it attaineth not, but worketh a contrary effect.

10. Eighthly, if a punishment be determined and prescribed in the law itself and after the crime committed there be a greater punishment inflicted, the excess is not punishment, but an act of hostility. For seeing the aim of punishment is not a revenge, but terror, and the terror of a great punishment unknown is taken away by the declaration of a less, the unexpected addition is no part

---

1 See also 31.40.

of the punishment. But where there is no punishment at all determined by the law, there whatsoever is inflicted hath the nature of punishment. For he that goes about the violation of a law, wherein no penalty is determined, expecteth an indeterminate, that is to say, an arbitrary punishment.

11. Ninthly, harm inflicted for a fact done before there was a law that forbade it is not punishment, but an act of hostility; for before the law, there is no transgression of the law; but punishment supposeth a fact judged to have been a transgression of the law; therefore harm inflicted before the law made is not punishment, but an act of hostility. *Hurt inflicted for a fact done before the law, no punishment.*

12. Tenthly, hurt inflicted on the representative of the commonwealth is not punishment, but an act of hostility, because it is of the nature of punishment to be inflicted by public authority, which is the authority only of the representative itself. *The representative of the commonwealth unpunishable.*

13. Lastly, harm inflicted upon one that is a declared enemy falls not under the name of punishment, because seeing they were either never subject to the law and therefore cannot transgress it or having been subject to it and professing to be no longer so, by consequence deny they can transgress it, all the harms that can be done them must be taken as acts of hostility. But in declared hostility all infliction of evil is lawful. From whence it followeth that if a subject shall by fact or word wittingly and deliberately deny the authority of the representative of the commonwealth (whatsoever penalty hath been formerly ordained for treason), he may lawfully be made to suffer whatsoever the representative will; for in denying subjection, he denies such punishment as by the law hath been ordained, and therefore suffers as an enemy of the commonwealth, that is, according to the will of the representative. For the punishments set down in the law are to subjects, not to enemies; such as are they that, having been by their own act subjects, deliberately revolting, deny the sovereign power. *Hurt to revolted subjects is done by right of war, not by way of punishment.*

14. The first and most general distribution of punishments is into *divine* and *human*. Of the former I shall have occasion to speak in a more convenient place hereafter.[1]

---

1 See 31.40.

15. *Human* are those punishments that be inflicted by the commandment of man; and are either corporal or pecuniary or ignominy or imprisonment or exile or mixed of these.

Punishments corporal. 16. *Corporal punishment* is that which is inflicted on the body directly and according to the intention of him that inflicteth it; such as are stripes or wounds or deprivation of such pleasures of the body as were before lawfully enjoyed.

Capital. 17. And of these, some be *capital*, some *less* than *capital*. Capital is the infliction of death, and that either simply or with torment. Less than capital are stripes, wounds, chains, and any other corporal pain not in its own nature mortal. For if upon the infliction of a punishment death follow, not in the intention of the inflicter, the punishment is not to be esteemed capital, though the harm [164] prove mortal by an accident not to be foreseen; in which case death is not inflicted, but hastened.

18. *Pecuniary punishment* is that which consisteth not only in the deprivation of a sum of money, but also of lands or any other goods which are usually bought and sold for money. And in case the law that ordaineth such a punishment be made with design to gather money from such as shall transgress the same, it is not properly a punishment, but the price of privilege and exemption from the law, which doth not absolutely forbid the fact but only to those that are not able to pay the money, except where the law is natural or part of religion; for in that case it is not an exemption from the law, but a transgression of it. As where a law exacteth a pecuniary mulct [fine] of them that take the name of God in vain, the payment of the mulct is not the price of a dispensation to swear, but the punishment of the transgression of a law indispensable. In like manner if the law impose a sum of money to be paid to him that has been injured, this is but a satisfaction for the hurt done him and extinguisheth the accusation of the party injured, not the crime of the offender.

Ignominy. 19. *Ignominy* is the infliction of such evil as is made dishonourable or the deprivation of such good as is made honourable by the commonwealth. For there be some things honourable by nature, as the effects of courage, magnanimity, strength, wisdom, and other abilities of body and mind, others made honourable by the commonwealth, as badges, titles, offices, or any other singular mark of the sovereign's favour. The former (though they may fail by nature or accident) cannot be taken away by a law; and therefore the loss of them is not punishment. But the latter may be taken away by the public authority that made them honourable, and are properly punishments; such are, degrading men condemned of their badges, titles, and offices, or declaring them incapable of the like in time to come.

20. *Imprisonment* is when a man is by public authority deprived of liberty and may happen from two divers ends, whereof one is the safe custody of a man accused, the other is the inflicting of pain on a man condemned. The former is not punishment, because no man is supposed to be punished before he be judicially heard and declared guilty. And therefore whatsoever hurt a man is made to suffer by bonds or restraint before his cause be heard, over and above that which is necessary to assure his custody, is against the law of nature. But the latter is punishment because evil and inflicted by public authority for somewhat that has by the same authority been judged a transgression of the law. Under this word imprisonment, I comprehend all restraint of motion caused by an external obstacle,[1] be it a house, which is called by the general name of a prison, or an island, as when men are said to be confined to it, or a place where men are set to work, as in old time men have been condemned to quarries, and in these times to galleys, or be it a chain or any other such impediment.

Imprisonment.

21. *Exile* (banishment) is when a man is for a crime condemned to depart out of the dominion of the commonwealth or out of a certain part thereof, and during a prefixed time or forever not to return into it; and [it] seemeth not in its own nature, without other circumstances, to be a punishment, but rather an escape or a public commandment to avoid punishment by flight. And Cicero says there was never any such punishment ordained in the city of Rome; but calls it a refuge of men in danger. For if a man banished be nevertheless permitted to enjoy his goods and the revenue of his lands, the mere change of air is no punishment; nor does it tend to

Exile.
[165]

---

1   Cf. 21.1.

that benefit of the commonwealth for which all punishments are ordained, that is to say, to the forming of men's wills to the observation of the law; but many times to the damage of the commonwealth. For a banished man is a lawful enemy of the commonwealth that banished him, as being no more a member of the same. But if he be withal deprived of his lands or goods, then the punishment lieth not in the exile, but is to be reckoned amongst punishments pecuniary.

The punishment of innocent subjects is contrary to the law of nature.

22. All punishments of innocent subjects, be they great or little, are against the law of nature; for punishment is only for transgression of the law; and therefore there can be no punishment of the innocent.[1] It is therefore a violation, first, of that law of nature which forbiddeth all men in their revenges to look at anything but some future good; for there can arrive no good to the commonwealth by punishing the innocent. Secondly, of that which forbiddeth ingratitude; for seeing all sovereign power is originally given by the consent of everyone of the subjects, to the end they should as long as they are obedient be protected thereby, the punishment of the innocent is a rendering of evil for good. And thirdly, of the law that commandeth equity, that is to say, an equal distribution of justice, which in punishing the innocent is not observed.

But the harm done to innocents in war, not so.

23. But the infliction of what evil soever on an innocent man that is not a subject, if it be for the benefit of the commonwealth and without violation of any former covenant, is no breach of the law of nature. For all men that are not subjects are either enemies or else they have ceased from being so by some precedent covenants. But against enemies, whom the commonwealth judgeth capable to do them hurt, it is lawful by the original right of nature to make war, wherein the sword judgeth not; nor doth the victor make distinction of nocent [guilty] and innocent as to the time past, nor has other respect of mercy than as it conduceth to the good of his own people. And upon this ground it is that also in subjects who deliberately deny the authority of the commonwealth

---

1 Hobbes is making a logical point. It is part of the meaning of the word "punishment" that whoever is punished is guilty. See also 17.11 and 28.3.

established, the vengeance is lawfully extended, not only to the fathers, but also to the third and fourth generation not yet in being, and consequently innocent of the fact for which they are afflicted, because the nature of this offence consisteth in the renouncing of subjection, which is a relapse into the condition of war commonly called rebellion; and they that so offend, suffer not as subjects, but as enemies.[1] For rebellion is but war renewed.

[166]

24. REWARD is either of gift or by contract. When by contract, it is called salary and wages, which is benefit due for service performed or promised. When of gift, it is benefit proceeding from the grace of them that bestow it, to encourage or enable men to do them service. And therefore when the sovereign of a commonwealth appointeth a salary to any public office, he that receiveth it is bound in justice to perform his office; otherwise, he is bound only in honour to acknowledgement and an endeavour of requital. For though men have no lawful remedy when they be commanded to quit their private business to serve the public without reward or salary; yet they are not bound thereto by the law of nature nor by the institution of the commonwealth, unless the service cannot otherwise be done, because it is supposed the sovereign may make use of all their means, insomuch as the most common soldier may demand the wages of his warfare as a debt.

Reward is either salary or grace.

25. The benefits which a sovereign bestoweth on a subject for fear of some power and ability he hath to do hurt to the commonwealth are not properly rewards; for they are not salaries, because there is in this case no contract supposed, every man being obliged already not to do the commonwealth disservice; nor are they graces, because they be extorted by fear, which ought not to be incident to the sovereign power; but [they] are rather sacrifices, which the sovereign, considered in his natural person and not in the person of the commonwealth, makes for the appeasing the discontent of him he thinks more potent than himself; and [such actions] encourage not to obedience, but, on the contrary, to the continuance and increasing of further extortion.

Benefits bestowed for fear are not rewards.

26. And whereas some salaries are certain and proceed from the public treasury, and others uncertain and

Salaries certain and casual.

---

1 Cf. 28.13.

casual, proceeding from the execution of the office for which the salary is ordained, the latter is in some cases hurtful to the commonwealth, as in the case of judicature. For where the benefit of the judges and ministers of a court of justice ariseth for the multitude of causes that are brought to their cognizance, there must needs follow two inconveniences: one is the nourishing of suits (for the more suits, the greater benefit); and another that depends on that, which is contention about jurisdiction (each court drawing to itself as many causes as it can). But in offices of execution[1] there are not those inconveniences, because their employment cannot be increased by any endeavour of their own. And thus much shall suffice for the nature of punishment and reward; which are, as it were, the nerves and tendons that move the limbs and joints of a commonwealth.

27. Hitherto I have set forth the nature of man, whose pride and other passions have compelled him to submit himself to government, together with the great power of his governor, whom I compared to Leviathan, taking that comparison out of the two last verses of the one-and-fortieth of Job where God, having set forth the great power of Leviathan,[2] calleth him king of the proud. *There is nothing,* saith he, *on earth to be compared with him. He is made so as not to be afraid. He seeth every high thing below him; and is king of all the children of pride.* But because he is mortal and subject to decay, as all other earthly creatures are, and because there is that in heaven, though not on earth, that he should stand in fear of and whose laws he ought to obey, I shall in the next following chapters speak of his diseases and the causes of his mortality, and of what laws of nature he is bound to obey.

[167]

---

1   See 23.10.
2   See also 17.13; Ps. 74:13-14 and 104:26; Job 3:8 and 41:1-34.
    In *A Midsummer's Night Dream,* Shakespeare uses Leviathan to express speed and strength (2.1.174). In "Anniversary of the Government under O.C. [Oliver Cromwell],"Andrew Marvell uses Leviathan to refer to a large ship.

Chapter XXIX

Of Those Things that Weaken or Tend to the Dissolution of a Commonwealth

1. Though nothing can be immortal which mortals make, yet if men had the use of reason they pretend to, their commonwealths might be secured, at least, from perishing by internal diseases. For by the nature of their institution, they are designed to live as long as mankind or as the laws of nature or as justice itself, which gives them life. Therefore when they come to be dissolved, not by external violence, but intestine disorder, the fault is not in men as they are the matter, but as they are the makers and orderers of them. For men, as they become at last weary of irregular jostling and hewing one another and desire with all their hearts to conform themselves into one firm and lasting edifice, so for want both of the art of making fit laws to square their actions by and also of humility and patience to suffer the rude and cumbersome points of their present greatness to be taken off, they cannot without the help of a very able architect be compiled into any other than a crazy building, such as, hardly lasting out their own time, must assuredly fall upon the heads of their posterity.

Dissolution of commonwealths proceedeth from their imperfect institution.

2. Amongst the *infirmities* therefore of a commonwealth, I will reckon in the first place those that arise from an imperfect institution and resemble the diseases of a natural body, which proceed from a defectuous [defective] procreation.

3. Of which this is one: *that a man to obtain a kingdom is sometimes content with less power than to the peace and defence of the commonwealth is necessarily required.* From whence it cometh to pass that when the exercise of the power laid by is for the public safety to be resumed, it hath the resemblance of an unjust act, which disposeth great numbers of men, when occasion is presented, to rebel, in the same manner as the bodies of children, gotten by diseased parents, are subject either to untimely death or to purge the ill quality derived from their vicious conception, by breaking out into biles and scabs. And when kings deny themselves some such necessary power, it is not always (though sometimes) out of ignorance of

Want of absolute power.

what is necessary to the office they undertake, but many times out of a hope to recover the same again at their pleasure;[1] wherein they reason not well, because such as will hold them to their promises shall be maintained against them by foreign commonwealths, who in order to the good of their own subjects let slip few occasions to weaken the estate of their neighbours. So was Thomas Becket,[2] Archbishop of Canterbury, supported against Henry the Second by the Pope, the subjection of ecclesiastics to the commonwealth having been dispensed with by William the Conqueror at his reception, when he took an oath not to infringe the liberty of the Church. And so were the barons, whose power was by William Rufus[3] (to have their help in transferring the succession from his elder brother to himself) increased to a degree inconsistent with the sovereign power, maintained in their rebellion against King John by the French.

4. Nor does this happen in monarchy only. For whereas the style of the ancient Roman commonwealth was, *The Senate and People of Rome*, neither Senate nor people pretended to the whole power; which first caused the seditions of Tiberius Gracchus, Caius Gracchus, Lucius Saturninus,[4] and others, and afterwards the wars between

---

1 Hobbes may be thinking of Charles I, who made concessions to Parliament in his "Reply to the Nineteen Propositions," which he probably intended to retract once he had sufficient power to do so.

2 Thomas à Becket (1118-70), English martyr. King Henry II appointed Becket archbishop of Canterbury with the expectation that he would support the king's position on the church. Becket did not, and when Henry in anger said, "Will none of those who live off my bounty relieve me of this troublesome clerk?," four of Henry's knights went off and murdered Becket in his cathedral.

3 William Rufus, King William II (1056-1100), was son of William the Conqueror (c. 1027-1087) and fought with Anselm of Canterbury over the issue of lay investiture. William was not well liked. He was shot in the back with an arrow during a hunting party; no one was ever prosecuted for the crime.

4 The Gracchi brothers, last third of the second century BCE, were Roman reformers, concerned about the political danger of enormous wealth in the hands of a few people. They were killed in riots. Saturninus (d. 100 BCE) ingratiated himself with ex-soldiers by proposing that each be given a tract of land in Africa; he

the Senate and the people under Marius and Sylla, and again under Pompey and Caesar, to the extinction of their democracy and the setting up of monarchy.

5. The people of Athens bound themselves but from one only action, which was that no man on pain of death should propound the renewing of the war for the island of Salamis; and yet thereby, if Solon[1] had not caused to be given out he was mad, and afterwards in gesture and habit of a madman, and in verse, propounded it to the people that flocked about him, they had had an enemy perpetually in readiness, even at the gates of their city; such damage or shifts are all commonwealths forced to that have their power never so little limited.

6. In the second place, I observe the diseases of a commonwealth that proceed from the poison of seditious doctrines, whereof one is that every private man is judge of good and evil actions.[2] This is true in the condition of mere nature, where there are no civil laws, and also under civil government in such cases as are not determined by the law. But otherwise, it is manifest that the measure of good and evil actions is the civil law; and the judge [is] the legislator, who is always representative of the commonwealth. From this false doctrine, men are disposed to debate with themselves and dispute the commands of the commonwealth, and afterwards to obey or disobey them as in their private judgements they shall think fit, whereby the commonwealth is distracted and weakened.

Private judgement of good and evil.

7. Another doctrine repugnant to civil society is that whatsoever a man does against his conscience is sin; and it dependeth on the presumption of making himself judge of good and evil. For a man's conscience and his judgement is the same thing; and as the judgement, so also the conscience may be erroneous.[3] Therefore, though he that is subject to no civil law sinneth in all he does against his conscience, because he has no other rule to follow but his own reason; yet it is not so with him that lives in a

Erroneous conscience.

[169]

---

exploited the reputation of the Gracchis for his own purposes. Hobbes's examples are of Roman "populists."

1 Solon (c. 639-559 BCE) was an Athenian reformer, statesman, and lawgiver. The rich opposed his reforms. Hobbes's source about Salamis is Plutarch's *Life of Solon.*

2 See also 6.7, 18.10, and 26.8.

3 See also 7.4 and 30.14.

commonwealth, because the law is the public conscience by which he hath already undertaken to be guided. Otherwise in such diversity as there is of private consciences, which are but private opinions, the commonwealth must needs be distracted, and no man dare to obey the sovereign power farther than it shall seem good in his own eyes.

Pretence of inspiration.

8. It hath been also commonly taught that faith and sanctity are not to be attained by study and reason, but by supernatural inspiration or infusion. Which granted, I see not why any man should render a reason of his faith, or why every Christian should not be also a prophet; or why any man should take the law of his country rather than his own inspiration for the rule of his actions. And thus we fall again into the fault of taking upon us to judge of good and evil, or to make judges of it such private men as pretend to be supernaturally inspired, to the dissolution of all civil government. Faith comes by hearing,[1] and hearing by those accidents which guide us into the presence of them that speak to us; which accidents are all contrived by God Almighty, and yet are not supernatural, but only, for the great number of them that concur to every effect, unobservable. Faith and sanctity are indeed not very frequent; but yet they are not miracles, but brought to pass by education, discipline, correction, and other natural ways by which God worketh them in his elect, at such time as he thinketh fit. And these three opinions, pernicious to peace and government, have in this part of the world proceeded chiefly from tongues and pens of unlearned divines, who, joining the words of Holy Scripture together otherwise than is agreeable to reason, do what they can to make men think that sanctity and natural reason cannot stand together.

Subjecting the sovereign power to civil laws.

9. A fourth opinion repugnant to the nature of a commonwealth is this: *that he that hath the sovereign power is subject to the civil laws.* It is true that sovereigns are all subject to the laws of nature,[2] because such laws be divine and cannot by any man or commonwealth be abrogated. But to those laws which the sovereign himself, that is, which the commonwealth, maketh, he is not subject. For to be subject to laws is to be subject to the

---

1 A reference to Rom. 10:17. See also 43.8.
2 See also 21.7 and 22.7.

commonwealth, that is, to the sovereign representative, that is, to himself, which is not subjection, but freedom from the laws. Which error, because it setteth the laws above the sovereign, setteth also a judge above him, and a power to punish him; which is to make a new sovereign; and again for the same reason a third, to punish the second; and so continually without end, to the confusion and dissolution of the commonwealth.

10. A fifth doctrine that tendeth to the dissolution of a commonwealth is that every private man has an absolute propriety in his goods, such as excludeth the right of the sovereign. Every man has indeed a propriety that excludes the right of every other subject;[1] and he has it only from the sovereign power, without the protection whereof every other man should have right to the same. But the right of the sovereign also be excluded, he cannot perform the office they have put him into, which is to defend them both from foreign enemies and from the injuries of one another, and consequently there is no longer a commonwealth.

Attributing of absolute propriety to subjects.

[170]

11. And if the propriety of subjects exclude not the right of the sovereign representative to their goods, [then] much less to their offices of judicature or execution in which they represent the sovereign himself.

12. There is a sixth doctrine, plainly and directly against the essence of a commonwealth, and it is this: *that the sovereign power may be divided.* For what is it to divide the power of a commonwealth, but to dissolve it; for powers divided mutually destroy each other. And for these doctrines men are chiefly beholding to some of those that, making profession of the laws, endeavour to make them depend upon their own learning, and not upon the legislative power.

Dividing of the sovereign power.

13. And as false doctrine, so also oftentimes the example of different government in a neighbouring nation disposeth men to alteration of the form already settled. So the people of the Jews were stirred up to reject God and to call upon the prophet Samuel for a king after the manner of the nations;[2] so also the lesser cities of Greece were

Imitation of neighbour nations.

---

1 See 24.7.
2 "Then all the elders of Israel gathered themselves together, and came to Samuel unto Ramah, and said unto him, 'Behold, thou are old, and thy sons walk not in thy ways: now (Continued)

continually disturbed with seditions of the aristocratical and democratical factions, one part of almost every commonwealth desiring to imitate the Lacedaemonians, the other, the Athenians. And I doubt not but many men have been contented to see the late troubles in England out of an imitation of the Low Countries, supposing there needed no more to grow rich than to change, as they had done, the form of their government. For the constitution of man's nature is of itself subject to desire novelty; when therefore they are provoked to the same by the neighbourhood also of those that have been enriched by it, it is almost impossible for them not to be content with those that solicit them to change; and [they] love the first beginnings, though they be grieved with the continuance, of disorder, like hot bloods that having gotten the itch, tear themselves with their own nails till they can endure the smart no longer.

Imitation of the Greeks and Romans. 14. And as to rebellion in particular against monarchy, one of the most frequent causes of it is the reading of the books of policy and histories of the ancient Greeks and Romans,[1] from which young men and all others that are unprovided of the antidote of solid reason, receiving a strong and delightful impression of the great exploits of war achieved by the conductors of their armies, receive withal a pleasing idea of all they have done besides; and [they] imagine their great prosperity not to have proceeded from the emulation of particular men, but from the virtue of their popular form of government, not considering the frequent seditions and civil wars produced by the imperfection of their policy. From the reading, I say, of

---

make us a king to judge us, like all the nations.' But the thing displeased Samuel, when they said, 'Give us a king to judge us'; and Samuel prayed unto the Lord. And the Lord said unto Samuel, 'Hearken unto the voice of the people in all that they say unto thee; for they have not rejected thee, but they have rejected me, that I should not reign over them'" (1 Sam. 8:4-7, Authorized Version).

1 Hobbes hated the political views of such thinkers as Aristotle, as represented by his *Politics*, not his *Rhetoric*, and Cicero, who was a republican. See also 46.11-14 and 47.16. Hobbes approved of other ancient Greek and Latin authors, such as Thucydides, whose history of the Peloponnesian war he translated.

such books, men have undertaken to kill their kings, because the Greek and Latin writers in their books and discourses of policy make it lawful and laudable for any man so to do, provided before he do it he call him tyrant. For they say not *regicide*, that is, killing of a king, but *tyrannicide*, that is, killing of a tyrant, is lawful. From the same books they that live under a monarch conceive an opinion that the subjects in a popular commonwealth enjoy liberty, but that in a monarchy they are all slaves. I say, they that live under a monarchy conceive such an opinion, not they that live under a popular government, for they find no such matter. In sum, I cannot imagine how anything can be more prejudicial to a monarchy than the allowing of such books to be publicly read, without present applying such correctives of discreet masters as are fit to take away their venom; which venom I will not doubt to compare to the biting of a mad dog, which is a disease that physicians call *hydrophobia* or *fear of water*. For as he that is so bitten has a continual torment of thirst and yet abhorreth water; and [he] is in such an estate as if the poison endeavoured to convert him into a dog; so when a monarchy is once bitten to the quick by those democratical writers that continually snarl at that estate, it wanteth nothing more than a strong monarch, which nevertheless out of a certain *tyrannophobia* or fear of being strongly governed, when they have him, they abhor. [171]

15. As there have been doctors that hold there be three souls in a man, so there be [they] also that think there may be more souls, that is, more sovereigns, than one in a commonwealth; and [they] set up a *supremacy* against the *sovereignty*, canons against *laws*, and a *ghostly authority* against the *civil*, working on men's minds with words and distinctions that of themselves signify nothing, but bewray [reveal], by their obscurity, that there walketh (as some think invisibly) another kingdom, as it were a kingdom of fairies, in the dark. Now seeing it is manifest that the civil power and the power of the commonwealth is the same thing; and that supremacy and the power of making canons and granting faculties implieth a commonwealth; it followeth that where one is sovereign, another supreme; where one can make laws and another make canons, there must needs be two commonwealths, of one and the same subjects; which is a kingdom divided in itself and cannot

stand. For notwithstanding the insignificant distinction of *temporal* and *ghostly*, they are still two kingdoms,[1] and every subject is subject to two masters.[2] For seeing the *ghostly* power challengeth the right to declare what is sin, it challengeth by consequence to declare what is law, sin being nothing but the transgression of the law; and again, the civil power challenging to declare what is law, every subject must obey two masters, who both will have their commands be observed as law, which is impossible. Or, if it be but one kingdom, [then] either the civil, which is the power of the commonwealth, must be subordinate to the ghostly, and then there is no sovereignty but the ghostly; or the ghostly must be subordinate to the temporal, and then there is no supremacy but the temporal. When therefore these two powers oppose one another, [172] the commonwealth cannot but be in great danger of civil war and dissolution. For the civil authority being more visible, and standing in the clearer light of natural reason, cannot choose but draw to it in all times a very considerable part of the people; and the spiritual, though it stand in the darkness of School distinctions and hard words; yet because the fear of darkness and ghosts is greater than other fears, [the spiritual] cannot want a party sufficient to trouble and sometimes to destroy a commonwealth. And this is a disease which not unfitly may be compared to the epilepsy or falling sickness (which the Jews took to be one kind of possession by spirits) in the body natural. For as in this disease there is an unnatural spirit or wind in the head that obstructeth the roots of the nerves, and moving them violently, taketh the motion which naturally they should have from the power of the soul in the brain, and thereby causeth violent and irregular motions, which men call convulsions in the parts, insomuch as he that is seized therewith falleth down sometimes into the water and sometimes into the fire, as a man deprived of his senses; so also in the body politic, when the spiritual power moveth the members of a commonwealth by the

---

1 Hobbes insisted that every citizen is subject to only one king-dom. This is one reason why he maintained that the kingdom of God did not exist at the present but would exist sometime in the indefinite future, with Christ as the sovereign.

2 Matt. 5:24: "No man can serve two masters." Hobbes applied this biblical aphorism to politics. See 42.102 and 42.123.

terror of punishments and hope of rewards (which are the nerves of it) otherwise than by the civil power (which is the soul of the commonwealth) they ought to be moved, and [when] by strange and hard words suffocates their understanding, it must needs thereby distract the people and either overwhelm the commonwealth with oppression or cast it into the fire of a civil war.

16. Sometimes also in the merely civil government there be more than one soul, as when the power of levying money, which is the nutritive faculty, has depended on a general assembly;[1] the power of conduct and command, which is the motive faculty, on one man;[2] and the power of making laws, which is the rational faculty, on the accidental consent, not only of those two, but also of a third;[3] this endangereth the commonwealth, sometimes for want of consent to good laws, but most often for want of such nourishment as is necessary to life and motion. For although few perceive that such government is not government, but division of the commonwealth into three factions, and call it mixed monarchy; yet the truth is that it is not one independent commonwealth, but three independent factions; nor one representative person, but three. In the kingdom of God there may be three persons independent, without breach of unity in God that reigneth; but where men reign, that be subject to diversity of opinions, it cannot be so. And therefore if the king bear the person of the people, and the general assembly bear also the person of the people, and another assembly bear the person of a part of the people, they are not one person, nor one sovereign, but three persons and three sovereigns.

Mixed government.

17. To what disease in the natural body of man I may exactly compare this irregularity of a commonwealth, I know not. But I have seen a man that had another man growing out of his side, with a head, arms, breast, and stomach of his own; if he had had another man growing out of his other side, the comparison might then have been exact.

[173]

---

1   The monarch depended on the House of Commons to approve funds.
2   Hobbes is thinking of the monarch of England.
3   Hobbes is probably thinking of the House of Lords as the third faculty.

18. Hitherto I have named such diseases of a commonwealth as are of the greatest and most present danger. There be other, not so great, which nevertheless are not unfit to be observed. As first, the difficulty of raising money for the necessary uses of the commonwealth, especially in the approach of war.[1] This difficulty ariseth from the opinion that every subject hath of a propriety in his lands and goods exclusive of the sovereign's right to the use of the same. From whence it cometh to pass that the sovereign power, which foreseeth the necessities and dangers of the commonwealth (finding the passage of money to the public treasury obstructed by the tenacity of the people), whereas it ought to extend itself to encounter and prevent such dangers in their beginnings, contracteth itself as long as it can; and when it cannot longer, [the sovereign power] struggles with the people by stratagems of law to obtain little sums, which, not sufficing, he is fain [required] at last violently to open the way for present supply or perish; and, being put often to these extremities, at last reduceth the people to their due temper or else the commonwealth must perish.[2] Insomuch as we may compare this distemper very aptly to an ague, wherein the fleshy parts being congealed or by venomous matter obstructed, the veins which by their natural course empty themselves into the heart are not (as they ought to be) supplied from the arteries, whereby there succeedeth at first a cold contraction and trembling of the limbs, and afterwards a hot and strong endeavour of the heart to force a passage for the blood; and before it can do that, contenteth itself with the small refreshments of such things as cool for a time, till, if nature be

---

1 Charles had trouble getting money from Parliament for his entire reign, beginning with his first year of rule, 1625, when, contrary to tradition, Parliament refused to grant him the right to levy tonnage and poundage (customs duties). His imposition of Ship Money in 1634 was legal but extremely unpopular. Charles called his first parliament since 1629 for the spring of 1640 in order to get it to approve funds to fight a second Bishops' War. When Parliament refused to consider levying money until after their grievances had been resolved, Charles dissolved it.

2 Although this looks like a prediction or generalization, Hobbes is thinking specifically of the English Civil War.

strong enough, it break at last the contumacy of the parts obstructed and dissipateth the venom into sweat; or, if nature be too weak, the patient dieth.

19. Again, there is sometimes in a commonwealth a disease which resembleth the pleurisy; and that is when the treasury of the commonwealth, flowing out of its due course, is gathered together in too much abundance in one or a few private men, by monopolies or by farms of the public revenues; in the same manner as the blood in a pleurisy, getting into the membrane of the breast, breedeth there an inflammation, accompanied with a fever and painful stitches.

Monopolies and abuses of publicans.

20. Also, the popularity of a potent subject, unless the commonwealth have very good caution of his fidelity, is a dangerous disease, because the people, which should receive their motion from the authority of the sovereign, by the flattery and by the reputation of an ambitious man, are drawn away from their obedience to the laws to follow a man of whose virtues and designs they have no knowledge. And this is commonly of more danger in a popular government than in a monarchy, because an army is of so great force and multitude as it may easily be made believe they are the people. By this means it was that Julius Caesar, who was set up by the people against the Senate, having won to himself the affections of his army, made himself master both of Senate and people. And this proceeding of popular and ambitious men is plain rebellion, and may be resembled to the effects of witchcraft.

Popular men.

[174]

21. Another infirmity of a commonwealth is the immoderate greatness of a town,[1] when it is able to furnish out of its own circuit the number and expense of a great army, as also the great number of corporations, which are as it were many lesser commonwealths in the bowels of a greater, like worms in the entrails of a natural man. To which may be added, the liberty of disputing against absolute power by pretenders to political prudence; which though bred for the most part in the lees [dregs] of the people; yet animated by false doctrines are perpetually meddling with the fundamental laws, to the molestation

Excessive greatness of a town or multitude of corporations.

Liberty of disputing against sovereign power.

---

1 Hobbes is thinking of London, which on the one hand often opposed the king, and on the other sometimes opposed Parliament. London raised its own army during the Civil War to protect against parliamentary troops.

of the commonwealth, like the little worms which physicians call *ascarides*.

22. We may further add the insatiable appetite or *bulimia* of enlarging dominion, with the incurable *wounds* thereby many times received from the enemy, and the *wens* [lumps] of ununited conquests, which are many times a burden, and with less danger lost than kept; as also [we may add] the *lethargy* of ease,[1] and *consumption* of riot and vain expense.

Dissolution of the commonwealth.

23. Lastly, when in a war, foreign or intestine, the enemies get a final victory, so as (the forces of the commonwealth keeping the field no longer) there is no further protection of subjects in their loyalty, then is the commonwealth DISSOLVED, and every man at liberty to protect himself by such courses as his own discretion shall suggest unto him. For the sovereign is the public soul, giving life and motion to the commonwealth, which expiring, the members are governed by it no more than the carcass of a man by his departed, though immortal, soul.[2] For though the right of a sovereign monarch cannot be extinguished by the act of another; yet the obligation of the members may. For he that wants protection may seek it anywhere; and, when he hath it, is obliged (without fraudulent pretence of having submitted himself out of fear) to protect his protection as long as he is able.[3] But when the power of an assembly is once suppressed, the right of the same perisheth utterly, because the assembly itself is extinct; and consequently, there is no possibility for sovereignty to re-enter.

[175]

Chapter XXX

Of the Office of the Sovereign Representative

The procuration of the good of the people.

1. The OFFICE of the sovereign (be it a monarch or an assembly) consisteth in the end for which he was trusted with the sovereign power, namely the procuration of the safety of the people, to which he is obliged by the law

---

1 See also 17.11.
2 See also 21.21 and 42.125.
3 Cf. "Review and Conclusion," 5.

of nature, and to render an account thereof to God, the Author of that law, and to none but him. But by safety here is not meant a bare preservation, but also all other contentments of life, which every man by lawful industry, without danger or hurt to the commonwealth, shall acquire to himself.

2. And this is intended should be done, not by care applied to individuals further than their protection from injuries when they shall complain, but by a general providence contained in public instruction, both of doctrine and example; and in the making and executing of good laws to which individual persons may apply their own cases. By instruction and laws.

3. And because, if the essential rights of sovereignty (specified before in the eighteenth chapter) be taken away, the commonwealth is thereby dissolved, and every man returneth into the condition and calamity of a war with every other man, which is the greatest evil that can happen in this life; it is the office of the sovereign to maintain those rights entire, and consequently against his duty, first, to transfer to another or to lay from himself any of them. For he that deserteth the means deserteth the ends; and he deserteth the means that, being the sovereign, acknowledgeth himself subject to the civil laws, and renounceth the power of supreme judicature; or of making war or peace by his own authority; or of judging of the necessities of the commonwealth; or of levying money and soldiers when and as much as in his own conscience he shall judge necessary; or of making officers and ministers both of war and peace; or of appointing teachers and examining what doctrines are conformable or contrary to the defence, peace, and good of the people. Secondly, it is against his duty to let the people be ignorant or misinformed of the grounds and reasons of those his essential rights, because thereby men are easy to be seduced and drawn to resist him when the commonwealth shall require their use and exercise. Against the duty of a sovereign to relinquish any essential right of sovereignty.

4. And the grounds of these rights have the rather need to be diligently and truly taught, because they cannot be maintained by any civil law or terror of legal punishment. For a civil law that shall forbid rebellion (and such is all resistance to the essential rights of sovereignty) is not (as a civil law) any obligation but by virtue only of the law [176]

of nature that forbiddeth the violation of faith;[1] which natural obligation, if men know not, they cannot know the right of any law the sovereign maketh. And for the punishment, they take it but for an act of hostility; which when they think they have strength enough, they will endeavour, by acts of hostility, to avoid.

Objection of those that say there are no principles of reason for absolute sovereignty.

5. As I have heard some say that justice is but a word, without substance, and that whatsoever a man can by force or art acquire to himself (not only in the condition of war, but also in a commonwealth) is his own, which I have already shown to be false;[2] so there be also [some] that maintain that there are no grounds nor principles of reason to sustain those essential rights which make sovereignty absolute. For if there were, they would have been found out in some place or other; whereas we see there has not hitherto been any commonwealth where those rights have been acknowledged or challenged. Wherein they argue as ill, as if the savage people of America should deny there were any grounds or principles of reason so to build a house as to last as long as the materials, because they never yet saw any so well built. Time and industry produce every day new knowledge. And as the art of well building is derived from principles of reason, observed by industrious men that had long studied the nature of materials and the divers effects of figure and proportion, long after mankind began, though poorly, to build; so, long time after men have begun to constitute commonwealths, imperfect and apt to relapse into disorder, there may principles of reason be found out by industrious meditation, to make their constitution, excepting by external violence, everlasting. And such are those which I have in this discourse set forth; which, whether they come not into the sight of those that have power to make use of them or be neglected by them or not, concerneth my particular interest, at this day, very little. But supposing that these of mine are not such principles of reason; yet I am sure they are principles from authority of Scripture, as I shall make it appear when I shall come to speak of the

---

1 The obligation not to rebel is more basic than any obligation in civil laws. It exists in virtue of the laws of nature, certainly the first, since rebellion is war, and obviously also the third, that people are to keep their covenants (15.1).

2 See 15.4-8.

kingdom of God, administered by Moses, over the Jews, his peculiar people by covenant.

6. But they say again that though the principles be right; yet common people are not of capacity enough to be made to understand them. I should be glad that the rich and potent subjects of a kingdom, or those that are accounted the most learned, were no less incapable than they. But all men know that the obstructions to this kind of doctrine proceed not so much from the difficulty of the matter, as from the interest of them that are to learn. Potent men digest hardly anything that setteth up a power to bridle their affections; and learned men, anything that discovereth their errors, and thereby their authority; whereas the common people's minds, unless they be tainted with dependence on the potent or scribbled over with the opinions of their doctors are like clean paper, fit to receive whatsoever by public authority shall be imprinted in them. Shall whole nations be brought to acquiesce in the great mysteries of Christian religion, which are above reason, and millions of men be made believe that the same body may be in innumerable places at one and the same time, which is against reason; and shall not men be able by their teaching and preaching, protected by the law, to make that received which is so consonant to reason that any unprejudicated man needs no more to learn it than to hear it?[1] I conclude therefore that in the instruction of the people in the essential rights which are the natural and fundamental laws of sovereignty, there is no difficulty, whilst a sovereign has his power entire, but what proceeds from his own fault or the fault of those whom he trusteth in the administration of the commonwealth; and consequently, it is his duty to cause them so to be instructed; and not only his duty, but his benefit also and security against the danger that may arrive to himself in his natural person from rebellion.

7. And (to descend to particulars) the people are to be taught, first, that they ought not to be in love with any form of government they see in their neighbour nations, more than with their own, nor (whatsoever present

Objection from the incapacity of the vulgar.

[177]

Subjects are to be taught not to affect change of government:

---

1   Since people have been taught to believe Christian mysteries and even some absurd doctrines, they certainly can be taught to believe the reasonable principles of political obedience.

prosperity they behold in nations that are otherwise governed than they) to desire change. For the prosperity of a people ruled by an aristocratical or democratical assembly cometh not from aristocracy nor from democracy, but from the obedience and concord of the subjects; nor do the people flourish in a monarchy because one man has the right to rule them, but because they obey him. Take away in any kind of state the obedience (and consequently the concord of the people) and they shall not only not flourish, but in short time be dissolved. And they that go about by disobedience to do no more than reform the commonwealth shall find they do thereby destroy it, like the foolish daughters of Peleus, in the fable, which desiring to renew the youth of their decrepit father, did by the counsel of Medea cut him in pieces and boil him, together with strange herbs, but made not of him a new man. This desire of change is like the breach of the first of God's commandments; for there God says, *Non habebis Deos alienos*:[1] Thou shalt not have the Gods of other nations; and in another place concerning *kings*, that they are *gods* [Psalm 82:6].

Nor adhere (against the sovereign) to popular men:

8. Secondly, they are to be taught that they ought not to be led with admiration of the virtue of any of their fellow subjects, how high soever he stand nor how conspicuously soever he shine in the commonwealth; nor [of the virtue] of any assembly (except the sovereign assembly), so as to defer to them any obedience or honour appropriate to the sovereign only, whom (in their particular stations) they represent; nor to receive any influence from them, but such as is conveyed by them from the sovereign authority. For that sovereign cannot be imagined to love his people as he ought that is not jealous of them, but suffers [allows] them by the flattery of popular men to be seduced from their loyalty, as they have often been, not only secretly, but openly, so as to proclaim marriage with them *in facie ecclesiae*[2] by preachers, and by publishing the same in the open streets; which may fitly be compared to the violation of the second of the Ten Commandments.

[178]

Nor to dispute the sovereign power:

9. Thirdly, in consequence to this, they ought to be informed how great a fault it is to speak evil of the sovereign

---

1   See also 42.37 and 45.10.

2   Latin: "In the appearance [that is, the presence] of the church."

representative (whether one man or an assembly of men) or to argue and dispute his power or any way to use his name irreverently, whereby he may be brought into contempt with his people, and their obedience (in which the safety of the commonwealth consisteth) slackened. Which doctrine the third Commandment by resemblance pointeth to.

10. Fourthly, seeing people cannot be taught this, nor, when it is taught, remember it, nor after one generation past so much as know in whom the sovereign power is placed, without setting apart from their ordinary labour some certain times in which they may attend those that are appointed to instruct them; it is necessary that some such times be determined wherein they may assemble together, and (after prayers and praises given to God, the Sovereign of sovereigns), hear those their duties told them, and the positive laws, such as generally concern them all, read and expounded, and be put in mind of the authority that maketh them laws. To this end had the Jews every seventh day a Sabbath, in which the law was read and expounded; and in the solemnity whereof they were put in mind that their king was God; that having created the world in six days, he rested on the seventh day; and by their resting on it from their labour, that that God was their king, which redeemed them from their servile and painful labour in Egypt, and gave them a time, after they had rejoiced in God, to take joy also in themselves, by lawful recreation. So that the first table of the commandments is spent all in setting down the sum of God's absolute power, not only as God, but as King by pact (in peculiar) of the Jews; and [the first table] may therefore give light to those that have sovereign power conferred on them by the consent of men, to see what doctrine they ought to teach their subjects.

And to have days set apart to learn their duty.

11. And because the first instruction of children dependeth on the care of their parents, it is necessary that they should be obedient to them whilst they are under their tuition; and not only so, but that also afterwards (as gratitude requireth) they acknowledge the benefit of their education by external signs of honour. To which end they are to be taught that originally the father of every man was also his sovereign lord, with power over him of life and death; and that the fathers of families, when by instituting

And to honour their parents.

a commonwealth they resigned that absolute power; yet it was never intended they should lose the honour due unto them for their education. For to relinquish such right was not necessary to the institution of sovereign power; nor would there be any reason why any man should desire to have children or take the care to nourish and instruct them, if they were afterwards to have no other benefit from them than from other men. And this accordeth with the fifth Commandment.

[179] And to avoid doing of injury.

12. Again, every sovereign ought to cause justice to be taught, which (consisting in taking from no man what is his) is as much as to say, to cause men to be taught not to deprive their neighbours by violence or fraud of anything which by the sovereign authority is theirs. Of things held in propriety, those that are dearest to a man are his own life and limbs; and in the next degree (in most men) those that concern conjugal affection; and after them riches and means of living. Therefore the people are to be taught to abstain from violence to one another's person by private revenges, from violation of conjugal honour, and from forcible rapine and fraudulent surreption of one another's goods. For which purpose also it is necessary they be shown the evil consequences of false judgement by corruption either of judges or witnesses, whereby the distinction of propriety is taken away, and justice becomes of no effect; all which things are intimated in the sixth, seventh, eighth, and ninth commandments.

And to do all this sincerely from the heart.

13. Lastly, they are to be taught that not only the unjust facts [actions], but the designs and intentions to do them (though by accident hindered) are injustice; which consisteth in the pravity [corrupt quality] of the will, as well as in the irregularity of the act. And this is the intention of the tenth commandment and the sum of the second table; which is reduced all to this one commandment of mutual charity, *Thou shalt love thy neighbour as thy self*, as the sum of the first table is reduced to *the love of God*; whom they had then newly received as their king.

The use of universities.

14. As for the means and conduits by which the people may receive this instruction, we are to search by what means so many opinions contrary to the peace of mankind, upon weak and false principles, have nevertheless been so deeply rooted in them. I mean those which I have in the precedent chapter specified, as that men shall

judge of what is lawful and unlawful, not by the law itself, but by their own consciences, that is to say, by their own private judgements;[1] that subjects sin in obeying the commands of the commonwealth, unless they themselves have first judged them to be lawful; that their propriety in their riches is such as to exclude the dominion which the commonwealth hath over the same; that it is lawful for subjects to kill such as they call tyrants; that the sovereign power may be divided,[2] and the like; which come to be instilled into the people by this means. They whom necessity or covetousness keepeth attent on their trades and labour, and they, on the other side, whom superfluity or sloth carrieth after their sensual pleasures (which two sorts of men take up the greatest part of mankind), being diverted from the deep meditation which the learning of truth, not only in the matter of natural justice, but also of all other sciences necessarily requireth, receive the notions of their duty chiefly from divines in the pulpit, and partly from such of their neighbours or familiar acquaintance, as having the faculty of discoursing readily and plausibly, seem wiser and better learned in cases of law and conscience than themselves. And the divines and such others as make show of learning derive their knowledge from the universities and from the schools of law or from the books which by men eminent in those schools and universities have been published. It is therefore manifest that the instruction of the people dependeth wholly on the right teaching of youth in the universities. But are not (may some man say) the universities of England learned enough already to do that? Or is it you [who] will undertake to teach the universities? Hard questions. Yet to the first, I doubt not to answer: that till towards the latter end of Henry the Eighth, the power of the Pope was always upheld against the power of the commonwealth principally by the universities; and that the doctrines maintained by so many preachers against the sovereign power of the king and by so many lawyers and others that had their education there, is a sufficient argument that, though the universities were not authors of those

---

1 See 29.6-7.
2 Many supporters of Parliament in the 1640s, and some royalists, thought that political authority in England was divided between the monarch and Parliament.

false doctrines, yet they knew not how to plant the true. For in such a contradiction of opinions, it is most certain that they have not been sufficiently instructed; and it is no wonder, if they yet retain a relish of that subtle liquor wherewith they were first seasoned against the civil authority. But to the latter question, it is not fit nor needful for me to say either aye or no; for any man that sees what I am doing may easily perceive what I think.

15. The safety of the people requireth further from him or them that have the sovereign power, that justice be equally administered to all degrees of people, that is, that as well the rich and mighty, as poor and obscure persons, may be righted of the injuries done them, so as the great may have no greater hope of impunity, when they do violence, dishonour or any injury to the meaner sort, than when one of these does the like to one of them; for in this consisteth equity; to which, as being a precept of the law of nature, a sovereign is as much subject as any of the meanest of his people. All breaches of the law are offences against the commonwealth; but there be some that are also against private persons. Those that concern the commonwealth only may without breach of equity be pardoned; for every man may pardon what is done against himself, according to his own discretion. But an offence against a private man cannot in equity be pardoned without the consent of him that is injured, or reasonable satisfaction.

16. The inequality of subjects proceedeth from the acts of sovereign power and therefore has no more place in the presence of the sovereign, that is to say, in a court of justice, than the inequality between kings and their subjects in the presence of the King of kings.[1] The honour of great persons is to be valued for their beneficence and the aids they give to men of inferior rank, or not at all. And the violences, oppressions, and injuries they do are not extenuated, but aggravated, by the greatness of their

---

1 Hobbes's assertion of the equality of all subjects is surprising since he had lived off nobility for most of his life. The surprise is moderated somewhat by the fact that the House of Commons abolished the House of Lords on 19 March 1649, the same day that it declared England to be a "Commonwealth and Free State," and two days after abolishing the office of king. See also chapter 21 and 30.25.

persons, because they have least need to commit them. The consequences of this partiality towards the great proceed in this manner. Impunity maketh insolence; insolence, hatred; and hatred, an endeavour to pull down all oppressing and contumelious greatness, though with the ruin of the commonwealth.

17. To equal justice appertaineth also the equal imposition of taxes; the equality whereof dependeth not on the equality of riches, but on the equality of the debt that every man oweth to the commonwealth for his defence. It is not enough for a man to labour for the maintenance of his life, but also to fight (if need be) for the securing of his labour. They must either do as the Jews did after their return from captivity in re-edifying the Temple, [namely,] build with one hand and hold the sword in the other, or else they must hire others to fight for them. For the impositions that are laid on the people by the sovereign power are nothing else but the wages due to them that hold the public sword to defend private men in the exercise of their several trades and callings. Seeing then the benefit that every one receiveth thereby is the enjoyment of life, which is equally dear to poor and rich; the debt which a poor man oweth them that defend his life is the same which a rich man oweth for the defence of his, saving that the rich, who have the service of the poor, may be debtors not only for their own persons, but for many more. Which considered, the equality of imposition consisteth rather in the equality of that which is consumed than of the riches of the persons that consume the same. For what reason is there, that he which laboureth much, and sparing the fruits of his labour, consumeth little, should be more charged than he that living idly, getteth little and spendeth all he gets, seeing the one hath no more protection from the commonwealth than the other? But when the impositions are laid upon those things which men consume, every man payeth equally for what he useth; nor is the commonwealth defrauded by the luxurious waste of private men.

18. And whereas many men, by accident inevitable, become unable to maintain themselves by their labour, they ought not to be left to the charity of private persons, but to be provided for, as far forth as the necessities of nature require, by the laws of the commonwealth. For as

[181] Equal taxes.

Public charity.

it is uncharitableness in any man to neglect the impotent; so it is in the sovereign of a commonwealth, to expose them to the hazard of such uncertain charity.

Prevention of idleness.

19. But for such as have strong bodies the case is otherwise; they are to be forced to work; and to avoid the excuse of not finding employment, there ought to be such laws as may encourage all manner of arts, as navigation, agriculture, fishing, and all manner of manufacture that requires labour. The multitude of poor and yet strong people still increasing, they are to be transplanted into countries not sufficiently inhabited; where nevertheless they are not to exterminate those they find there, but constrain them to inhabit closer together, and not range a great deal of ground to snatch what they find, but to court each little plot with art and labour, to give them their sustenance in due season. And when all the world is overcharged with inhabitants, then the last remedy of all is war, which provideth for every man, by victory or death.

Good laws, what.

[182]

20. To the care of the sovereign belongeth the making of good laws. But what is a good law? By a good law, I mean not a just law; for no law can be unjust. The law is made by the sovereign power; and all that is done by such power is warranted and owned by every one of the people; and that which every man will have so, no man can say is unjust. It is in the laws of a commonwealth, as in the laws of gaming: whatsoever the gamesters all agree on is injustice to none of them. A good law is that which is *needful*, for the *good of the people*, and withal *perspicuous*.

Such as are necessary.

21. For the use of laws (which are but rules authorised) is not to bind the people from all voluntary actions, but to direct and keep them in such a motion as not to hurt themselves by their own impetuous desires, rashness, or indiscretion, as hedges are set, not to stop travellers, but to keep them in the way. And therefore a law that is not needful, having not the true end of a law, is not good. A law may be conceived to be good when it is for the benefit of the sovereign, though it be not necessary for the people, but it is not so. For the good of the sovereign and people cannot be separated. It is a weak sovereign that has weak subjects, and a weak people whose sovereign wanteth power to rule them at his will. Unnecessary laws are not good laws, but traps for money which, where

the right of sovereign power is acknowledged, are superfluous; and where it is not acknowledged, insufficient to
defend the people.

22. The perspicuity consisteth not so much in the   Such as are
words of the law itself, as in a declaration of the causes   perspicuous.
and motives for which it was made. That is it that shows
us the meaning of the legislator; and the meaning of the
legislator known, the law is more easily understood by
few than many words. For all words are subject to ambiguity; and therefore multiplication of words in the body
of the law is multiplication of ambiguity; besides it seems
to imply (by too much diligence) that whosoever can
evade the words is without the compass of the law. And
this is a cause of many unnecessary processes. For when
I consider how short were the laws of ancient times, and
how they grew by degrees still longer, methinks I see a
contention between the penners and pleaders of the law;
the former seeking to circumscribe the latter and the latter to evade their circumscriptions; and that the pleaders
have got the victory. It belongeth therefore to the office of
a legislator (such as is in all commonwealths the supreme
representative, be it one man or an assembly) to make the
reason perspicuous why the law was made, and the body
of the law itself as short, but in as proper and significant
terms, as may be.

23. It belongeth also to the office of the sovereign to   Punishments.
make a right application of punishments and rewards. And
seeing the end of punishing is not revenge and discharge
of choler [anger], but correction either of the offender
or of others by his example,[1] the severest punishments
are to be inflicted for those crimes that are of most danger to the public; such as are those which proceed from
malice to the government established; those that spring
from contempt of justice; those that provoke indignation
in the multitude; and those which, unpunished, seem au-   [183]
thorised, as when they are committed by sons, servants,
or favourites of men in authority; for indignation carrieth
men, not only against the actors and authors of injustice,
but against all power that is likely to protect them, as in
the case of Tarquin, when for the insolent act of one of

---

1   Hobbes's views about punishment are enlightened. See 15.19,
    28.1, and 28.9.

his sons he was driven out of Rome and the monarchy itself dissolved.[1] But crimes of infirmity, such as are those which proceed from great provocation, from great fear, great need, or from ignorance whether the fact be a great crime or not, there is place many times for lenity, without prejudice to the commonwealth; and lenity, when there is such place for it, is required by the law of nature. The punishment of the leaders and teachers in a commotion, not the poor seduced people, when they are punished, can profit the commonwealth by their example. To be severe to people is to punish ignorance which may in great part be imputed to the sovereign, whose fault it was they were no better instructed.

Rewards.   24. In like manner it belongeth to the office and duty of the sovereign to apply his rewards always so as there may arise from them benefit to the commonwealth; wherein consisteth their use and end; and is then done when they that have well served the commonwealth are with as little expense of the common treasury as is possible, so well recompensed as others thereby may be encouraged, both to serve the same as faithfully as they can and to study the arts by which they may be enabled to do it better. To buy with money or preferment from a popular ambitious subject [his agreement] to be quiet and desist from making ill impressions in the minds of the people, has nothing of the nature of reward (which is ordained not for disservice, but for service past); nor a sign of gratitude, but of fear; nor does it tend to the benefit, but to the damage of the public. It is a contention with ambition, like that of Hercules with the monster Hydra, which, having many heads, for every one that was vanquished there grew up three. For in like manner, when the stubbornness of one popular man is overcome with reward, there arise many more by the example, that do the same mischief in hope of like benefit; and as all sorts of manufacture, so also malice increaseth by being vendible. And though sometimes a civil war may be deferred by such ways as that; yet the danger grows still the greater, and the public ruin more assured. It is therefore against the duty of the sovereign, to whom

---

1 The monarchy was abolished after Tarquin's son, Sextus Tarquinus, raped Lucretia, the wife of his cousin Cullatinus, in 508/07 BCE. The entire Tarquin family was exiled.

the public safety is committed, to reward those that aspire to greatness by disturbing the peace of their country, and not rather to oppose the beginnings of such men with a little danger, than after a longer time with greater.

25. Another business of the sovereign is to choose good counsellors; I mean such whose advice he is to take in the government of the commonwealth. For this word counsel (*consilium*, corrupted from *considium*) is of a large signification and comprehendeth all assemblies of men that sit together, not only to deliberate what is to be done hereafter, but also to judge of facts past and of law for the present. I take it here in the first sense only; and in this sense, there is no choice of counsel, neither in a democracy nor aristocracy, because the persons counselling are members of the person counselled. The choice of counsellors therefore is proper to monarchy, in which the sovereign that endeavoureth not to make choice of those that in every kind are the most able, dischargeth not his office as he ought to do. The most able counsellors are they that have least hope of benefit by giving evil counsel and most knowledge of those things that conduce to the peace and defence of the commonwealth. It is a hard matter to know who expecteth benefit from public troubles; but the signs that guide to a just suspicion is the soothing of the people in their unreasonable or irremediable grievances by men whose estates are not sufficient to discharge their accustomed expenses, and may easily be observed by any one whom it concerns to know it. But to know who has most knowledge of the public affairs is yet harder; and they that know them need them a great deal the less. For to know who knows the rules almost of any art is a great degree of the knowledge of the same art, because no man can be assured of the truth of another's rules but he that is first taught to understand them. But the best signs of knowledge of any art are much conversing in it and constant good effects of it. Good counsel comes not by lot nor by inheritance; and therefore there is no more reason to expect good advice from the rich or noble in matter of state,[1] than in delineating the dimensions of a fortress; unless we shall think there needs no method in the study of the politics (as there does in the study of geometry)

Counsellors.

[184]

---

1 Another attack on the nobles. See also 30.16.

but only to be lookers on; which is not so. For the politics is the harder study of the two. Whereas in these parts of Europe it hath been taken for a right of certain persons to have place in the highest council of state by inheritance, it derived from the conquests of the ancient Germans; wherein many absolute lords, joining together to conquer other nations, would not enter into the confederacy without such privileges as might be marks of difference in time following between their posterity and the posterity of their subjects; which privileges being inconsistent with the sovereign power, by the favour of the sovereign they may seem to keep; but contending for them as their right, they must needs by degrees let them go and have at last no further honour than adhereth naturally to their abilities.

26. And how able soever be the counsellors in any affair, the benefit of their counsel is greater when they give every one his advice and the reasons of it apart, than when they do it in an assembly by way of orations, and when they have premeditated, than when they speak on the sudden, both because they have more time to survey the consequences of action and are less subject to be carried away to contradiction through envy, emulation, or other passions arising from the difference of opinion.

27. The best counsel in those things that concern not other nations, but only the ease and benefit the subjects [185] may enjoy, by laws that look only inward, is to be taken from the general informations and complaints of the people of each province, who are best acquainted with their own wants, and ought therefore, when they demand nothing in derogation of the essential rights of sovereignty, to be diligently taken notice of. For without those essential rights, as I have often before said, the commonwealth cannot at all subsist.

Commanders.   28. A commander of an army in chief, if he be not popular, shall not be beloved, nor feared as he ought to be by his army, and consequently cannot perform that office with good success. He must therefore be industrious, valiant, affable, liberal and fortunate, that he may gain an opinion both of sufficiency and of loving his soldiers. This is popularity and breeds in the soldiers both desire and courage to recommend themselves to his favour; and protects the severity of the general in punishing, when need is, the mutinous or negligent soldiers. But this love of soldiers, if caution be not given of the commander's fidelity, is a dangerous thing to sovereign power, especially when it is in the hands of an assembly not popular. It belongeth therefore to the safety of the people, both that they be good conductors and faithful subjects, to whom the sovereign commits his armies.

29. But when the sovereign himself is popular, that is, reverenced and beloved of his people, there is no danger at all from the popularity of a subject. For soldiers are never so generally unjust as to side with their captain, though they love him, against their sovereign, when they love not only his person, but also his cause. And therefore those who by violence have at any time suppressed the power of their lawful sovereign before they could settle themselves in his place, have been always put to the trouble of contriving their titles to save the people from the shame of receiving them. To have a known right to sovereign power is so popular a quality, as he that has it needs no more for his own part to turn the hearts of his subjects to him, but that they see him able absolutely to govern his own family; nor, on the part of his enemies, but a disbanding of their armies. For the greatest and most active part of mankind has never hitherto been well contented with the present.

30. Concerning the offices of one sovereign to another, which are comprehended in that law which is commonly called the law of nations, I need not say anything in this place, because the law of nations and the law of nature is the same thing. And every sovereign hath the same right in procuring the safety of his people, that any particular man can have in procuring the safety of his own body. And the same law that dictateth to men that have no civil government what they ought to do, and what to avoid in regard of one another, dictateth the same to commonwealths, that is, to the consciences of sovereign princes and sovereign assemblies; there being no court of natural justice, but in the conscience only,[1] where not man, but God reigneth, whose laws, such of them as oblige all mankind, in respect of God, as he is the author of nature, [186]

---

1   See also 15.36.

are *natural*;[1] and in respect of the same God, as he is King of kings, are *laws*. But of the kingdom of God, as King of kings, and as King also of a peculiar people, I shall speak in the rest of this discourse.

Chapter XXXI

Of the Kingdom of God by Nature

The scope of the following chapters.

1. That the condition of mere nature, that is to say, of absolute liberty, such as is theirs that neither are sovereigns nor subjects, is anarchy and the condition of war; that the precepts by which men are guided to avoid that condition, are the laws of nature; that a commonwealth without sovereign power is but a word without substance and cannot stand; that subjects owe to sovereigns simple obedience in all things wherein their obedience is not repugnant to the laws of God, I have sufficiently proved in that which I have already written. There wants only for the entire knowledge of civil duty to know what are those laws of God. For without that, a man knows not when he is commanded anything by the civil power, whether it be contrary to the law of God or no; and so, either by too much civil obedience offends the Divine Majesty, or, through fear of offending God, transgresses the commandments of the commonwealth. To avoid both these rocks, it is necessary to know what are the laws divine. And seeing the knowledge of all law dependeth on the knowledge of the sovereign power, I shall say something in that which followeth of the KINGDOM OF GOD.

2. *God is King, let the earth rejoice*, saith the psalmist. And again, *God is King though the nations be angry; and he that sitteth on the cherubim, though the earth be moved.* Whether men will or not, they must be subject always to the divine power. By denying the existence or providence of God, men may shake off their ease, but not their yoke. But to call this power of God, which extendeth itself not only to man, but also to beasts and plants and bodies

Ps. 97:1.

Ps. 99:1. Who are subjects in the kingdom of God.

---

1 This is evidence that the laws of nature are genuine laws. If they are not, sovereigns seem to have less incentive for obeying them.

inanimate, by the name of kingdom, is but a metaphorical use of the word. For he only is properly said to reign that governs his subjects by his word and by promise of rewards to those that obey it, and by threatening them with punishment that obey it not. Subjects therefore in the kingdom of God are not bodies inanimate, nor creatures irrational, because they understand no precepts as his, nor atheists,[1] nor they that believe not that God has any care of the actions of mankind, because they acknowledge no word for his, nor have hope of his rewards or fear of his threatenings. They therefore that believe there is a God that governeth the world and hath given precepts and propounded rewards and punishments to mankind are God's subjects; all the rest are to be understood as enemies.

[187]

3. To rule by words requires that such words be manifestly made known; for else they are no laws; for to the nature of laws belongeth a sufficient and clear promulgation, such as may take away the excuse of ignorance; which in the laws of men is but of one only kind, and that is, proclamation or promulgation by the voice of man. But God declareth his laws three ways: by the dictates of *natural reason*, by *revelation*, and by the *voice* of some *man* to whom, by the operation of miracles, he procureth credit with the rest. From hence there ariseth a triple word of God, *rational*, *sensible*, and *prophetic*; to which correspondeth a triple hearing: *right reason, sense supernatural,* and *faith*. As for sense supernatural, which consisteth in revelation or inspiration, there have not been any universal laws so given, because God speaketh not in that manner but to particular persons and to divers men divers things.

A threefold word of God, reason, revelation, and prophecy.

4. From the difference between the other two kinds of God's word, rational and prophetic, there may be attributed to God a twofold kingdom, *natural* and *prophetic*: natural, wherein he governeth as many of mankind as acknowledge his providence by the natural dictates of right reason; and prophetic, wherein having chosen out one peculiar nation, the Jews, for his subjects, he governed

A twofold kingdom of God, natural and prophetic.

---

1 Hobbes was criticized for excluding atheists from the kingdom of God because it meant that atheists could not sin. Hobbes's reply is that atheists will be treated as enemies of God because they do not acknowledge him. See also 28.13, 31.5, and 42.103.

them, and none but them, not only by natural reason, but by positive laws, which he gave them by the mouths of his holy prophets. Of the natural kingdom of God I intend to speak in this chapter.

The right of God's sovereignty is derived from his omnipotence.

5. The right of nature whereby God reigneth over men and punisheth those that break his laws is to be derived, not from his creating them, as if he required obedience as of gratitude for his benefits, but from his *irresistible power*. I have formerly shown how the sovereign right ariseth from pact; to show how the same right may arise from nature requires no more but to show in what case it is never taken away. Seeing all men by nature had right to all things, they had right everyone to reign over all the rest. But because this right could not be obtained by force, it concerned the safety of everyone, laying by that right, to set up men (with sovereign authority) by common consent, to rule and defend them; whereas if there had been any man of power irresistible, there had been no reason why he should not by that power have ruled and defended both himself and them, according to his own discretion. To those therefore whose power is irresistible, the dominion of all men adhereth naturally by their excellence of power; and consequently it is from that power

[188] that the kingdom over men and the right of afflicting men at his pleasure belongeth naturally to God Almighty, not as Creator and gracious, but as omnipotent. And though punishment be due for sin only, because by that word is understood affliction for sin; yet the right of afflicting is not always derived from men's sin, but from God's power.

Sin not the cause of all affliction.

6. This question, *why evil men often prosper; and good men suffer adversity*, has been much disputed by the ancients, and is the same with this of ours, *by what right God dispenseth the prosperities and adversities of this life*, and is of that difficulty, as it hath shaken the faith, not only of the vulgar, but of philosophers and, which is more, of the saints, concerning the Divine Providence. *How good*, saith David, *is the God of Israel to those that are upright in heart; and yet my feet were almost gone, my treadings had well-nigh slipped; for I was grieved at the wicked, when I saw the un-*

Ps. 72:1-3.

godly in such prosperity. And Job, how earnestly does he expostulate with God for the many afflictions he suffered, notwithstanding his righteousness? This question in the case of Job is decided by God himself, not by arguments derived from Job's sin, but his own power.[1] For whereas the friends of Job drew their arguments from his affliction to his sin, and he defended himself by the conscience of his innocence; God himself taketh up the matter and, having justified the affliction by arguments drawn from his power, such as this, *Where wast thou when I laid the foundations of the earth*,[2] and the like, both approved Job's innocence and reproved the erroneous doctrine of his friends. Conformable to this doctrine is the sentence of our Saviour concerning the man that was born blind, in these words, *Neither hath this man sinned, nor his fathers; but that the works of God might be made manifest in him.*[3] And though it be said, *that death entered into the world by sin* (by which is meant that if Adam had never sinned, he had never died, that is, never suffered any separation of his soul from his body), it follows not thence that God could not justly have afflicted him, though he had not sinned, as well as he afflicteth other living creatures that cannot sin.

Job 38:4.

7. Having spoken of the right of God's sovereignty as grounded only on nature, we are to consider next what are the divine laws, or dictates of natural reason; which laws concern either the natural duties of one man to another, or the honour naturally due to our Divine Sovereign. The first are the same laws of nature, of which I have spoken already in the fourteenth and fifteenth chapters of this treatise, namely, equity, justice, mercy, humility, and the rest of the moral virtues. It remaineth therefore that we consider what precepts are dictated to men by their natural reason only, without other word of God, touching the honour and worship of the Divine Majesty.

Divine laws.

---

1 The book of Job proposes many solutions to the problem of evil. Hobbes's preferred solution might be called "The God-Above-Justice Solution." Being almighty, God has a natural authority over humans, that is, is sovereign over them and hence cannot be unjust to them.

2 This verse contains a solution to the problem of evil that might be called "The Unanswerable-Question Solution." Humans do not have enough information to be able to answer the question. This solution is different from the God-Above-Justice Solution.

3 This verse from the gospel of John 9:3 expresses still another solution, different from those mentioned above. It does not occur in Job.

8. Honour consisteth in the inward thought and opinion of the power and goodness of another; and therefore to honour God is to think as highly of his power and goodness as is possible. And of that opinion, the external signs appearing in the words and actions of men are called *worship*;[1] which is one part of that which the Latins understand by the word *cultus*; for *cultus* signifieth properly and constantly that labour which a man bestows on anything with a purpose to make benefit by it. Now those

[189]

things whereof we make benefit are either subject to us, and the profit they yield followeth the labour we bestow upon them as a natural effect; or they are not subject to us, but answer our labour according to their own wills. In the first sense the labour bestowed on the earth is called *culture*; and the education of children, a *culture* of their minds. In the second sense, where men's wills are to be wrought to our purpose, not by force, but by complaisance, it signifieth as much as courting, that is, a winning of favour by good offices; as by praises, by acknowledging their power, and by whatsoever is pleasing to them from whom we look for any benefit. And this is properly *worship*; in which sense *publicola* is understood for a worshipper of the people; and *cultus Dei*, for the worship of God.

9. From internal honour, consisting in the opinion of power and goodness, arise three passions: *love*, which hath reference to goodness; and *hope*, and *fear*, that relate to power; and three parts of external worship: *praise*, *magnifying*, and *blessing*; the subject of praise being goodness; the subject of magnifying and blessing being power; and the effect thereof felicity. Praise and magnifying are signified both by words and actions: by words, when we say a man is good or great; by actions, when we thank him for his bounty and obey his power. The opinion of the happiness of another can only be expressed by words.

10. There be some signs of honour (both in attributes and actions) that be naturally so, as amongst attributes, *good*, *just*, *liberal*, and the like; and amongst actions, *prayers*, *thanks*, and *obedience*. Others are so by institution or custom of men; and in some times and places are

---

1 Hobbes distinguishes between honor and worship on the basis of what is internal and external. This contrast is continued in 31.9.

honourable; in others, dishonourable; in others, indifferent; such as are the gestures in salutation, prayer, and thanksgiving, in different times and places, differently used. The former is *natural*; the latter *arbitrary* worship.

11. And of arbitrary worship, there be two differences; for sometimes it is *commanded*, sometimes a *voluntary* worship: commanded, when it is such as he requireth who is worshipped; free, when it is such as the worshipper thinks fit. When it is commanded, not the words or gesture, but the obedience is the worship. But when free, the worship consists in the opinion of the beholders; for if to them the words or actions by which we intend honour seem ridiculous and tending to contumely, [then] they are no worship, because no signs of honour; and [they are] no signs of honour, because a sign is not a sign to him that giveth it, but to him to whom it is made, that is, to the spectator.

12. Again there is a *public* and a *private* worship. Public is the worship that a commonwealth performeth, as one person. Private is that which a private person exhibiteth. Public, in respect of the whole commonwealth, is free; but in respect of particular men it is not so. Private is in secret free; but in the sight of the multitude it is never without some restraint either from the laws or from the opinion of men; which is contrary to the nature of liberty.

13. The end of worship amongst men is power. For where a man seeth another worshipped, he supposeth him powerful and is the readier to obey him; which makes his power greater. But God has no ends; the worship we do him proceeds from our duty and is directed according to our capacity by those rules of honour that reason dictateth to be done by the weak to the more potent men, in hope of benefit, for fear of damage, or in thankfulness for good already received from them.

14. That we may know what worship of God is taught us by the light of nature, I will begin with his attributes. Where, first, it is manifest, we ought to attribute to him *existence*;[1] for no man can have the will to honour that which he thinks not to have any being.

---

1 In this and the following paragraphs, Hobbes is saying what "we ought to attribute" to God and not necessarily what is literally true of God. It happens to be the case that God exists and that we ought to attribute existence to him, (Continued)

15. Secondly, that those philosophers who said the world, or the soul of the world, was God spake unworthily of him, and denied his existence; for by God is understood the cause of the world; and to say the world is God[1] is to say there is no cause of it, that is, no God.

16. Thirdly, to say the world was not created, but eternal (seeing that which is eternal has no cause) is to deny there is a God.

17. Fourthly, that they who, attributing (as they think) ease to God, take from him the care of mankind, take from him his honour; for it takes away men's love and fear of him, which is the root of honour.

18. Fifthly, in those things that signify greatness and power, to say he is *finite* is not to honour him; for it is not a sign of the will to honour God to attribute to him less than we can, because to finite, it is easy to add more.

19. Therefore to attribute *figure* to him is not honour; for all figure is finite:

20. Nor to say we conceive, and imagine, or have an *idea* of him in our mind; for whatsoever we conceive is finite:

21. Nor to attribute to him *parts* or *totality*; which are the attributes only of things finite:

22. Nor to say he is in this or that *place*; for whatsoever is in place is bounded and finite:

23. Nor that he is *moved* or *resteth*; for both these attributes ascribe to him place:

24. Nor that there be more gods than one, because it implies them all finite; for there cannot be more than one infinite:

25. Nor to ascribe to him (unless metaphorically, meaning not the passion, but the effect) passions that partake of grief, as *repentance, anger, mercy*; or of want, as *appetite, hope, desire*; or of any passive faculty; for passion is power limited by somewhat else.

---

but God is literally in some place because he is a body and all bodies are in some place, but we are not to attribute being in a place to him because it suggests that he is finite, and that dishonors him. See 31.22 and 31.33.

1 If the world is defined as the totality of bodies, God is part of the world since God is a body. But he is not identical with the world. Cf. 34.2

26. And therefore when we ascribe to God a *will*, it is not to be understood, as that of man, for a *rational appetite*; but as the power by which he effecteth everything.

27. Likewise when we attribute to him *sight*, and other acts of sense, as also *knowledge* and *understanding*, which in us is nothing else but a tumult of the mind, raised by external things that press the organical parts of man's body; for there is no such thing in God, and being things that depend on natural causes, cannot be attributed to him.

28. He that will attribute to God nothing but what is warranted by natural reason must either use such negative attributes as *infinite, eternal, incomprehensible*;[1] or superlatives, as *most high, most great*, and the like; or indefinite, as *good, just, holy, creator*, and in such sense as if he meant not to declare what he is (for that were to circumscribe him within the limits of our fancy), but how much we admire him, and how ready we would be to obey him; which is a sign of humility and of a will to honour him as much as we can;[2] for there is but one name to signify our conception of his nature, and that is I Am;[3] and but one name of his relation to us, and that is God, in which is contained Father, King, and Lord. [191]

29. Concerning the actions of divine worship, it is a most general precept of reason that they be signs of the intention to honour God; such as are, first, *prayers*; for not the carvers, when they made images, were thought to make them gods, but the people that prayed to them.

Actions that are signs of honour divine.

30. Secondly, *thanksgiving*, which differeth from prayer in divine worship no otherwise than that prayers precede, and thanks succeed, the benefit, the end both of the one and the other being to acknowledge God for author of all benefits as well past as future.

---

1 These attributes are negative because "infinite" means not finite, "eternal" means not temporal and "incomprehensible" means not comprehensible.

2 Many philosophers have been insensitive to the fact that language is used to do many more things than just state the facts. Even indicative sentences can be used for nondescriptive purposes. Hobbes's point is that a sentence such as "God is good" should be understood not as describing God but as worshipping him. See also 36.9.

3 "I am" is a translation from the Greek of the name God gave as his own to Moses, which in Hebrew is "Yahweh."

31. Thirdly, *gifts*; that is to say, sacrifices and oblations (if they be of the best) are signs of honour; for they are thanksgivings.

32. Fourthly, *not to swear* by any but God is naturally a sign of honour; for it is a confession that God only knoweth the heart and that no man's wit or strength can protect a man against God's vengeance on the perjured.

33. Fifthly, it is a part of rational worship to speak considerately of God; for it argues a fear of him, and fear is a confession of his power. Hence followeth, that the name of God is not to be used rashly and to no purpose; for that is as much as in vain; and it is to no purpose unless it be by way of oath and by order of the commonwealth, to make judgements certain; or between commonwealths, to avoid war. And that disputing of God's nature is contrary to his honour; for it is supposed that in this natural kingdom of God, there is no other way to know anything but by natural reason, that is, from the principles of natural science, which are so far from teaching us anything of God's nature, as they cannot teach us our own nature, nor the nature of the smallest creature living.[1] And therefore, when men out of the principles of natural reason dispute of the attributes of God, they but dishonour him; for in the attributes which we give to God, we are not to consider the signification of philosophical truth, but the signification of pious intention to do him the greatest honour we are able. From the want of which consideration have proceeded the volumes of disputation about the nature of God that tend not to his honour, but to the honour of our own wits and learning; and are nothing else but inconsiderate and vain abuses of his sacred name.

34. Sixthly, in *prayers, thanksgivings, offerings* and *sacrifices*, it is a dictate of natural reason that they be every [192] one in his kind the best and most significant of honour. As, for example, that prayers and thanksgiving be made in words and phrases not sudden, nor light, nor plebeian, but beautiful and well composed; for else we do not God as much honour as we can. And therefore the heathens did absurdly to worship images for gods, but their doing

---

1 Human reason is so limited that it cannot discover the nature of even the smallest living being. So it is not surprising that God would be beyond the ken of science, if for no other reason.

it in verse and with music, both of voice and instruments, was reasonable. Also that the beasts they offered in sacrifice, and the gifts they offered, and their actions in worshipping, were full of submission and commemorative of benefits received, was according to reason, as proceeding from an intention to honour him.

35. Seventhly, reason directeth not only to worship God in secret, but also and especially in public and in the sight of men; for without that, that which in honour is most acceptable, the procuring others to honour him, is lost.

36. Lastly, obedience to his laws (that is, in this case to the laws of nature) is the greatest worship of all. For as obedience is more acceptable to God than sacrifice, so also to set light by his commandments is the greatest of all contumelies.[1] And these are the laws of that divine worship which natural reason dictateth to private men.

37. But seeing a commonwealth is but one person, it ought also to exhibit to God but one worship; which then it doth when it commandeth it to be exhibited by private men, publicly. And this is public worship, the property whereof is to be uniform;[2] for those actions that are done differently by different men cannot be said to be a public worship. And therefore, where many sorts of worship be allowed, proceeding from the different religions of private men, it cannot be said there is any public worship, nor that the commonwealth is of any religion at all.

Public worship consisteth in uniformity.

38. And because words (and consequently the attributes of God) have their signification by agreement and constitution of men, those attributes are to be held significative of honour that men intend shall so be; and whatsoever may be done by the wills of particular men, where there is no law but reason, may be done by the will of the commonwealth by laws civil. And because a commonwealth hath no will nor makes no laws but those that are made by the will of him or them that have the

All attributes depend on the laws civil.

---

1 Hobbes may have in mind Amos 5:21-24, where God says, "I hate, I despise your feast days ... Though ye offer me burnt offerings and grain offerings, I will not accept them," because the Israelites were not obeying him.

2 Cf. 47.20. Since the Commonwealth did not have any uniform public worship, Hobbes is indicating that England no longer has any religion. He is probably criticizing the Commonwealth.

sovereign power; it followeth that those attributes which the sovereign ordaineth in the worship of God for signs of honour ought to be taken and used for such by private men in their public worship.

Not all actions.

39. But because not all actions are signs by constitution, but some are naturally signs of honour, others of contumely, these latter, which are those that men are ashamed to do in the sight of them they reverence, cannot be made by human power a part of divine worship; nor the former, such as are decent, modest, humble behaviour, ever be separated from it. But whereas there be an infinite number of actions and gestures of an indifferent nature, such of them as the commonwealth shall ordain to be publicly and universally in use, as signs of honour [193] and part of God's worship, are to be taken and used for such by the subjects. And that which is said in the Scripture, *It is better to obey God than man*, hath place in the kingdom of God by pact, and not by nature.

Natural punish-
ments.

40. Having thus briefly spoken of the natural kingdom of God, and his natural laws, I will add only to this chapter a short declaration of his natural punishments. There is no action of man in this life that is not the beginning of so long a chain of consequences as no human providence is high enough to give a man a prospect to the end. And in this chain there are linked together both pleasing and unpleasing events; in such manner as he that will do anything for his pleasure, must engage himself to suffer all the pains annexed to it; and these pains are the natural punishments of those actions which are the beginning of more harm than good. And hereby it comes to pass that intemperance is naturally punished with diseases; rashness, with mischances; injustice, with the violence of enemies; pride, with ruin; cowardice, with oppression; negligent government of princes, with rebellion; and rebellion, with slaughter. For seeing punishments are consequent to the breach of laws, natural punishments must be naturally consequent to the breach of the laws of nature, and therefore follow them as their natural, not arbitrary, effects.[1]

The conclusion
of the second
part.

41. And thus far concerning the constitution, nature, and right of sovereigns, and concerning the duty of sub-

---

1 See also 28.8.

jects, derived from the principles of natural reason. And now, considering how different this doctrine is from the practice of the greatest part of the world, especially of these western parts that have received their moral learning from Rome and Athens, and how much depth of moral philosophy is required in them that have the administration of the sovereign power, I am at the point of believing this my labour as useless as the commonwealth of Plato; for he also is of opinion that it is impossible for the disorders of state and change of governments by civil war, ever to be taken away till sovereigns be philosophers. But when I consider again that the science of natural justice is the only science necessary for sovereigns and their principal ministers, and that they need not be charged with the sciences mathematical, as by Plato they are, further than by good laws to encourage men to the study of them; and that neither Plato nor any other philosopher hitherto hath put into order and sufficiently or probably proved all the theorems of moral doctrine, that men may learn thereby both how to govern and how to obey, I recover some hope that one time or other this writing of mine may fall into the hands of a sovereign who will consider it himself (for it is short, and I think clear) without the help of any interested or envious interpreter; and by the exercise of entire sovereignty, in protecting the public teaching of it, convert this truth of speculation into the utility of practice.

A REVIEW and CONCLUSION

1. From the contrariety of some of the Natural Faculties of the Mind, one to another, as also of one Passion to another, and from their reference to Conversation, there has been an argument taken, to inferre an impossibility that any one man should be sufficiently disposed to all sorts of Civill duty. The Severity of Judgement, they say, makes men Censorious and unapt to pardon the Errours and Infirmities of other men: and on the other side, Celerity of Fancy makes the thoughts lesse steddy than is necessary, to discern exactly between Right and Wrong. Again, in all Deliberations, and in all Pleadings, the faculty of solid Reasoning, is necessary; for without it, the Resolutions of men are rash, and their Sentences unjust: and yet if there be not powerful Eloquence, which procureth attention and Consent, the effect of Reason will be little. But these are contrary Faculties; the former being grounded upon principles of Truth; the other upon Opinions already received, true, or false; and upon the Passions and Interests of men, which are different, and mutable.

2. And amongst the Passions, *Courage*, (by which I mean the Contempt of Wounds, and violent Death) enclineth men to private Revenges, and sometimes to endeavour the unsettling of the Publique Peace: And *Timorousnesse*, many times disposeth to the desertion of the Publique Defence. Both these they say cannot stand together in the same person.

3. And to consider the contrariety of mens Opinions, and Manners in generall, It is they say, impossible to entertain a constant Civill Amity with all those, with whom the Businesse of the world constrains us to converse: Which Businesse, consisteth almost in nothing else but a perpetuall contention for Honour, Riches, and Authority.

4. To which I answer, that these are indeed great difficulties, but not Impossibilities: For by Education, and Discipline, they may bee, and are sometimes reconciled. Judgement, and Fancy may have place in the same man; but by turnes, as the end which he aimeth at requireth. As the Israelites in Egypt, were sometimes fastened to their labour of making Bricks, and other times were ranging

abroad to gather Straw: So also may the Judgement sometimes be fixed upon one certain Consideration, and the Fancy at another time wandring about the world. So also Reason, and Eloquence, (though not perhaps in the Natural Sciences, yet in the Morall) may stand very [390]   well together. For wheresoever there is place for adorning and preferring of Errour, there is much more place for adorning and preferring of Truth, if they have it to adorn. Nor is there any repugnancy between fearing the Laws, and not fearing a publique Enemy; nor between abstaining from Injury, and pardoning it in others. There is therefore no such Inconsistence of Humane Nature, with Civill Duties, as some think. I have known cleernesse of Judgement, and largenesse of Fancy; strength of Reason, and graceful Elocution; a Courage for the Warre, and a Fear for the Laws, and all eminently in one man; and that was my most noble and honoured friend, Mr. *Sidney Godolphin*; who hating no man, nor hated of any, was unfortunately slain in the beginning of the late Civill warre, in the Publique quarrell, by an undiscerned, and an undiscerning hand.

5. To the Laws of Nature, declared in the 15. Chapter, I would have this added, *That every man is bound by Nature, as much as in him lieth, to protect in Warre the Authority, by which he is himself protected in time of peace.* For he that pretendeth a Right of Nature to preserve his owne body, cannot pretend a Right of Nature to destroy him, by whose strength he is preserved: It is a manifest contradiction of himselfe. And though this Law may bee drawn by consequence, from some of those that are there already mentioned; yet the Times require to have it inculcated, and remembered.

6. And because I find by divers English Books lately printed, that the Civill warres have not yet sufficiently taught men, in what point of time it is, that a Subject becomes obliged to the Conquerour; nor what is Conquest; nor how it comes about, that it obliges men to obey his Laws:[1] Therefore for farther satisfaction of men therein, I say, the point of time, wherein a man becomes subject

---

1 Hobbes is probably thinking of the *de facto* theorists, according to whom a person owes obligation to whoever holds power. For Hobbes, power must be combined with the consent of the subject ("Review and Conclusion," 7). See also 20.10 and 21.21.

to a Conquerour, is that point, wherein having liberty to submit to him, he consenteth, either by expresse words, or by other sufficient sign, to be his Subject. When it is that a man hath the liberty to submit, I have shewed before in the end of the 21. Chapter; namely, that for him that hath no obligation to his former sovereign but that of an ordinary Subject, it is then, when the means of his life is within the Guards and Garrisons of the Enemy; for it is then, that he hath no longer Protection from him, but is protected by the adverse party for his Contribution. Seeing therefore such contribution is every where, as a thing inevitable, (not withstanding it be an assistance to the Enemy,) esteemed lawfull; a totall Submission, which is but an assistance to the Enemy, cannot be esteemed unlawful. Besides, if a man consider that they who submit, assist the Enemy but with part of their estates, whereas they that refuse, assist him with the whole, there is no reason to call their Submission, or Composition an Assistance; but rather a Detriment to the Enemy. But if a man, besides the obligation of a Subject, hath taken upon him a new obligation of a Souldier, then he hath not the liberty to submit to a new Power, as long as the old one keeps the field, and giveth him means of subsistence, either in his Armies or Garrisons: for in this case, he cannot complain of want of Protection, and means to live as a [391] Souldier: But when that also failes, a Souldier also may seek his Protection wheresoever he has most hope to have it; and may lawfully submit himself to his new Master. And so much for the time when he may do it lawfully, if hee will. If therefore he doe it, he is undoubtedly bound to be a true Subject: For a Contract lawfully made, cannot lawfully be broken.

7. By this also a man may understand, when it is, that men may be said to be Conquered; and in what the nature of Conquest, and the Right of a Conquerour consisteth: For this Submission is it [that] implyeth them all. Conquest, is not the Victory it self; but the Acquisition, by Victory, of a Right, over the persons of men. He therefore that is slain, is overcome, but not Conquered: He that is taken, and put into prison, or chaines, is not Conquered, though Overcome; for he is still an Enemy, and may save himself if hee can: But he that upon promise of Obedience, hath his Life and Liberty allowed him,

is then Conquered, and a Subject; and not before. The Romans used to say, that their Generall had *Pacified* such a *Province*, that is to say, in English, *Conquered* it; and that the Countrey was *Pacified* by Victory, when the people of it had promised *Imperata facere*, that is, *To doe what the Romane People commanded them*: This was to be Conquered. But this promise may be either expresse, or tacite: Expresse, by Promise: Tacite, by other signes. As, for example, a man that hath not been called to make such an expresse Promise, (because he is one whose power perhaps is not considerable;) yet if he live under their Protection openly, hee is understood to submit himselfe to the Government: But if he live there secretly, he is lyable to any thing that may bee done to a Spie, and Enemy of the State. I say not, hee does any Injustice, (for acts of open Hostility bear not that name); but that he may be justly put to death. Likewise, if a man, when his Country is conquered, be out of it, he is not Conquered, nor Subject: but if at his return he submit to the Government, he is bound to obey it. So that *Conquest* (to define it) is the Acquiring of the Right of Soveraignty by Victory. Which Right is acquired in the people's Submission, by which they contract with the Victor, promising Obedience, for Life and Liberty.

8. In the 29. Chapter I have set down for one of the causes of the Dissolutions of Common-wealths, their Imperfect Generation, consisting in the want of an Absolute and Arbitrary Legislative Power; for want whereof, the Civill Soveraign is fain to handle the Sword of Justice unconstantly, and as if it were too hot for him to hold: One reason whereof (which I have not there mentioned) is this, That they will all of them justifie the War, by which their Power was at first gotten, and whereon (as they think) their Right dependeth, and not on the Possession. As if, for example, the Right of the Kings of England did depend on the goodnesse of the cause of *William* the Conquerour, and upon their lineall, and directest Descent from him; by which means, there would perhaps be no tie of the Subjects obedience to their Soveraign at [392] this day in all the world: wherein whilest they needlessely think to justifie themselves, they justifie all the successfull Rebellions that Ambition shall at any time raise against them and their Successors. Therefore I put down for one

of the most effectuall seeds of the Death of any State, that the Conquerors require not onely a submission of mens actions to them for the future, but also an Approbation of all their actions past; when there is scarce a Common-wealth in the world, whose beginnings can in conscience be justified.

9. And because the name of Tyranny,[1] signifieth nothing more, nor lesse, than the name of Soveraignty, be it in one, or many men, saving that they that use the former word, are understood to bee angry with them they call Tyrants; I think the toleration of a professed hatred of Tyranny, is a Toleration of hatred to Common-wealth in generall, and another evill seed, not differing much from the former. For to the Justification of the Cause of a Conqueror, the Reproach of the Cause of the Conquered, is for the most part necessary: but neither of them necessary for the Obligation of the Conquered. And thus much I have thought fit to say upon the Review of the first and second part of this Discourse.

10. In the 35. Chapter,[2] I have sufficiently declared out of the Scripture, that in the Common-wealth of the Jewes, God himselfe was made the Soveraign, by Pact with the People; who were therefore called his *Peculiar People*, to distinguish them from the rest of the world, over whom God reigned not by their Consent, but by his own Power: And that in this Kingdome Moses was Gods Lieutenant on Earth; and that it was he that told them what Laws God appointed them to be ruled by. But I have omitted to set down who were the Officers appointed to doe Execution; especially in Capitall Punishments; not then thinking it a matter of so neccssary consideration as I find it since. Wee know that generally in all Common-wealths, the Execution of Corporeall Punishments was either put upon the Guards, or other Souldiers of the Sovereign Power; or given to those, in whom want of means, contempt of honour, and hardnesse of heart concurred, to make them sue for such an Office. But amongst the Israelites it was a Positive Law of God their Soveraign, that he that was convicted of a capitall Crime, should be stoned to death by the People; and that the Witnesses should cast

---

1 See also 19.2 and 46.35.
2 See 35.5.

the first Stone, and after the Witnesses, then the rest of the People. This was a Law that designed who were to be the Executioners; but not that any one should throw a stone at him before Conviction and Sentence, where the Congregation was Judge. The Witnesses were neverthelesse to be heard before they proceeded to Execution, unlesse the Fact were committed in the presence of the Congregation it self, or in sight of the lawfull Judges; for then there needed no other Witnesses but the Judges themselves. Neverthelesse, this manner of proceeding, being not thoroughly understood, hath given occasion to a dangerous opinion, that any man may kill another, in some cases, by a Right of Zeal, as if the Executions done upon Offenders in the Kingdome of God in old time, [393] proceeded not from the Soveraign Command, but from the Authority of Private Zeal: which, if we consider the texts that seem to favour it, is quite contrary.

11. First, where the Levites fell upon the People, that had made and worshipped the Golden Calfe, and slew three thousand of them; it was by the Commandement of Moses, from the mouth of God, as is manifest, *Exod.*, 32. 27. And when the Son of a woman of Israel had blasphemed God, they that heard it, did not kill him, but brought him before Moses, who put him under custody, till God should give Sentence against him; as appears, *Levit.* 24. 11, 12. Again, (*Numbers* 25. 6, 7.) when Phinehas killed Zimri and Cosbi, it was not by Right of Private Zeale: Their Crime was committed in the sight of the Assembly; there needed no Witnesse; the Law was known, and he the heir apparent to the Soveraignty; and, which is the principall point, the Lawfulnesse of his Act depended wholly upon a subsequent Ratification by Moses, whereof he had no cause to doubt. And this Presumption of a future Ratification, is sometimes necessary to the safety of a Common-wealth; as in a sudden Rebellion, any man that can suppresse it by his own Power in the Countrey where it begins, without expresse Lawe or Commission, may lawfully doe it, and provide to have it Ratified, or Pardoned, whilst it is in doing, or after it is done. Also, *Numb. 35.30* it is expressly said, *Whosoever shall kill the Murtherer, shall kill him upon the word of Witnesses*: but Witnesses suppose a formall Judicature, and consequently condemn that pretence of *Jus Zelotarum*. The Law of

Moses concerning him that enticeth to Idolatry, (that is to say, in the Kingdome of God to a renouncing of his Allegiance (*Deut.* 13. 8.) forbids to conceal him, and commands the Accuser to cause him to be put to death, and to cast the first stone at him; but not to kill him before he be Condemned. And (*Deut.* 17. Ver. 4, 5, 6) the Processe against Idolatry is exactly set down: For God there speaketh to the People, as Judge, and commandeth them, when a man is Accused of Idolatry, to Enquire diligently of the Fact, and finding it true, then to Stone him; but still the hand of the Witnesse throweth the first stone. This is not Private Zeale, but Publique Condemnation. In like manner when a Father hath a rebellious Son, the Law is (*Deut.* 21. 18.) that he shall bring him before the Judges of the Town, and all the people of the Town shall Stone him. Lastly, by pretence of these Laws it was, that St. Stephen was Stoned, and not by pretence of Private Zeal: for before hee was carried away to Execution, he had Pleaded his Cause before the High Priest. There is nothing in all this, nor in any other part of the Bible, to countenance Executions by Private Zeal; which being oftentimes but a conjunction of Ignorance and Passion, is against both the Justice and Peace of a Common-wealth.

12. In the 36. Chapter I have said, that it is not declared in what manner God spoke supernaturally to Moses: Not that he spake not to him sometimes by Dreams and Visions, and by a supernaturall Voice, as to other Prophets: For the manner how he spake unto him from the Mercy-Seat, is expressely set down *Numbers* 7.89 in these words, [394] *From that time forward, when Moses entred into the Tabernacle of the Congregation to speak with God, he heard a Voice which spake unto him from over the Mercy-Seat, which is over the Arke of the Testimony; from between the Cherubims he spake unto him.* But it is not declared in what consisted the praeeminence of the manner of Gods speaking to Moses, above that of his speaking to other Prophets, as to Samuel, and to Abraham, to whom he also spake by a Voice, (that is, by Vision) Unlesse the difference consist in the clearnesse of the Vision. For *Face to Face,* and *Mouth to Mouth,* cannot be literally understood of the Infinitenesse, and Incomprehensibility of the Divine Nature.[1]

---

1 See also 36.13.

13. And as to the whole Doctrine, I see not yet, but the Principles of it are true and proper; and the Ratiocination solid. For I ground the Civill Right of Soveraigns, and both the Duty and Liberty of Subjects, upon the known naturall Inclinations of Mankind, and upon the Articles of the Law of Nature; of which no man, that pretends but reason enough to govern his private family, ought to be ignorant. And for the Power Ecclesiasticall of the same Soveraigns, I ground it on such Texts, as are both evident in themselves, and consonant to the Scope of the whole Scripture. And therefore am perswaded, that he that shall read it with a purpose onely to be informed, shall be informed by it. But for those that by Writing, or Publique Discourse, or by their eminent actions, have already engaged themselves to the maintaining of contrary opinions, they will not bee so easily satisfied. For in such cases, it is naturall for men, at one and the same time, both to proceed in reading, and to lose their attention, in the search of objections to that they had read before: Of which, in a time wherein the interests of men are changed (seeing much of that Doctrine, which serveth to the establishing of a new Government, must needs be contrary to that which conduced to the dissolution of the old,) there cannot choose but be very many.

14. In that part which treateth of a Christian Common-wealth, there are some new Doctrines, which, it may be, in a State where the contrary were already fully determined, were a fault for a Subject without leave to divulge, as being a usurpation of the place of a Teacher. But in this time, that men call not onely for Peace, but also for Truth, to offer such Doctrines as I think True, and that manifestly tend to Peace and Loyalty, to the consideration of those that are yet in deliberation, is no more, but to offer New Wine, to bee put into New Casks, that both may be preserved together. And I suppose, that then, when Novelty can breed no trouble, nor disorder in a State, men are not generally so much inclined to the reverence of Antiquity as to preferre Ancient Errors, before New and well proved Truth.

15. There is nothing I distrust more than my Elocution; which neverthelesse I am confident (excepting the Mischances of the Presse) is not obscure. That I have neglected the Ornament of quoting ancient Poets, Orators,

and Philosophers, contrary to the custome of late time, (whether I have done well or ill in it,) proceedeth from my judgement, grounded on many reasons. For first, [395] all Truth of Doctrine dependeth either upon *Reason*, or upon *Scripture*; both which give credit to many, but never receive it from any Writer. Secondly, the matters in question are not of *Fact*, but of *Right*, wherein there is no place for *Witnesses*. There is scarce any of those old Writers, that contradicteth not sometimes both himself, and others; which makes their Testimonies insufficient. Fourthly, such Opinions as are taken onely upon Credit of Antiquity, are not intrinsecally the Judgement of those that cite them, but Words that passe (like gaping) from mouth to mouth. Fifthly, it is many times with a fraudulent Designe that men stick their corrupt Doctrine with the Cloves of other mens Wit. Sixtly, I find not that the Ancients they cite, took it for an Ornament, to doe the like with those that wrote before them. Seventhly, it is an argument of Indigestion, when Greek and Latine Sentences unchewed come up again, as they use to doe, unchanged. Lastly, though I reverence those men of Ancient time that either have written Truth perspicuously, or set us in a better way to find it out our selves; yet to the Antiquity it self I think nothing due: For if we will reverence the Age, the Present is the Oldest; if the Antiquity of the Writer, I am not sure that generally they to whom such honour is given, were more Ancient when they wrote, than I am that am Writing: But if it bee well considered, the praise of Ancient Authors, proceeds not from the reverence of the Dead, but from the competition, and mutuall envy of the Living.

16. To conclude, there is nothing in this whole Discourse, nor in that I before of the same subject in Latine,[1] as far as I can perceive, contrary either to the Word of God, or to good Manners; or [tending][2] to the disturbance of the Publique Tranquillity. Therefore I think it may be profitably printed, and more profitably taught in the Universities, in case they also think so, to whom the judgement of the same belongeth. For seeing the Universities are the Fountains of Civill and Morall Doctrine, from whence the Preachers, and the Gentry, drawing

---

1 Hobbes is referring to *De Cive*.
2 The word "tending" occurs here in the manuscript version.

such water as they find, use to sprinkle the same (both from the Pulpit, and in their Conversation) upon the People, there ought certainly to be great care taken, to have it pure, both from the Venime of Heathen Politicians, and from the Incantation of Deceiving Spirits. And by that means the most men, knowing their Duties, will be the less subject to serve the Ambition of a few discontented persons, in their purposes against the State; and be the lesse grieved with the Contributions necessary for their Peace, and Defence; and the Governours themselves have the lesse cause, to maintain at the Common charge any greater Army, than is necessary to make good the Publique Liberty, against the Invasions and Encroachments of forraign Enemies.

17. And thus I have brought to an end my Discourse of Civill and Ecclesiasticall Government, occasioned by the disorders of the present time, without partiality, without application, and without other designe, than to set before [396] mens eyes the mutuall Relation between Protection and Obedience; of which the condition of Humane Nature, and the Laws Divine, (both Naturall and Positive), require an inviolable observation. And though in the revolution of States, there can be no very good Constellation for Truths of this nature to be born under, (as having an angry aspect from the dissolvers of an old Government, and seeing but the backs of them that erect a new); yet I cannot think it will be condemned at this time, either by the Publique Judge of Doctrine, or by any that desires the continuance of Publique Peace. And in this hope I return to my interrupted Speculation of Bodies Naturall; wherein, (if God give me health to finish it,) I hope the Novelty will as much please, as in the Doctrine of this Artificial Body it useth to offend. For such Truth, as opposeth no man's profit, nor pleasure, is to all men welcome.

FINIS

Appendix A: From Robert Filmer, Observations Concerning the Original of Government, Upon Mr Hobbes's "Leviathan," Mr Milton Against Salmasius, H. Grotius "De Jure Belli" (R. Royston, 1652)

[Robert Filmer (c. 1588-1653) was a gentleman educated at Trinity College, Cambridge. Little noted in his own day, he is now best known as the target of John Locke's criticisms in the first of the *Two Treatises of Government*. Like Hobbes, Filmer believed in absolute sovereignty, as indicated by the title of his book, *The Necessity of the Absolute Power of all Kings* (1648). Filmer published *Observations Concerning the Original of Government, Upon Mr Hobbes's "Leviathan," Mr Milton against Salmasius, H. Grotius "De Jure Belli"* in 1652. His theory is patriarchal; that is, he believes that a ruler's right comes from a father's right to rule. To put this slightly differently, the basis for political authority is the same as that for the authority of a father over his family. Filmer also believes political authority is grounded upon divine right; sovereigns govern by the authority of God. Although Hobbes gives lip service to the divine-right theory and thinks that fathers often gave rise to governments by extracting an implicit covenant from their family members, he does not subscribe to the divine-right theory or to patriarchalism.

Filmer's page references to *Leviathan* are to the original edition; these page numbers are printed in brackets in the margins of the text of this edition of *Leviathan*.]

I

If God created only Adam, and of a piece of him made the woman; [and] if by generation from them two as parts of them all mankind be propagated; [and] if also God gave to Adam not only the dominion over the woman and the children that should issue from them, but also over the whole earth to subdue it and over all the creatures on it, so that as long as Adam lived no man could claim or enjoy anything but by donation, assignation, or permission from him; [then] I wonder how the right of nature can be imagined by Mr. Hobbes, which he says, page 64, is a liberty for each man to use his own power as he will himself for preservation of his own life; a condition of war of everyone against everyone; a right of every man to everything, even to one another's body, especially since he himself affirms, page 178, that originally the father of every man [Adam] was also his Sovereign Lord with power over him of life and death.[1]

II

Mr. Hobbes confesses and believes it was never generally so, that there was such a *jus naturae* [right of nature]; and if not generally, then not at all; for one exception bars all if he mark it well; whereas he imagines such a right of nature may now be practiced in America, he confesses a government there of families, which government how small or brutish soever (as he calls it) is sufficient to destroy his *jus naturale* [natural right].

III

I cannot understand how this right of nature can be conceived without imagining a company of men at the very first to have been all created together without any dependency one of another; or as mushrooms (*fungorum more*) [as if] they all on a sudden were sprung out of the earth without any obligation one to another, as Mr. Hobbes' words are in his book *De Cive*, chapter 8, section 3: The Scripture teaches us otherwise, that all men came by succession, and generation from one man. We must not deny the truth of the history of the creation.

IV

It is not to be thought that God would create man in a condition worse than any beasts, as if he made men to no other end by nature but to destroy one another, a right for the father to destroy or eat his children; and for children to do the like by their parents, is worse than cannibals [*De Cive*, 1.10]. This horrid condition of pure nature when Mr. Hobbes was charged with, his refuge was to answer, that no son can be under-stood to be in this state of nature. Which [this] is all one with denying his own principle; for if men be not free-born, it is not possible for him to assign and prove any other time for them to claim a right of nature to liberty, if not at their birth.

V

But if it be allowed (which is yet most false) that a company of men were at first without a common power to keep them in awe, [then] I do not see why such a condition must be called a state of war of all men against all men. Indeed if such a multitude of men should be created as the earth could not well nourish, there might be cause for men to de-

---

1   [The state of nature is not a state of war.]

stroy one another rather than perish for want of food; but God was no such niggard in the creation; and there being plenty of sustenance and room for all men, there is no cause or use of war till men be hindered in the preservation of life, so that there is no absolute necessity of war in the state of pure nature. It is the right of nature for every man to live in peace, that so he may tend the preservation of his life, which whilst he is in actual war he cannot do. War of itself, as it is war, preserves no man's life; it only helps us to preserve and obtain the means to live. If every man tend the right of preserving life, which may be done in peace, there is no cause of war.

VI

But admit the state of nature were the state of war; [then] let us see what help Mr. Hobbes hath for it. It is a principle of his that "the law of nature is a rule found out by reason" (I do think it is given by God), page 64, "forbidding a man to do that which is destructive to his life, and [forbidding him] to omit that by which he thinks it may be best preserved." If the right of nature be a liberty for a man to do anything he thinks fit to preserve his life, then in the first place nature must teach him that life is to be preserved, and so consequently forbids to do that which may destroy or take away the means of life, or to omit that by which it may be preserved. And thus the right of nature and the law of nature will be all one;[1] for I think Mr. Hobbes will not say [that] the right of nature is a liberty for a man to destroy his own life. The law of nature might be better have been said to consist in a command to preserve or not to omit the means of preserving life, than in a prohibition to destroy, or to omit it.

VII

Another principle I meet with, page 65. "If other men will not lay down their right as well as he, then there is no reason for any to divest himself of his." Hence it follows that if all the men in the world do not agree, no commonwealth can be established. [But], it is a thing impossible for all men in the world, every man with every man, to covenant to lay down their right. Nay it is not possible to be done in the smallest kingdom, though all men should spend their whole lives in nothing else but in running up and down to covenant.

[...]

---

1 According to Filmer, it follows from the right of nature and the law of nature that they are identical.

IX

[...]

To authorize and give up his right of governing himself, to confer all his power and strength, and to submit his will to another is to lay down his right of resisting; for if right of nature be a liberty to use power for preservation of life, [then] laying down of that power must be a relinquishing of power to preserve or defend life; otherwise a man relinquishes nothing.

To reduce all the wills of an assembly by plurality of voices to one will is not a proper speech; for it is not a plurality but a totality of voices which makes an assembly be of one will; otherwise it is but the one will of a major part of the assembly; the negative voice of any one hinders the being of the one will of the assembly. There is nothing more destructive to the true nature of a lawful assembly, than to allow a major part to prevail when the whole only hath right. For a man to give up his right to one that never covenants to protect is a great folly, since it is neither "in consideration of some right reciprocally transferred to himself, nor can he hope for any other good, by standing out of the way, that the other may enjoy his own original right without hindrance from him by reason of so much diminution of impediments," page 66.

X

The liberty, saith Mr. Hobbes, *whereof there is so frequent and honourable mention in the histories and philosophy of the ancient Greeks and Romans, and in the writings and discourse of those that from them have received all their learning in the politics, is not the liberty of particular men, but the liberty of the commonwealth. Whether a commonwealth be monarchical or popular, the freedom is still the same* [page 110]. Here I find Mr. Hobbes is much mistaken. For the liberty of the Athenians and Romans was a liberty only to be found in popular estates [states], and not in monarchies. This is clear by Aristotle, who calls a city a community of freemen, meaning every particular citizen to be free. Not that every particular man had a liberty to resist his governor or do what he list [liked], but a liberty only for particular men, to govern and to be governed by turns, archein and archesthai are Aristotle's words. This was a liberty not to be found in hereditary monarchies. So Tacitus mentioning the several governments of Rome, joins the consulship and liberty to be brought in by Brutus, because by the annual election of Consuls, particular citizens came in their course to govern and to be governed. This may be confirmed by the complaint of our author, which follows: *It is an easy thing for men to be deceived by the specious name of liberty; and for want of judgement to ... mistake that for their pri-*

vate inheritance or birthright which is the right of the public only; and when the same error is confirmed by the authority of men in reputation for their writings on this subject, it is no wonder if it produce sedition and change of government [page 110].

[...]

XIII

I cannot but wonder [that] Master Hobbes should say, page 112, the consent of a subject to sovereign power is contained in these words, *I authorize and do take upon me all his actions* [page 87], in which there is no restriction at all of his own former natural liberty. Surely here Master Hobbes forgot himself; for before he makes the resignation to go in these words also, *I give up my right of governing myself to this man* [page 87]. This is a restriction certainly of his own former natural liberty when he gives it away; and if a man allow his sovereign to kill him which Mr. Hobbes seems to confess, how can he reserve a right to defend himself?[1] And if a man have a power and right to kill himself, [then] he does not authorize and give up his right to his sovereign, if he do not obey him when he commands him to kill himself.

[...]

XV

... He [Hobbes] says, page 66, *A man cannot lay down the right of resisting them that assault him by force to take away his life; the same be said of wounds, chains and imprisonment.* Page 69. *A covenant to defend myself from force by force is void.* Page 68. *Right of defending life and means of living can never be abandoned.*

These last doctrines are destructive to all government whatsoever, and even to the *Leviathan* itself. Hereby any rogue or villain may murder his sovereign, if the sovereign but offer by force to whip or lay him in the stocks, since whipping may be said to be wounding, and putting in the stocks an imprisonment; so likewise every man's goods being means of living, if a man cannot abandon them, no contract among men, be it never so just, can be observed. Thus we are at least in as miserable a condition of war as Mr. Hobbes at first by nature found us.

---

1 According to Filmer, Hobbes's theory is contradictory.

Appendix B: *From George Lawson,* An Examination of the Political Part of Mr. Hobbs His Leviathan *(Printed by R. White for Francis Tyton, 1657)*

[George Lawson (1598-1678), educated at Emmanuel College, Cambridge, a Puritan college, nonetheless was an Arminian; that is, he believed in free will. Although he was a protégé of the archbishop of Canterbury, William Laud, who had been executed in 1645, Lawson was able to live undisturbed in England during the Civil Wars, and took the Engagement, a sworn oath to support the Commonwealth, in 1650. He published *An Examination of the Political Part of Mr Hobbs His Leviathan* in 1657. His more important book is *Politica Sacra & Civilis: or A Model of Civil and Ecclesiastical Government* (1660). Unlike Hobbes, who believes that God's natural sovereignty over human beings comes from his absolute power, Lawson holds that God has supreme authority over the universe because he created it.

Lawson's page references to *Leviathan* are to the original edition; these page numbers are printed in brackets in the margins of this edition of *Leviathan*.]

The Epistle to the Reader

To glorify God and benefit man, both by doing good and preventing and removing evil, should be the endeavor, as it's the duty, of every Christian in his station.... [When] I understood by divers learned and judicious friends, that it *[Leviathan]* took much with many gentlemen and young students in the universities, and though it was judged to be a rational piece, I wondered; for though I knew the distemper of the times to be great, yet by this I found it to be far greater than I formerly suspected.... When thou has read this brief Examination, thou mayest, if judicious and impartial, easily judge, whether there be any thing in Mr. *Hobbs* which is either excellent or extraordinary: and whether there be not many things inconsistent, not only with the sacred Scriptures, but with the rules of right reason....

Cap. [Chapter] I.
Of Mr. Hobbs his Leviathan, concerning the Causes, Generation, and Definition of a Commonwealth.

Civil government derives its being from heaven;[1] for it is a part of God's government over mankind, wherein he uses the ministry of angels and the service of men; yet so, as that he reserves the supreme and universal power in his own hands, with a liberty to dispose the rulers of the world at will and pleasure, and transfer the government of one nation to another; to lay the foundation of great empires, and again to destroy them for their iniquity. To think that the sole or principal cause of the constitution of a civil state is the consent of men, or that it aims at no further end than peace and plenty, is too mean a conceit of so noble an effect. And in this particular I cannot excuse Mr. Hobbs, who in the modelling both of a civil, and also of an ecclesiastical commonwealth, proceeds upon principles not only weak, but also false and dangerous.... And my intention is not to inform my betters, who know the vanity and absurdity of his discourse, but to undeceive the ignorant reader, who may too easily be surprised.

The ... seventeenth of his book, does inform us,
First, *That the end of civil government is security.*
Secondly, *This security cannot be had in the state of nature, because it is the state of war; nor by a weak, nor a great multitude, except united by one perpetual judgement.*
Thirdly, *A great multitude are thus united, when they confer all their power and strength upon one man or assembly of men, that may reduce all their wills by plurality of voices to one will, etc. From whence arises a common wealth.*
Fourthly, *This common-wealth is defined and distributed.*

Against all this, something may be excepted. For first, that the state of nature is the state of war, may be doubted, if not denied. For man is a rational creature; and if he act according to his nature, he must act rationally. And though he may seek to preserve himself, and [do] that sometimes with the damage or destruction of another, yet he cannot, [and] may not do this unjustly, but [only] according to the laws of nature; which are two:

The first, *Love thy neighbour as thy self.*
The second, *Do as thou would be done unto.*

---

1 According to Lawson, human rulers have their authority by divine right, that is, given by God.

These tend directly unto peace, not unto war, which is unnatural; and they may be kept by multitudes of men not united in a civil state, or under a form of government. And this is evident from divine and profane histories. For families ... and also states both by confederation and without any such thing have lived peaceably together. When the Apostle [Paul] says, *The gentiles which have not the law, by nature do the things contained in the Law*, he does not mean by *nature* a commonwealth or form of government civil. It's true, the Apostle brings in a bill of indictment against all mankind, and accuses them, *that their feet are swift to shed blood. Destruction and calamity or misery are in their ways. And the way of peace they have not known*, Rom. 3:15-17. Yet he understands this not of nature, but the corruption of nature; and the parties here accused are not men only as in the state of nature, but also under a government, and that [government] not only civil but ecclesiastical too. For such the Jews here charged, were. So that all that can be either by him evidently proved, or by others granted, is that if *by nature*, he mean corruption of nature, and the same not only original and native, but also acquired by perpetual acts, so far as to quench the light of nature and suppress the vigour of those principles which God left as relics of his image, then his position may be true, [namely] that the state of nature is the state of war. Secondly, that by a well-constituted civil government, to which nature inclines man, the laws of nature and peace may be more easily and better observed.

[...]

T.H. [Thomas Hobbes]: *The sovereign's actions cannot be accused of injustice by the subject, because he hath made himself author of all his actions. And no man can do injustice to himself. The sovereign may do iniquity, but not injustice.*
G.L. [George Lawson] 1. The sovereign's actions are to punish the evil and protect the good. As a sovereign, he can do no other actions, and these cannot be justly accused. 2. Neither can the consent of the people, nor does a commission of God give him any power to act contrary to these. 3. When he acts unjustly (for so he may do, and all iniquity is injustice) neither God nor the people are authors of such action; for he was set up by them to do justly, and no ways else. 4. Civil justice and injustice, as they consist in formalities, differ much from moral and essential justice and injustice. In this respect a prince may be civilly just and morally unjust. 5. To accuse may be judicial, or extra-judicial. Judicially, a prince as a prince cannot be accused by his subject as such. Yet the subject may represent unto his sovereign his faults, and by way of humble petition, desire them to be reformed.

[...]

T.H. [page 93]: *If there had not first been an opinion received of the greatest part of England, that these powers were divided between the king, and the Lords and the Commons, the people had never been divided and fallen into these civil wars.*

G.L.: The cause moral of these wars was our sins. The political cause was the mal-administration; yet so, that all sides have offended through want of wisdom, and many other ways. The ignorance of politics in general, and of our own constitution in particular, cannot be excused or excepted. What the ancient constitution was, we know not certainly, though some relics of the same continued till our times. But the whole frame was strangely altered and corrupted. Many different opinions there be concerning our government; yet three amongst the rest are most remarkable. [First,] for one party conceives the king to be an absolute monarch. A second determines, the king, peers, and Commons to be three co-ordinate powers; yet so that some of them grant three negatives, some only two. A third party gives distinct rights unto these three; yet in this they are sub-divided, and they would be thought to be more rational, who give the legislative power unto the Lords and Commons in one house; the judicial, to the Lords in a distinct house; and the executive to the king, who was therefore trusted with the sword both of war and justice. None of these can give satisfaction. There is another opinion, which puts the supreme power radically in the 40 counties, to be exercised by king, Peers and Commons, according to certain rules, which by antiquaries in law, together with some experienced states-men of this nation, might be found out, but are not. The seeds of this division were sown and began to appear before the wars; and the opinion that all these were only in one man, that is the king absolutely, some say, was the greatest cause, not only of the last, but also of other civil wars in former times; and it hath been observed, that every man liked that opinion best, which was most suitable to his own interest. Our several opinions in religion have heightened our differences, and hindered our settlement; yet religion is but pretended [a pretense]; for every party aims at civil power, not spiritual liberty from sin. And the power to settle us, thus woefully distracted, is only in God; and if he ever will be thus merciful unto us, the way whereby he will effect it, will be by giving the greatest power to men of greatest wisdom and integrity, not by reducing us unto one opinion, that all the powers civil must be in one, as the author does fondly fancy. Let the form be the best in the world, yet without good governors it's in vain.

[...]

This man [Hobbes] deserves to be a perpetual slave; his intention is to make men believe that the kings of England were absolute monarchs, their subjects slaves, without propriety of goods or liberty of person, the parliaments of England merely nothing but shadows, and the members thereof but so many carriers of letters and petitions between home and the court. What he means by subordinate representatives, I know not. I think his intention is to oppose those who affirmed king, Peers, and Commons to be co-ordinate, not subordinate powers, and all of them jointly to make up one supreme. Subordinate representatives or powers he may safely and must grant in all states. The word *representative* he either does not understand, or if he does, he intolerably abuses his unwary and unlearned reader by that term. A representative in the civil law, called *topoteretes*, is one who by his presence supplies the place of another that is absent, for some certain end, as to act that which another should do, but in his own person does not, yet with the consent of the person represented, so far as that the thing is judged to be done by him. And in this sense, the person representing is judged to be one with the person represented by fiction of law. And one may represent another as a superior, who may represent another in any act, so far as that other is in his power; or as an inferior, by a power derived from his superior; or as an equal by consent, so far as the person represented is willing, and the person representing will undertake to act for him. In all these representations, the *representee* and the representer are judged one person. In a free-state, a parliament is a representative of the whole body of the people; this we call a general representative. The reason of this representation is, because the whole body of a people cannot well act personally. What kind of representative the parliament of England was, is hard to know, except we knew certainly the first institution, which, by tract of time and many abuses of that excellent Assembly, is now unknown. It was certainly trusted with the highest acts of legislation, judgement, [and] execution. The whole body consisted of several orders and ranks of men, as of kings, peers, commons, the clergy. Whether they might meddle with the constitution or no, is not so clear; it's conceived they could not alter it, though they might declare it what it was. Their power was great without all doubt, yet not so great, but that it was bounded, and a later parliament might alter and reform what a former had established, which argues, that the 40 counties, and the whole body of the people whence all parliaments have their original [origin] and being, as they are parliaments, were above them. In this great assembly, the knights and burgesses did represent the counties and the boroughs, the convocation [represented] the whole body of the clergy; the peers, by ancient tenure, [represented] their families, vassals and dependants. But whom the king should represent is hard to determine. If the law did consider him as an infant, and this according to the constitution, he could represent no other person or persons. And if this be so, then there is plain reason why he never should have the title of representative; yet evident reason there is, why the rest should be called a representative; and the people are not representers, as he fondly imagines, but the persons represented.

[...]

T.H.: *That by the liberty of the subject, the sovereign's power of life and death is neither abolished nor limited.*
G.L.: It's certain that the sovereign's power and the subject's liberty are consistent. For the sovereign may take away the life of his subject; yet according to the evidence of judgement, agreeable to law; [and] no otherwise. Yet he presupposes, 1. That the king is supreme and [is] the primary subject, owner and possessor of the original power, which sometimes may be; yet with us it's far otherwise. 2. That the power of civil sovereigns is absolute. For with him,
T.H.: [page 109] *Nothing the sovereign representative can do to a subject on what pretence so ever, can properly be called injustice or injury ...*
G.L.: Here he seems to contradict himself. For he grants two things. 1. That the sovereign is subject to God. 2. That in that respect he is bound to observe the laws of nature; yet he says, he can do no injustice to the subject, and that he hath right to anything, so yet as he is limited by subjection to God and the laws of nature....

[But] if he be God's subject, as certainly he is, it follows that in that respect he is but trusted as a servant with the administration of the power civil; [and it follows] that he is fellow-subject with his subjects; [and it follows that] he may do injustice, as one fellow subject may wrong another.

Secondly, if he be bound to observe the laws of nature, which are the laws of God; then, 1. he is not absolute, or *solutus legibus* [*free of the laws*]. His power is limited and bounded by these laws. 2. Then he hath no power to murder, oppress, and destroy his innocent subjects, who are more God's than his, and only trusted by God in his hands for to be protected, righted in all just causes, and vindicated from all wrongs. 3. No prince or sovereign can assume, or any people give to any person or persons, any the least power above, or contrary unto the laws of nature. These laws are the moral precepts of eternal justice and equity, from which all civil laws have their rise, and are either conclusions drawn from them, or certain rules tending to the better observation of them. Which things well considered, do make it very evident how little the power of civil lords and princes must needs be. In some few indifferent things, they may be absolute, have arbitrary power, and be in some respect above those constitutive laws which they themselves enact....

[But] let me digress a little and search out the reason and cause of the power of life and death, as in the hands of civil sovereigns. To this end, observe that no man hath absolute power of his own life, as he hath of his goods. Man may have the use and possession, but not the propriety [property] and dominion of it. Therefore it's granted on all hands that though a man's life be said to be his own; yet he may not also be *felo de se*, and kill himself; he is not master of his life so far, as to have any power or liberty to do any such thing. It is true that God, who is Lord of life and death, gives liberty to man in some cases to hazard, [and] in some he commands to lay down his life. He may hazard it in a just war and defense of his own country, and also of himself, against an unjust invader. He must lay down his life; and God commands it for the testimony of Christ, in which case he that loses it shall find it. From all this it follows that no people can, by making a sovereign, give any absolute power of life and death unto him. For nothing can give that which it hath not; neither can they make themselves authors of the unjust acts of their sovereign, much less of his murders, and taking away the lives of their innocent subjects. *Id enim quisque potest quod jure potest.* [*Anyone can do that which can be done by right.*] If thus it be, then they must have the power to take away life, from God who alone hath power of life; and this power he only gives in case the subject be guilty of such crimes as by his laws are capital.

[...]

T.H. (pages 111-13): *The liberty of the subject is in such things as are neither determined by his first submission to the sovereign power, nor by the laws.* G.L.: ... [W]hen a subject is not bound either by the laws of the constitution or administration, he is free according to Mr. Hobbs his judgement. Yet in proper sense in both these cases, he is no subject; but *dominus* [lord] and far more than *liber* [free]. The civilians [civil lawyers] do better determine the liberty of the subject to be *potestatem agendi sub publicae defensionis praesidio* [the power of acting under the protection of the public defense] though this be no perfect definition. As before, so now I say, that liberty here is not opposed to obligation, but servitude. For to be subject to a wise sovereign according to just laws is so much liberty as any reasonable man can desire; for in this respect he is rather subject to God than man; and to serve him is doubtless perfect freedom. As no sovereign should be denied so much power as to protect the least, if innocent, and to punish the greatest, if guilty; so no subject should be bound to do evil, which is servitude and bondage indeed, or restrained from doing that good which God commands him. Civil government was never ordained by God to be destructive either of moral or divine virtues, or of the noble condition of man as a rational creature. Therefore regular submission unto supreme power, will never stand with any obligation unto evil, or contract for protection except in innocency ...

[...]

Of the Second Part, the Twenty-fourth of the Book;
Of Nutrition and Procreation of a Commonwealth.

Two things only in this Cap. I question: the 1. concerning the original of propriety [property]. The 2. concerning a standing revenue of the crown....

For 1. we find propriety of goods and lands in several families, which are of no commonwealth. 2. The constitution of any commonwealth does presuppose this propriety, without which there can be no buying, selling, exchanging, stealing, restitution; otherwise the eighth commandment, *Thou shalt not steal*, could not be a law of nature, nor bind any man, except in a commonwealth; and so before a commonwealth be instituted in a community or people, there could be no sin in stealing. 3. All that may be granted in this point is that the sovereign may preserve and regulate propriety, both by laws and judgements. Yet the author makes all men brutes, nay wild and ravenous beasts, and birds of prey, until they have made themselves slaves unto some absolute sovereign, and such they must be, either beasts by the law of nature, or slaves by the law of the civil state. 4. As for his instance in the land of Canaan divided by lots to be chosen before Eleazer the high Priest, and Joshua the general, it's impertinent and false. [See *Leviathan* 24.6.] For, 1. Israel before it was molded into a commonwealth, had propriety in their goods. 2. The propriety of that land was at the first and continued in God; for they were but God's tenants in a special and peculiar manner, so as no people in the world was; therefore no man could alienate nor mortgage beyond the year of Jubilee, at which time God seemed to renew their leases ... 3. When they had in common conquered, and taken possession of the land, it was theirs, so far as God had conveyed it, in common. 4. It was for peace and order, as also for to preserve the distinction of tribes divided; yet so as the sovereign dividing it was God, who ordered the lot. Eleazer and Joshua were but superintendents of the lot, and no sovereigns; neither had they any the least propriety more than others of the people ...

Of the Second Part. The 25th of the Book "Of Counsel"

... [G.L.]: That command should be for the benefit of the party commanding, and counsel for the good of the party counselled, is merely accidental in ways essential to them. And though sometimes both the intention and the event of both may be such as he determines, yet we know it is many times otherwise. For commands may sometimes, nay often, be beneficial to the party commanded, and intended to be so; as counsel may be intended, not only for the good of the party counseled, but also counseling; and also prove so to be.

[...]

For one and the same sentence may be a command, a counsel and an exhortation too, yet in different respects; as it binds [it is] a command, as it directs a counsel, as it incites an exhortation.

T.H.: *The legislator in all commonwealths is the sovereign. Again, the commonwealth is the legislator by the representative.*[1]

G.L.: That *pars imperans* [the commanding part] is the legislator in every state must needs be granted; but that the commonwealth should be the legislator, either by or without *pars imperans*, the sovereign, I do not understand. For it consists of two parts, the sovereign and the subject; and if the whole commonwealth make laws, then the subject as well as the sovereign is legislator. In a republic or free-state, there is a difference between the sovereign and the subject, much more in other models and forms. Therefore he must needs speak either improperly or untruly, when he says the state is legislator.

T.H.: ... *The sovereign is not subject to the civil laws, because he hath power to make and repeal them at pleasure.*[2]

G.L.: That the sovereign in divers respects and especially as a sovereign is not subject unto but [is] above the laws is a certain truth. For laws do bind the subject, not the sovereign, to obey or be punished; but the sovereign does command as superior, not obey as inferior; [and he] does punish [and] is not punished. The power to make a law, when there is none, and to repeal after that it's made, is sufficient evidence of his superiority, as also dispensations in judgements and pardons be. Yet this supreme will, legislative over men, is subject to the superior will of God, and must neither make, nor repeal laws, but according to wisdom and justice.

T.H.: ... *Custom is not law by long continuance of time, but by consent of the sovereign.*[3]

---

1 See 26.5.

2 See 26.6.

3 It is not clear which passage Lawson has in mind. See *Dialogue Between a Philosopher and a Student of the Common Laws*, etc. in *English Works*, ed. Molesworth, vol. 6, p. 61, and *De Cive* 14.15.

G.L.: ... For if the sovereign only be the legislator, then continuance of time and practice of the people, though universal, cannot make a law. The sovereign must give either an express or tacit consent; and this consent is then most evident when he makes the custom a rule in judgement and observes it. And the civilians [civil lawyers] well observe that besides continuance of time and the sovereign's consent, a third thing is required, and that is, that the beginning of it be reasonable, as the author here does note.

T.H.: ... *The law of nature and the civil law contain each other, and are of equal extent. For the laws of nature, which consist in equity, justice, gratitude and other moral virtues on these depending, in the condition of mere nature, are not properly laws, but qualities, that dispose men to peace and obedience; when a commonwealth is once actually settled, then are they laws, etc.*[1]

G.L.: 1. This is no conclusion from the definition, except he mean that the rule of right and wrong be the law of nature. 2. The laws of nature are the laws of God, and not of man; and not only subjects, but sovereigns are bound by them. 3. Therefore they bind not as commanded by the civil sovereign, but as written by the hand of heaven in the heart of man. Neither is that which afterwards he makes the difference between the law of nature and the law of civil governors, any difference at all, that the one is written, the other not. For both are written, one by the hand of man, though every civil law be not written, and the other by the hand of God: the one in the heart, the other upon some other material substance; and that which is written in the heart, may be written out of it. 4. Equity, justice, gratitude and other moral virtues, are not laws of nature, but either habitual or actual conformities unto the laws of nature. 5. How the laws of nature, and laws civil should be of equal extent, and yet contain one another, and be parts one of another, I do not understand. 6. A law of nature is only then a civil law, when it's declared to be so by the civil sovereign, yet it's a law before. 7. For the most part, learned men do understand by the laws of nature certain divine principles imprinted upon the heart of man; by the laws of nations, more immediate; by the laws civil, more remote conclusions of constitutive laws civil.

T.H.: *1. How can a man without supernatural revelation, be assured of the revelation received by the declarer of those laws?*[2]

2. How can he be bound to obey them?

The answer to the first, by sanctity, miracle, wisdom, success, without particular revelation, it's impossible for a man to have assurance of a revelation made to another. Therefore no man can infallibly know by natural reason that another hath had a supernatural revelation of God's will, but only a belief.

---

1 See 26.8.
2 See 26.40.

G.L.: This presupposes, 1. That there is a positive law of God. 2. This positive law is declared and witnessed to be the law of God. 3. That this testimony concerning this law is divine and infallible. 4. That it is such, because it's grounded on and agreeable to an immediate revelation from God of that law to him that does declare it, as to Moses, the Prophets or Apostles. For God formerly spoke unto the fathers by the prophets, in the latter times to their children by his son first and after by his Apostles. The question here is not how we shall attain a demonstrative, clear or intuitive knowledge of the matter of the law, nor the manner of the revelation; but how we may be assured that the declaration or testimony of him to whom the revelation was made, is divine, that we may believe it as divine and from God. The means whereby the divinity of the testimony was made evident at the first were extraordinary as signs, wonders, and divers miracles and gifts of the Holy Ghost, according to his own will (Heb. 2:4). But after that, upon these divine attestations, the Gospel was generally received in all nations, and the prophecies of the Old Testament in this particular fulfilled, these ceased; yet one thing always did, and ever will manifest the testimony and doctrine of the Gospel to be divine, and that is the Holy Ghost, who (by his powerful working upon the hearts of men, seriously attending to this truth, whereby a great change both inwardly in their hearts, and outwardly in their lives is wrought) does mightily confirm it. And those who find, and feel in themselves the effects of sanctification and heavenly comfort, can no ways doubt, but are assured that God was in the Prophets and Apostles, and did speak by them. Besides when we consider, 1. That the more we understand them, the more excellency of wisdom we find in them. 2. That these positives are agreeable and no ways contrary to pure morals. 3. That they conduce effectually to holiness and eternal life. 4. That they were approved, received by the best men in the world, and sealed with the blood of many martyrs, we must needs be fully satisfied that they are not false, feigned, fantastic conceits of deluded men, and not only so, but all these things may persuade any rational man to try upon practice, whether they be divine or no. And this never any did, but found the Apostles' doctrine to be of God. If we had nothing but the universal and perpetual agreement and tradition of the Church of all places and times, affirming the Scripture to be the Word of God, it were sufficient to produce in a rational man a greater measure of belief, than any book or history in the world can possibly require or deserve. For this universal testimony of the best in several parts of the world, at such a distance as that they in their time neither heard of, nor knew one another, makes it more credible than any humane history can be. But to return unto Mr. Hobbs, I say it's possible, and not impossible to know the divinity of the testimony or declaration immediately, but not of the revelation or matter revealed. Yet that such a revelation, and such a thing revealed there was, is known in some measure by consequence. And the divine authority of this testimony may be infallibly known, and that by natural reason, yet by it as elevated and more perfected by outward representation and inward sanctification. And the matter of the revelation to another, together with the manner, may be believed, though not known. For when we once know that God hath revealed it, we believe the thing revealed to be true, though by artificial and intrinsical arguments we cannot prove it to be so. For the testimony of God may be evident, though the thing testified be hidden and above our reason. The conclusion is that we may have an infallible knowledge of the positive laws of God, so far as to know that they are from him, and are his laws, and that without particular revelation, that they were revealed to another.

[...]

T.H.: *That the subject in the first constitution laid aside his power of self-preservation by hurting, subduing, killing others in his own defense; and so did not give it, but left to the sovereign.*[1]
G.L.: This is ridiculous, absurd, and grounded upon his false principles. For, 1. The sovereign is the minister of God and is bound to do (so that he keep within the compass of his commission) that which God would do, and that is to punish evil. And as all his power of making laws, judgement, peace, war, etc. are from God, so is this amongst the rest. By whom he is made a sovereign, from him he hath the sword to punish. Men may give their consent that such a man or such a company of men shall reign, but the power is from God, not them. 2. In the constitution of a supreme governor, no man can covenant to be protected or defended in doing evil. Neither can any or all higher powers in the world justly promise to protect any in evil; neither hath any man any power unjustly to preserve himself. For that of the author, that in the state of nature every man hath right to every thing, is absolutely false and abominable. When a man subjects himself unto a sovereign ordained of God, not only to protect the good, but to punish the evil, he cannot except himself from his punitive power, if he do ill; because he subjects according to the just laws of God and cannot lawfully do any other ways. So that power to punish is given by God, not left by man unto higher powers civil.

[...]

---

1 See 28.2.

T.H.: *A second cause of weakening and dissolving a state are certain doctrines. The first, that every private man is judge of good and evil actions.*[1]

G.L.: Judgement is public or private; public no private man can pass; private he may; and that most of his own actions, and others too. The acts of others are private and public; of both these he may judge. Public acts of the governors are laws, judgements, [and] execution. Even of laws he may, he must within himself, so far as they are a rule and bind him, enquire, examine and determine, whether good or evil. Otherwise, he can perform but only a blind obedience to the best; and if he conform unto the unjust, he in obeying man, disobeys God, which no good man will do. In other acts which are apparently just, we may judge of them truly as they are, and no otherwise. Yet this must not be done to palliate our disobedience to that which is just, or raise sedition, or rebel; but we may complain to God, and by our humble prayers seek redress.

[...]

T.H.: *A fourth opinion repugnant to the nature of a commonwealth is this, that he that hath the sovereign power, is subject to the civil laws.*[2]

G.L.: There is no doubt but that this is destructive of government and contrary to the very nature and essence of a commonwealth; the essential parts whereof are, *imperans & subditus* [commanding and being subdued], the sovereign and the subject; take this difference away, [and] you confound all, and turn the commonwealth into a community; yet though sovereigns are above their own laws, (how otherwise could they dispense with them and repeal them?) wise men have given advice to princes for to observe their own laws, and that for example unto others; and good princes have followed this advice. Sovereigns are to govern by laws, not to be subject unto them. But what this man means by sovereign, in the hypothesis, is hard to know. For he presupposes all sovereigns absolute, and all kings of England such sovereigns; and so in general it may be granted, that all sovereigns are above the laws civil; yet the application of this rule to particular princes of limited power, may be false and no ways tolerable....

T.H.: *A fifth doctrine which tends to the dissolution of a commonwealth is that every man hath an absolute propriety in his goods, such as excludes the right of the sovereign.*[3]

G.L.: 1. If the subject have propriety, as the author grants, it must needs be absolute and must needs exclude not only the right of the fellow-subject, but of the sovereign too. For propriety in proper sense is an

---

1   See 29.6.
2   See 29.9.
3   See 29.10.

independent right of total alienation, without any license of a superior or any other. 2. This propriety is not derived from the sovereign, except he be despotical; and such indeed the author affirms all sovereigns to be; and in that respect the subjects can neither have propriety nor liberty; therefore he contradicts himself, when he says in many places, that the sovereign is absolute, and here, that the subject hath propriety. 3. It's to be granted that even in a free-state the subjects' propriety cannot [be] free from the public charges; for as a member of the whole body, he is bound to contribute to the maintenance of the state, without the preservation whereof he cannot so well preserve his own private right. 4. Propriety is by the law of nature and nations at least agreeable unto both. And when men agree to constitute a commonwealth, they retain their proper right, which they had unto their goods before the constitution, which does not destroy, but preserve propriety, if well ordered. For men may advance a sovereign without any alienation of their estates. No man hath any propriety from God, but so as to be bound to give unto the poor, relieve the distressed, and maintain the sovereign in his just government; yet this does not take away, but prove propriety, because every one gives, even unto the commonwealth, that which is his own, not another man's, nor his sovereign's, who may justly in necessary cases, for the preservation of the state, impose a just rate upon the subject.

But if the reader seriously consider the author's discourse in other parts of his book, he may easily know whereat he aims. For, 1. he makes all sovereigns absolute. 2. The kings of England to be sovereigns. And 3. in that respect to have a power to raise subsidies and moneys without a parliament. And 4. hath made that a mortal disease of our state, which is a great preservative of our liberty. For the people always bear the purse and could not by the king be charged with the least, without their consent by their representative in the parliament. This did poise and limit the regal power, prevented much riot and excess in the court, made the prince frugal, and hindered unnecessary wars. Yet good princes and frugal, never wanted money, were freely supplied by their subjects, whilst they required in their need any thing extraordinary above the public revenue, in a right way by Parliament.

[...]

T.H.: *And as to rebellion in particular against monarchy, one of the most frequent causes is the reading of the books of policy and histories of the ancient Greeks and Romans, etc.*[1]

---

1   See 29.14.

G.L.: This has been formerly examined. The reading of these books cannot do so much hurt, as this *Leviathan* may do. For it is far more dangerous and destructive of good government than any of their histories, which can do no hurt to any but such as are ignorant and ill-disposed. In those books they may read of kings and emperors, and of monarchies as well as free-states; and few are so void of understanding, but that they well know they are bound to their own form of government, and are not to covet every model they read of. Such men as he do shamefully debase free-state, as forms unlawful in themselves, and so flatter limited princes, as though they were absolute lords, and advance monarchy so high, as though it were the only form of government, so instituted by God and commanded; that all nations were bound unto it, and whosoever does not bow unto it, is a rebel against God. Yet he [God] never instituted immediately any commonwealth but one, and that was a free-state [Israel]; and when a king was desired, he was offended, and under a regal government it came to ruin. Whereas he thinks these books do teach regicide and killing of kings, he is much mistaken. For subjects to murder their lawful sovereigns, is an horrid crime, and so much the more to be detested, if done under the name of *tyrannicide*. To plead for tyrants really such as such, is to be abhorred. They pervert the very end of all government, abuse their power, act contrary to the laws of God and men, to the ruin of the state, are enemies of mankind, the chiefest agents for the devil. The question is, whether a people having power in their hands may not restrain or remove or put to death such men, as being guilty of many crimes, which the laws of God have made universally capital, so that no man in the world can plead exemption? Some think that they are to be left to God, and subjects must seek deliverance by prayers and tears; and the truth is, Christians as Christians, have no other remedy. Others conceive [that] they may be restrained, and that by force, and their own subjects do it. Others give this power only unto magistrates or to such as share with them in the supreme power: Others are of a mind that seeing [since] they cease to be kings or sovereigns, they may be lawfully tried and put to death, as well as private men; and that without any ordinary jurisdiction. Others determine this to be lawful in such states as that of Lacedemon in Greece and Aragon in Spain. What the doctrine of the Church of Rome is cannot be unknown. For the Pope does arrogate an universal ecclesiastical jurisdiction, whereby he may excommunicate any Christian king that shall not obey his canons [laws] and edicts; and upon this sentence once given, he may depose him, free his subjects from their allegiance, and command them as Catholics to rise in rebellion against him; and some of them have taught, that it's a meritorious art to poison, stab, or any other way to murder kings for the promotion of the Catholic cause. This question, after the terms thereof clearly explicated, is of very great moment; and let men advise well how they do determine either in their own judgement privately, or before others.

[...]

T.H.: *Some make the power of levying money depend upon a general assembly; of conduct and command upon one man; of making laws upon the accidental consent of three. Such government is no government, but a division of the commonwealth into three independent factions, etc.*[1]

G.L.: Here again he hath made the Parliament, which is the bulwark of, and best remedy for to preserve our liberty, a disease; and hath turned the king, peers, and Commons into three independent factions; and this government, he says, some call a mixed monarchy. Whether there can be a mixed state is a question in politics; yet if we understand what mixture is and could determine whether this mixture be in the supreme power as fixed in the constitution or exercised in the administration, we might more easily satisfy ourselves. But this hath not been exactly done. For it's probable that in the exercise of the supreme power, in the three acts of legislation, judgement, execution, there might be a mixture, and these brought to a just and regular temperament. But a mixed monarchy in proper sense there cannot be. Yet a limited and well-poised monarch there may be. To place the power legislative, which includes all the rest, in three co-ordinate parties, granting to every one of them severally a negative, to me seems irrational; for it may easily turn them who should be one, into three factions, as here it is affirmed. At least it will retard all businesses, which for dispatch, require secrecy and expedition. But to place the universal power originally in the general assembly without any negative; the judicial in the Lords, and the executive in the king, seems to be far more agreeable to the rules of reason. This some think was our ancient constitution, and the same excellent.

Difficulty of raising monies necessary for the defense and preservation of state, monopolies, [and] popularity in a subject are diseases which much weaken a state; there is no doubt of this. That one city should engross the wealth and strength of a nation, and be so rich and populous as to be able to set forth a potent army and maintain it, may be judged very dangerous to a commonwealth, as Mr. Hobbs informs us ...

After all these diseases from within, which weaken and may dissolve a government, he informs of a destructive cause, and that is a foreign or intestine war, wherein the enemy obtains a final victory, so that the sovereign cannot protect his subjects in their loyalty. This indeed may cut off a line, change the governors, and alter the form of government.

---

1 See 29.16.

Yet in all this, the community may continue and never be like a subject matter without any form; but the government may be the same and the governors only altered; nay the constitution may stand firm, and the administration only varied; or if the form be changed, yet the privation of the former is an introduction of the latter. Here it's confessed that when the power of protection fails in the sovereign, obligation in the subject is taken away. But he starts a question, though with him no question, whether the right of a sovereign monarch can be extinguished by the act of another? He says it cannot. Yet experience tells us, it may. For a conquered monarch, fallen into the power of another, ceases to be a sovereign, and this is by the act of another. And again, if God by another take away his sword, though his person escape and be at liberty, he hath but the name and not the thing or real title. If his subjects, freed from obligation, because he can give no protection, do submit themselves unto another; yet he thinks, that if the power of an assembly be suppressed, their right is extinct. The assembly in an aristocracy or democracy, for such he means, may be extraordinary or ordinary; and the same [may be] the immediate subject of the supreme power or only trusted for a time with the administration and exercise thereof. And the power of an assembly may be suppressed for a time, and so only suspended, the assembly remaining still. Except he let us know what kind of assembly he understands, and what kind of suppression of power he means, he does nothing. An assembly whose power depends on a certain place, time, number, may lose their right, if once they be scattered or defective in that circumstance.

[...]

Many of his rules [in chapter 20] I confess are good, but most of them are such as are very ordinary and commonly known. But in those points wherein he is singular, he can hardly be excused from errour. His first and chiefest care after the good of the people is to preserve the absolute power of rulers, which he asserts to be their due; and lest they should lose any of them, he renews his catalogue of them again. These must be taught [to] the people, that they may know themselves to be absolute slaves. And princes must take heed of transferring any of sovereign rights unto another. But this was needless; for they have a desire of power before they do obtain it. And after they are once possessed of it, they not only keep that which is due, but also usurp far more than either God or man hath given them. Kings, who are but trusted with a limited power, endeavour to make themselves absolute lords; and despotical sovereigns must be petty deities. The best princes had always a greater care to exercise their power well than to enlarge it. And by their wisdom and justice have governed more happily than any of these absolute sovereigns, who desire rather to be great than good, and themselves more honourable than the people happy.

The errours of this author, vented in this part, as that sovereign power civil is absolute; a civil law against rebellion is no obligation; a good law is not a just law, because no law can be unjust. All his rules of government may be proved out of scripture and other such like, I will not here examine, because some of them are ridiculous; some of them have been formerly answered: and his proof of these in his next part shall be discussed.

Of ... the 31st of the Book. Of the Kingdom of God by Nature.

This chapter is the conclusion of the second part, the *Leviathan*, and makes way for the third following. The principal subject hereof is the laws of nature as distinct to laws supernatural. For he truly and wisely makes God the king and lawgiver both in the kingdom of God by nature and above nature. That God is the universal king by nature, he seems to prove out of the Scripture ...

Obedience is due to God not merely as gratitude to a benefactor, but as a duty unto him as a lawgiver. For as a creator he may have a right to command, because by creation he hath an absolute propriety in his being, which is such as he is capable of a law. And creation is not considered as any kind of benefit, but such a benefit as his rational being was wholly derived from it, and also wholly and perpetually depends upon his preservation, and his eternal happiness upon his legislation and government....

If they [sovereigns] have no better directions, they may make use of his principles, as some have done to their ruin. Princes and ministers of state have no need to be taught them. For they know them too well and follow them too much.

Appendix C: From John Bramhall, The Catching of Leviathan, or the Great Whale *(Printed by E. T. for John Crook, 1658)*

[John Bramhall (1594-1663), educated at Sidney Sussex College, Cambridge, made a good career in the Church of England. Having supported Thomas Wentworth's oppressive but efficient governance of Ireland in the early 1630s, he was made bishop of Derry in 1634. A royalist, he fled England with William Cavendish, then marquis of Newcastle, after the battle of Marston Moor (1644). At the Restoration, Bramhall was made archbishop of Armagh, primate of Ireland. In Paris, a debate with Hobbes on free will conducted in front of Newcastle resulted in an exchange of treatises in the 1650s. Bramhall's *The Catching of Leviathan* was published (with the date 1658) as an appendix to *Castigations of Mr Hobbes His Last Animadversions in the Case Concerning Liberty, and Universal Necessity* (1658).

References that appear in the margin of the original edition of *The Catching of Leviathan* have been placed within the body of the text within parentheses. Page references to *Leviathan* are to the edition of 1651.]

The Catching of Leviathan, or the Great Whale

Demonstrating, out of Mr. Hobbs his own works, That no man who is thoroughly an Hobbist, can be a good Christian, or a good commonwealth's man or reconcile himself to himself. Because his principles are not only destructive to all religion, but to all societies; extinguishing the relation between prince and subject, parent and child, master and servant, husband and wife: and abound with palpable contradictions....

Every man therefore ought to consider who is the sovereign prophet, that is to say, who it is that is God's vicegerent upon earth, and hath next under God the authority of governing Christian men ... (*Lev.* p. 232). Upon his principles the case holds as well among Jews and Turks and heathens, as Christians. Then he that teaches transubstantiation in France, is a true prophet, he that teaches it in England, a false prophet....

And howsoever in words he deny all resistance to the sovereign, yet indeed he admits it. *No man is bound by his pacts whatsoever they be, not to resist him, who brings upon him death or wounds, or other bodily damage* (*DC* 2.18). (By this learning, the scholar, if he be able, may take the rod out of his master's hand and whip him.) ... *In case a great many men together have already resisted the sovereign power unjustly, or committed some capital crime, for which every one of them expects death, whether have they not the liberty to join together, and assist and defend one another? Certainly they have, for they do but defend their lives, which the guilty man may as well do, as the innocent* ... (*Lev.* p. 112). Why should we not change the name of Leviathan into the Rebel's Catechism? Observe the difference between the primitive spirit, and the Hobbian spirit. The Theban Legion of known valour in a good cause, when they were able to resist, did choose rather to be cut in pieces to a man, than defend themselves against their Emperor by arms, because they would rather die innocent, than live nocent [guilty]. But T.H. allows rebels and conspirators to make good their unlawful attempts by arms. Was there ever such a trumpeter of rebellion heard of before? Perhaps he may say that he allows them not to justify their unlawful acts, but to defend themselves. First this is contrary to himself, for he allows them *to maintain what they had unjustly done.* This is too much and too intolerable, but this is not all. Secondly, if they chance to win the field, [then] who must suffer for their faults? Or who dare thenceforward call their acts unlawful?

[...]

His ... [next] excess is a grievous one, that *before the institution of a commonwealth, every man had a right to do whatsoever he thought necessary to his own preservation, subduing, hurting, or killing any man, in order thereunto. And this is the foundation of that right of punishing which is exercised in every commonwealth* (*Lev.* p. 161). And his sentence in brief is this; that if the magistrate do examine and condemn the delinquent, then it is properly punishment; if not, it is an hostile act, but both are justifiable. Judge reader, whether thou wilt trust St. Paul or T.H. St. Paul tells us, that the magistrate is *the ordinance of God, the minister of God, the revenger of God* (Rom. 13:2, 13:4), the sword-bearer of God *to execute wrath upon him that does evil.*

No, says T.H.; punishment is not an act of the magistrate as he is a magistrate, or as he is an officer of God to do justice, or a revenger of evil deeds; but as he is the only private man who has not laid down his natural right to kill any man at his own discretion, if he do but suspect that he may prove noisome to him, or conceive it necessary for his own preservation. Who ever heard of such a right before, so repugnant to the laws of God and Nature? But observe reader what is the result of it, that the sovereign may lawfully kill any of his subjects, or as many of them as he pleases, without any fault of theirs, without any examination on his part, merely upon suspicion of the least crime, if he do but judge him to be hurtful or noisome, as freely as a man may pluck up a weed, because it hinders the nourishment of better plants. *Before the institution of a commonwealth every one may lawfully be spoiled or killed by every one, but in a commonwealth only by one (DC* 10.1), that is the sovereign. And *by the right of nature we destroy without being unjust, all that is noxious, both beasts and men.* He makes no difference between a Christian and a wolf. Would you know what is noxious with him, even *whatsoever he thinks can annoy him (Q* pp. 116 and 140). Who would not desire to live in his commonwealth, where the sovereign may lawfully kill a thousand innocents every morning to his breakfast? Surely this is a commonwealth of fishes, where the great ones eat the lesser.

It were strange if his subjects should be in a better condition for their fortunes than they are for their lives, no I warrant you; do but hear him. *Thy dominion and thy property is so great, and lasts so long, as the commonwealth* (that is, the sovereign) *will (DC* 12.7). Perhaps he means in some extraordinary cases? Tush, in all cases, and at all times. When thou did choose a sovereign, even in choosing him thou made him a deed of gift of all thou has. *Et tu ergo tuum jus civitate concessisti, and therefore thou has granted all thy right to the commonwealth* (ibid.) ...

Another of his whimsies is: *that no law can be unjust; by a good law I mean, not just a law, for no law can be unjust, etc. It is in the laws of the commonwealth, as in the laws of gaming. Whatsoever the gamesters all agree on, is injustice to none of them (Lev.* p. 182). An opinion absurd in itself, and contradictory to his own ground. There may be laws tending to the contumely of God, to atheism, to denial of God's providence, to idolatry, all which he confesses to be crimes of high treason against God. There may be laws against the law of nature, which he acknowledges to be the *divine law, eternally, immutable, which God hath made known to all men, by his eternal word born in themselves, that is to say, natural reason (DC* 14.4).... The true ground of this and many other of his mistakes, is this, that he fancies no reality of any natural justice or honesty, nor any relation to the law of God or nature, but only to the laws of the commonwealth. So from one absurdity being admitted, many others are apt to follow.

His economics are no better than his politics. He teaches parents *that they cannot be injurious to their children, so long as they are in their power (DC* 9.7). Yes, too many ways, both by omission and commission. He teaches mothers *that they may cast away their infants, or expose them at their own discretion lawfully (DC* 9.2)....

What horrid doctrines are these? It may be he will tell us that he speaks only of the state of mere nature, but he does not; for he speaks expressly of commonwealths and parallels fathers with kings and lords, to whom he ascribes absolute dominion, who have no place in his state of mere nature; for therein, according to his grounds, the children have as much privilege to kill their parents, as the parents to kill their children, seeing he supposes it to be a state of war of all men against men.

And if he did speak of the state of mere nature, it were all one. For first his state of mere nature is a drowsy dream of his own feigning, which looks upon *men as if they were suddenly grown out of the ground like mushrooms* (*DC* 8.1). The primogenious and most natural state of mankind was in Adam before his fall, that is, the state of innocence. Or suppose we should give way to him to expound himself of the state of corrupted nature, that was in Adam and his family after his fall. But there was no such state of mere nature as he imagines. There was religion, there were laws, government, society; and if there ever were any such barbarous savage rabble of men, as he supposes, in the world, it is both untrue and dishonourable to the God of nature, to call it the state of mere nature, which is the state of degenerated nature. He might as well call an hydropical distemper, contracted by intemperance or any other disease of that nature, the natural state of men. But there never was any such degenerate rabble of men in the world, that were without all religion, all government, all laws, natural and civil, no, not amongst the most barbarous Americans (who except some few criminal habits, which those poor degenerate people, deceived by national custom, do hold for noble) have more principles of natural piety, and honesty, and morality, than are readily to be found in his writings. As for the times of civil war, they are so far from being without all pacts and governors, that they abound overmuch with pacts and governors making policy not only to seem, but to be double....

My ... harping-iron is aimed at the head of his Leviathan, or the rational part of his discourse, to show that his principles are contradictory one to another, and consequently destructive one of another. It is his own observation: *That which takes away the reputation of wisdom in him that formeth a religion or addeth to it when it is already formed is an enjoining a belief of contradictories; for both parts of a contradiction cannot possibly be true. And therefore to enjoin the belief of them, is an argument of ignorance* (*Lev.* p. 58). How he will free himself from his own censure, I do not understand; let the reader judge.

He affirms that an hereditary kingdom is the best form of government: *We are made subjects to him upon the best condition, whose interest it is that we should be safe and sound. And this comes to pass when we are the sovereign's inheritance* (that is, in an hereditary kingdom), *for every one does of his own accord study to preserve his own inheritance* (*DC* 10.18). Now let us hear him retract all this: *There is no perfect form of government where the disposing of the succession is not in the present sovereign* (*Lev.* p. 99). And whether he *transfer it by testament, or give it, or sell it, it is rightly disposed* (*DC* 9.13; *Lev.* p. 193).

He affirms *that which is said in the Scripture, it is better to obey God than man, has place in the kingdom of God by pact, and not by nature.* One can scarcely meet with a more absurd senseless paradox, that in God's own kingdom of nature (where he supposes all men equal, and no governor but God) it should not be better to obey God than man, the Creator than the created, the sovereign rather than a fellow-subject. Of the two it had been the less absurdity to have said that it had place in the kingdom of God by nature, and not by pact, because in the kingdom of God by pact, sovereigns are as *mortal gods.*

Now let us see him Penelope-like, unweave in the night what he had woven in the day: *It is manifest enough, that when man receives two contrary commands, and knows that one of them is God's, he ought to obey that, and not the other, though it be the command even of his lawful sovereign* (*Lev.* p. 321). Take another place more express, speaking of the first kingdom of God by pact with Abraham, etc. He has these words: *Nor was there any contract which could add to, or strengthen the obligation, by which both they and all man else were bound naturally to obey God Almighty* (*Lev.* p. 249). ... But in Abraham's time, and before his time, the world was full of kings; every city had a king; was it not better for their subjects to obey God than them? Yet that was the kingdom of God by nature, or no kingdom of God at all.

Sometimes he says the laws of nature are laws: *whose laws (such of them as oblige all mankind) and in respect of God, as he is the god of nature, are natural, in respect of the same God, as he is King of Kings, are laws* (*Lev.* p. 185); and *right reason is a law* (*DC* 2.1). And he defines the law of nature to be *the dictate of right reason.* Where by the way observe what he makes to be the end of the laws of nature: *the long conservation of our lives and members, so much as in our power.* By this the reader may see what he believes of honesty, or the life to come. At other times he says that they are no laws. *Those which we call the laws of nature, being nothing else but certain conclusions understood by reason of things to be done; or to be left undone. And a law, if we speak properly and accurately, is the speech that commands something by right to others, to be done, or not to be done, speaking properly, they are not laws, as they proceed from nature* (*DC* 3.33).

It is true, he adds in the same place, that *as they are given by God in holy Scripture, they are most properly called laws, for the holy Scripture is the voice of God ruling all things for the greatest right.* But this will not solve the contradiction, for so the laws of nature shall be no laws to any but those who have read the Scripture, contrary to the sense of all the world. And even in this he contradicts himself also. *The Bible is a law? to whom? to all the world; he knows it is not: how came it then to be a law to us? Did God speak it vive voce to us? Have we any other warrant for it than the word of the prophets? Have we seen the miracles? Have we any other assurance of their certainty, than the authority of the Church?* (*Q* p. 136). And so he concludes that the authority of the Church is the authority of the commonwealth, the authority of the commonwealth, the authority of the sovereign, and his authority was given him by us. And so *the Bible was made law by the assent of the subjects* (ibid.). And *the Bible is their only law, where the civil Sovereign has made it so* (*Lev.* p. 332). Thus in seeking to prove one contradiction we have met with two.

He teaches: *that the laws of nature are eternal and immutable, that which they forbid can never be lawful, that which they command never unlawful* (*DC* 3.29). At other times he teaches, that *in war, and especially in a war of all men against all men, the laws of nature are silent* (*DC* 5.2). And that they do not oblige as laws, before there be a commonwealth constituted. *When a commonwealth is once settled, then are they actually laws, and not before* (*Lev.* p. 138).

He says *true religion consists in obedience to Christ's lieutenants, and in giving God such honour, both in attributes and actions, as they in their several lieutenancies, shall ordain* (*Q* pp. 334, 341). Which lieutenant upon earth is the *supreme civil magistrate.* And yet contrary to this he excepts from the obedience due to sovereign princes, *all things that are contrary to the laws of God, who rules over rulers.* Adding that *we cannot rightly transfer the obedience due to him upon men* (*DC* 6.13). ...

He affirms that *if a sovereign shall grant to a subject any liberty inconsistent with sovereign power, if the subject refuse to obey the sovereign's command, being contrary to the liberty granted, it is a sin, and contrary to his duty, for he ought to take notice of what is inconsistent with sovereignty, etc. And that such liberty was granted through ignorance of the evil consequence thereof* (*Lev.* p. 157). Then a subject may judge not only what is fit for his own preservation, but also what are the essential rights of sovereignty, which is contrary to his doctrine elsewhere. *It belongs to kings to discern what is good and evil; and private men, who take to themselves the knowledge of good and evil, do covet to be as kings, which consisteth not with the safety of the commonwealth* (*DC* 12.1); which he calls *a seditious doctrine,* and one of the *diseases of a commonwealth* (*Lev.* p. 168). Yet such is his forgetfulness that he himself licenses his own book *for the press,* and to *be taught in the universities,* as containing nothing contrary to the *word of God or good manners,* or to *the disturbance of public tranquility* (Lev. p. 395). Is not this to take to himself the knowledge of good and evil?

In one place he says that *the just power of sovereigns is absolute, and to be limited by the strength of the commonwealth, and nothing else* (*DC* 6.18). In other places he says his power is to be limited by the laws of God and nature. As *there is that in heaven, though not on earth, which he should stand in fear of, and whose laws he ought to obey* (*Lev.* p. 167). And *it is true, that sovereigns are all subject to the laws of nature, because such laws be divine, and cannot by any man or commonwealth be abrogated* (*Lev.* pp.

199, 169). In one place he maintains that *all men by nature are equal among themselves* (*DC* 1.3). In another place, that *the father of every man was originally his sovereign Lord, with power over him of life and death* (*Lev.* p. 178).

... *All punishments of innocent subjects, be they great or little, are against the law of nature. For punishment is only for transgression of the law, and therefore can be no punishment of the innocent* (2 Chron. 25:4).Yet within few lines after he changes his note. *In subjects who deliberately deny the authority of the commonwealth established, the vengeance is lawfully extend-ed, not only to the fathers, but also to the third and fourth generation* (ibid.). His reason is because *this offence consists in renouncing of subjection: so they suffer not as subjects, but as enemies.*Well, but the children were born subjects as well as the father, and they never renounced their subjection, how come they to lose their birth-right, and their lives for their fathers' fault, if there can be no punishment of the innocent; so the contradiction stands still.

But all this is but a copy of his countenance, I have showed formerly expressly out of his principles, *that the foundation of the right of punishing, exercised in every commonwealth*, is not the right of the sovereign for crimes committed, but *that right which every man by nature had to kill every man.* Which right, he says, every subject has renounced, but the sovereign, by whose authority punishment is inflicted, hath not. So if he do examine the crime in justice, and condemn the delinquent, then it is properly punishment. If he do not, then it is an hostile act, but both ways just and allowable. Reader, if thou please to see what a slippery memory he has, [then] for thine own satisfaction, read over the beginning of the eight and twentieth chapter of his *Leviathan.* Innocents cannot be justly punished, but justly killed upon his principles.

But this very man, who would seem so zealous sometimes for human justice, that there can be no just punishment, but for crimes committed, how stands he affected to divine justice? He regards it not at all, grounding everywhere God's right to afflict the creatures upon his omnipotence: and maintaining that God may as justly afflict with eternal torments without sin, as for sin. *Though God have power to afflict a man, and not for sin, without injustice, shall we think God so cruel, as to afflict a man, and not for sin, with extreme and endless torments? Is it not cruelty? No more than to do the same for sin, when he that afflicts might without trouble have kept him from sinning* (*Q* p. 13).Whether God do afflict eternally, or punish eternally; whether the sovereign proceed judicially, or in a hostile way, so it be not for any crime committed; it is all one as to the justice of God and the sovereign, and all one as to the sufferings of the innocent. But *it may and doth often happen in commonwealths that a subject may be put to death by the command of the sovereign power, and yet neither do the other wrong* (*Lev.* p. 105); that is to say, both be innocent, for that is the whole scope of the place. It is against the law of nature to punish innocent subjects, says one place, but innocent subjects may lawfully be killed or put to death, says another.

Sometimes he makes the institution of sovereignty to be only the laying down the right of subjects, which they had by nature ... ([see] *Lev.* p. 65). And elsewhere, *The subjects did not give the sovereign that right, but only in laying down theirs, strengthened him to use his own, etc.* (*Lev.* p. 162).... He might as well have said, and with as much sense: *the transferring of right doth consist in not transferring of right.*[1] At other times he makes it to be a surrender, *or giving up of the subjects right to govern himself to this man* (*Lev.* p. 87). And *David did no injury to Uriah, because the right to do what he pleased, was given him by Uriah himself* (*Lev.* p. 109). Before we had a transferring without transferring; now we have a giving up without giving up, an appointing or constituting, without appointing or constituting, a subjection without subjection, an authorizing without authorizing. What is this? ...

A principal cause of his errours is a fancying to himself a general state of nature, which is so far from being general, that there is not an instance to be found of it in the nature of things, where mankind was altogether without laws and without governors, guided only by self interest, without any sense of conscience, justice, honesty, or honour. He may search all the corners of America with a candle and lantern at noon day, and after his fruitless pains, return a *non est inventus* [it has not been found].

Yet all plants and living creatures are subject to degenerate and grow wild by degrees. Suppose it should so happen that some remnant of men, either chased by war or persecution or forced out of the habitable world for some crimes by themselves committed or being cast by shipwreck upon some desert, by long conversing with savage beasts, lions, bears, wolves and tigers, should in time becomes more brutish (it is his own epithet,) than the brutes themselves, would any man in his right wits make that to be the universal condition of mankind, which was only the condition of an odd handful of men or that to be the state of nature, which was not the state of nature, but an accidental degeneration?

He that will behold the state of the nature rightly, must look upon the family of Adam and his posterity in their successive generations from the creation to the deluge and from the deluge until Abraham's time, when the first kingdom of God by pact as supposed by T.H. to begin. All this while (which was a great part of that time the world has stood) from the creation lasted the kingdom of God by nature, as he

---

1 According to Bramhall, Hobbes contradicts himself by holding that people give up their rights to govern themselves and do not give up this right.

phrases it. And yet in those days there were laws and government, and more kings in the world, than there are at this present. We find nine kings engaged in one war; and yet all their dominions but a narrow circuit of land (Gen. 14). And so it continued for divers hundreds of years after, as we see by all those kings which Joshua discomfited in and of Canaan. Every city had its own king. The reason is evident; the original right of fathers of families was not then extinguished.

Indeed *T.H.* supposes that men did spring out of the earth like mushrooms or mandrakes: *That we may return again to the state of nature, and consider men as if they were even now suddenly sprouted and grown out of the earth, after the manner of mushrooms, without any obligation of one to another* (*DC* 8.1). But this supposition is both false and atheistical, howsoever it dropped from his pen. Mankind did not spring out of the earth, but was created by God, not many suddenly, but one to whom all his posterity were obliged as to their father and ruler.

A second ground of his errours is his gross mistake of the laws of nature, which he relates most imperfectly, and most untruly. A moral heathen would blush for shame to see such a catalogue of the laws of nature.

First he makes the laws of nature to be laws and no laws: just as *a man and no man, hit a bird and no bird, with a stone and no stone, on a tree and no tree*: not *laws* but *theorems*, laws which require not *performance* but *endeavours*, laws which were silent, and could not be put in execution in the state of nature. *Where nothing was another man's, and therefore a man could not steal; where all things were common, and therefore no adultery; where there was a state of war, and therefore it was lawful to kill; where all things were defined by a man's own judgement, and therefore what honours he pleased to give unto his father; and lastly, where there were no public judgements, and therefore no use of witnesses* (*DC* 14.9). As for the first table he does not trouble himself much with it, except it be to accommodate it unto kings. Every one of these grounds here alleged are most false, without any verisimilitude in them; and so his superstructure must needs fall flat to the ground.

Secondly he relates the laws of nature most imperfectly, smothering and concealing all those principal laws, which concern either piety, and our duty towards man.

Thirdly, sundry of those laws which he is pleased to take notice of are either misrelated or misinterpreted by him. He makes the only end of all the laws of nature to be *the long conservation of a man's life and members*, most untruly. He makes every man by nature *the only judge of the means of his own conservation*, most untruly. His father and sovereign in the weightiest cases is more judge than himself. He says that *by the law of nature every man has right to all things, and over all persons*, most untruly. He says the natural condition of mankind is *a war of all men against all men*, most untruly. And that *nature dictates to us to relinquish this* feigned *right of all men to all things*, most untruly. And that *nature dictates to a man to retain his right of preserving his life and limbs, though against a lawful magistrate*, lawfully proceeding, most untruely. I omit his uncouth doctrine about pacts made in the state of nature, and that he knoweth no gratitude, but where there is a trust, *fiducia*. These things are unsound, and the rest of his laws, for the most part, poor trivial things, in comparison of those weightier dictates of nature, which he has omitted.

All other writers of politics do derive commonwealths from the sociability of nature, which is in mankind, most truly. But he will have the beginning of all human society to be from mutual fear, as much contrary to reason as to authority. We see some kind of creatures delight altogether in solitude, rarely, or never in company. We see others (among which is mankind) delight altogether in company, rarely, or never in solitude. Let him tell me what mutual fear of danger did draw the silly bees into swarms; or the sheep and doves into flocks; and what protection they can hope for, one from another? and I shall conceive it possible, that the beginning of human society might be from fear also.

And thus having invented a fit foundation for his intended building, ycleped [called] *the state of mere nature*, which he himself first devised for that purpose, he hath been long modelling and framing to himself a new form of policy, to be built upon it. But the best is, it has only been in paper. All this while he has never had a finger in mortar. This is the new frame of *absolute sovereignty*, which T.H. knew right well would never stand; nor he should be ever permitted to rear it up in our European climes [territory] or in any other part of the habitable world, which had ever seen any other form of civil government. Therefore he has sought out for a fit place in America, among the savages, to try if perhaps they might be persuaded that the laws of God and nature, the names of good and evil, just and unjust, did signify nothing but at the pleasure of the sovereign prince.

And because there has been much clashing in these quarters about religion, through the distempered zeal of some, the seditious orations of others, and some pernicious principles, well meant at first, but ill understood, and worse pursued. To prevent all such garboiles [disturbances] in his commonwealth, he has taken an order to make his sovereign to be *Christ's lieutenant upon earth, in obedience to whose commands true religion doth consist.*[1] Thus making policy to be the building, and religion the hangings, which must be fashioned just according to the

---

1 See 42.11.

proportion of the policy; and (not as Mr. [Thomas] Cartwright[1] would have had it) making religion to be the building, and policy the hangings, which must be conformed to religion.

Well the law is costly, and I am for an accommodation, that T.H. should have the sole privilege of setting up his form of government in America, as being calculated and fitted for that meridian. And if it prosper there, then to have the liberty to transplant it hither: who knows (if there could but be some means devised to make them understand his language) whether the Americans might not choose him to be their sovereign? But all the fear is that if he should put his principles in practice, as magisterially as he does dictate them, his supposed subjects might chance to tear their *mortal God* in pieces with their teeth, and entomb his sovereignty [in] their bowels.

---

1 Thomas Cartwright (c. 1535-1603), Calvinist theologian who had a famous debate (1574-77) with John Whitgift (1530-1604), later archbishop of Canterbury. Cartwright's views were Presbyterian, and he held that church and state were independent while Whitgift upheld the official view of the Church of England.

Appendix D: From William Lucy, Observations, Censures and Confutations of Notorious Errours in Mr. Hobbes His Leviathan (Printed by J. G. for Nath. Brooke, 1663)

[William Lucy (1594-1677) received his BA from Trinity College, Oxford, and then studied law at Lincoln's Inn but never practiced because he took a position at Caius College, Cambridge. He became bishop of St. David's at the Restoration. His *Observations, Censures and Confutations of Divers Errours in the 12, 13, and 14 Chap. of Mr Hobs His Leviathan* appeared in 1657, under the pseudonym William Pyke, Christophilus [lover of Christ]. It was enlarged and republished under the title used in this appendix in 1663. Lucy was a conventional thinker of the mid-seventeenth century, an Arminian in theology, and an Aristotelian scholastic in philosophy. Hobbes refers to Lucy, under the name "Pike," in *Considerations Upon the Reputation and Loyalty, Manners, and Religion of Thomas Hobbes* (ed. Molesworth, vol. 4, p. 435) and *Six Lessons to the Savilian Professors of the Mathematics* (ed. Molesworth, vol. 7, p. 354).]

[Hobbes says] *every man hath so much experience, as to have seen the Sun, or other visible objects, by reflection in the water, and the glasses, and this alone is sufficient for this conclusion, that* colour *and* image *may be there where the thing seen is not* [*Elements of Law, Natural and Politic*, Part 1, c. 2, sec. 5] ... He should have proved first that colour and image are the same, which he knows is denied by all his adversaries; colour is in the object of sight, but there is no need of the image, where the substance is, nor can the image of colour be in the same subject with the colour.... I say then that colour is in the object, but image is not....

But he [Hobbes] urgeth again that *divers times men see the same object double, as two candles for one, which may happen by distemper* [ibid.] ... I answer to this that this double sight may be two ways, either by a distemper of the organ or by a false reflection in the medium. The first I have had and have been cured by physick. The second is easy, for there may be multiplying glasses, and may such instruments, which may deliver the species double, and then the colour or object must appear such; but here is no reason to prove that the colour is not in the object, because *Quicquid recipitur, recipitur ad modum recipientis* [Whatever is received is received according to the mode of the thing receiving]. If the eye be indisposed, it must needs follow that the species shall be qualified accordingly. And for the medium or middle place or mean, which transports the species to the eye, it must needs be that the liquor will taste of that tap out of which it runs; that every story is enlarged or lessened, multiplied or diminished, according to the disposition of the deliverer, and so the indisposition of the medium varying the species, it must needs be that the colour must appear such, although it be other.... [T]he image or species ... is not in the object, but the colour is.

He [Hobbes] begins thus: *The fool hath said in his heart there is no such thing as justice; and sometimes also with his tongue seriously alleging that every man's conservation and contentment being committed to his care, there could be no reason why every man might not do what he thought conduced thereunto; and therefore also to make or not make, keep or not keep, covenants, was not against reason, when it conduced to one's benefit* (p. 72). Thus he makes the fool to confirm his wicked conclusion; and for my part, I think the fool's argument is unanswerable, out of Mr Hobbes his principles. For if it be true, as he hath supposed, that every man hath a natural right to every thing, and every man's conservation and contentment is committed to his own charge, and that no man can renounce by any covenant his right to defend himself from death, wounds, imprisonment, which he delivered in his 66 page ... then he can by no covenant be obliged to forsake any thing, but only such little things as are scarcely considerable in justice.

... If a man take from any act or habit those circumstances which make it evil, [then] it will be good; but I am persuaded that a fear of God is so rooted in the hearts of men, that although men may darken the light, and clear light out of it, with wicked reasoning; although men may hinder the vivacity in the opposition of it, by customary inhabiting, reigning sins; yet it cannot be so extirpated, but that it will appear and break out sometimes in action. And although a fool or wicked man may sometimes *say so*; yet other times he will not believe his own words, and must oft fear he is in the wrong. This kind of reasoning either Mr. Hobbes taught, or learned from him; for I am persuaded never man disputed so high conclusions out of such impossible supposals, as he hath; such is this, *if there were no fear of God*. Let us see the force of the fool's argument; it seems to affirm that injustice, *taking away the fear of God, will stand with that reason which dictateth to every man his own good*; I am persuaded it is good when injustice may be committed where is no commonwealth, when men commit injustice so secretly that no magistrate may take notice of it; for if no God, no heaven or hell ... for good or ill actions; and then a man's considerations are chiefly about his own ease, pleasure, and contentment in his bodily and sensitive life; but yet I must add one restraint to the fool's proposition. Injustice may stand with that reason which prescribes his own good, that is, his pleasure or contentment; but not with right reason, for right reason prefers the public good before the private, which cannot subsist without justice.

[...]

The question, according to his [Hobbes's] own framing is *whether it be profitable to deceive or not*; his answer is drawn from a declaration that that man [the fool] should make, [namely] *that he thinks it fit to deceive*, which no man but a verier [bigger] fool than he ... did ever do.[1] There is no power to act any great wickedness; but under the show of piety, not by professing to deceive, but by professing not to deceive. Oaths, covenants, protestations, cursing of themselves, are the horrid masks of impiety, which wicked men use to deceive with. The devil can no way so efficaciously deceive, as by putting on the shape or likeness of an angel; ... sometimes urging the Scripture itself, as with our Saviour. That child of the devil, who will prosper in this world, must not protest and declare that he will deceive, but protest against it....

Now my conclusion is that all deceit is injustice, all injustice unprofitable, because against the most sacred lawmaker, who will avenge it here or hereafter, whether men take notice of it or no. Evil and injustice will hunt the wicked person; only honesty and justice will bring a man peace and prosperity at the last....

A person is he who doth or speaks any thing [p. 80], and this is as full as his [Hobbes's definition]; for whosoever doth or speaks his words or deeds are considered either as his own or another's.... *When they are considered as his own* (that is, those actions or words) *then is he called a* Natural Person; *and when they are considered as representing the words and actions of another then he is a* feigned *or* artificial person. Thus may a man be distinguished into a true and counterfeit[2] man; and no more than the picture or the image of a man is a true man, no more is *a feigned or artificial person*, a true *person*; and yet this *feigned or artificial person* does as fully agree to his definition, as the *true person*; which shows the definition to be to blame. The *metaphysicians* have an undoubted axiom, that *ens* and *verum convertuntur* [being and truth are interchangeable]; what is not truly such is not such. If then such a man, whom he names be but a *feigned person*, he is not a *person truly*, and then not *a person*; yet

---

1 Lucy is calling attention to an ambiguity in Hobbes's discussion of the problem of the fool. If the fool is clever, he will not tell people that he thinks it is right to deceive them. And against this fool, Hobbes has no good answer, according to Lucy. But in the passage that Lucy alludes to, "he which declares he thinks it reason to deceive those that help him can in reason expect no other means of safety" (15.5), the fool is foolish because he admits to being a deceiver. Although Hobbes is able to refute this foolish fool, he fails to refute the clever fool, a person all too well known in the world, according to Lucy.

2 Lucy is unfairly taking "feigned" to mean "counterfeit" and thus concluding that a feigned or artificial person is not really a person. By "feigned" in "feigned person," Hobbes simply means a person who is created by human beings.

we shall find him endeavouring to set him out, as the only *true person*, presently afterward with his grammar rules....

So (saith he) *that a* person *is the same that an* actor *is, both on the stage and in common conversation; and, to* personate, *is to* act *or* represent *himself or another*. This is it I foretold you of, that although a *feigned* thing cannot be a *true* thing, yet he makes the *feigned* only the true, and the *representer* only to be the true *person*, not to be who is *represented*; and although in his definition he said that *a person is he whose words or actions are considered as his own, etc.* and in his following division there was a *natural* and a *feigned* person; yet here he makes all persons *feigned*, and their words or actions to be others. If he answer that his words were *represent himself or another,* then if he *act himself,* it is enough to constitute him a person. I reply that what it is to *act himself,* he has expressed in the words immediately preceding, *a person is the same that an actor is, both on the stage and in common conversation.* Now no man can properly be said to *act himself* or *represent himself,* for the actor and the acted, the representer and the represented are two. He proceeds, *and he that acteth another is said to bear his person, or act in his name.* Very true, but if he bears *another's person,* the *other* is the *person,* not he that bears it. The constable bears [and] represents the person of a King, but is not his person; so doth a player; this makes all against himself ... [Hobbes] labours to show that the representer is the person, but his argument proves only the represented is the person; and this we shall find in the ancient tragedies and comedies put out. The critics, which puts them out, calls the *persons* those which were *represented,* not the *actors,* as is to be seen in *Seneca* and *Terence,*[1] etc.; not that I deny this word has sometimes been used by writers, as Mr. *Hobbes* expresses it; but I deny that that is the universal acception of that word, or that Mr. *Hobbes* his argument doth show, that it was ever so accepted. But rather clean contrary; the *person* is he who is represented, not the representer....

A *person* then, taken in the most received conceit [concept] that *divines* and *philosophers* acknowledge is defined by Boethius, [in] *De duabus naturis,* to be *rationalis, naturae individua substantia:An individual substance of a rational nature:* This definition is most generally received, and I doubt not, but it will abide the test, when it is clearly explained, which I shall endeavour to do ...[2]

First, a *person* is a *substance*; by that term it is opposed to all *accidents,* and things only *imaginary*; it is an *individual substance,* by that term it

---

1 Lucius Annaeus Seneca (c. 3 BCE-65 CE) and Publius Terentius Afer (195/185-159 BCE) were Roman playwrights.

2 Lucy is simply unwilling to consider Hobbes's unconventional definitions of persons. Lucy is refusing to understand "person" in any sense other than the conventional scholastic definition that originated with Boethius (c. 480-c. 586).

is opposed to those [that] are called *second substances*, ... as a man or a lion.... The last term in this definition is that it is *rationalis*, of a *reasonable nature*: this word *reasonable* must be understood of any intellectual nature, whether by discourse or else, and so it comprehends all divine, angelical, or whatsoever.... Mr. *Hobbes* [should] have not suffered himself to be transported with the imagination of how this word is used upon the *stage* ... [I]n words, we are not always to consider their etymology, but how they are used....

In the 82 page, ... he saith that *the true God may be personated*. This phrase gave me an amazement, for I cannot call to mind any such expression made either in *Scripture* or orthodox *ecclesiastical* writers, and understanding *personating* in that sense that Mr Hobbes doth.... [T]o say that *the true God may be personated* by any thing which is not God was too great an exaltation of the *creature*, and diminution of his excellency; but yet thus he doth, as appears by his instance *as he was first by Moses, who governed the Israelites (that were not his, but God's people) not in his own name with* hoc dicit Moses [Moses says this], *but in God's name with* hoc dicit Dominus [the Lord says this], *first by Moses.* I am persuaded he can never show me that the true God was ever personated by Moses....

Appendix E: From Thomas Tenison, The Creed of Mr. Hobbes Examined; in a Feigned Conference between Him and a Student in Divinity (Printed for Francis Tyton, 1670)

[Thomas Tenison (1636-1715) received his BA from Corpus Christi College (at that time Bene't College), Cambridge, and was privately ordained a priest by the bishop of Salisbury in 1657 because the Commonwealth had outlawed the episcopal Church of England. During the Restoration, he was made a fellow of Corpus Christi College, but he also held Church offices that gave him a good living. He became bishop of Lincoln in 1692 and archbishop of Canterbury in 1695.

It was at Corpus Christi College that he became influenced by the Cambridge Platonists, especially Ralph Cudworth. He, like the Cambridge Platonists, abhorred Hobbes's materialism. Thus, in *The Creed of Mr Hobbes Examined in a Feigned Conference*, published in 1670, Tenison asserts that God is not a body and that Hobbes confuses an idea with an image. Humans can have an idea of God without having an image of him, because, being immaterial, God cannot be sensed.]

I have sometimes heard the substance of them [Hobbes's views] comprised in twelve Articles, which sound harshly to men professing Christianity; and they were delivered under the Title of the *Hobbist's Creed*, in such phrase and order as followeth.

"I believe that God is Almighty matter; that in him there are three Persons, he having been thrice represented on earth; that it is to be decided by the Civil Power, whether he created all things else; that angels are not incorporeal substances (those words implying a contradiction), but preternatural impressions on the brain of man; that the soul of man is the temperament of his body; that the liberty of will in that soul is physically necessary; that the prime Law of Nature in the soul of man is that of self-love; that the law of the civil sovereign is the obliging rule of good and evil, just and unjust; that the books of the Old and New Testaments are made canon and law by the civil powers; that whatsoever is written in these books, may lawfully be denied even upon oath (after the laudable doctrine and practice of the Gnostics) in times of persecution, when men shall be urged by the menaces of authority; that hell is a tolerable condition of life, for a few years upon earth, to begin at the general resurrection; and that heaven is a blessed estate of good men, like that of Adam before his fall beginning at the general resurrection, to be from thenceforth eternal upon earth in the Holy-Land." ...

[Concerning Ideas, Images, and God]

Student: If God be a body, seeing man may have an image of extension and of all the possible figures, which may be made by the varieties of extension in matter, what hindereth that we may not have, in your gross way, an image of God? But because he is an immaterial substance, we cannot indeed have any bodily remembrance of him; but there is in every man a power to have an idea of him.[1] For, although it hath been said that there have been found whole nations (as in the Western World in Brazil) who have lived without the least suspicion of an infinite being, yet there is no nation so very barbarous, wherein the inhabitants have no faculty at all of exciting in them this idea of God. And here I cannot but reprehend it, as a very shameful error, in a man who placeth truth in the right ordering of names, and pretendeth to begin the sciences, by settling first the significations of their words, to confound the names of *image* and *idea*, as if they were terms of equal importance. It is also an argument of thickness of mind, of a soul not yet advanced above the power of fancy, to say that no man hath or can have any kind of conception without an image, as if nothing were authentically written upon the table of our minds, without a real and sensible impression affixed to it.... By [an] idea is understood, not merely a corporeal similitude, but any notion without imagery, and whatsoever occureth in any perception: the very form of cogitation, whereby I become conscious to my self that I have perceived, is an idea.... [There is a] difference betwixt the idea of God in a perspicuous mind, and the notion of a God taken through the pictures of imagination.

---

1 Tenison criticizes Hobbes for refusing to recognize a distinction between an image, which is closely connected with sensation, and an idea, which is conceptual. We cannot imagine things that are not material or could not be sensed, but that does not mean that they cannot be conceived of or understood by the human mind, according to Tenison. He thinks that humans have no image of God because God is not a body, but humans can have an idea of God. It is not clear whether Tenison has adequately explained what an idea is: "By [an] idea is understood, not merely a corporeal similitude, but any notion without imagery, and whatsoever occureth in any perception: the very form of cogitation, whereby I become conscious to my self that I have perceived, is an idea."

Appendix F: From Samuel Pufendorf, Of the Law of Nature and of Nations, in Eight Books *(1672)*

[Samuel Pufendorf (1632-94), born in Saxony, was educated at Leipzig and then Jena. In Jena he read the works of both Hugo Grotius (1583-1645), a famous Dutch political philosopher, and Hobbes. He taught philosophy first at the university in Heidelberg and then at the University of Lund, Sweden. In addition to his university teaching, Pufendorf at various times was a tutor and historiographer.

His first book, *Elementorum jurisprudentiae universalis* (*Elements of Universal Jurisprudence*), was published in 1660. His most important book was *De Jure Naturae et Gentium* (*Of the Law of Nature and Nations*), published in 1672. The translation used in this appendix is by Basil Kennett, the third edition of which appeared in 1717. Pufendorf's goal in *Of the Law of Nature and of Nations* was to build on but also to correct, by his lights, the natural-law theories of Grotius and Hobbes. From Grotius, Pufendorf took the idea that man was sociable, if not naturally, then at least by necessity, and also the idea that natural-law theory can achieve the same rigour as mathematics. On another matter Pufendorf parted with Grotius. Grotius was notorious in some circles for saying that the law of nature would "apply though we should even grant, what without the greatest wickedness cannot be granted, that there is no God, or that he has no care of [providence over] human affairs" ("Prolegomena," *De Jure Belli ac Pacis Libri Tres* [*Three Books on the Law of War and Peace*]). Pufendorf refused to countenance the possibility that God might not exist. From Hobbes, Pufendorf took the idea that human desire for self-preservation was fundamental to natural law and also the idea that natural theory should argue from a priori premises. In contrast to Hobbes, Pufendorf thought that humans were by necessity sociable, as mentioned above.]

... It may not be improper here to examine that assertion of Mr. Hobbs which he hath laid down in ... his *Leviathan* ... *Now seeing all men, by nature, had a right to all things, they had a right every one of them to reign over all the rest. But because this right could not be obtained by force, it concerned the safety of everyone laying aside that right, to set up men with sovereign authority by common consent to rule and defend them: Whereas if there had been any man of power irresistible, there had been no reason why he should not by that power have ruled and defended both himself and them according to his own discretion....* [*Lev.* 187]. Now in this discourse there are several things that deserve to be censured. For, in the first place, it may be questioned whether or no those two expressions, *A right of sovereignty* (upon account of strength) *is granted by nature*, and *A right of, etc, is not taken away by nature*, hang very well together. Because in most cases, my not taking away a thing is by no means an argument that I therefore grant it.[1] And since *not to be taken away* and *to be granted* are different things, such a right may seem to be granted by some other principle than nature, though nature doth not *take it away*. Besides, that maxim, *All men by nature had a right to everything*, ought to be interpreted with great caution. By *right* he means liberty, which every man hath of using his natural faculties according to reason. Therefore his principle, in a sound sense, will amount to no more than this: By nature, that is, upon the removal of all law, every man may fairly use his natural strength against those whom his reason instructs him thus to deal with, for the sake of his preservation. But it does not hence follow that barely by natural strength an obligation, properly so called, may be laid on another. For to *compel* and to *oblige* are different matters; and though natural strength may be sufficient for the former, yet the latter cannot be performed by that superiority alone.[2] For even according to Mr. Hobbes's own notion, as one man hath a right of compelling others, so those others have a right of resisting him. But now obligation cannot stand with a right of resisting, because it presupposes such reasons as inwardly affecting men's consciences make them conclude, by the judgement of their own mind, that they cannot honestly and therefore rightly resist. And though it be irrational to contend violently against a superior strength and by that means to draw upon ourselves greater mischiefs; yet there remains in us a right of trying all ways either to drive off the force by the dexterous application of other force or to elude it by subterfuge and escape. But neither can this right consist with that obligation which is precisely so termed, and which Grotius commonly opposeth to extrinsical. So that, on the whole matter, by bare force, not the right of resistance, but only the exercise of it, is extinguished.... Mr. Hobbes himself acknowledgeth that a captive of war, although capable of obligation, yet is under none whilst he is restrained only by natural bond and before the interposition of any faith or compact; and that therefore such an one may give his conqueror the slip or may assault him violently, as soon as he finds the opportunity....

---

1 For example, it may be the case that Ava does not take Bill's apple from him, but she did not give it to him.

2 Obligation is a normative notion. It requires some moral or political force. Compelling something is not a normative notion. It involves only physical force. If a person has an obligation to someone, he does not have a right to resist that person.

When we pay those things which are due upon the pact of a society with a member or a member with a society, ... we are said to exercise distributive justice. For whenever a man is received into a society, a pact is either expressly or at least tacitly made between the society and the member now to be introduced, by which the society engageth to give him a just share and proportion of the goods which it enjoys as a common body; and the member promiseth that he will bear his proper and equal part of those burdens which conduce to the preservation of the society, considered as such. The exact determination of the proper share of goods to be assigned to the member is made according to the rule and value of the pains or charges employed by him towards preserving the common society in proportion to the pains or charges contributed by the other members. On the other hand, the determination of the proper share of burdens to be laid on the members is made according to the value of the benefits received by him from the society, considered in proportion to the advantages which the rest of the members enjoy. Hence, since it generally happens that one member contributes more towards the preservation of the society than another and that one likewise exceeds another in deriving advantage from it, the reason is very apparent why, upon the supposal of many persons, and of this inequality amongst them, we ought in the exercise of distributive justice, to observe a comparative equality.... Thus, for instance, if six things of the same value are to be distributed amongst Caius, Seius, and Titius, upon supposition that Titius exceeds Caius in a triple proportion, and Seius in a double, Titius shall have three, Seius two, and Caius one. Nor is it requisite to this equality that the reward fully answer and come up to the merits of the person.... And the same rule must be followed in distributing burdens....

As for what Mr. Hobbes allegeth to overthrow this reflective equality, that *I may of my own goods distribute least to him that deserves most, and most to him that deserves least, provided I pay but for what I bargain for*; and useth the authority of our Saviour, in the 20th of St. Matt. ver. 13, etc. to confirm his opinion. All this, if rightly considered, makes nothing to the purpose. For in the place of Scripture cited above, it is shown indeed that he doth not offend against commutative justice (which governs the contracts about hire, etc.) who out of his liberality gives to some a larger reward than their service deserves; or who, to the wages due upon this commutative justice, adds something out of free bounty, which is comprehended under universal justice....

Mr. Hobbes hath advanced one single notion of justice to comprehend every kind, making it nothing else but a keeping of faith and fulfilling of covenants, which opinion he borrowed from Epicurus. (See Diogenes Laertius, Book 10 near the end.) Commutative justice, he says, takes place in contracts, as in buying and selling, hiring and letting to hire, lending and borrowing, exchanging, bartering, and the like. Distributive justice (though improperly so called) is, he says, *the justice of an arbitrator, which being trusted by them who make him arbitrator, if he perform his trust, he is said to distribute to every man his own.* Nor will he allow any other equality to be observed but this, that since we are all equal by nature, one man ought not to arrogate to himself more right than he allows another, unless he hath obtained a greater right than ordinary, by the intervention of covenants. Farther, since according to his sentiments an injury or an unjust action or omission is nothing else but the violation of a covenant, he hence infers that we cannot offer an injury to a man unless we have before covenanted with him. This assertion is founded on his old maxim of *the right of every man to all things,* which he hath stretched far beyond its just limits; so that he imagines before any covenant is made ... every man hath a right of doing to others what he pleaseth; and thus, only using his right, he cannot be said to commit an injury. But ... nature allows a man to use all such means as reason shall judge conducible to his firm and lasting preservation, as indeed Mr. Hobbes himself in his definition of right inserts the use of reason. But now sound reason will never advise us, out of our own pleasure and humour, to put such affronts on another, as cannot but provoke him to war or to a reciprocal desire of hurting us. Besides it implies a manifest contradiction to say that upon the supposal of many men equal in rights, each of them hath a right to all things; since the right of one man to all things, if it hath any effect, must extinguish the rights of the rest; and if the right hath no effect upon the others, it is useless, absurd, and ridiculous. For in moral account, *not to be* and *not to be effectual* are much the same. And indeed, how can we call that a right which another may oppose with an equal right? Who would say, *I had the right of commanding a man,* if he, by the same right of commanding a man, might despise my order? Or that I had a right of beating another when he too had a right of returning my blows, and, if he pleased, with advantage and increase? 'Tis certain therefore that he that doth these things to another hath no right of doing them and consequently is injurious. On the contrary, the other party hath a right that such things should not be put upon him and is therefore injured. Thus we see that such right as being violated produceth an injury is not only acquired by covenant, but was given at first by nature without the intervention of any human act....

Having arrived to know what justice is, we may easily settle our notions of injustice, and of its several species. An action, then, is unjust either when we apply it designedly to a person to whom we owed a different action, or when we deny another somewhat which was really his due. That is, we are equally guilty of a breach of justice by doing any evil to another which we had no right to do, and by taking from another or denying him any good which he had a fair title to require....

But an unjust action, proceeding from intention, and trespassing on the perfect right of another, is in one word called *injury*. By the natural state of man in our present inquiry, we do not mean that condition which is ultimately designed [for] him by nature, as the most perfect and most agreeable; but such state as we may conceive man to be placed in by his bare nativity, abstracting from all the rules and institutions, whether of human invention or of the suggestion and revelation of heaven....

We are ready to acknowledge it for a most certain truth that all mankind did never exist together in a mere natural state, inasmuch as upon the divine authority of Scriptures, we believe all human race to have proceeded from one original pair. Now it's plain that Eve was subject to Adam, Gen. 3:16, and those who were born of these primitive parents, and so on, did immediately fall under paternal authority and under family government. But such a state might have befallen mankind if, as some of the heathens believed, they had in the beginning of their being, leapt out of the earth like frogs or had come up from seed, like Cadmus's human crop (Ovid. *Metamorphoses* Book 3, vv. 122-3), which fable is, methinks, a very exact representation of that state of nature and of that war of all men against all, which Hobbes would introduce....

A state of nature then did never naturally exist unless qualified and, as it were, in part; namely, while some party of men joined with some more in a civil body or in some confederacy like that; but still retained a natural liberty against all others.

[...]

As to Mr. Hobbes's reasons, they are easily answered. In the first place, those cannot immediately hurt one another who are divided by distance of place; for he who is absent cannot hurt me, except by some body else who is present, and my possessions cannot be destroyed unless by one upon the spot. Therefore, those who live separately or at a distance from one another can offer no mutual hurt so long as they continue thus distant, it doth not appear why such men should not rather be reckoned friends than enemies.

[Hobbes] acknowledgeth no more than one covenant of each man to each man; frequently representing and declaring that there passeth no covenant between the prince or the senate and his subjects. Indeed, we may easily gather from the design of his books of policy, which is clearly discovered in his *Leviathan*, the reason that put him upon his assertion. His principal aim was to oppose those seditious and turbulent spirits who in his time laboured to bring down the regal power to their own model and either utterly to extinguish or to render it inferior to the subjects. To cut off from these men their ordinary plea for rebellion which was that there is a reciprocal faith between the prince and the people, and that when the former departs from what he engaged by promise, the latter are released from their obedience, as also to hinder restless and factious persons from interpreting every action of their prince, which suited not with their own humour, as a breach of his faith; he resolves to deny that there is any such thing as a covenant between subjects and their sovereign.... [However] this consideration doth by no means make it necessary for us to deny what is as clear as the light and to acknowledge no covenant in a case where there is certainly a mutual promise for the performance of duties not before required. Whilst I voluntarily subject myself to a prince, I promise obedience and engage his protection; on the other hand, the prince when he receives me as a subject, promiseth his protection, and engageth my obedience. Before this reciprocal promise, neither was he bound to protect me, nor I to obey him, at least by any perfect obligation. And who will not pretend to say that an act of this kind doth not fall under the head of covenants? Nor is this covenant useless because they who by their own free choice appoint a king over themselves seem beforehand to have entered into an agreement for the advancing such a particular person to the throne. For as the bare election without the acceptance of the party elected confers on him no power over the rest, so 'tis plain enough from the nature of the business that they who freely put themselves under the power of another desire he should in the exercise of that power pursue the end for which it was given him; and that he received the power on this condition that those who conferred it on him should not, by his means, miss their aim. They who create a sovereign, therefore, as they at the same time promise whatever the nature of subjection requires; so, on the other part, engage him to endeavour the procuring of all those benefits for the sake of which civil governments are introduced. And what can we call this but the entering into covenant?

Appendix G: From *Edward Hyde,* A Brief View and Survey of the Dangerous and Pernicious Errors to Church and State in Mr Hobbes's Book Entitled Leviathan *(Oxford, 1676)*

[Edward Hyde (1609-74), like Hobbes, was born in Wiltshire and attended Magdalen Hall, Oxford, though Hyde was twenty years younger. He was a member of Lord Falkland's intellectual circle at Great Tew, where he may have met Hobbes. He was a moderate monarchist, opposing the doctrine of absolute sovereignty but stalwart in defending the monarchy. He thought that parliament was not an independent political entity but was part of "the king in parliament." Although he voted to impeach Strafford (see p. 223, note 4, above), he eventually sided with the king in the Civil War.

He came to know Hobbes well when they were both in exile in Paris. At the Restoration, Hyde was made earl of Clarendon and was one of Charles II's most important counselors until, being made a scapegoat, he was again forced to flee to Paris. Bitter in exile, he might have fumed over the good fortune of Hobbes, a summer patriot, and not even a sunshine soldier, while he, faithful Hyde, was disgraced and in effect ostracized. He vented his spleen in *A Brief View and Survey of the Dangerous and Pernicious Errors to Church and State in Mr Hobbes's Book Entitled Leviathan,* published in 1676, two years after his death. While he had liked Hobbes's *De Cive* (1642, 1647), he hated *Leviathan*; and he surmises in various places that Hobbes had altered his theory in order to ingratiate himself with the "usurper" Oliver Cromwell.

If Hyde's many criticisms are reduced to three, they are that Hobbes is wrong in holding that all people are born equal, that Hobbes's political theory is inconsistent with English law, and that the lessons of biblical history show Hobbes's theory to be false.

Hyde's prose is maddeningly prolix and serpentine. Many of the deletions indicated in the text are cut from the middle of a sentence.

All internal page references are to the 1651 edition of *Leviathan*.]

The Introduction

... [T]here are many who, being delighted with some new notions and the pleasant and clear style throughout the book, have not taken notice of those down-right conclusions which overthrow or undermine all those principles of government, which have preserved the peace of this kingdom through so many ages, even from the time of its first institution; or restored it to peace, when it had at some times been interrupted; and [they have taken] much less [notice] of those odious insinuations and perverting [of] some texts of Scripture, which do dishonour and would destroy the very essence of the religion of Christ. And when I called to mind the good acquaintance that had been between us and what I had said to many who I knew had informed him of it, and which indeed I had sent to himself upon the first publishing of his *Leviathan*, I thought myself even bound to give him some satisfaction why I had entertained so evil an opinion of his Book.

[...]

The Survey of Chapters 13, 14 , 15, 16.

... [U]nder the pretence of examining, ... what the natural condition of mankind is, he takes many things for granted which are not true, as that *nature has made all men equal in the faculties of body and mind* (p. 60), and imputes that to the nature of man in general, which is but the infirmity of some particular men; and by a mist of words, under the notion of explaining common terms (the meaning whereof is understood by all men, and which his explanation leaves less intelligible than they were before), he dazzles men's eyes from discerning those fallacies upon which he raises his structure.... And whosoever looks narrowly to his preparatory assertions shall find such contradictions as must destroy the foundation of all his new doctrine in government, of which some particulars shall be mentioned anon.[1] So that if his maxims of one kind were marshalled together, collected out of these four chapters, and applied to his other maxims which are to support his whole *Leviathan*, the one would be a sufficient answer to the other; and so many inconsistencies and absurdities would appear between them, that they could never be thought links of one chain.... [How can] a man of Mr. Hobbes's sagacity ... reproach the Schools for absurdity in saying that *heavy bodies fall downwards out of an appetite to rest, thereby ascribing knowledge to things inanimate* (p. 4); and himself [in] ... describing the nature of foul weather, say, *that it lieth not in a shower or two of rain, but in an inclination thereto of many days together* (p. 62), as if foul weather were not as inanimate a thing as heavy bodies, and inclination did not imply as much of knowledge as appetite does. In truth, neither ... signi-

---

1 According to Hyde, Hobbes often contradicts himself.

fies in the before-mentioned instances more than a natural tendency to motion and alteration.

When God vouchsafed [condescended] to make man after his own image and in his own likeness ..., it cannot be imagined but that at the same time he endued him with reason and all the other noble faculties which were necessary for the administration of that empire and the preservation of the several species which were to succeed the creation. And therefore to uncreate him to such a baseness and villainy in his nature ... is a power that God never gave to the devil; nor has any body assumed it, till Mr. Hobbes took it upon him. Nor can anything be said more contrary to the honour and dignity of God almighty than that he should leave his master workmanship, man, in a condition of war of every man against every man,[1] in such a condition of confusion *that every man has a right to every thing, even to one another's body* (p. 64), inclined to all the malice, force and fraud that may promote his profit or his pleasure, and without any notions of, or instinct towards, justice, honour, or good nature, which only makes mankind superior to the beasts of the wilderness. Nor had Mr. Hobbes any other reason to degrade him to this degree of bestiality, but that he may be fit to wear those chains and fetters which he has provided for him. He deprives man of the greatest happiness and glory that can be attributed to him, ... that gentleness and benevolence towards other men, by which he delights in the good fortune and tranquility that they enjoy.... Man only [according to Hobbes] ... is obliged for his own benefit and for the defence of his own right to worry and destroy all of his own kind, until they all become yoked by a covenant and contract that Mr. Hobbes has provided for them, and which was never yet entered into by any one man, and is in nature impossible to be entered into.[2]

... [T]he instances and arguments given by him are very unweighty and trivial to conclude the nature of man to be so full of jealousy and malignity, as he would have it believed to be from that common practice of circumspection and providence which custom and discretion has introduced into human life. For men shut their chests in which their money is, ... as that it may be preserved from thieves; and they lock their doors [in order] that their houses may not be common; and [they] ride armed and in company, because they know that there are ill men, who may be inclined to do injuries if they find an opportunity.[3] Nor is

---

1 According to Hyde, it is an insult to God to claim that the natural condition of human beings is a state of war.

2 According to Hyde, no one has ever entered into a covenant or contract in the state of nature; and it is impossible to do so.

3 According to Hyde, people lock doors and chests to protect against the very few people who are criminals.

a wariness to prevent the damage and injury that thieves and robbers may do to any man an argument that mankind is in that man's opinion inclined and disposed to commit those outrages. If it be known that there is one thief in a city, all men have reason to shut their doors and lock their chests; and if there be two or three drunkards in a town, all men have reason to go armed in the streets to control the violence or indignity they might receive from them. Princes are attended by their guards in progress and all their servants [are] armed when they hunt without any apprehension of being assaulted, custom having made it so necessary, that many men are not longer without their swords than they are without their doublets, who never were jealous that any man desired to hurt them....

... He is very much offended with Aristotle, for saying in the first book of his *Politics*, that by nature some are fit to command, and others to serve; which he says is not only against reason, but also against experience, for *there are very few so foolish that had not rather govern themselves, than be governed by others* (p. 77). Which proposition does not contradict anything said by Aristotle, the question being whether nature has made some men worthier, not whether it has made all others so modest as to confess it; and [his view] would have required a more serious disquisition, since it is no more than is imputed to horses and other beasts, whereof men find by experience that some by nature are fitter for nobler uses and others for vile and to be only beasts of burden. But, indeed, [this] he says is the law of nature: *that every man must acknowledge every other man for his equal by nature* (p. 77); which may be true as to the essentials of human nature; and yet there may be inequality enough as to a capacity of government.[1] ... And 'tis very true, that Aristotle did believe that Divine Providence does show and demonstrate who are fit and proper for low and vile offices, not only by very notable defects in their understandings, incapable of any cultivation, but by some eminent deformity of the body (though that does not always hold) which makes them unfit to bear rule. And without doubt, the observation of all ages since that time has contributed very much to that conclusion which Mr. Hobbes so much derides, of inequality by nature, and that nature itself has a bounty which she extends to some men in a much superior degree than she does to others. Which is not contradicted by seeing many great defects and indigencies [deficiencies] of nature in some men, wonderfully corrected and repaired by industry, education, and above all, by conversation [social interaction]; nor by seeing some early blossoms in others, which raise a great expectation of rare perfection, that suddenly decay and insensibly wither away by not being cherished and improved

---

1 According to Hyde, it is a simple fact that some people by nature are more fit to govern than others.

by diligence, or rather by being blasted by vice or supine laziness. Those accidents may sometimes happen, do not very often, and are necessary to awaken men out of the lethargy of depending wholly upon the wealth of nature's store....

But where are those maxims to be found which Mr. Hobbes declares and publishes to be the laws of nature, in any other author before him?[1] That is only properly called the Law of Nature that is dictated to the whole species, as to defend a man's self from violence and to repel force by force. [Laws of Nature are] not all that results upon prudential motives unto the mind of such as have been cultivated by learning and education.... For under what other notion can that reasonable conclusion ... be called the law of nature, which is his fifteenth law, *That all men that mediate peace be allowed safe conduct?* (p. 78). And of this kind much of the body of his law of nature is compiled; which I should not dislike, the style being in some sense not improper, but that I observe that from some of these conclusions which he pronounces to be *immutable and eternal as the laws of nature* (p. 79), he makes deductions and inferences to control opinions he dislikes and to obtain concessions which are not right, by amusing men with his method and confounding, rather than informing, their understandings by a chime of words in definitions and pleasant instances.... And it is an unanswerable evidence of the irresistible force and strength of truth and reason that whilst men are making war against it with all their power and stratagems, somewhat does still start up out of the dictates and confessions of the adversary that determines the controversy and vindicates the truth from the malice that would oppress it. How should it else come to pass that Mr. Hobbes, while he is demolishing the whole frame of nature for want of order to support it and makes it unavoidably necessary for every man to cut his neighbour's throat, to kill him who is weaker than himself and to circumvent and by any fraud destroy him who is stronger [would] set down such a body of laws prescribed by nature itself, as are *immutable and eternal?*[2] ... If the law of the Gospel [be], *Whatsoever you require that others should do to you, that do ye to them*, ... [and] if it be the law of nature that every man strive to accommodate himself to the rest, as he says it is, and *that no man by deed, word, countenance or gestures, declare hatred or contempt for another* (p. 76); [and] if all men are bound by the law of nature *that they that are at controversy, submit their right to the judgement of an arbitrator* (p. 78), ... [then] how come they to fall into that condition

---

1   According to Hyde, Hobbes's supposed laws of nature are not genuinely such because he is the only one who affirms them; and genuine laws of nature need to be known by all people.

2   According to Hyde, it is not possible for Hobbes's laws of nature to exist and for people in their natural condition to be in a state of war.

of war, as to be every one against everyone, and to be without any other cardinal virtues, but of force and fraud? It is a wonderful thing that a man should be so sharp-sighted, as to discern mankind so well enclosed and fortified by the wisdom of nature and so blind as to think him in a more secure estate by his transferring of right to another man, which yet he confesses is impossible entirely to transfer....[1]

What greater contradiction can there be to the peace which he would establish upon those unreasonable conditions than this liberty, which he says can never be abandoned, and which yet may dissolve the peace every day?[2] ...

Without doubt, no man is *dominus vitae suae* [lord of his own life], and therefore cannot give that to another, which he has not in himself. God only has reserved that absolute dominion and power of life and death to himself, and by his putting the sword into the hand of the supreme magistrate, has qualified and enabled him to execute that justice which is necessary for the peace and preservation of his people, which may seem in a manner to be provided for by Mr. Hobbes's law of nature, if what he says be true, *that right to the end contains right to the means* (p. 68). And this sole proposition, that men cannot dispose of their own lives, has been always held as a manifest and undeniable argument, that sovereigns never had, nor can have their power from the people....

The Survey of Chapters 17, 18

Mr. Hobbes having taken upon himself to imitate God and [having] created man after his own likeness, given him all the passions and affections which he finds in himself, he prescribes him [man] to judge of all things and words, according to the definitions he sets down, with the authority of a Creator.... He comes at last to institute such a commonwealth as never was in nature or ever heard of from the beginning of the world till this structure of his, and ... [he] gives the man he hath made the sovereign command and government of with such an extent of power and authority as the Great Turk hath not yet appeared to affect.

... He will not find one government in the world, of what kind soever, so instituted, as he dogmatically declares all government to be; nor was mankind in any nation since the creation upon such a level, as to institute their government by such an assembly and election, and covenant,

---

1 According to Hyde, it is incredible that Hobbes should think that people are intelligent enough to deduce the laws of nature and so stupid as to transfer their rights to others.

2 According to Hyde, for Hobbes to hold that people retain the liberty of self-preservation contradicts his view about how peace is established.

and consent, as he very unwarrantedly more than supposes. And it was an undertaking of the more impertinence, since by his own rule, *where there is already erected a sovereign power* (p. 95), which was then and still is in every kingdom and state in Europe, and for aught we know in the whole world, *there can be no other representative of the people, but only to certain particular ends limited by the sovereign* [p. 95]. So that he could have no other design but to shake what was erected; and the government was not at that time in any suspense but in his own country, by the effect of an odious and detestable rebellion....

It had been kindly done of Mr. Hobbes, if according to his laudable custom of illustrating his definitions by instances, ... he had to this his positive determination added one instance of a government so instituted. There is no doubt there are in all governments many things done by and with the consent of the people; ... but that any government was originally instituted by an assembly of men equally free and that they ever elected the person who should have the sovereign power over them is yet to be proved; and till it be proved, must not be supposed, to raise new doctrines, upon which shake all government.

... [I]f Mr. Hobbes did not affect to be of the humour of those unreasonable gamesters, [whom he describes on p. 19], ... he might with as much reason, ... because it would have carried with it more equality and consequently more security, have supposed a covenant to be on the sovereign's part.... [He] will not admit that they who are his subjects make any covenant with their sovereign to obey him; which if he did, he could as well covenant again with them to govern righteously[1] without making them the judges of his justice or himself liable to their control and jurisdiction. So that the sovereign hath no security for the obedience of his people, but the promise they have made to each other; and consequently if they rebel against him, he cannot complain of any injustice done to him, because they have broke no promise they made to him. And truly, by his own logic, they may release to one another when they think it convenient.[2] Whereas if the promises be mutual, I do not say *conditional*, the sovereign must not be at the mercy of his subjects; but as they put themselves under his power, so tyrannically (which will be a proper and significant word against all his interpretation) by which they have as much obligation upon him to be just, as he hath upon them to be obedient, which is no other, than that they swerve from justice, if they withdraw their obedience from him....

---

1 According to Hyde, Hobbes should have had people make a covenant with their sovereign to govern righteously.
2 According to Hyde, Hobbes's views make government unstable because subjects are free to release each other from their covenant.

It is to no purpose to examine the prerogatives he [Hobbes] grants to his sovereign, because he founds them all upon a supposition of a contract and covenant that never was in nature nor ever can reasonably be supposed to be; yet he confesses it to be *the generation of the great Leviathan* (p. 87), and which, falling to the ground, all his prerogatives must likewise fall too; and so much to the damage of the sovereign power, (to which most of the prerogatives are due) that men will [be] apt to suppose that they proceed from a ground which is not true, and so be the more inclined to dispute them. Whereas those prerogatives are indeed vested in the sovereign by his being sovereign; but he does not become sovereign by virtue of such a contract and covenant, but are of the essence of his sovereignty.... And here he supposes again that whatsoever a sovereign is possessed of is of his sovereignty; and therefore he will by no means admit that he shall part with any of his power which he calls *essential and inseparable rights* [p. 93], and that whatever grant he makes of such power, the same is void; and he does believe that this sovereign right was at the time when he published his book so well understood (that is, [Oliver] Cromwell liked his doctrine so well) that it would be generally acknowledged in England at the next return of peace. Yet he sees ·himself deceived. It hath pleased God to restore a blessed and a general peace, and neither king nor people believe his doctrine to be true or consistent with peace.

... And there is too much cause to fear that the unhappy publication of this doctrine against the liberty and propriety [property][1] of the subject (which others had the honour to declare before Mr. Hobbes, though they had not the good fortune to escape punishment as he hath done, I mean Dr. [Roger] Manwaring, and Dr. [Robert] Sibthorpe)[2] contributed too much thereunto.

... [Hobbes's ignorance causes him to marvel that] he that had the sovereignty [in England] from a descent of six hundred years was alone called *sovereign*, had the title of *Majesty* from every one of his subjects, and was unquestionably taken by them for their king, was notwithstanding never considered as their representative, that name without

---

1 "But one man's liberty can be another man's slavery.... For the Parliamentary electorate—gentry and merchants—the most important liberty to be defended was the sanctity of private property; and the institution on which they relied to safeguard property was Parliament, the representative body of the propertied class. For most of the population, owning no property or very little, the sanctity of private property was not a major issue." Christopher Hill, *Liberty Against the Law* (London: Penguin Books, 1997), pp. 19-20. Hyde was an MP in the 1640s but ultimately sided with the king.

2 Roger Manwaring (1589-1653) and Robert Sibthorpe (d. 1662) both maintained that the king of England was an absolute monarch. Both were punished by parliament for their views.

contradiction, passing for the title of those men which at his command were sent up by the people to carry their petitions and give him, if he permitted it, their advice; which he says *may serve as an admonition for those that are the true and absolute representative of a people* (which he hath made his sovereign to be) *to take heed how they admit of any other general representative upon any occasion whatsoever* (p. 95).... And if Mr. Hobbes did not make war against all modesty, he would rather have concluded that the title of the representative of the people was not to be affected by the king than that, for want [lack] of understanding, his Majesty should neglect to assume it or that his faithful counsel and his learned judges, who cannot be supposed to be ignorant of the regalities of the crown, should fail to put him in mind of so advantageous a plea, when his fundamental rights were so foully assaulted and in danger.[1] But though the king knew too well the original [source] of his own power to be contented to be thought the representative of the people; yet if Mr. Hobbes were not strangely unconversant with the transactions of those times, he would have known ... that the king frequently and upon all occasions reprehended [reprimanded] the two Houses, both for assuming the style and appellation of parliament, which they were not, but in and by his Majesty's conjunction with them, and for calling themselves the Representative of the People, which they neither were, or could be to any other purpose than to present their petitions and humbly to offer their advice, when and in what his Majesty required it; and this was as generally understood by men of all conditions in England, as it was that rebellion was treason. But they who were able by false pretences and under false protestations to raise an Army, found it no difficult matter to persuade that army and those who concurred with them, that they were not in rebellion....

The Survey of Chapter 20

... And in the first place we must deny ... *that war is founded in nature,* which gives the stronger a right to whatever the weaker is possessed of;[2] so that there can be no peace or security from oppression, till such covenants are made, as may appoint a sovereign to have all that power which is necessary to provide for that peace and security; and out of and by this institution, his magistrate grows up to the greatness and size of his Leviathan. But we say that peace is founded in nature and that when the God of nature gave his creature, man, the dominion

---

1 According to Hyde, the king of England is the sovereign of the people, not their representative.

2 According to Hyde, peace is founded in nature; and God gave people the skills to govern the world.

over the rest of his creation, he gave him likewise natural strength and power to govern the world with peace and order. And how much soever he lost by his own integrity by falling from his obedience to his creator and how severe a punishment soever he underwent by that his disobedience, it does not appear that his [Adam's] dominion over mankind was in any degree lessened or abated. So that we cannot but look upon him [Adam], during his life, as the sole monarch of the world; and that lasted so long, as we may reasonably compute, that a very considerable part of the world that was peopled before the Flood was peopled in his life, ... so that his dominion was over a very numerous people. And during all that time, we have no reason to imagine that there was any such instrument of government by covenants and contracts....

... After the Flood, we cannot but think that Noah remained the sole monarch of the world during his life....

The Survey of Chapter 21

... And it is not Mr. Hobbes's authority that will make it believed that he who desires more liberty demands an exemption from all laws, by which all other men may be masters of their lives, and that every subject is author of every act the sovereign doth, upon the extravagant supposition of a consent that never was given; and if it were possible to have been given, must have been void at the instant it was given, by Mr. Hobbes's own rules, as shall be made out in its place....

Mr. Hobbes is too much conversant in both those learned languages to wish that the Western world were deprived of the Greek and Latin tongues for any mischief they have done; and upon my conscience, whatever errors may have been brought into philosophy by the authority of Aristotle, no man ever grew a rebel by reading him.... And if Mr. Hobbes would take a view of the insurrections and the civil wars which have at any time been stirred up in the Western parts, he will not find that they have been contrived or fomented by men who had spent much time in the reading Greek or Latin authors.... And I believe had Mr. Hobbes been of this opinion when he taught Thucydides to speak English, which book contains more of the science of mutiny and sedition, and teaches more of the oratory that contributes thereunto, than all that Aristotle and Cicero have, he would not have communicated such materials to his countrymen....

But [in order] that this supreme sovereign, whom he hath invested with the whole property and liberty of all his subjects and so invested him in it that he hath not power to part with any of it by promise or donation or release, may not be too much exalted with his own greatness, he [Hobbes] hath humbled him sufficiently by giving his subjects leave to withdraw their obedience from him when he hath most need of their assistance; for *the obligation of subjects to the sovereign is understood* (he says) *to last as long, and no longer, than the power lasts to protect them* (p. 114). So that as soon as any town, city, or province of any prince's dominions is invaded by a foreign enemy or possessed by a rebellious subject that the prince for the present cannot suppress, ... the people may lawfully resort to those who are over them; and for their protection [the people may] perform all the offices and duties of good subjects to them. *For the right men have by nature to protect themselves when none else can protect them, can by no covenant be relinquished, and the end of obedience is protection, which wherever a man sees it either in his own or in another's sword, nature applies his obedience to it, and his endeavours to maintain it* (p. 114). And truly it is no wonder if ... subjects take the first opportunity to free themselves from such a sovereign as he hath given them, and choose a better for themselves. Whereas the duty of subjects is ... another kind of duty and obedience to their sovereign than to withdraw their subjection because he is oppressed; and [true subjects] will prefer poverty and death itself before they will renounce their obedience to their natural prince or do any thing that may advance the service of his enemies. And since Mr. Hobbes gives so ill a testimony of his government *that it is in its own nature not only subject to violent death by foreign war, but also from the ignorance and passion of men that it hath in it from the very institution many seeds of natural mortality by internal discord* (p. 114), worse than which he cannot say of any government, we may very reasonably prefer the government we have and under which we have enjoyed much happiness, before his which we do not know, nor any body hath had experience of....

Whether the relation of subjects be extinguished in all those cases, which Mr. Hobbes takes upon him to prescribe, as [for example] imprisonment, banishment, and the like, I leave to those who can instruct him better in the Law of Nations, by which they must be judged, notwithstanding all his appeals to the Law of Nature; and I presume if a banished person *during which*, he says, *he is not the subject* (p. 114), shall join in an action under a foreign power against his country, wherein he shall with others be taken prisoner, ... he shall be judged as a traitor and rebel, which he could not be, if he were not a subject.... Surely this woeful desertion and defection in the cases above mentioned, which hath been always held criminal by all law that hath been current in any part of the world, received so much countenance and justification by Mr. Hobbes his book and more by his conversation that Cromwell found the submission to those principles produced a submission to him [Cromwell], and the imaginary relation between protection and allegiance, so positively proclaimed by him, prevailed for many years to extinguish all visible fidelity to the King, whilst he [Hobbes] persuaded many to take the Engagement as a thing lawful and to become subjects to the usurper [Cromwell], as to their legitimate sovereign ...

It appears at last why by his institution he would have the power and security of his sovereign wholly and only to depend upon the contracts and covenants which the people make one with another, to transfer all their rights to a third person (who shall be sovereign) without entering into any covenant with the sovereign himself, which would have divested them of that liberty to disobey him.... [T]hen he says, *if a monarch shall relinquish the sovereignty both for himself, and his heirs, his subjects return to the absolute liberty of nature. Because though nature may declare who are his sons and who are the nearest of his kin, yet it dependeth on his own will who shall be his heir; and if he will have no heir, there is no sovereignty or subjection* [p. 114]. This seems the hardest condition for the poor subject that he can be liable unto, that when he hath divested himself of all the right he had, only for his sovereign's protection, that he may be redeemed from the state of war and confusion that nature hath left him in and hath paid so dear for that protection, it is left still in his sovereign's power to withdraw that protection from him, to renounce his subjection, and without his consent to transfer the sovereignty to another, to whom he hath no mind to be subject. One might have imagined that this new trick of transferring and covenanting had been an universal remedy, that being once applied would forever prevent the ill condition and confusion that nature had left us in, and that such a right would have been constituted by it, that sovereignty would never have failed to the world's end. And that when the subject can never retract or avoid the bargain he hath made, how ill soever he likes it or improve it by acquiring any better conditions in it, it shall notwithstanding be in the sovereign's power ... to leave him without any protection, without any security, and as a prey to all who are too strong for him. This indeed is the greatest prerogative that he hath conferred upon his sovereign, when he had given him all that belongs to his subjects, that when he is weary of governing, he can destroy them by leaving them to destroy one another.... And whereas he hath in his eighteenth chapter pronounced *the right of Judicatory of hearing and deciding all controversies which concern law, either civil or natural, or concerning fact* (p. 91) to be inseparably annexed to the sovereignty, and incapable of being aliened and transferred by him; and afterwards [he] declares *that the judgements given by judges qualified and commissioned by him to that purpose are his own proper judgements and to be regarded as such,* which is a truth generally confessed; in this chapter, against all practice and all reason, he degrades him from at least half that power, and fancies a judge to be such a party that if the litigant be not pleased with the opinion of his judge in matter of law or matter of fact, he may therefore (*because they are both subjects to the sovereign* [p. 125]) appeal from his judge, and ought to be tried before another: for those the sovereign may hear and determine the cause himself if he please; yet if he will appoint another to be judge, it must be such a one as they shall both agree upon.

... Notwithstanding that *the law is reason* and *not the letter, but that which is according to the intention of the legislator (that is of the sovereign) is the law* (p. 139), yet when there is any difficulty in the understanding the law, the interpretation thereof may reasonably belong to learned judges, who by their education and the testimony of their known abilities before they are made judges, and by their oaths to judge according to right, are the most competent to explain those difficulties, which no sovereign as sovereign can be presumed to understand or comprehend. And the judgements and decisions those judges make are the judgements of the sovereigns who have qualified them to be judges and who are to pronounce their sentence according to the reason of the law, not the reason of the sovereign. And therefore Mr. Hobbes would make a very ignorant judge, when he would not have him versed in the study of the laws, but only a man of good natural reason and of a right understanding of the Law of Nature. ... For to what purpose is all the distinction and division of laws into human and divine, into natural and moral, into distributive and penal, when [a person is the] sovereign? *[T]he Law of Nature is a part of the civil law in all commonwealths in the world,* and that though *it be naturally reasonable, yet it is by the sovereign power that it is law,* and he says likewise, *that all laws written and unwritten, and the Law of Nature itself, have need of interpretation* (p. 138). And then he makes his supreme sovereign the only legitimate interpreter. So that he hath the Law of Nature as much in his power as under his jurisdiction, as any other part of the civil law. And yet he confesses his subject is not bound to pay obedience to any thing that his sovereign enjoins against the Law of Nature. In such labyrinths men entangle themselves who obstinately engage in opinions relating to a science they do not understand.... I believe every man who reads Mr. Hobbes observes that when he entangles himself in the Laws of England and affects to be more learned in them than the Chief Justice Cook [Edward Coke], the natural sharpness and vigour of his reason is more flat and insipid than upon other arguments, and he makes deductions which have no coherence, and in a word loses himself in a mist of words that render him less intelligible than at other times....

The Survey of Chapter 28

...There cannot be a more pernicious doctrine and more destructive to peace and justice, than that all men who are not subjects are enemies, and that against enemies, whom the commonwealth judges capable to do them hurt, it is lawful by the original right of nature to make war;

which would keep up a continual war between all princes, since they are few who are not capable to do hurt to their neighbours. Nor can this mischief be prevented by any treaty or league; for whilst they are capable of doing hurt, the lawfulness still remains, and being the original right of nature, cannot be extinguished....

The Survey of Chapter 30

Mr. Hobbes having invested his sovereign with so absolute power and omnipotence, we have reason to expect that in this Chapter of his office, he will enjoin him to use all the authority he has given him.... And least [lest] he should forget the rights and power he hath bestowed upon him, he recollects them all in three or four lines, amongst which he puts him in mind that he hath power to levy money when, and as much as in his own conscience, he shall judge necessary. And then [Hobbes] tells him [the sovereign] that it is against his duty to let the people be ignorant or misinformed of the grounds and reasons of those his essential rights, that is, that he is obliged to make his Leviathan canonical scripture, there being no other book ever yet printed that can inform them of those rights, and the grounds and reason of them.

... In the meantime he must not take it ill that I observe his extreme malignity to the Nobility, by whose bread he hath been always sustained [and] who must not expect any part, at least any precedence in his institution [government]; that in this his deep meditation upon the ten commandments and in a conjuncture when the Levellers were at highest and the reduction of all degrees to one and the same was resolved upon and begun and exercised towards the whole Nobility with all the instances of contempt and scorn he chose to publish his judgement, as if the safety of the people required an equality of persons....

The Survey of Chapter 31

... It is one of the unhappy effects, which a too gracious and merciful indulgence ever produces in corrupt and proud natures, that they believe that whatsoever is tolerated in them is justified and commended; and because Mr. Hobbes hath not received any such brand which the authors of such doctrine have been usually marked with, nor hath seen his book burned by the hand of the hangman, as many more innocent books have been, he is exalted to a hope that the supreme magistrate will at some time so far exercise his sovereignty, as to protect the public teaching his principles and convert the truth of his speculation into the utility of practice. But he might remember, and all those who are scandalized, that such monstrous and seditious discourses have so long escaped a judicial examination and punishment, must know that Mr.

Hobbes his *Leviathan* was printed and published in the highest time of Cromwell's wicked usurpation; for the vindication and perpetuating whereof, it was contrived and designed, and when all legal power was suppressed; and upon his Majesty's blessed return, that merciful and wholesome Act of Oblivion, which pardoned all treasons and murders, sacrilege, robbery, heresies and blasphemies, as well with reference to their writings as their persons, and other actions, did likewise wipe out the memory of the enormities of Mr. Hobbes and his *Leviathan*....

We shall conclude here our disquisition of his policy and government of his commonwealth with the recollecting and stating the excellent maxims and principles upon which his government is founded and supported, [in order] that when they appear naked and uninvolved in his magisterial discourses, men may judge of the liberty and security they should enjoy, if Mr. Hobbes's doctrine were inculcated into the minds of men ...

1. *That the king's word is sufficient to take any thing from any subject [more] than there is need, and that the king is judge of that need. Page 106, cap. 20. part. 2.*
2. *The liberty of a subject lieth only in those things, which in regulating their actions, the sovereign hath pretermitted [passed over], such as is the liberty to buy and sell, and otherwise to contract with one another; to choose their own abode, their own diet, their own trade of life, and institute their children as they themselves think fit, and the like. Page 109, cap. 21. part. 2.*
3. *Nothing the sovereign can do to a subject, on what pretence soever, can properly be called injustice or injury. Page 109.*
4. *When a sovereign prince putteth to death an innocent subject, though the action be against the Law of Nature, as being contrary to equity, yet it is not an injury to the subject, but to God. Page 109.*
5. *No man hath liberty to resist the word of the sovereign; but in case a great many men together, have already resisted the sovereign power unjustly, or committed some capital crime, for which every one of them expecteth death, they have liberty to join together, and to assist and defend one another. Page 112.*
6. *If a sovereign demand, or take any thing by pretence of his power, there lieth in that case no action at law. Page 112.*
7. *If a subject be taken prisoner in war, or his person or his means of life be within the guards of the enemy, and hath his life and corporal liberty given him on condition to be subject to the victor, he hath liberty to accept the condition, and having accepted it, is the subject of him that took him. Page 114.*
8. *If the sovereign banish the subject, during the banishment he is no subject. Page 114.*

9. *The obligation of subjects to the sovereign, is as long, and no longer than the power lasteth, by which he is able to protect them. Page 124.*
10. *What ever promises or covenants the sovereign makes are void. Page 89.*
11. *He whose private interest is to be judged in an assembly, may make as many friends as he can; and though he hires such friends with money, yet it is not injustice. Page 122, cap. 22. part. 2.*
12. *The propriety which a subject hath in his lands, consisteth in a right to exclude all other subjects from the use of them, and not to exclude their sovereign. Page 128, cap. 24. part. 2.*
13. *When the sovereign commandeth a man to do that which is against law, the doing of it is totally excused; when the sovereign commandeth anything to be done against law, the command as to that particular fact is an abrogation of the law. Page 157, cap. 27. part. 2.*
14. *Though the right of a sovereign monarch cannot be extinguished by the act of another, yet the obligation of the members may; for he that wants protection, may seek it anywhere, and when he hath it, is obliged (without fraudulent pretence of having submitted himself out of fear) to protect his protector as long as he is able. Page 174, cap. 29. part. 2.*

If upon the short reflections we have made upon these several doctrines, as they lie scattered over his book and involved in other discourses, the view of the naked propositions by themselves, without any other clothing or disguise of words, may better serve to make them odious to king and people; and that the first will easily discern, to how high a pinnacle of power soever he would carry him, he leaves him upon such a precipice, from whence the least blast of invasion from a neighbour or from rebellion by his subjects may throw him headlong to irrecoverable ruin. And the other [the people] will as much abhor an allegiance of that temper that by any misfortune of their prince they may be absolved from, and cease to be subjects, when their sovereign hath most need of their obedience. And surely if these articles of Mr. Hobbes's creed be the product of right reason and the effects of Christian obligations, the Great Turk may be looked upon as the best philosopher and all his subjects as the best Christians.

Appendix H: From Thomas Hobbes, An Answer to a Book Published by Dr. Bramhall, late Bishop of Derry; called The Catching of the Leviathan (London: W. Crooke, 1682)

[Hobbes replied to Bramhall's criticisms (see Appendix C) in this book, which he seems to have written only after Bramhall had died; and it was published only after Hobbes had died. His general estimate of Bramhall's criticisms applies equally well to his other critics: Bramhall presented Hobbes's conclusions "without their proofs" and claimed that they were "atheism, blasphemy, impiety, [and] subversion of religion." Hobbes urged his readers "to turn to the place itself, and see whether they be well proved, and how to be understood" ("To the Reader").

In his reply to Bramhall, Hobbes quotes a passage from Bramhall, indicated by "J.D.," for "John of Derry," followed by Hobbes's response indicated by "T.H."]

To the Reader

As in all things which I have written, so also in this piece, I have endeavoured all I can to be perspicuous; but yet your own attention is always necessary. The late Lord Bishop of Derry published a book called *The Catching of the Leviathan*, in which he hath put together divers sentences picked out of my *Leviathan*, which stand there plainly and firmly proved, and sets them down without their proofs, and without the order of their dependance one upon another; and calls them atheism, blasphemy, impiety, subversion of religion, and by other names of that kind. My request unto you is, that when he cites my words for erroneous, you will be pleased to turn to the place itself, and see whether they be well proved, and how to be understood.... If you want leisure or care of the questions between us, I pray you condemn me not upon report. To judge and not examine is not just.

Farewell.
T. Hobbes

An Answer, etc. That the Hobbian Principles are Destructive to Christianity and all Religion

J.D. The image of God is not altogether defaced by the fall of man, but that there will remain some practical notions of God and goodness; which when the mind is free from vagrant desires, and violent passions, do shine as clearly in the heart, as other speculative notions do in the head. Hence it is, that there was never any nation so barbarous or savage throughout the whole world, which had not their God.... Hence it is, that the greatest atheists in any sudden danger do unwittingly cast their eyes up to heaven, as craving aid from thence, and in a thunder creep into some hole to hide themselves. And they who are conscious to themselves of any secret crimes, though they be secure enough from the justice of men, do yet feel the blind blows of a guilty conscience, and fear Divine vengeance. This is acknowledged by T.H. himself in his lucid intervals....

T.H. Hitherto his Lordship discharges me of atheism. What need he to say that *all nations, how barbarous soever, yet have their Gods and religious rites, and atheists are frighted with thunder, and feel the blind blows of conscience?* It might have been as apt a preface to any other of his discourses as this. I expect therefore in the next place to be told, that I deny again my afore-recited doctrine.

J.D. Yet, to let us see how inconsistent and irreconcilable he is with himself, elsewhere reckoning up all the laws of nature at large, even twenty in number, he hath not one word that concerneth religion, or hath the least relation in the world to God.... Thus in describing the laws of nature, this great clerk forgetteth the God of nature, and the main and principal laws of nature, which contain a man's duty to his God, and the principal end of his creation.

T.H. After I had ended the discourse he mentions of the laws of nature, I thought it fittest in the last place, once for all, to say they were the laws of God, then when they were delivered in the word of God; but before, being not known by men for any thing but their own natural reason, they were but theorems, tending to peace, and those uncertain, as being but conclusions of particular men, and therefore not properly laws. Besides, I had formerly in my book *De Cive*, cap. IV, proved them severally, one by one, out of the Scriptures: which his Lordship had read and knew. It was therefore an unjust charge of his to say, I had not one word in them that concerns religion, or that hath the least relation in the world to God; and this upon no other ground than that I added not to every article, *this law is in the Scripture.* But why he should call me (ironically) a great clerk, I cannot tell. I suppose he would make men believe, I arrogated to myself all the learning of a great clerk, bishop, or other inferior minister.... But his Lordship was pleased to use any artifice to disgrace me in any kind whatsoever.

J.D. Perhaps he will say that he handleth the laws of nature there, only so far as may serve to the constitution or settlement of a commonwealth. In good time, let it be so. He hath devised us a trim commonwealth, which is founded neither upon religion towards God, nor justice towards man; but merely upon self-interest, and self-preservation. Those rays of heavenly light, those natural seeds of religion, which God himself hath imprinted in the heart of man, are more efficacious towards preservation of a society, whether we regard the nature of the thing, or the blessing of God, than all his *pacts*, and *surrenders*, and *translations of power*. He who unteacheth men their duty to God, may make them eye-servants, so long as their interest doth oblige them to obey; but is no fit master to teach men conscience and fidelity.

T.H. He has not yet found the place where I contradict either the existence, or infiniteness, or incomprehensibility, or unity, or ubiquity of God. I am therefore yet absolved of atheism. But I am, he says, inconsistent and irreconcilable with myself; that is, I am (though he says not so) he thinks, a forgetful blockhead. I cannot help that: but my forgetfulness appears not here. Even his Lordship, where he says, "those rays of heavenly light, those seeds of religion, which God himself hath imprinted in the heart of man (meaning natural reason), are more efficacious to the preservation of society, than all the *pacts*, *surrenders*, and *translating of power*," had forgotten to except the old pact of the Jews, and the new pact of Christians.[1] But pardoning that, did he hope to make any wise man believe, that when this nation very lately was an anarchy, and dissolute multitude of men, doing every one what his own reason or imprinted light suggested, they did again out of the same light call in the king, and peace again, and ask pardon for the faults, which that their illumination had brought them into, rather than out of fear of perpetual danger and hope of preservation?[2]

J.D. Without religion, societies are like but soapy bubbles, quickly dissolved. It was the judgement of as wise a man as T.H. himself, though perhaps he will hardly be persuaded to it, that Rome owed more of its grandeur to religion, than either to strength or stratagems. We have not exceeded the Spaniards in number, nor the Gauls in strength, nor the Carthaginians in craft, nor the Grecians in art, &c. but we have overcome all nations by our piety and religion.

---

1 Hobbes's point is that both the Old and New Testaments are pacts or covenants. In fact, Old and New Covenants is a more accurate translation of the original language than "Testament" is.

2 Hobbes's philosophy describes the actual causes that lead people to form governments.

T.H. Did not his Lordship forget himself here again, in approving this sentence of Tully,[1] which makes the idolatry of the Romans, not only better than the idolatry of other nations; but also better than the religion of the Jews, whose law Christ himself says he came not to destroy but to fulfill?[2] And that the Romans overcame both them and other nations by their piety, when it is manifest that the Romans overran the world by injustice and cruelty, and that their victories ought not to be ascribed to the piety of the Romans, but to the impiety as well of the Jews as of other nations? ...

J.D. Among his laws he inserteth *gratitude* to men as the third precept of the law of nature; but of the gratitude of mankind to their Creator, there is a deep silence. If men had sprung up from the earth in a night, like mushrooms or excrescences, without all sense of honour, justice, conscience, or gratitude, he could not have vilified the human nature more than he doth.

T.H. My Lord discovers here an ignorance of such method as is necessary for lawful and strict reasoning, and explication of the truth in controversy. And not only that, but also how little able he is to fix his mind upon what he reads in other men's writings. When I had defined ingratitude universally, he finds fault that I do not mention ingratitude towards God, as if his Lordship knew not that an universal comprehends all the particulars. When I had defined equity universally, why did he not as well blame me for not telling what that equity is in God? ...

J.D. From this shameful omission or preterition of the main duty of mankind, a man might easily take the height of T.H. his religion. But he himself putteth it past all conjectures. His principles are brim full of prodigious impiety. *In these four things, opinions of ghosts, ignorance of second causes, devotion to what men fear, and taking of things casual for prognostics, consisteth the natural seed of religion....*

T.H. ... Fear of invisible powers, what is it else in savage people, but the fear of somewhat they think a God? What invisible power does the reason of a savage man suggest unto him, but those phantasms of his sleep, or his distemper, which we frequently call ghosts, and the savages thought gods; so that the fear of a God, though not of the true one, to them was the beginning of religion, as the fear of the true God was the beginning of wisdom to the Jews and Christians? Ignorance of second causes made men fly to some first cause, the fear of which bred devotion and worship. The ignorance of what that power might do, made them observe the order of what he had done; that they might guess by the like

---

1 Marcus Tullius Cicero (106-43 BCE), Roman senator, philosopher, and orator.
2 Hobbes, like other Protestant thinkers, often objected to using pagan authors to justify Christian doctrines.

order, what he was to do another time. This was their prognostication. What prodigious impiety is here? How confutes he it? Must it be taken for impiety upon his bare calumny? I said superstition was fear without reason. Is not the fear of a false God, or fancied demon, contrary to right reason? And is not atheism boldness grounded on false reasoning, such as is this, the *wicked prosper, therefore there is no God*? He offers no proof against any of this; but says only I make atheism to be more reasonable than superstition; which is not true: for I deny that there is any reason either in the atheist or in the superstitious. And because the atheist thinks he has reason, where he has none, I think him the more irrational of the two. But all this while he argues not against any of this; but enquires only, what is become of my natural worship of God, and of his existency; infiniteness, incomprehensibility, unity, and ubiquity. As if whatsoever reason can suggest, must be suggested all at once....

J.D. For T.H. his God is not the God of Christians, nor of any rational men....

T.H. Though I believe the omnipotence of God, and that he can do what he will, yet I dare not say how every thing is done, because I cannot conceive nor comprehend either the Divine substance, or the way of its operation. And I think it impiety to speak concerning God any thing of my own head, or upon the authority of philosophers or Schoolmen, which I understand not, without warrant in the Scripture: and what I say of omnipotence, I say also of ubiquity....

J.D. Our God is a perfect, pure, simple, indivisible, infinite essence; free from all composition of matter and form, of substance and accidents. All matter is finite, and he who acteth by his infinite essence, needeth neither organs nor faculties ..., nor accidents, to render him more complete. But T.H. his God is a divisible God, a compounded God, that hath matter, or qualities, or accidents. Hear himself. I argue thus: *The Divine substance is indivisible; but eternity is the Divine substance. The major is evident, because God is* actus simplicissimus;[1] *the minor is confessed by all men, that whatsoever is attributed to God, is God.* Now listen to his answer: *The major is so far from being evident, that* actus simplicissimus *signifieth nothing. The minor is said by some men, thought by no man; whatsoever is thought is understood.* The major was this, *the Divine substance is indivisible.* Is this far from being evident? Either it is indivisible, or divisible. If it be not indivisible, then it is divisible, then it is materiate, then it is corporeal, then it hath parts, then it is finite by his own confession. *Habere partes, aut esse totum aliquid, sunt attributa finitorum.* [To have parts or to be a whole something is an attribute of finite things.] Upon this silly conceit he chargeth me for saying, that *God is*

---

1   "The most simple act." The view here is that God has no parts of any kind and has no potentiality. His being is always actual or complete.

not just, but justice itself; not eternal, but eternity itself; which he calleth *unseemly words to be said of God*. And he thinketh he doth me a great courtesy in not adding *blasphemous and atheistical*. But his bolts are so soon shot, and his reasons are such vain imaginations, and such drowsy phantasies, that no sober man doth much regard them. Thus he hath already destroyed the ubiquity, the eternity, and the simplicity of God. I wish he had considered better with himself, before he had desperately cast himself upon these rocks.... My next charge is, that he destroys the very being of God, and leaves nothing in his place, but an empty name. For by taking away all incorporeal substances, he taketh away God himself. The very name, saith he, of an incorporeal substance, is a *contradiction*. And *to say that an angel or spirit, is an incorporeal substance, is to say in effect, that there is no angel or spirit at all*. By the same reason to say, that God is an incorporeal substance, is to say there is no God at all. Either God is incorporeal; or he is finite, and consists of parts, and consequently is no God. This, that there is no incorporeal spirit, is that main root of atheism, from which so many lesser branches are daily sprouting up.

T.H. God is indeed a perfect, pure, simple, infinite substance; and his name incommunicable, that is to say, not divisible into this and that individual God, in such manner as the name of man is divisible into Peter and John. And therefore God is individual; which word amongst the Greeks is expressed by the word indivisible. Certain heretics in the primitive church, because special and individual are called particulars, maintained that Christ was a particular God, differing in number from God the Father. And this was the doctrine that was condemned for heresy in the first council of Nice [Nicea], by these words, *God hath no parts*....

Matter is the same with *body*; but never without respect to a body which is made thereof. *Form* is the aggregate of all accidents together, for which we give the matter a new name; so *albedo, whiteness*, is the form of *album*, or *white body*. So also humanity is the essence of man, and Deity the essence of Deus.

Spirit is thin, fluid, transparent, invisible body. The word in Latin signifies breath, air, wind, and the like. In Greek *pneuma* from *pneo, spirō, flo*.

I have seen, and so have many more, two waters, one of the river, the other a mineral water, so like that no man could discern the one from the other by his sight; yet when they have been both put together, the whole substance could not by the eye be distinguished from milk. Yet we know that the one was not mixed with the other, so as every part of the one to be in every part of the other, for that is impossible, unless two bodies can be in the same place. How then could the change be made in every part, but only by the activity of the mineral water, changing it every where to the sense, and yet not being every where, and in every part of the water? If then such gross bodies have so great activity, what shall we think of spirits, whose kinds be as many as there be kinds of liquor, and activity greater? Can it then be doubted, but that God, who is an infinitely fine Spirit, and withal intelligent, can make and change all species and kinds of body as he pleaseth? But I dare not say that this is the way by which God Almighty worketh, because it is past my apprehension: yet it serves very well to demonstrate that the omnipotence of God implieth no contradiction; and is better than by pretence of magnifying the fineness of the Divine substance, to reduce it to a spright or phantasm, which is nothing.

A *person* (Latin, *persona*) signifies an intelligent substance that acteth any thing in his own or another's name, or by his own or another's authority. Of this definition there can be no other proof than from the use of that word, in such Latin authors as were esteemed the most skilful in their own language, of which number was Cicero. But Cicero, in an epistle to Atticus, saith thus: *Unus sustineo tres personas, mei, adversarii, et judicis*: that is, "I that am but one man, sustain three persons; mine own person, the person of my adversary, and the person of the judge." Cicero was here the substance intelligent, one man; and because he pleaded for himself, he calls himself his own person: and again, because he pleaded for his adversary, he says, he sustained the person of his adversary: and lastly, because he himself gave the sentence, he says, he sustained the person of the judge. In the same sense we use the word in English vulgarly, calling him that acteth by his own authority, his own person, and him that acteth by the authority of another, the person of that other. And thus we have the exact meaning of the word person. The Greek tongue cannot render it; for *prosōpon* is properly a face, and, metaphorically, a vizard of an actor upon the stage. How then did the Greek Fathers render the word person, as it is in the blessed Trinity? Not well. Instead of the word *person* they put *hypostasis*, which signifies substance; from whence it might be inferred, that the three persons in the Trinity are three Divine substances, that is, three Gods....

J.D. When they have taken away all incorporeal spirits, what do they leave God himself to be? He who is the fountain of all being, from whom and in whom all creatures have their being, must needs have a real being of his own. And what real being can God have among bodies and accidents? For they have left nothing else in the universe....

T.H. To his Lordship's question here: *What I leave God to be?* I answer, I leave him to be a most pure, simple, invisible spirit corporeal. By corporeal I mean a substance that has magnitude, and so mean all learned men, divines and others, though perhaps there be some common people so rude as to call nothing body, but what they can see and feel. To his second question: *What real being He can have amongst bodies and accidents?* I answer, the being of a spirit, not of a spright. If I should ask any the most subtile distinguisher, what middle nature there were between an infinitely subtile substance, and a mere thought or phantasm, by what name could he call it? He might call it perhaps an incorporeal substance; and so *incorporeal* shall pass for a middle nature between *infinitely subtile* and *nothing*, and be less *subtile* than infinitely subtile, and yet more subtile than a thought....

J.D. We have seen what his principles are concerning the Deity, they are full as bad or worse concerning the Trinity. Hear himself: *A person is he that is represented as often as he is represented. And therefore God who has been represented, that is personated thrice, may properly enough be said to be three persons, though neither the word Person nor Trinity be ascribed to him in the Bible....*

T.H. As for the words recited, I confess there is a fault in the ratiocination,[1] which nevertheless his Lordship hath not discovered, but no impiety. All that he objecteth is, that it followeth hereupon, that there be as many persons of a king, as there be petty constables in his kingdom. And so there are, or else he cannot be obeyed. But I never said that a king, and every one of his persons, are the same substance. The fault I here made, and saw not, was this; I was to prove that it is no contradiction, as Lucian[2] and heathen scoffers would have it, to say of God, he was one and three. I saw the true definition of the word *person* would serve my turn in this manner; God, in his own person, both created the world, and instituted a church in Israel, using therein the ministry of Moses: the same God, in the person of his Son God and man, redeemed the same world, and the same church; the same God, in the person of the Holy Ghost, sanctified the same church, and all the faithful men in the world.... His Lordship all this while hath catched nothing. It is I that catched myself, for saying, instead of by the ministry of Moses, in the person of Moses. But this error I no sooner saw, than I no less publicly corrected than I had committed it, in my *Leviathan* converted into Latin, which by this time I think is printed beyond the seas with this alteration, and also with the omission of some such passages as strangers are not concerned in. And I had corrected this error sooner, if I had sooner found it. For though I was told by Dr. Cosins, now Bishop of Durham, that the place above-cited was not applicable enough to the doctrine of the Trinity, yet I could not in reviewing the same espy the defect, till of late ... when [I began] to translate the book into Latin.... But how concludes his Lordship out of this, that I put out of the creed these words, *the Father eternal, the Son eternal, the Holy*

---

1 A rare admission by Hobbes of a substantive mistake.
2 Lucian of Samosata (c. 125-180 CE), a Syrian or Assyrian satirist who wrote in Greek.

Ghost eternal? Or these words, *let us make man after our image*, out of the Bible? Which last words neither I nor Bellarmine put out of the Bible, but we both put them out of the number of good arguments to prove the Trinity; for it is no unusual thing in the Hebrew, as may be seen by Bellarmine's quotations, to join a noun of the plural number with a verb of the singular. And we may say also of many other texts of Scripture alleged to prove the Trinity, that they are not so firm as that high article requireth. But mark his Lordship's Scholastic charity in the last words of this period: such *bold presumption requireth another manner of confutation*. This bishop, and others of his opinion, had been in their element, if they had been bishops in Queen Mary's time.[1] ...

J.D. And touching the prophetical office of Christ, I do much doubt whether he do believe in earnest, that there is any such thing as prophecy in the world. He maketh very little difference between a *prophet* and a *madman*, and a *demoniac. And if there were nothing else*, says he, *that bewrayed [betrayed] their madness, yet that very arrogating such inspiration to themselves is argument enough*. He maketh the pretence of inspiration in any man to be, and always to have been, *an opinion pernicious to peace, and tending to the dissolution of all civil government*. He subjecteth all prophetical revelations from God, to the sole pleasure and censure of the sovereign prince, either to authorize them, or to exauctorate them....

T.H. To remove his Lordship's doubt in the first place, I confess there was true prophesy and true prophets in the church of God, from Abraham down to our Saviour, the greatest prophet of all, and the last of the Old Testament, and first of the New. After our Saviour's time, till the death of St. John the apostle, there were true prophets in the church of Christ, prophets to whom God spake supernaturally, and testified the truth of their mission by miracles.[2] Of those that in the Scripture are called prophets without miracles, (and for this cause only, that they spake in the name of God to men, and in the name of men to God), there are, have been, and shall be in the church, innumerable. Such a prophet was his Lordship, and such are all pastors in the Christian church. But the question here is of those prophets that from the mouth of God foretell things future, or do other miracle. Of this kind I deny there has been any since the death of St. John the Evangelist. If any man find fault with this, he ought to name some man or other, whom

---

1 Hobbes is suggesting that Bramhall would like to act as Mary I ("Bloody Mary"), the Roman Catholic monarch, did and have those whom he considered heretics executed.

2 Hobbes is expressing a common Protestant view. Once the work of redemption was done and revelation complete, there was no more need for prophets who performed miracles. See Calvin, *Institutes of the Christian Religion*, Book IV, chapter xix, section 18.

we are bound to acknowledge that they have done a miracle, cast out a devil, or cured any disease by the sole invocation of the Divine Majesty. We are not bound to trust to the legend of the Roman saints, nor to the history written by Sulpitius of the life of St. Martin, or to any other fables of the Roman clergy, nor to such things as were pretended to be done by some divines here in the time of king James. Secondly, he says I make little difference between a *prophet*, and a *madman* or *demoniac*; to which I say, he accuses me falsely. I say only thus much, *that I see nothing at all in the Scripture that requireth a belief, that demoniacs were any other thing than madmen*. And this is also made very probable out of Scripture, by a worthy divine, Mr. Mede.[1] ...

J.D. We are taught in our creed to believe the catholic or universal church. But T.H. teacheth us the contrary: *That if there be more Christian churches than one, all of them together are not one church personally.* And more plainly: *Now if the whole number of Christians be not contained in one commonwealth, they are not one person, nor is there an universal church, that hath any authority over them.* And again: *The universal church is not one person, of which it can be said, that it hath done, or decreed, or ordained, or excommunicated, or absolved.* This doth quite overthrow all the authority of general councils.

All other men distinguish between the church and the commonwealth; only T.H. maketh them to be one and the same thing. *The commonwealth of Christian men, and the church of the same, are altogether the same thing, called by two names for two reasons. For the matter of the church and of the commonwealth is the same, namely, the same Christian men; and the form is the same, which consisteth in the lawful power of convocating them.* And hence he concludeth, that *every Christian commonwealth is a church endowed with all spiritual authority.* And yet more fully: *The church if it be one person, is the same thing with the commonwealth of Christians; called a commonwealth, because it consisteth of men united in one person their sovereign; and a church, because it consisteth in Christian men united in one Christian sovereign.* Upon which account there was no Christian church in these parts of the world, for some hundreds of years after Christ, because there was no Christian sovereign.

T.H. For answer to this period, I say only this; that taking the *church*, as I do, in all those places, for a company of Christian men on earth incorporated into one person, that can speak, command, or do any act of a person, all that he citeth out of what I have written is true; and that all private conventicles, though their belief be right, are not properly called churches; and that there is not any one universal church here on earth, which is a person indued with authority universal to govern all

---

1 Joseph Mede (1586-1639) was a well-respected, respectable, and pious biblical scholar, and the first to argue that demoniacs were madmen.

Christian men on earth, no more than there is one universal sovereign prince or state on earth, that hath right to govern all mankind. I deny also that the whole clergy of a Christian kingdom or state being assembled, are the representative of that church further than the civil laws permit; or can lawfully assemble themselves, unless by the command or by the leave of the sovereign civil power. I say further, that the denial of this point tendeth in England towards the taking away of the king's supremacy in causes ecclesiastical. But his Lordship has not here denied any thing of mine, because he has done no more but set down my words. He says further, that this doctrine destroys the authority of all general councils; which I confess. Nor hath any general council at this day in this kingdom the force of a law, nor ever had, but by the authority of the king.[1]

J.D. Neither is he more orthodox concerning the holy Scriptures: hitherto, that is, for the books of Moses, *the power of making the Scripture canonical, was in the civil sovereign*. The like he saith of the Old Testament, made canonical by Esdras. And of the New Testament, that *it was not the apostles which made their own writings canonical, but every convert made them so to himself*: yet with this restriction, that *until the sovereign ruler had prescribed them, they were but counsel and advice, which whether good or bad, he that was counselled might without injustice refuse to observe, and being contrary to the laws established, could not without injustice observe*.... Thus if Christian sovereigns, of different communications, do clash one with another, in their interpretation, or misinterpretation of Scripture, as they do daily, then the word of God is contradictory to itself; or that is the word of God in one commonwealth, which is the word of the Devil in another commonwealth. And the same thing may be true, and not true at the same time: which is the peculiar privilege of T.H. to make contradictories to be true together.

T.H. There is no doubt but by what authority the Scripture or any other writing is made a law, by the same authority the Scriptures are to be interpreted, or else they are made law in vain. But to obey is one thing, to believe is another; which distinction perhaps his Lordship never heard of. To obey is to do or forbear as one is commanded, and depends on the will; but to believe, depends not on the will, but on the providence and guidance of our hearts that are in the hands of God Almighty. Laws only require obedience; belief requires teachers and arguments drawn either from reason, or from some thing already believed. Where there is no reason for our belief, there is no reason we should believe. The reason why men believe, is drawn from the authority of those men

---

1 Hobbes adheres to the legal doctrine of the church in England. Bramhall supported the independence of the Church, as the Pope had done during the quarrel with King Henry VIII.

whom we have no just cause to mistrust, that is, of such men to whom no profit accrues by their deceiving us, and of such men as never used to lie, or else from the authority of such men whose promises, threats, and affirmations, we have seen confirmed by God with miracles. If it be not from the king's authority that the Scripture is law, what other authority makes it law? ... All that the Bishop does in this argument is but a heaving at the King's supremacy. Oh, but, says he, if two kings interpret a place of Scripture in contrary senses, it will follow that both senses are true. It does not follow. For the interpretation, though it be made by just authority, must not therefore always be true. If the doctrine in the one sense be necessary to salvation, then they that hold the other must die in their sins, and be damned. But if the doctrine in neither sense be necessary to salvation, then all is well, except perhaps that they will call one another atheists, and fight about it.[1]

J.D. Sometimes he is for holy orders, and giveth to the pastors of the church the right of ordination and absolution, and infallibility, too much for a particular pastor, or the pastors of one particular church. *It is manifest, that the consecration of the chiefest doctors in every church, and imposition of hands, doth pertain to the doctors of the same church. And, it cannot be doubted of, but the power of binding and loosing was given by Christ to the future pastors, after the same manner as to his present apostles. And, our Saviour hath promised this infallibility in those things which are necessary to salvation, to his apostles, until the day of judgement, that is to say, to the apostles, and pastors to be consecrated by the apostles successively, by the imposition of hands.*

But at other times he casteth all this meal down with his foot. *Christian sovereigns are the supreme pastors, and the only persons whom Christians now hear speak from God, except such as God speaketh to in these days supernaturally.* What is now become of the promised infallibility? ...

T.H. ... The bishop consecrates, but the king both makes him bishop and gives him his authority. The head of the church not only gives the power of consecration, dedication, and benediction, but may also exercise the act himself if he please. Solomon did it; and the book of canons says, that the King of England has all the right that any good king of Israel had; it might have added, that any other king or sovereign assembly had in their own dominions. I deny that any pastor or any assembly of pastors in any particular church, or all the churches on earth though united, are infallible: yet I say, the pastors of a Christian church assembled are, in all such points as are necessary to salvation.

---

1 Hobbes emphasizes the sense in which the Bible is part of the law in England. What he says is correct. His distinction between what one must do out of obedience versus what one may believe is helpful, but would not satisfy Bramhall, who wants the Bible to have an independent claim to being normative.

J.D. ... Who supposeth that *when a man dieth, there remaineth nothing of him but his carcase?* Who maketh the word *soul* in Holy Scripture to signify always either the life, or the living creature; and expoundeth the casting of body and soul into hell-fire, to be *the casting of body and life into hell-fire?* Who maketh this orthodox truth, that the souls of men are substances distinct from their bodies, to be *an error contracted by the contagion of the demonology of the Greeks, and a window that gives entrance to the dark doctrine of eternal torments?* ...

T.H. He comes here to that which is a great paradox in School-divinity. The grounds of my opinion are the canonical Scripture, and the texts which I cited I must again recite, to which I shall also add some others. My doctrine is this: first, *that the elect in Christ, from the day of judgement forward, by virtue of Christ's passion and victory over death, shall enjoy eternal life, that is, they shall be immortal.* Secondly, *that there is no living soul separated in place from the body, more than there is a living body separated from the soul.*[1] Thirdly, *that the reprobate shall be revived to judgement, and shall die a second death in torments, which death shall be everlasting.*

J.D. A fourth aphorism may be this, *that, which is said in the Scripture, it is better to obey God than man, hath place in the kingdom of God by pact, and not by nature.* Why? Nature itself doth teach us it is better to obey God than men. Neither can he say that he intended this only of obedience in the use of indifferent actions and gestures, in the service of God, commanded by the commonwealth: for that is to obey both God and man. But if Divine law and human law clash one with another, without doubt it is evermore better to obey God than man.

T.H. Here again appears his unskilfulness in reasoning. Who denies, but it is always, and in all cases, better to obey God than man? But there is no law, neither Divine nor human, that ought to be taken for a law, till we know what it is; and if a Divine law, till we know that God hath commanded it to be kept. We agree that the Scriptures are the word of God. But they are a law by pact, that is, to us who have been baptized into the covenant. To all others it is an invitation only to their own benefit. It is true that even nature suggesteth to us that the law of God is to be obeyed rather than the law of man. But nature does not suggest to us that the Scripture is the law of God, much less how every text of it ought to be interpreted. But who then shall suggest this? Dr. Bramhall? I deny it. Who then? The stream of divines? Why so? Am I, that have the Scripture itself before my eyes, obliged to venture my eternal life upon their interpretation, how learned soever they pretend to be, when no

---

1 Hobbes again commits himself to the primacy of the Bible for Christian doctrine. He is right in holding that there is no doctrine of the immortality of the soul in the Bible.

counter-security, that they can give me, will save me harmless? If not the stream of divines, who then? The lawful assembly of pastors, or of bishops? But there can be no lawful assembly in England without the authority of the King. The Scripture, therefore, what it is, and how to be interpreted, is made known unto us here, by no other way than the authority of our sovereign lord both in temporals and spirituals, the King's Majesty. And where he has set forth no interpretation, there I am allowed to follow my own, as well as any other man, bishop or not bishop. For my own part, all that know me, know also it is my opinion, that the best government in religion is by episcopacy, but in the King's right, not in their own....

J.D. His sixth paradox is a rapper: *The civil laws are the rules of good and evil, just and unjust, honest and dishonest; and therefore what the lawgiver commands, that is to be accounted good, what he forbids, bad.* And a little after: *Before empires were, just and unjust were not, as whose nature is relative to a command, every action in its own nature is indifferent. That is, just or unjust proceedeth from the right of him that commandeth. Therefore lawful kings make those things which they command just, by commanding them, and those things which they forbid, unjust by forbidding them. To this add his definition of a sin, that which one doth, or omitteth, saith, or willeth, contrary to the reason of the commonwealth, that is, the (civil) laws.* Where by the laws he doth not understand the written laws, elected and approved by the whole commonwealth, but the verbal commands or mandates of him that hath the sovereign power, as we find in many places of his writings. *The civil laws are nothing else but the commands of him, that is endowed with sovereign power in the commonwealth, concerning the future actions of his subjects. And the civil laws are fastened to the lips of that man who hath the sovereign power....*

T.H. My sixth paradox he calls a rapper. A rapper, a swapper, and such like terms, are his Lordship's elegancies. But let us see what this rapper is: it is this; the civil laws are the rules of good and evil, just and unjust, honest and dishonest. Truly, I see no other rules they have. The Scriptures themselves were made law to us here, by the authority of the commonwealth, and are therefore part of the law civil. If they were laws in their own nature, then were they laws over all the world, and men were obliged to obey them in America, as soon as they should be shown there, though without a miracle, by a friar. What is unjust, but the transgression of a law? *Law* therefore was before unjust: and the law was made known by sovereign power before it was a law: therefore *sovereign power* was antecedent both to *law* and *injustice*.[1] Who then made unjust but sovereign kings or sovereign assemblies? Where is now the wonder of this rapper, *that lawful kings make those things which they com-*

---

1 Hobbes is talking here about only the laws of a civil state.

mand just, by commanding them, and those things which they forbid unjust, by forbidding them? Just and unjust were surely made. If the king made them not, who made them else? For certainly the breach of a civil law is a sin against God. Another calumny which he would fix upon me, is, that I make the King's verbal commands to be laws. How so? Because I say, *the civil laws are nothing else but the commands of him that hath the sovereign power, concerning the future actions of his subjects.* What verbal command of a king can arrive at the ears of all his subjects, which it must do ere it be a law, without the seal of the person of the commonwealth, which is here the Great Seal of England? Who, but his Lordship, ever denied that the command of England was a law to Englishmen? ...

J.D. Something there is which he hath confused glimmering of ..., which he is not able to apprehend and express clearly. We acknowledge, that though the laws or commands of a sovereign prince be erroneous, or unjust, or injurious, such as a subject cannot approve for good in themselves; yet he is bound to acquiesce, and may not oppose or resist, otherwise than by prayers and tears, and at the most by flight. We acknowledge that the civil laws have power to bind the conscience of a Christian.... But in plain cases, which admit no doubt, it is always better to obey God than man.... God help us, into what times are we fallen, when the immutable laws of God and nature are made to depend upon the mutable laws of mortal men, just as one should go about to control the sun by the authority of the clock.

T.H. ... *We acknowledge, saith he, that though the laws or commands of a sovereign prince be erroneous, or unjust, or injurious, such as a subject cannot approve for good in themselves, yet he is bound to acquiesce, and may not oppose or resist otherwise than by prayers and tears, and at the most by flight.* Hence it follows clearly, that when a sovereign has made a law, though erroneous, then, if his subject oppose it, it is a sin. Therefore I would fain know, when a man has broken that law by doing what it forbad, or by refusing to do what it commanded, whether he have opposed this law or not. If to break the law be to oppose it, he granteth it. Therefore his Lordship has not here expressed himself so clearly, as to make men understand the difference between breaking a law and opposing it. Though there be some difference between breaking of a law, and opposing those that are sent with force to see it executed; yet between breaking and opposing the law itself, there is no difference. Also, though the subject think the law just, as when a thief is by law condemned to die, yet he may lawfully oppose the execution, not only by prayers, tears, and flight, but also (as I think) any way he can. For though his fault were never so great, yet his endeavour to save his own life is not a fault. For the law expects it, and for that cause appointeth felons to be carried bound and encompassed with armed men to execution. Nothing is opposite to law, but sin: nothing opposite to the sheriff, but force. So that his Lordship's sight was not sharp enough to see the difference between the law and the officer.... *But*, saieth he, *in evident cases which admit no doubt, it is always better to obey God than man.* Yes, and in doubtful cases also, say I. But not always better to obey the inferior pastors than the supreme pastor, which is the king. But what are those cases that admit no doubt? I know but very few, and those are such as his Lordship was not much acquainted with.

J.D. ... *There can be no contradiction between the laws of God, and the laws of a Christian commonwealth.* Yet, we see Christian commonwealths daily contradict one another.

T.H. ...[H]is Lordship's instance, *that Christian commonwealths contradict one another*, has nothing to do here. Their laws do indeed contradict one another, but contradict not the law of God. For God commands their subjects to obey them in all things, and his Lordship himself confesseth that their laws, though erroneous, bind the conscience. But Christian commonwealths would seldom contradict one another, if they made no doctrine law, but such as were necessary to salvation.

J.D. ... *No man giveth but with intention of some good to himself. Of all voluntary acts, the object is to every man his own good.* Moses, St. Paul, and the Decii[1] were not of his mind.

T.H. That ... Moses, St. Paul, and the Decii were not of my mind, is false. For the two former did what they did for a good to themselves, which was eternal life; and the Decii for a good fame after death. And his Lordship also, if he had believed there is an eternal happiness to come, or thought a good fame after death to be anything worth, would have directed all his actions towards them, and have despised the wealth and titles of the present world.[2] ...

J.D. His whole works are a heap of mis-shapen errors, and absurd paradoxes, vented with the confidence of a juggler, the brags of a mountebank, and the authority of some Pythagoras,[3] or third Cato,[4] lately dropped down from heaven.

Thus we have seen how the Hobbian principles do destroy the existence, the simplicity, the ubiquity, the eternity, and infiniteness of God,

---

1 Three generations of men in the fourth and third centuries BCE, each with the name "Publius Decius Mus," were renowned for their altruistic behavior on behalf of Rome.
2 Hobbes is accusing Bramhall, who amassed significant wealth as a bishop, of valuing worldly wealth over divine reward.
3 Pythagoras (c. 570-495 BCE), Greek mathematician and founder of a religious school.
4 Marcus Porcius Cato Uticensis (95-46 BCE), Roman statesman, enemy of Julius Caesar, and Stoic, known for his integrity and admired by Roman republicans.

the doctrine of the Blessed Trinity, the hypostatical union, the kingly, sacerdotal, and prophetical office of Christ, the being and operation of the Holy Ghost, heaven, hell, angels, devils, the immortality of the soul, the Catholic and all national churches; the holy Scriptures, holy orders, the holy sacraments, the whole frame of religion, and the worship of God; the laws of nature, the reality of goodness, justice, piety, honesty, conscience, and all that is sacred. If his disciples have such an implicit faith, that they can digest all these things, they may feed with *ostriches*.

T.H. He here concludes his first chapter with bitter reproaches, to leave in his reader, as he thought, a sting; supposing perhaps that he will read nothing but the beginning and end of his book, as is the custom of many men. But to make him lose that petty piece of cunning, I must desire of the reader one of these two things. Either that he would read with it the places of my *Leviathan* which he cites, and see not only how he answers my arguments, but also what the arguments are which he produceth against them; or else, that he would forbear to condemn me, so much as in his thought: for otherwise he is unjust. The name of Bishop is of great authority; but these words are not the words of a bishop, but of a passionate Schoolman, too fierce and unseemly in any man whatsoever. Besides, they are untrue. Who that knows me will say that I have the confidence of a juggler, or that I use to brag of anything, much less that I play the mountebank? What my works are, he was no fit judge.... He accuses me first of destroying the existence of God; that is to say, he would make the world believe I were an atheist. But upon what ground? Because I say, that God is a spirit, but corporeal. But to say that, is allowed me by St. Paul, that says (1 Cor. xv. 44): *There is a spiritual body, and there is an animal body.* He that holds there is a God, and that God is really somewhat, (for *body* is doubtlessly a *real substance*), is as far from being an atheist, as it is possible to be. But he that says God is an *incorporeal substance*, no man can be sure whether he be an atheist or not. For no man living can tell whether there be any *substance* at all, that is not also corporeal. For neither the word *incorporeal*, nor *immaterial*, nor any word equivalent to it, is to be found in Scripture, or in reason. But on the contrary, that *the Godhead dwelleth bodily in Christ*, is found in Colos. ii. 9; and Tertullian[1] maintains that God is either a *corporeal substance* or *nothing*. Nor was he ever condemned for it by the church. For why? Not only Tertullian, but all the learned, call *body*, not only that which one can see, but also whatsoever has magnitude, or that is somewhere; for they had greater reverence for the divine substance, than that they durst think it had no *magnitude*, or was *nowhere*. But they that hold God to be a phantasm, as did the

---

1 Quintus Septimius Florens Tertullianus (c. 160-c. 220), Western Christian theologian.

exorcists in the Church of Rome, that is, such a thing as were at that time thought to be the sprights, that were said to walk in churchyards and to be the souls of men buried, do absolutely make God to be nothing at all. But how? Were they atheists? No. For though by ignorance of the consequence they said that which was equivalent to atheism, yet in their hearts they thought God a substance, and would also, if they had known what *substance* and what *corporeal* meant, have said he was a corporeal substance. So that this *atheism by consequence* is a very easy thing to be fallen into, even by the most godly men of the church. He also that says that God is *wholly here*, and *wholly there*, and *wholly every where*, destroys by consequence the unity of God, and the infiniteness of God, and the simplicity of God. And this the Schoolmen do, and are therefore *atheists by consequence*, and yet they do not all say in their hearts that there is no God. So also his Lordship by exempting the will of man from being subject to the necessity of God's will or decree, denies by *consequence* the Divine prescience, which also will amount to *atheism by consequence*. But out of this, that God is a *spirit corporeal* and *infinitely pure*, there can no unworthy or dishonourable consequence be drawn....

Select Bibliography

Bowle, John. *Hobbes and his Critics*. London: Jonathan Cape, 1951.

Hampton, Jean. *Hobbes and the Social Contract Tradition*. Cambridge: Cambridge UP, 1986.

Hoekstra, K. "Hobbes and the Foole." *Political Theory* 25 (1997): 620-54.

Kavka, Gregory. *Hobbesian Moral and Political Theory*. Princeton, NJ: Princeton UP, 1986.

Lloyd, S.A. *Ideals as Interests in Hobbes's Leviathan*. Cambridge: Cambridge UP, 1992.

———. *Morality in the Philosophy of Thomas Hobbes: Cases in the Law of Nature*. Cambridge: Cambridge UP, 2008.

———, ed. *Special Issue on Recent Work on the Moral and Political Philosophy of Thomas Hobbes*. *Pacific Philosophical Quarterly* 82 (2001).

Martinich, A.P. *Hobbes*. London: Routledge, 2005.

———. *Hobbes: A Biography*. Cambridge: Cambridge UP, 1999.

———. *A Hobbes Dictionary*. Oxford: Blackwell, 1996.

Mintz, Samuel. *The Hunting of the Leviathan*. Cambridge: Cambridge UP, 1962; rept. Bristol: Thoemmes Press, 1996.

Nagel, Thomas. "Hobbes's Concept of Obligation." *Philosophical Review* 68 (1959): 53-68.

Ryan, G.A.J., and Alan Ryan, eds. *Perspectives on Thomas Hobbes*. Oxford: Clarendon P, 1988.

Skinner, Quentin. *Visions of Politics, Volume III: Hobbes and Civil Science*. Cambridge UP, 2002.

Sorell, Tom. *Hobbes*. London: Routledge & Kegan Paul, 1986.

———, ed. *The Cambridge Companion to Hobbes*. Cambridge: Cambridge UP, 1996.

Springborg, Patricia, ed. *Cambridge Companion to Hobbes's Leviathan*. Cambridge: Cambridge UP, 2007.

Tuck, Richard. *Hobbes*. Oxford: Oxford UP, 1989.

Wright, George. *Religion, Politics, and Thomas Hobbes*. Dordrecht: Springer, 2006.

Index

commutative justice, 141-42, 366
compassion. *See* pity
compatibilism, 11, 74n1
competition, 103, 123, 157
complaisance (5th law of nature), 142
compounded imagination, 43
concourse of people, 208, 209-10
conditional knowledge, 91. *See also* science
confidence, 71, 106
conflict, 15
  causes of, 16
conjuring, 115
conquest, 179. *See also* commonwealth by acquisition
  conquered monarch no longer sovereign, 344
conscience, 147, 275-76, 290-91
  erroneous, 275
  laws of nature and, 78, 218, 251, 299
consent, 141
Considerations Upon the Reputation and Loyalty (Hobbes), 357
conspiracies, 208-09
Constantine I, Emperor of Rome, 101n2
contempt (8th law of nature), 68, 69, 143
contentment and commodious living, 285
contract, 131, 142, 379. *See also* covenant; promise
  definition, 129
  dominion by, 182
  express signs of, 129
  impossible in state of nature, 372
contumely, 143, 144
corporeality. *See* (in)corporeality
Cosin, John, 12
Council of Lateran (fourth), 45
counsel and counsellors, 35, 215, 297-98, 335, 336
  applies only to monarchy, 297

best to one not an assembly, 172, 224, 228, 298
  different from command, 222, 223, 225
  examples from Scripture, 225
  fit and unfit counsellors, 224-29
courage, 71, 140, 195, 196
courts of justice, 213-14
covenant, 36, 131-33, 139, 158, 190, 368, 379, 388
  to accuse self, 134, 195
  with actor or representative, 150
  but words without the sword, 155, 162
  definition, 129
  every man with every man, 16, 158, 194
  extorted by fear, 133
  former covenant voids a later, 134
  with God only through a representative, 132, 133, 161
  God with Abraham, 117, 247, 289
  impossible in state of nature, 372
  master-servant, 183
  no covenant with beasts, 132
  not discharged by vice of recipient, 140
  not to defend self, 134, 194
  subject and sovereign, 369, 376, 378, 381
  validity of, 131, 132, 133, 134, 137, 150, 194, 195
covetousness, 71, 255, 256
cowardice, 11
craft, 83
creation, 324, 325, 345, 354, 379, 387, 389
  origin of human beings, 368, 372
Creed, 79
The Creed of Mr Hobbes Examined in a Feigned Conference (Tenison), 362, 363
crime
  comparison from effect, 262-64
  definition, 250

LIST
of products used:

1,351 lb(s) of Rolland Enviro100 Print
100% post-consumer

Generated by : www.cascades.com/calculator

Sources : Environmental Paper Network (EPN)
www.papercalculator.org

RESULTS
Based on the Cascades products you selected
compared to products in the industry made with
100% virgin fiber, your savings are:

 11 trees

 11,177 gal. US of water
121 days of water consumption

 1,413 lbs of waste
13 waste containers

 3,673 lbs CO$_2$
6,964 miles driven

18 MMBTU
87,104 60W light bulbs for one hour

 11 lbs NOx
**emissions of one truck during 15
days**